THE LIVING HISTORY OF PAKISTAN

Judges & Generals in Pakistan

Volume IV

by

INAM R SEHRI

CONTEMPORARY HISTORY IS NOT
THAT WHAT HAS BEEN HAPPENING AROUND?
IT IS THE STATEMENT OF FACTS
ABOUT WHAT THE PEOPLE
CONSIDERED SIGNIFICANT

Grosvenor House
Publishing Limited

All rights reserved
Copyright © Inam R Sehri, 2014

(However, scholars & students are permitted
to use material of this book by quoting the exact reference)
The right of Inam R Sehri to be identified as the author of this
work has been asserted by him in accordance with Section 78
of the Copyright, Designs and Patents Act 1988

Re-Print June 2017

The book cover picture is copyright to Avid Creative

This book is published by
Grosvenor House Publishing Ltd
28-30 High Street, Guildford, Surrey, GU1 3EL.
www.grosvenorhousepublishing.co.uk

This book is sold subject to the conditions that it shall not, by way of
trade or otherwise, be lent, resold, hired out or otherwise circulated
without the author's or publisher's prior consent in any form of binding
or cover other than that in which it is published and
without a similar condition including this condition being imposed
on the subsequent purchaser.

A CIP record for this book
is available from the British Library

[All page with usual statements ending with]

ISBN 978-1-78148-673-3

On **18**th **September 2011**: [BERN] Director Swiss Bank said
<u>ABOUT THIS COUNTRY</u>:

'Pakistanis are poor but Pakistan isn't a poor country; that 97 billion dollars of Pakistan is deposited in respective banks and if this money would be utilized for the welfare of Pakistan and its people then Pakistan can make tax-less budget for 30 years, can create 60 million jobs, can carpet four lanes road from any village to Islamabad, endless power supply to five hundred social projects, every citizen can get 20000 rupees salary for the next 60 years and there is no need to see IMF and any World Bank for loans.'

[Daily 'the Nation' & 'Pakistan Today'
dated **19**th **September 2011** is referred]

Other Books from

INAM R SEHRI

KHUDKUSHI
(on Suicide) [in Urdu]   (1983)
{Details of historical perspective of 'Suicide' in various societies; & investigation techniques differentiating in Murder & Suicides}

WARDI KAY ANDAR AADMI
(Man in uniform) [in Urdu]   (1984)
{Collection of short stories keeping a sensitive policeman in focus}

AURAT JARAIM KI DALDAL MEIN
(on Female Criminality) [in Urdu]   (1985)
{Describing various theories and cultural taboos concerning Female Criminal Behaviour}

POLICE AWAM RABTAY
(on Police Public relationship) [in Urdu]   (1986)
{Essays describing importance of mutual relationships}

DEHSHAT GARDI
(on Terrorism) [in Urdu]   (1987)
{Various theories and essays differentiating between Freedom Fighting & Terrorism in Middle Eastern perspective}

QATL
(on Murder) [in Urdu]   (1988)
{The first book written for Police students & Lawyers to explain techniques of investigation of (difficult) Murder cases}

SERVICE POLICING IN PAKISTAN
[in English]   (1990)
{A dissertation type book on which basis the PM Benazir Bhutto, in 1990, had okayed the Commissionerate System of Policing in Pakistan. Taking Karachi as the pilot project, later, it was levied for all major cities and still going on as such}

SHADI
   (on Marriages) [in Urdu]   (1998)
{A detailed exposition of Marriage explained in various religions, cultures, countries and special groups; much applauded & commented upon on PTV in 1998-99}

All the above books were published by Pakistan's number one publisher

SANG E MEEL PUBLICATIONS,
25 - The Lower Mall LAHORE, Pakistan

And are normally available with them in latest re-prints.

Judges & Generals in Pakistan VOL-I
   [in English]   (2012)

Judges & Generals in Pakistan VOL-II
   [in English]   (2012)

Judges & Generals in Pakistan VOL-III
   [in English]   (2013)

Published by

Grosvenor House Publishing Ltd
28-30 High Street, Guildford
SURREY UK GU1 3HY

It's me; my Lord!

INAM R SEHRI

- Born in Lyallpur (Pakistan) in April 1948

- First Degree from Government College Lyallpur (1969)

- Studied at Government College Lahore & got first Master's Degree from Punjab University Lahore (1971);

- Attachment with AJK Education Service (1973-1976)

- Central Superior Services (CSS) Exam passed (batch 1975)

- Civil Service Academy Lahore (joined 1976)

- National Police Academy Islamabad (joined 1977)

- LLB from BUZ University Multan (1981)

- Master's Degree from Exeter University of UK (1990)

- Regular Police Service: District Admin, Police College, National Police Academy, the Intelligence Bureau (IB), Federal Investigation Agency (FIA) [1977-1998] then migrated to the UK permanently.

A part-script copied from the earlier volumes:

Just spent a normal routine life; with hundreds of mentionable memoirs allegedly of bravery & glamour as every uniformed officer keeps, some times to smile at and next moment to repent upon but taking it just normal except one or two spills.

During my tenure at IB HQ Islamabad I got chance to peep into the elite civil and military leadership of Pakistan then existing in governmental dossiers and database.

During my stay at FIA I was assigned to conduct special enquiries & investigations into some acutely sensitive matters like Motorway Scandal, sudden expansion and build-up of Sharif family's industrial empire, Sharif's accounts in foreign countries; Alleged Financial Corruptions in Pakistan's Embassies in Far-Eastern Countries; Shahnawaz Bhutto's murder in Cannes (France); Land Scandals of CDA's Estate

Directorate; Ittefaq Foundry's 'custom duty on scrap' scam, Hudaibya Engineering & Hudaibya Paper Mills enquiries, Bhindara's Murree Brewery and tens more cases like that.

> [*Through these words I want to keep it on record that during the course of the above mentioned, (and also which cannot be mentioned due to space limits) investigations or enquiries, the then Prime Minister Benazir Bhutto, or [late] Gen Naseerullah Babar the then Federal Interior Minister, or G Asghar Malik the then DG FIA, had never ever issued direct instructions or implicit directions or wished me to distort facts or to go malafide for orchestrating a political edge or other intangible gains.*
>
> *Hats off to all of them!*]

I should feel proud that veracity and truthfulness of none of my enquiry or investigation could be challenged or proved false in NAB or Special Courts; yes, most of them were used to avail political compromises by Gen Musharraf's government.

That's enough, my dear countrymen.

Contents

My Apologies; One Time More:

This VOLUME-IV mainly encompasses the real facts of corruption, financial and intellectual both, done by Pakistan's ruling elite, Bhutto's poor and deprived party PPP and its associates – but never mind it was all done in the name of democracy.

Equally important topic engulfed in the coming pages is related with [so called?] national honour and *ghairat* [killing others mainly the women over flimsy traditions] of Pakistan's general populace, but how their successive rulers behaved like slaves before their foreign masters just for peanuts, those too not for the poor people but to be sent directly to their family Swiss accounts. Also see details of Osama Bin Laden's killing inside.

Let us take start from few years back;

Wherein, after general elections of 1977, when Z A Bhutto's dubious National Assembly met in Islamabad on 28th March [1977], only the PPP members had shown up. Mr Bhutto floated an offer to enter into a dialogue with the opposition thinking that it would settle for increased representation in the Assembly's session but miserably failed.

Soon after, Mr Bhutto declared a national emergency and used *'Defence of Pakistan Rules'* under which all the opposition leaders were arrested. He called for his political opponents to negotiate a solution but they did not trust Bhutto and the demonstrations continued throughout April till June 1977.

Tired of the strikes and agitations, once Mr Bhutto called an emergency meeting, where Gen Ziaul Haq and Gen Faiz Ali Chishti were also present amongst other key persons, and said:

'Gentlemen, I've decided to resign; Brother Ziaul Haq would take over.'

In the meeting, Gen Chishti had the courage to say:

'Sir, I'm personally your humble servant but cannot guarantee the behaviour of jawans who believe that the elections were vastly rigged.'

Gen Ziaul Haq stood up with his right hand on chest; little bowed down and said that:

> *'Sir, Army is with you; you are Fakhr e Asia, have been the Chairman Islamic Summit Conference [1974]; you will not resign whatsoever.'*

The irony of fate: Mr Bhutto was confident that with the allegiance of the Pak - Army under Gen Ziaul Haq he would be able to control the situation, but he was at fault to understand the General's inner side. The result was that Mr Bhutto was first sent to prison and then to the gallows; a chapter closed.

Another page from two years later when the Pak - Army Generals unilaterally decided to pose their nose into the affairs of others – when they decided to jump into Afghani sandgrave; those army Generals named Ziaul Haq, Akhtar Abdul Rehman and some others could not conceive that if they were going to spread bullets and gunpowder in their neighbouring country, the same kind of stuff would also be seen in their own regions of Pakistan.

Later the poor people of Pakistan had to go through the same burning fires along with two more versatile nuisances; Kalashnikov culture and drugs in abundance. Pakistan's present youth has taken birth amidst the whiffs of the same two menaces of killing devices; they have never breathed the clean air as available to the rest of the world.

That group of few Army Generals had decided at their own, purportedly on behalf of the nation - only that ruler would occupy the presidency in Kabul to whom they would give the clearance chit, to whom they would allow to pass through the green signal; how innocent [*do not say them fools*] they were.

They were wise enough to handle the bags full of American dollars which were continuously pouring in their villas in the name of 'war money'. Their few families were happy but they had pushed their *jawans,* JCOs & Commissioned officers of Pak-Army and the next generations into the hell of miseries, gloom, and depression amidst showers of blood and arson.

The above were the stratagems and deceptions which brought Pakistanis to see huge paintings pasted on the walls of global village. A leaked *Wikileaks* cable *of 4*th *February 2009* suggested, citing a briefing prepared for the US embassy in Islamabad by US special envoy to Pakistan and Afghanistan, Richard Holbrooke that:

> '......*being a failed state, Pakistan is facing rough and tough challenges. Pakistan army is facing shortage of weaponry while the president Zardari is blind to key challenges his country is countering.*'

Late Richard Halbrooke had not declared Pakistan a 'failed state' in 2009 but in 2011, while giving statement before the Abbotabad Commission, Pakistan's ISI Chief Gen Ahmed Shuja Pasha openly admitted on record that Pakistan, though not a [complete] failed state yet but *'a failing state'* – meaning thereby that 'failing process' was in progress.

Another script;

Pakistan's contemporary history seems exhausted while narrating the stories of Lawyer's *Long March dated 15*th *March 2009*, supposedly escorted by Nawaz Sharif of PML(N) from Lahore, at the end of which Chief Justice Iftikhar M Chaudhry and his team were saddled back into their seats. Let us peep into the phases through which that reinstatement process had been moving.

In June 2008, there had been efforts for the restoration of the deposed judges in the name of achieveing the ultimate objective of an independent judiciary and the move also came from Gen Musharraf. Some of the deposed judges were ready for a compromise to accept the PCO judges as their colleagues in return for their reinstatement.

> *'Some top lawyers' leaders, too, in their off-the-record discussions, talk of having no option but to accept the PCO judges whereas the champion of the pro-Nov 2 judiciary, the PML-N, also seems to be showing some flexibility on its principled stand.*
>
> *....... some of the deposed judges are frustrated to get back to their chambers at any cost; these deposed judges are willing to serve alongside the PCO judges.*
>
> *The compromise solution appears strange because the deposed judges would work with the PCO judges, who would be in a majority in a 29-member full court. The role of the restored judges would also*

be limited through some person-specific amendments to be made in the Constitution'.

(Ref: **The News London 19**[th] **June 2008**)

Though the deposed CJ Iftikhar M Chaudhry, who had symbolized the ongoing struggle for an independent judiciary, had rejected the continuation of the PCO judges upon reinstatement of the deposed judges, but the PML(N), which had gained a lot of popularity for its clear stance on the judges issue, had started reflecting vague notions.

While PML(N) leader Nawaz Sharif was categorically stating that he would not accept the PCO judges, his lieutenants were talking of a possible compromise as acceptable. Astonishing enough, it was then confirmed that the proposal to increase the strength of the Supreme Court judges was given by the PML(N) and that his party would completely support the Finance Bill, including the contentious proposal.

'How can we oppose it as we ourselves have suggested it? Rather we are thankful to the PPP to have it included in the budget document," one PML(N) leader, known to be very near to Mr Zardari was quoted as saying.

When asked how his party could accept regularization of the PCO judges, the same PML(N) leader had openly claimed before media that: *'it has been done in consultation with the deposed judges and the lawyer's leadership.'*

The days, however, passed amidst roaring voices till March 2009 AND the superior judiciary was restored at last.

Then started another phase of jealousy, suspicion and intrigues within the ruling political elite. Recall the days when the CJP Iftikhar M Chaudhry gave 120 days to get the NRO reframed or accented from the Parliament which comprised of the PPP members and its allies but they failed.

The people knew that the whole game of NRO was intelligently played by PM Yousaf Raza Gilani to settle his scores with the presidency because the relationship between the two bigs was at the height of humiliation; at that moment for both. The last episode was considered most damaging; it was the then on-going CEC meeting in which repeated mention of rebirth of Farooq Legharis within the PPP was made throwing arrows at the PM by Zardari loyalists meaning that he was a traitor.

'It was in this desperate state of mind that Gilani took his revenge and forced his law minister [Mr Afzal] to go out and announce to the world the notorious list of thieves and crooks who had first robbed the country dry and then had taken refuge behind a disgraceful deal with a dictator. He was paying back his critics, in kind.' [**The News of 23**rd **November 2009** is referred]

Another fact revealed;

On 18th September 2011: [BERN] Director Swiss Bank said:

'Pakistanis are poor but Pakistan isn't a poor country; that 97 billion dollars of Pakistan is deposited in respective banks and if this money would be utilized for the welfare of Pakistan and its people then Pakistan can make taxless budget for 30 years, can create 60 million jobs, can carpet four lanes road from any village to Islamabad, endless power supply to five hundred social projects, every citizen can get 20000 rupees salary for the next 60 years and there is no need to see IMF and any World Bank for loans.'

More gimmicks;

Justice Saqib Nisar's Judicial Commission [*on Saleem Shahzad's murder*] in its report, released in early 2012, had observed that:

'Agencies and bureaucracy are strong in Pakistan because political leaders are corrupt and self-centered. They use these institutes when it suits them and try to level blames when it does not.

In the name of supremacy of parliament, government is trying to cover up corruption of individuals in its ranks. At the same time in the name of peoples' power, important issues of national interest are side lined such as Memo-gate scandal.'

Referring to 'the News' of 29th June 2013, former Prime Minister Raja Pervez Ashraf **on his last day in office [15**th **March 2013]** lifted ban on cutting of trees in Gilgit - Baltistan causing a loss of Rs:8 billion to the national exchequer. That lifting of ban also brought cutting of 350 old trees in the area which was a major source of attraction for the tourists from home and abroad. The ban was imposed in 2008. National Assembly directed the government to constitute an inter-ministerial committee to probe the issue and present report on the floor in that regard but, never mind; Committees and their reports are not taken seriously in Pakistan.

It has also been witnessed by the history that Barrister Aitzaz Ahsan, who was the key character in calling the defunct judiciary back; once in July 2007 by pleading Justice Iftikhar M Chaudhry's case and then by launching his famous **'Black Coat Revolution'** through the long march of 16th March 2009; had always advised his PPP's government that:

> *'In Zardari's context, the executive should write a letter to the Swiss government.'*

But on 2nd February 2012, Justice Naseerul Mulk, head of 7 member's bench of the SC, during a case hearing, had to remark that:

> *'Mr Ahsan, since the last three years your stance on the said issue have been known to all but today you are pleading exactly at 180 angle; why so'.*

Aitzaz Ahsan had lost in vacuum, he had no words to answer thus he lost the day and the cause, of course.

Never mind; his palms were properly greased; immediately before, Aitzaz Ahsan was awarded the Senator's ticket from the PPP and it was fair in Pakistan's democracy.

Now the tail piece:

On *12th October 2011,* in a debate in the National Assembly, on the anniversary of the Oct 1999's military coup, PML(N) members demanded for initiating a treason case against Gen Musharraf and accused the PPP rulers of providing protection to him under a clandestine deal.

PPP's legislator Nadeem Afzal Chan counter attacked that:

> *'Why had the PML(N) singled out Gen Musharraf and spared others, including the judges who had allowed a man in uniform to carry out changes in the Constitution.*
>
> *PML(N) should not claim the credit for the reinstatement of superior court judges, including the Chief Justice who had been reinstated because of the intervention of the ISI and not because of the opposition's long march.*
>
> *Long march was just a drama and a farce. The judiciary was restored when the ISI wanted it. It was on ISI's directives that the Chief Justice*

took a stand and said 'no' to Gen Musharraf when the former president had asked him to resign on 9th March 2007.

PML(N) should also demand action against the army Generals who had been with Gen Musharraf in the past and were nowadays playing golf in Punjab.'

{An essay published at *pakspectators.com* on *9th February 2012* is referred}

But when PML(N) got their turn of rule after May 2013's elections, their leadership was not initially serious to take Gen Musharraf through that treason mill – although the retired General was physically there in Pakistan and under arrest. However, during the first week of November 2013, the treason case was given the formal approval under the provisions of an Act of 1976.

(Inam R Sehri)
Manchester UK
December 2013

Scenario 73

LUTTO – TAY HORE LUTTO

[CORRUPTION SCANDALS IN PAKISTAN]

PAK-LEGISLATORS PAY NO TAX:

On 2nd **March 2010,** there was leading news in the whole print and electronic media that many Pakistani legislators had businesses and property portfolios in other parts of the world worth millions of dollars. Going through the filed statements of assets of members of the National Assembly, dozens of names appeared to have either a foreign business or owned some property abroad.

Arbab Alamgir Khan and his spouse Asma Alamgir Arbab [MNA on reserved seat] of the Pakistan People's Party [PPP] owned an apartment in Marina Dubai worth Rs: 30m; Makhdoom Amin Fahim owned a 2.2m Dirham worth apartment number 217 - Al-Dahsara-2, Greens Dubai.

The then National Assembly Speaker Dr Fehmida Mirza had mentioned in her assets declaration that she had paid an advance amount of Rs: 7.3m against an overseas apartment. Sherry Rehman's spouse also owned a residential apartment in London worth Rs: 59m and Farahnaz Ispahani, wife of Hussain Haqqani and herself an MNA from PPP' s gifted seats, had an apartment number 3005 at 4301 Massachusetts Avenue, Washington DC 20036 worth $675,000 then.

Engineer Usman Tarkai had one house in Doha, Qatar valued at Rs:15m; Munir Khan Orakzai had an investment of $225,000 in transport business in Doha.

M Jamil Malik owned a house in Rotterdam, Holland, valued at 60,249 euros [only?]. He also owned a shop worth 250,000 euro and an investment of one million euros in food business named Malik Eastern Food in Netherlands.

Khwaja Asif had an investment of $25,000 in Zen Japanees Rest; brought $88,243 in Pakistan as remittances also. Ch Iftikhar Nazir had an investment of Rs: 41m in Weal AG Cooperation and Welcon International of Hong Kong having branches in Lahore.

Zahid Iqbal owned a house in London worth £0.9m, a restaurant and property business in London with £2m. Ch Nazir Ahmad Jatt had an investment of $0.5 million in Eihar Construction of Riyadh, Saudi Arabia.

Dr Talat Iqbal Mahesar owned an apartment in Houston USA worth $55K. Sohail Mansoor Khwaja had an investment as 18, Craneborne Chase, White Church Stoufville, Canada, worth Canadian $0.32m. He also owned Unit no: 12, worth $0.47m in 9088 Halston Court, Burnby BC, Canada.

Farhat M Khan had house no: 21744, Marigot Dr Boca Raton Fl-33428-USA worth $0.9m. He had an investment of $0.55m in Petroleum Cord, 4400 Federal Hwy Ft Lauderdale, FL USA. Anousha Rehman owned a house in UK worth Rs:50m and Begum Ishrat Ashraf and her spouse had flat in the UK valued at Rs: 9.2m.

The real point of disturbance for the people of Pakistan was that none of the above mentioned [and others too] parliamentarians had disclosed that whether they had bought the respective properties from the money on which tax had been paid to the national exchequer and how much. Fact remained that majority of them had turned out to be tax dodgers; the GUARDIAN dated 12th December 2012' once mentioned in detail.

A year long study report, published jointly by two civil society organizations — the Centre for Peace and Development Initiatives and the Centre for Investigative Reporting in Pakistan — did not take into account the tax paid by politicians on their parliamentary salaries, which used to be automatically deducted by the government. Instead, it focused on the lawmakers' declarations of supplemental income from property, professional practices, and other sources of revenue.

Tax evasion has been a social norm in Pakistan since sixty years; people never considered it a crime. The country has been at chronically low rate of income tax collection. Of the country's 180 million people, only 2 percent are registered to pay tax, and less than a quarter of those actually pay, according to the report. [Only 260,000 out of 180 million citizens paid tax consecutively for the last three years, according to the Federal Board of Revenues (FBR) data]

Income tax evasion is particularly high among the wealthiest Pakistanis, leaving the country with the lowest ratio of tax to gross domestic product in South Asia. Meanwhile, the poor bear a disproportionately high tax burden because of indirect taxes on electricity, food and other goods.

Pakistan's flawed tax system had long been an issue for Western donors, who doled out the Pakistani government billions of dollars as development loans / aid over the past decade and supported bailout programs from multinational institutions like the International Monetary Fund [IMF] and World Bank.

In a Congress session of 2010, the US Secretary Hillary Clinton had said:

> *"They don't tax income. They don't tax land. And a lot of the wealth is held in these huge feudal estates. They have no public education system to speak of, and it's because the very well off, of whom there is a considerable number, do not pay their fair share."*

Pakistan's refusal to implement sweeping tax reform was instrumental in the collapse of $11.3 billion IMF bailout programme in November 2010.

Most Pakistani feudal avoid taxation because their income is largely derived from agriculture, a sector that is exempt from federal taxation — a longstanding complaint of the country's urban middle classes. The point is not that 70% don't file their returns, it's that those who do file fictitious returns and do not declare the true extent of their income. The problem is not limited to lawmakers; it's the entire prosperous class of Pakistan. Their lifestyles are totally out of sync with their declared income.

Another difficulty remained that, even when breaches of the tax laws were discovered, the rich and politically connected were never prosecuted. Law enforcement in Pakistan is in general very weak and if you happen to be an influential and powerful person like a politician, then it goes weaker. Those who make revenue policies run the government; they have not been able to set good examples for others.

The report carried the figures that out of 446 members of the Senate and National Assembly, 300 did not file their tax returns. And those who submitted the income tax return statement had paid an insignificant amount that didn't match with their princely living standards and expenses.

Out of 126 tax return-filing lawmakers from both the Houses, the National Assembly & the Senate, only 15 paid tax above one million rupees and 68 paid below Rs:100K each. All the MNAs and senators were sent a letter asking them for tax details. Only two MNAs, Pervaiz Malik and Arbab Muhammad Zahir, responded positively. The National Tax Numbers [NTNs] and Computerised National Identity Cards [CNICs] of the lawmakers were collected from their nomination papers and used for checking their tax information through sources with access to their data.

Prime Minister Raja Pervaiz Ashraf paid an insignificant amount of tax, Rs:142,536 in 2011. Out of his 54-member jumbo size cabinet, 34 didn't file tax returns. Prominent among them were Ch Pervaiz Elahi, Ch Wajahat Hussain, Haji Ghulam Ahmed Bilour, Rehman Malik, Nazar Mohammad Gondal, Farzana Raja and Makhdoom Amin Fahim. *This 70-page report that contained all tax-related details of the MPs could be accessed through the CIRP website.*

The number of tax-dodgers increased over the years. A study based on the 2008's nomination papers record of the lawmakers found that 61% of them had admitted in their papers having not paid a penny in taxes the year they contested elections. Of the remaining 39% taxpaying lawmakers, only 9% paid tax above one million rupees.

Prime Minister Yusaf Raza Gilani and his 25 cabinet members had paid zero tax, including the then sitting Finance Minister Hafeez Sheikh and Foreign Minister Hina Rabbani Khar. Mr Gilani himself registered for NTN in July 2010.

The latest report *"An Analysis of MPs' Income Tax Returns for 2011,"* available with media told that in the Senate, Aitzaz Ahsan was the highest taxpayer who paid Rs:12.97 million; followed by Abbas Khan Afridi, Talha Mehmood, Farogh Naseem and Osman Saifullah. *Mushahid Hussain was the lowest taxpaying senator as he paid only Rs:82 in 2011.* Karim Ahmad Khawaja, Haji Saifullah Bangash, Naseema Ehsan, and Malik Salah-ud-Din Dogar were other four lowest taxpaying Senators. No political party had shown significant compliance with the tax laws making it mandatory to file the tax returns.

Jehangir Tareen [later joined PTI] was the highest taxpaying MNA with Rs:17.05 million in September 2011. He was followed by Hamid Yar Hiraj, Hamza Shahbaz Sharif, Attiya Inayatullah and Humayun Saifullah Khan. Sheikh Rohail Asghar of the PML(N) was the lowest taxpaying MNA among those who had then paid Rs:16,893 only. Ghulam Murtaza Jatoi, Asim Nazir, Engineer Amir Muqam, and Rana Afzaal Hussain had followed Sheikh Rohail in the bottom-five list.

There were 88 senators and MNAs who didn't have their NTNs even. Among them were included Commerce Minister Makhdoom Amin Faheem, Deputy Speaker National Assembly Faisal Karim Kundi, Senator Pervez Rashid, Aftab Sherpao, Faisal Saleh Hayat, Samina Khalid Ghurki, Zubaida Jalal and Mehboobullah Jan, who was declared the richest MNA in 2009 otherwise.

There were 35 senators and MNAs registered for NTN only after their elections of 2008. Prominent among them were Yusuf Raza Gilani, Maulana Fazlur-Rehman, Zahid Khan and two federal ministers, Sardar Bahadur Khan Sehar and Kh Sheraz Mahmood. Although, Gilani was no more in the PM House after mid 2012 but he was an MNA and PM in 2011 when the tax returns were filed and thus considered for study.

There were 10 key-position holders in the Senate like the Chairman and Deputy Chairman Senate and parliamentary leaders of different parties. Among them the highest taxpayer was Abbas Khan Afridi mentioned above and Ishaq Dar [*the Federal Finance Minister in PML's government in 1997-99*] the lowest taxpayer among them with Rs:32,750. Deputy Chairman Senate Sabir Baloch didn't file the tax return.

There were 12 MNAs holding key positions in the National Assembly. Among them, Dr Fehmida Mirza, Speaker National Assembly, was the highest taxpayer who paid Rs:0.649 million and Ghulam Murtaza Jatoi, the parliamentary leader of the National Peoples' Party (NPP) was the lowest taxpayer who had paid Rs:21,993. Ch Nisar Ali Khan, the Leader of the Opposition, paid Rs:153,940 as income tax in 2011.

The Pakistani elite class has been the biggest tax evaders. Right from Gen Ziaul Haq to President Zardari, no leader filed tax returns regularly. In the case of Gen Zia, the report quoted his speech of 1986 where he had urged Islamic punishment for the tax evaders [*Gen Zia had said if Islamic law called for the amputation of the hands of thieves, tax evaders should have their entire arm cut off*] but the tax authorities revealed later that Gen Zia himself had never filed a tax return right from 1969 to 1988; his family was finally forced to do so.

Pakistan's tax to GDP ratio of 9.2% had been [still it is] significantly lower amongst other countries like India (16 percent), Sri Lanka (13 percent), Indonesia (14 percent), Malaysia (15 percent), Thailand (17 percent), Philippines (14 percent), and South Korea (16 percent). It is even lower than Ethiopia (10 percent) and Afghanistan (9.4 percent). *The National Assembly was informed on 7th June 2011 that Pakistan was second from the bottom among 154 countries on the tax to GDP ratio ranking.*

In Pakistan, the tax malpractices on the part of elite have always discouraged the common citizens to pay taxes who already feel overburdened through indirect taxes. The low tax to GDP ratio had been a major revenue issue confronting Pakistan; as a result, its economy has long been dependent on foreign aid and loans, even more these days.

On 22nd April 2011, an FBR report for 2008-09 presented before the Public Accounts Committee (PAC) made a startling disclosure that banks withheld an amount of Rs:13.696 billion collected as tax but did not deposit the same in government treasury. 24 banks collected from the public a sum of Rs:22 billion in 2007-08 in taxes; they deposited only Rs:8 billion in government treasury and retained the rest of more than Rs:13 billion.

As per details; 232 companies in the public sector distributed profit of Rs:145 billion on which Rs:14.55 billion was realized as tax. However only Rs:5.42 billion were deposited in govt account and Rs:9.12 billion were not. Only four of 38 sections under the head of withholding tax for 2008-09 were subjected to scrutiny which revealed that Rs:45 billion of withholding tax were not deposited in govt account.

On the whole PAC termed the performance of FBR disappointing; its orders and directions had not been implemented seriously. It was noted that out of a population of 180 million, only 3.136 million people paid taxes. Out of those there were 47,412 companies, 1,716,375 traders, 1,230,165 salaried people and 141,672 associations of persons (small businessmen).

Pakistan Revenue Auto Machine Ltd (PRAL), functioning under FBR's administrative control was declared involved in embezzlement of Rs:18 m but the Accounts Officer culprit was restricted only to removal from service and FBR officials could not unearth the assets of the accused even in ten years. PRAL was functioning as a private company but public revenue was used to run that private company; salaries were being paid by FBR. The said concern was working as an e-filing unit and that 200,000 people benefited from it through electronic refunds and receipts.

During the fiscal year 2008-09, cases of recovery of Rs:120 billion on behalf of FBR were pending in the courts and the government had to promulgate three ordinances to recover Rs:51 billion. It was on record that for under trial cases, the counsels were paid from Rs:10K to Rs:1m as fee.

LIQUID NATURAL GAS [LNG] SCAM:

On 5th April 2010, the Supreme Court [SC] of Pakistan directed the Ministry of Petroleum to file complete record by 14th April regarding a 25 billion dollar Liquid Natural Gas (LNG) scam. A 3-member bench of the apex court comprising CJP Iftikhar M Chaudhry, Justice Ch Ijaz Ahmed, and Justice Ghulam Rabbani Rabbani gave the directives while hearing a *suo moto* case.

Reportedly, the government of Pakistan had suffered a loss of $1.33 billion in 3.5 million LNG deal worth $25 billion. The Federal Minister for Petroleum maintained that the government had not sustained loss; rather the country would get profit of the same amount after finalising this project. The Petroleum Ministry had clarified their position before the National Assembly Standing Committee on Petroleum and Natural Resources and according to the Committee's report submitted in the house on 9th April 2010, the alleged scam was termed baseless.

Media investigative reports had revealed that the PPP's top guns awarded a multibillion dollars contract for 3.5 milion tons LNG import to a French firm after ignoring the lowest bid jointly offered by the Fauji Foundation and the Vitol. Former Finance Minister Shaukat Tareen had filed a reply before the apex court saying that there was a clear lapse when the Fauji - VITOL proposal was not shared with the Economic Coordination Committee (ECC).

Managing Director Fauji Foundation Lt Gen (retd) Hamid Rab Nawaz alleged that they were intentionally dropped from the bidding as contract was awarded to a French firm on the pressure of Qatari high ups. Secretary Finance informed the court that the Petroleum Ministry had not placed complete details of the bidding before the ECC; a little more details below.

A secret letter No: Met/354/40, dated 4th February 2010 written by Qatar's Energy Minister Abdullah Bin Hamad to Petroleum Minister Naveed Qamar, pleading for the contract to be awarded to Shell, only five days before the ECC meeting on 9th February, was confident to getting this multi-billion dollar contract as the Qatari minister had invited Mr Qamar to visit Doha to witness the signing of the agreement to import the LNG.

Shaukat Tarin, the then Finance Minister sitting in the ECC meeting, rejected the recommendations of the Petroleum Ministry to award the contract to Shell and, instead, recommended to award it to the GDF Suez. *This became the main reason behind the annoyance of the President Zardari and Mr Tarin was sent home next day.*

The two official letters of the global head of the LNG Shell, De Ia Rey Ventor, and Qatar's Deputy Minister for Energy and Industry Abdullah

Bin Hamad Al Attiyah, were placed before the Supreme Court to prove how massive irregularities were committed in the award of this contract and how political clout was used to make last minute changes in the official summary.

Letters dated 10th & 18th February 2010, written by Petroleum Ministry's Special Secretary G A Sabri, to Shaukat Tarin [*informing him that the petroleum minister had stopped him from giving any reason for ignoring the lowest bidder, FF / Vitol, and that the minister would personally handle the matter*] were also made part of the court file. Fauji Foundation / Vitol's bid, claiming that it was the lowest by about $400 million from the GDF-Suez, was also presented before the SC. Replies of Mr Tarin, Finance Ministry, Petroleum Ministry and MD FF Gen Rab Nawaz to the notices issued on 2nd April 2010 were also duly submitted to the SC's bench.

Meanwhile, investigations revealed that the evaluation committee, headed by G A Sabri, was in favour of the FF / Vitol because their bid was cheaper for a five-year term, while the GDF-Suez was cheaper for a 20-year import contract. So, both were recommended for the contract. When Shell came to know that its bid was being ignored, its chairman met one of the top guns of Pakistan to seek his help. Consequently, Minister for Petroleum Naveed Qamar received a letter, dated 4th February, from De La Rey Venter, saying that:

> *"......Having considered what you shared with us and in view of our understanding of your requirements, we wish by this letter to provide you with an amended proposal. We believe this accommodates what you require without forgetting the long-term supply security for Pakistan."*

In this letter, Shell offered to supply 2.5 million tons of LNG [from Qatar] against the tender of 3.5 million tons for six years; also enclosed a new bid in the light of long discussions at the Presidency.

On the same day, Naveed Qamar received another letter from Qatari Minister Abdullah Bin Hamad saying that '*a decision on the LNG receiving terminal from Shell / Qatar has been taken in principle by you in the cabinet. I would like to congratulate you on achieving such a significant milestone on the route to LNG. ..... Thereafter would be pleased to invite you to Doha to witness signing of the relevant documents in due course*'.

When these two letters arrived at the ministry, the evaluation team was asked to "accommodate" Shell at all costs. The official summary was sent to the ECC replacing the name of FF / Vitol with Shell. The report of the consultant opposing the award of contract to Shell was thrown in the dustbin. But, finally it was decided to allow GDF-Suez to supply LNG for 20 years and Shell was recommended for five years. However, when the summary was presented before the ECC, Shaukat Tarin straightaway rejected the recommendation of the petroleum ministry to award the contract to Shell and instead awarded it to GDF-Suez.

In the ECC meeting, the name of FF / Vitol was not mentioned even being lowest. When Shaukat Tarin wrote to the Petroleum Ministry asking why it had never mentioned the bid of FF / Vitol in the official summary to the ECC. After eight days Sabri sent in a brief reply saying: *"Minister Naveed Qamar says he would handle the matter personally"*.

Shaukat Tarin was sent home *on 28*[th] *February 2010* thus the whole issue was buried. Gen Rab Nawaz of the Fauji Foundation wrote to PM Secretariat and even complained to ISI to investigate the matter; but there was no one to ask Naveed Qamar or G A Sbari and others – it was democratic Pakistan.

On 29th **April 2010,** the reporter who broke the story of LNG scam was misbehaved by the Chief Executive Officer [CEO] Stephen Hamilton of GDF Suez London, in the lobby of the apex court. GDF official Stephen gripped him from his arm and said *'Hello Mr, you defamed our company by filing a news story and we would precede a case against you in the London court.'*

The reporter replied that he had no concern with GDF but he only highlighted the irregularities in the Ministry of Petroleum; adding that *'you have no right to deal me in such a rude manner while showing your old colonial mentality, we are not your slaves.'*

The matter was brought in the notice of the apex court during that day's hearing and Abdul Hafeez Pirzada, the counsel for DGF Suez, and S M Zafar, the counsel for Petroleum Ministry had to apologise for that misconduct of top GDF official.

Full details are available in former petroleum secretary G A Sabri's book [*The Proclaimed LNG Scam – a Treatise in Perspective*] on this scam, released *on 18*[th] *June 2013* which narrated how the LNG project went dead due to controversies during the PPP government.

The book disclosed big names who were allegedly involved in failing that LNG import project; Pakistan could have been in a position to import LNG at $11 per mmbtu against the price of over $17 per mmbtu quoted by different suppliers.

THE FACTS remained that the import of 500 Million Cubic Feet per Day (MMCFD) of LNG project was scraped because of vested interest, intensifying the energy crisis in Pakistan. The government negotiated a price of $13.819 per MMBTU with potential suppliers, the ECC of the Cabinet gave the project go-ahead but because of certain reasons, the import of LNG went impossible till mid 2013 at least.

In 2013, the LNG price in the international market went up to $18 per MMBTU because of a higher demand in Japan, UK and India. In 2010, countries like Iran and Turkmenistan had quoted $15 per MMBTU but due to over enthusiasm of the Supreme Court, exhibited through the *suo-moto,* the project could not be finalized.

The nominated Price Negotiating Committee comprising of G A Sabri [Chairman] with Pervaiz Butt of the Planning Commission, Iqbal Awan of the Ministry of Finance, and Naeem Sharafat of the Sui Southern Gas Company had achieved a reduction of almost 46% resulting in a saving of over $1 billion per annum. The terminal tariff was also brought down by the PNC from $1.5 per MMBTU to $0.5 per MMBTU. Even the 2013's lowest tender price, not yet finalized, was higher by 28%.

Had Pakistan gone ahead seriously with the Vitol / Fauji or with GDF Suez, that saving could increase to almost $721 million per annum. *"In addition, the indirect cost of industrial sector's losses because of the energy crisis and its impact on the country's economy is yet to be quantified,"* the media reports held. The said quoted book loudly told that:

> *"Thus with irregularities of the people concerned and the omissions and prejudices of the judiciary, this wonderful deal, possibly the only transparent mega project in Pakistan at least in the last decade, died its poison injected death, ruining the energy sector and ultimately Pakistan's economy at large."*

The ECC had considered the summary on 26th January 2010 and directed the Ministry of PNR to resubmit it with additional reports from Asif Bajwa, Special Secretary Finance and Masroor Qureshi, DG Debt Management (DGDM) of the MoF. The revised summary was submitted on 8th February 2010; on 9th February 2010 the ECC approved the project with GDF Suez.

No sooner did the ECC decision become public, various mafias jumped in. A news report captioned *'$1 billion LNG scam lands in federal Cabinet'* by *Rauf Klasra* was published in two installments in the daily *'the News' of 29th & 31st March 2010*. It was evident that both articles were sponsored to malign the Award.

BISP's FAKE RECRUITMENTS:

The BISP was established through an Ordinance in 2009 to provide financial support, assistance and other opportunities, such as education, vocational training, skills development, welfare programme, livelihood programme, health insurance, accidence insurance and access to micro-finance. As per provisions, BISP was aimed to strive to achieve the three objectives like enhance financial capacity of the poor and their dependant family members, formulate and implement comprehensive policies and targeted programme and reduce poverty and promote equitable distribution of wealth, especially for the low-income groups.

On 4th April 2011; President Zardari was briefed on Benazir Income Support Programme [BISP]'s appointments by Farzana Raja at Naudero. Farzana Raja had recruited an exact number of 100 officers & staff for its Sindh chapter all with a concocted and fake table exercise. When the news was leaked to the media, Farzana Raja had defended these appointments but the programme's Media Director in BISP Shoaib Khan stood in the way; thus the appointments had to be cancelled as they were not approved by the BISP management.

The cancellation was announced as the officers at management level had refused to become part of those appointments and had approached the Chief Justice of Pakistan with the request to inquire into the matter to get these appointments cancelled and protect them from being targeted. The officer, Shoaib Khan was then surrendered to the Establishment Division making him a target for refusing to own up what he called the forged call letters issued under his fake signatures.

The said appointments caused a considerable embarrassment for Mr Zardari who did not know that those appointment letters, already issued to the candidates concerned, had become controversial as the officer concerned had refused to own them.

[*Here the story of* **A KETCHUP GIRL:** *Asif Ali Zardari, when used to appear in NAB Courts of Rawalpindi, was always surrounded by his usual courtiers who competed with each other to please the boss. The crony-in-chief, later in-charge of President's golden brief case, jail doctor Qayyum Soomro once brought biscuits and patties and were being served. An overly made-up woman suddenly dashed to Asif Zardari to pour ketchup in his plate and then turned around to inform others, "Asif Sahib likes his patty with ketchup."*

As Zardari gave her an approving smile she suddenly broke up in water melon sized tears. A little taken aback, Zardari was explained that her husband Pir Muqaram Ali Shah was also in jail for a printing case fraud. Everybody was moved—Asif Zardari the most. Asif told the nearby party workers that she would miss her husband's hearing but never his own. No surprises there. When Zardari affectionately said, 'come on girlie, give me a little more ketchup'. Instantly, she cheered up like a doll.

After 14 years, Farzana Raja was the biggest star and PPP's poster girl. She made great speeches and was seen shouldering Asif Zardari in every second picture; she had outsmarted the other two competing party Effs—Fehmida and Farahnaz—by miles. She was later the most powerful person in the PPP being in-charge minister of the Benazir Income Support Programme (BISP).

Every PPP member had to approach her for funds. The media could not dare to touch her as she had cleverly allocated a large amount of money for TV advertisements. One word against her and the ads involving tens of millions of rupees could be retracted. On Benazir Bhutto's death anniversaries, she used to be portrayed as the god mother of Benazir's children.

In her life, Benazir Bhutto disliked her because she once pulled a smart trick on her. Benazir had Jahangir Badr seated with her in a party meeting. He got up for a minute for some task and Farzana sat there pretending as if she had something to say to her. And then she got her photographed sitting next to her and got it flashed all around. Benazir was furious and asked Naheed not to let her come close to her again. Benazir was angry when Asif got her a Sindh Assembly seat in 2002.

Hats off to Zafar Bakhtawari of D Watson Islamabad with whom Farzana used to plan various politico - cultural activities in Islamabad. She used to visit various dignitaries for sponsoring certain events.

Once she went to get favours from Printing Press of Pakistan's Chairman, Pir Mukarram and he never returned - she got managed to marry Pir Sahib. Since those days on, she never looked back even when the poor Pir got jailed in corruption cum political victimization cases.]

On 9th April 2011; when the media broke the story and disclosed that the BISP's Sindh Chief had alleged that 100 "forged" appointment letters of assistant directors, complaint assistants and others had been issued to favourite candidates, the BISP Chairperson started blaming the officer of having been involved in a case of sexual harassment. Interestingly, former DG Sindh Akbar Aleem Shamim, on 6th April 2011 had written to the Secretary of the BISP Islamabad and other concerned and insisted that he had not signed what he called the "bogus offer letters".

Referring to *the 'Nation' dated 15th July 2013;* the Auditor General of Pakistan [AGP] detected irregularities and non-compliances of about Rs:147 billion in the accounts of the BISP in the audit year of 2013. The short comings were:

- *BISP management paid Rs:12.22 million to one Anjum Asim Shahid Rehman, a chartered accountant, vide cheque No.865129 on account of Nationwide Rollout of Poverty Scoreboard during 2011-12 ignoring the selection criteria of the firm.*

- *BISP management paid Rs:3.734 million to the nine deputationists under the head of house rent allowances despite the fact that they were allotted government accommodations; they were not entitled to monthly house rent.*

- *Rs:21.583 million were spent in adoption of special pay scale by BISP board without the concurrence and approval of Finance Division; thus the payments were irregular and unauthorised.*

- *Rs:2.746 million were paid in violation of the government's instruction; the officers appointed on contract basis were not entitled to benefit from arrears.*

- *Rs:1647.486 million were spent under the head of selection of four advertising firms without due evaluation, the entire process of short-listing and final selection was done without the involvement of Press Information Department; thus the whole process was termed as irregular.*

- *Rs: 2747.256 million were spent on irregular appointment of State Life Insurance Corporation [SLIC] without open competition while the invitations for 'Health Insurance' were advertised in leading newspapers. Appointment of SLIC without open competition and ignoring the eight competitors without observing the laid down rules was irregular.*

- *Rs:74412.364 million were spent in making payments during 2010-12 under Poverty Scorecard System, Parliamentarian System, Waseela-e-Haq, Waseela-e-Rozgar, Waseela-e-Sehat, Emergency Relief Packages and IDPs, the spending outlets not included in the BISP Act 2010.*

- *Rs:7.665 million were spent in the head of provision of vehicles to unauthorised officers and Rs:1.930 million was paid in irregular and unauthorised payment to cash reward to World Bank consultants.*

- *Rs:2648.747 million were spent in undue favour to SLIC as the BISP Board decided to provide life Insurance worth Rs:100,000 to the primary bread-earners of the families which was not authorised by the BISP Act.*

- *Rs:73.752 million were given to NADRA without open competition for printing and distribution of 184,379 Benazir Smart Cards at the rate of Rs:400 per card thus termed as irregular and unauthorized.*

- *Rs:65098 million were spent on agreements with Pakistan Post and commercial banks, which contained provision of reconciliation of funds disbursed before next payment. The amounts disbursed to Pakistan Post and commercial banks were not reconciled as required by the accounting procedure.*

- *Rs:48.049 million were spent for the printing work which was awarded to Pakistan Post Foundation Press without observing the prescribed rules and procedures.*

- *Rs:66.968 million were over-paid to Pakistan Post and no efforts were made to recover it back.*

- *Rs:305.577 million were **paid to ineligible beneficiaries**; there was no application control and responsibility was not fixed for those [bogus] payments.*

[The President of Pakistan is chief patron and prime minister is executive patron of BISP while a federal minister manages its operations as chairpersons with the help of board constituted by the President on the advice of the PM.]

ANJUM AQEEL OF PML(N) CASE:

On 31st March 2011; PML(N)'s MNA Anjum Aqeel agreed to hand over land and cash worth Rs:7b to the treasury under a deal struck with federal investigators to resolve the National Police Foundation (NPF) scandal. The recovery was made by the joint inquiry committee, comprising members of the Federal Investigation Agency (FIA) and the NPF. The committee, headed by Zafar Ahmad Qureshi, the Managing Director of NPF and Additional DG of FIA, conducted the inquiry on the orders of the Supreme Court and the interior secretary.

According to the deal struck between FIA officials, NPF authorities and Anjum Aqeel, the MNA had undertaken to hand over the possession of a 2.75 acre commercial plot worth Rs:2.2b located in Crystal Court Centre in Islamabad, besides taking on the liability of a 3.25 acre plot valued at Rs:2.6b. Aqeel had fraudulently obtained allotment letters of six acres of land from NPF. However, he was still the legal owner of all six acres and had Aqeel sold off the additional land, the NPF was responsible to give the land to the buyers. After the deal, the NPF's liability was apparently waived off.

Anjum Aqeel had also pledged to give possession of another 6,655 sq yard plot valued at Rs:240m; he was made bound by the agreement to deposit about Rs:2b in NPF account against the price of a 25-acre plot within one year. The price of the said land was to be assessed by the committee headed by the Secretary Interior.

MD NPF Zafar Qureshi told the media that the inquiry was almost finalised and its recommendations were ready to be placed before the apex court. Also that, on papers, as many as 59 persons were allotted lands, who did not actually exist, adding that if other people were also allotted 3.25 acres of land, they would also be included in the victims' list.

On 21st June 2011; the Supreme Court, on a *suo moto* notice, directed the MD NPF to initiate criminal action against MNA Anjum Aqeel involved in Rs:6b land scam case. The 3-member bench comprising Chief Justice Iftikhar M Chaudhry, Justice Tariq Parvez and Justice Amir Hani Muslim in its order observed that the NPF Committee had established irregularities and corruption in purchase of land and directed that all responsible should be dealt strictly as no one was above the law.

The NPF MD was also directed to proceed against those officials who arbitrarily and illegally got more than ten and 15 plots and caused huge loss. *"Prima facie, from land agreements it appears that those were not transparent. Go by the law, let the law prevail,"* the bench held.

The CJP expressed his displeasure that why a case was not registered against an MNA who had deprived the police employees of their lands; FIR should have been registered against the man who had embezzled Rs:6b. MD NPF informed the bench that NPF had taken back 25 kanals of land worth Rs:2b out of total 126 kanals from the MNA. The MD NPF confirmed that one director housing had grabbed 15 plots while one widow PSP officer was deprived of her plot.

On 15th July 2011, a mob comprising of local members of PML(N) raided the Shalimar Police Station Islamabad where MNA Anjum Aqeel was going to be kept in police custody for involvement in the above mentioned NPF land grabbing case [*termed as old tested modus-operandi of the PML(N) by the media – recall the stinking episode of November 1997 while attacking the SC premises*]. It was also noticed by the media and the high ups of police that the said fleeing away occurred with the connivance or at least with the consent of DSP In-charge and the concerned SHO. Thus a case was registered against both police officers on charges of rendering negligence in the line of duty; both officers were arrested too.

According to details, while MNA Anjum Aqeel was being brought to Shalimar Police Station, the police mobile van came under attack by PML(N)'s activists who shifted Anjum Aqeel in their car and fled away. On media pressure, Anjum Aqeel surrendered before the police next day and he along with those who kidnapped him from the police mobile were taken into custody and later an ATC court sent them to jail. A day after, however, the Rawalpindi ATC court approved bails of 31 persons including the MNA.

Meanwhile, one college lecturer named Shabhahat Ali, got registered a case against Anjum Aqeel alleging that the MNA had sold a plot for Rs:0.95m to him in the National Police Foundation housing scheme but the plot never materialised and neither was the huge sum returned by the accused. The matter went to court where the MNA's lawyer told the court that his client had made a compromise with the complainant and had returned the money.

On 12th August 2011, Special Judge Central, S Akhlaq Ahmed, granted a post-arrest bail to MNA Anjum Aqeel. The court also extended interim bail granted to him and to Director Housing Maj Laeeq Khan till

7th September in another case of alleged corruption in purchases of land for NPF.

Ironically, when MD Zafar Qureshi left the NPF in November 2011, the FIA declared the said MNA 'innocent'; *Dawn dated 15th Nov 2011* is referred, though Babar Sayeed Butt, counsel for the NPF had raised the dissenting voice.

As per interim report released by the FIA, Anjum Aqeel's Estate Company Land Linkers had received a payment of Rs:441,178,375 for 608 kanals. However, the Capital Development Authority [CDA] transferred only 563 kanals to the NPF. Of the remaining 45 kanals that were not transferred, 22 kanals were short because of duplication / triplication in transfers; 21 kanals were short due to change of ownership made on the directive of the Supreme Court; and two kanals were short due to sale of excess share. The fact sheet also absolved Anjum Aqeel of embezzlement of land in two other agreements as well.

Regarding another accused of the land scam – Maj (Rtd) Laeeq Ahmed Khan, ex-Director Housing – the FIA interim fact sheet said that he was not posted at that post in 1997 when the first agreement for purchase of land was signed between NPF and Land Linkers. However, he was allotted two plots in his own name and three plots were allotted to his son and daughter but no illegality came on record in this allotment.

Likewise, the Golra police also decided to withdraw a case registered against Anjum Aqeel and others on charges of breach of trust and trespass. The case was registered on 26th October in response to a complaint lodged by one retired SP of Sindh named Raja Ayub. Anjum Aqeel was declared innocent during investigation saying it was a civil matter not criminal.

The FIR contained that on 27th September, MNA Anjum Aqeel, Tahir Mehmood and Mansoor Khan, from whom SP Raja Ayub had purchased the land and paid the amount, re-occupied the land forcefully. Later the NPF converted its status from residential to commercial and transferred it to the accused MNA.

On 3rd December 2011, MNA Anjum Aqeel was arrested from courtroom after the Special Court rejected his bail plea in the Rs:6b NPF land scam case. The MNA appeared to the jury where the judge refused to extend his interim bail, rejecting his plea, after which FIA officials arrested him from the court premises. Another point surfaced that Aqeel was not the only owner of the land but there was another share holder with him who had got stay order of the court. MNA Aqeel had taken oath in the court to withdraw from 23-kanal land but as he had been given 14 extensions in the case, the Court ultimately handed him over to the FIA.

On 24th December 2011; Senior Civil Judge Mahmood Haroon referred NPF land scam case to Rawalpindi Special Court due to non-appearance of three accused including MNA Anjum Aqeel. NPF Secretary Abdul Hannan and former Director Iftikhar Ahmed had not appeared before the court on medical grounds. Ironically, all the three medical examinations were compiled by one Dr Akhtar Ali Badshah, Assistant Professor of Cardiology PIMS Islamabad.

FIA's AD Legal informed the court that the case was registered against above mentioned persons on orders of the Supreme Court [SC] during a *suo motu* notice case on 21st June. The MNA's company, Land Linkers, was chosen to procure land for the housing scheme in Sector E-11 for police personnel. The civil court was told that the value of just one piece of land of Crystal Courts, measuring 48 kanal was Rs:4b and the remaining land was residential, of over Rs:2b. Thus a heavy loss was caused to NPF in this allotment in connivance with some dishonest officers of NPF.

The ratio of affiliation of land of private owners as decided by CDA Board on 9th October 2002 could be 54% share of private owners. By this way 162 kanals developed land was allotted to the MNA.

On that very pretext of land scam, Anjum Aqeel lost his bright political carreer. He had previously been the elected MNA of Islamabad on PML(N) ticket. For general elections of May 2011, PML(N) did not consider his candidature thus Makhdoom Javed Hashmi of PTI won that seat.

Three months later, Anjum Aqeel's name was again considered by PML(N) high ups alongwith of Hanif Abbasi and Advocate Ashraf Gujjar to contest supplementary elections on the same constituency of Islamabad as Javed Hashmi had vacated the seat. Hot disussions were held in PM House for all the three but Ashraf Gujjar succeeded in getting more favours. That was another hard luck that PML(N) lost that seat against the PTI's candidate again.

Referring to Rauf Klasra's essay in *daily 'Dunya' of* 28th *April 2013:*

'Anjum Aqeel was the luckiest person of the lot. His principals, Sharif family people, were being dragged in courts since the last 15 years but could not get relief. Anjum started his career as a school teacher and sailed in the billionair's boat just within years.

He once escaped the police lock up through attack on police station by his companions; he paid bucks to the whole PS and judicial crew and got acquitted.

In another lower court for a similar land-fraud case, the judge asked him that the court could summon the newspaper reporter for publishing news against him because the complaint is being thrown out.

In the last the FIA had withdrawn that Rs:6 billion case from the court because everyone including DG FIA, IGP Islamabad Binyamin, Secretary Interior, Principal Secretary Kh Siddique Akbar, retiring MD NPF Zahid Mahmood and the whole PML(N) were all on his side.'

Never mind, everything is fair in love, war and Pakistan.

REKO DIQ GOLD MINES:

On 7th *April 2011*; Chief Justice Iftikhar M Chaudhry observed that when there were already rules for exploration and mining then why new rules were made; specially designed to facilitate companies involved in Reko Diq site in Balochistan.

[*Reko Diq is a small town in Chagai District of Balochistan in a desert area, 70 kilometres northwest of Naukundi, close to Pakistan's border with Iran and Afghanistan. The area is located in Tethyan belt that stretches all the way from Turkey and Iran into Pakistan.*

According to Dr Samar Mubarakmand, former Chairman Pak Atomic Energy Commission (PAEC), Geological Survey of Pakistan had discovered the Reko Diq reserves as far as in 1978. Its vast Gold and Copper reserves are known to all; believed to be the world 5th largest gold mine.]

A 3-member bench of the apex court, comprising CJP Iftikhar M Chaudhry, Justice M Sair Ali and Justice Ghulam Rabbani, was hearing a case against leasing of Reko Diq gold and copper mines in Balochistan worth over $260b [*to Tethyan Copper Company (TCC), a Canadian and Chilean consortium of Barrick Gold and Antofagasta Minerals*] by the federal and provincial governments in violation of then prevailing laws. The TCC had got the exploration licence for just $100 with a condition to find out something in six months and then come into an alliance and be a partner with Balochistan government in investment and profit.

The court observed that the original license holder company [BHP] had been investing millions of dollars in the project since ten years then could they sell the licence only for 100 dollars? TCC's lawyer told the court that the new company was to invest $3 million within six months and $100 was just a token consideration in the agreement. BHP was exhausted investing in this project so they invited the new company [TCC] and gave them full rights of exploration for the next six months; the companies were to be turned into a joint venture later.

Balochistan's Advocate General Ammanullah Kanrani objected the TCC counsel on the grounds that relaxation was against the rules and had never been approved by the chief minister; the TCC held that the summery of the joint venture was duly approved by the CM, the Balochistan government issued a notification and the then governor had issued the agreement. First notification for relaxation of rules was issued on 20th January 1994 and then under new rules it was re-written on 3rd April 2002.

The Balochistan's AG told the apex court that the BHP had made an agreement with a man namely Atta Muhammad who had since been sacked on corruption charges. TCC was ready to settle the matter with mutual cooperation but the AG told the apex court that the Balochistan government wanted a court decision on the project on merit instead of settling it through consultations.

Meanwhile, the federal government [of the PPP] distanced itself from that multi-billion dollar Reko Diq saga by refusing to pay Balochistan the Rs:450m it needed to pay legal experts to fight the international arbitration case filed by the TCC. TCC had opened litigation with Pakistan at the International Centre for Settlement of Disputes in Washington and was hoping for an out-of-court settlement. The panel of legal experts representing Pakistan included Cherie Blair, wife of former British PM Tony Blair, Barrister Mehnaz Malik, AG Amanullah Kanrani and Ahmer Bilal Soofi.

TCC had filed its case for international arbitration in November 2011 after Balochistan government blocked the company from mining copper and gold by rejecting its application. TCC had submitted the feasibility report to the provincial government in August 2010 and applied for a mining licence in February 2011.

Tethyan Copper Company had hired SNC-Lavalin, one of the top three feasibility study companies in the world, to prepare a feasibility study which cost them around $220m and took around three to four years to be completed.

Islamabad had also refused to pay damages had the TCC won the case in the international court. Several foreign companies refused to make investment in Pakistan after TCC went to international court. TCC, represented by Antofagasta of Chile and Barrick Gold of Canada, held 75% share in the project while Balochistan had 25% stake.

TCC claimed it had invested over $500 million in exploration, scoping and feasibility studies on the project; while total investment was projected to be $5 billion over a period of five years. Earlier, Balochistan government had once refused TCC's proposal to become a partner by financing 25% of the project. Basically, the TCC was concerned about purported involvement of a Chinese company in the same project.

In a letter written to the then Federal Petroleum Minister Naveed Qamar in September 2009, Pakistan's Ambassador to Chile Burhanul Islam wrote that it was not a good idea to entertain Chinese company MCC in the same mining site, which had been offered to TCC with all commitment, responsibility, investment and legal claims. He suggested that the Chinese, if aspiring for a project, could be offered a separate mining site.

Quoting *'the Express Tribune' dated 3*rd *August 2012* on the subject:

> *'In a feasibility report submitted to the Balochistan government, TCC projected a turnover of over $60 billion for the gold and copper project over a span of 56 years. This projection was based on the price of $2.2 per pound of copper and $925 per ounce of gold in 2009. The mine has estimated reserves of 11.65 million tons of copper and 21.18 million ounces of gold.'*

The mineral resource at Reko Diq is estimated at 5.9 billion tonnes with an average copper grade of 0.41% and an average gold grade of 0.22 g / tonne; with an annual production estimated at 200,000 tons of copper and 250,000 ounces of gold contained in 600,000 tons of concentrate. The $3.3 billion Reko Diq project was the largest foreign direct investment mining project in Pakistan.

Tethyan completed the feasibility study of Reko Diq project and placed their findings before the Government of Balochistan in August 2010. The company estimated that it had spent more than $345 million on project acquisition, exploration and feasibility studies. *On 15*[th] *February 2011*, Tethyan preferred an application to the Balochistan government for a mining lease. *On 15*[th] *November 2011*, TCC was notified by the government that its application for a mining lease had been turned down.

On 7th January 2013; the Supreme Court declared the Reko Diq agreement void. In its 16-page judgment, a 3-judge bench of the apex court, headed by Chief Justice Iftikhar M Chaudhry, stated that the agreement reached on 23rd July 1993 was in conflict with the laws of the country. The bench added that all amendments made to the agreement after its signing were unlawful and in contradiction with the agreement. Cases pertaining to Reko Diq mining lease dispute were being heard in courts for the past five years. The SC held:

> *"The CHEJVA dated 23.07.1993 is held to have been executed contrary to the provisions of the Mineral Development Act, 1948, the Mining Concession Rules of 1970 framed there under, the Contract Act 1872, the Transfer of Property Act 1882, etc., and is even otherwise not valid, therefore, the same is declared to be illegal, void and non est.*
>
> *The agreement was not permissible under the Balochistan Mining Rules (BMR) 2002 as well as the Rules of Business of the Government of Balochistan (GOB), particularly Rule 7."*

Earlier, *on 15*[th] *December 2012,* the International Centre for Settlement of Investment Disputes (ICSID) had given a go-ahead to the Balochistan government and prominent nuclear scientist Dr Samar Mubarakmand to carry out the mining and smelting project in Reko Diq area. The ICSID had rejected the TCC's demand for *'provisional measures'* for *'protecting'* two of its deposit areas.

The ICSID was seized with a dispute between Pakistan and TCC after the latter's application was rejected by the mining authority of Balochistan on the grounds that the company had submitted feasibility reports of only six kilometres area comprising two deposits, whereas it wanted to acquire 99 kilometres which contained 14 deposits. The ICSID tribunal, which had reserved its ruling on 6th November 2012, released a 45-page unanimous decision allowing the Balochistan government to carry out the mining activity.

Established under the auspices of the World Bank, the ICSID comprising Dr Klaus Sachs, Dr Stanimir Alexandrov and Lord Hoffman had, however, asked the provincial government to keep it abreast of all activities on a regular basis to be carried out in Reko Diq by Dr Samar and his team. Dr Samar Mubarak had also appeared before the tribunal in London to explain technical details about his project.

Barrick and Antofagasta Minerals took a $345 million gamble to develop Reko Diq, the first world-class mining project in Pakistan, only to lose the battle in Pakistan's Supreme Court.

The consortium had tried to force the Balochistan government to stop work in an area spread over 99 square kilometers including the area where Mubarakmand was working. Local authorities in Balochistan had refused to meet with TCC before rejecting the consortium's bid for Reko Diq.

On 31ˢᵗ January 2013; Governor Balochistan Nawab Zulfiqar Magsi chaired a high-level meeting during which Dr Samar Mubarik Mund gave briefing about the excavation work on the Reko Diq Copper Project. Provincial government aimed to execute the copper project on its own as it got clean chit from the Supreme Court. It was resolved that in its first phase, excavation work would be carried out on first-line reserves that contain 2.2 billion of tons of copper and gold worth 104 billion dollar.

Under the project, 15,000 of copper and gold reserves in raw form would be extracted annually enabling provincial government to get $321 million per annum. In the provincial PSDP for 2012-13, Rs:1400m had already been allocated for the project while Rs:1980m were earmarked for the provision of water in the Reko Diq area. The Governor Magsi also issued directives for making appointments of local people in the project and to ensure foolproof security measures in place besides establishing office at Quetta and Reko Diq instead of making the same at Islamabad.

PPP's government was over on 16ᵗʰ March 2013. In a mysterious development, the TCC consortium, which was thrown out from Pakistan by the SC, landed in Islamabad again in 2ⁿᵈ week of April 2013, to start top-level negotiations with the caretaker government to get back the Reko Diq project.

TCC's delegation was there in Islamabad because a delegation headed by Minister of Petroleum and Natural Resources Naveed Qamar, Finance Minister and Chairman BOI Saleem Mandviwalla and Sharmila Farooqi, a lady adviser of the Sindh government had visited Canada to invite Barrick Gold Co to Pakistan again. There were some lower level officials from other provinces as well for routine discussions.

What these three high-level officials discussed with Barrick executives in Canada was not known exactly but the media got air of those secret negotiations; thus the matter was in lime light once more. The basis of those fresh negotiations were that during hearing in ICSID Tribunal *"Pakistan, through the Baluchistan government, had proposed to restrict any activity to just the H4 deposit at Reko Diq and not touch the massive H14 and H15 copper-gold deposits."*

Pakistan had also promised not to contract with third parties for that work nor expand its activities beyond H4. It also said mining rights wouldn't be granted to any third parties. The TCC held that:

> *"The said decision helps preserve the possibility of the company ultimately receiving a mining lease for the Reko Diq area by significantly limiting the steps Pakistan and the Province of Balochistan may take regarding Reko Diq.*
>
> *We will carefully monitor the information Pakistan provides pursuant to the Tribunal's order, and we remain prepared to seek further relief from the Tribunal if Pakistan breaks any of the assurances it gave to the Tribunal during the upcoming merits phase of the hearings throughout 2013.*
>
> *[But] the company still prefers a negotiated solution to the current impasse and is open to holding talks with the Pakistan and Balochistan governments to reach a beneficial outcome for both the company and the people of Balochistan and Pakistan."*

However, the TCC could not get through the secret deal then [*or the asking price of negotiators was high*]. That was why *on 8th May 2013*, TCC announced that it had withdrawn its request for 'specific performance / mining license' in both international arbitrations [i.e, ICC & ICSID] and went for seeking claims for monetary damages only including lost profits for the mining operations; TCC had in fact given up hope of eventually mining Reko Diq. Instead, they opted to seek monetary damages as compensation for Pakistan's breaches of contract and treaty rights, and those of the region, Balochistan.

The TCC's statement, however, made no mention of the amount to be claimed as compensation.

On 4th July 2013; the Senate Standing Committee on Petroleum and Natural Resources was informed by Dr Imran Ahmed Khan, DG Geological Survey of Pakistan [GSP] that in Reko Diq area of Balochistan total gold and copper reservoirs, besides precious stones, are over five billion tons, worth over dollar one trillion.

Referring to *'the News' dated 21st September 2013,* the said Canadian company which carried out the controversial feasibility study into the Reko Diq gold and copper mines had been declared by the World Bank as the *world's most corrupt corporation* and blacklisted in dozens of countries.

According to the blacklist of the World Bank released on 19th September 2013, out of the 250 companies, 119 belong to this one Canadian giant, LNC-Lavalin, which had the highest number of corrupt and fraudulent companies. After the 119 Canadian companies, 46 US firms, 43 Indonesian, over 20 Chinese and even one Pakistani company have also been blacklisted.

The Montreal-based SNC-Lavalin Group Inc appeared on the list 58 times as a Canadian subsidiary and 14 times as an American company, with many more SNC subsidiaries named all over the world. It had been banned in Malaysia, Malta, Saudi Arabia, US, Canada, Algeria, Angola, Austria, Chile, Columbia, Costa Rica, Mexico, Egypt, India, Dominican Republic, Russia, Nigeria, Tunisia, Korea, Barbados, Mongolia, Panama, Peru, Brazil, Peuto Rico, South Africa and Uruguay.

Lavalin officials were accused of bribing officials in many countries and at least $56 million were doled out to the corrupt officials for various favours and illegal things that the company was involved in.

Lavalin carried out the feasibility report on the Reko Diq mines on behalf of Barrick Gold at a cost of US$70 million only but was demanding $400 million through the world tribunals preferring an out of court settlement. The company had quoted in every document that it had spent $345 m on the project whereas it was $70m only.

FLOOD SURCHARGE ON POOR ONLY:

In late July 2010, floods resulting from heavy monsoon rains attacked all the four provinces simultaneously in Pakistan; also affected the Indus

River basin. About one-fifth of Pakistan's total land area was underwater; approximately 796,095 square kilometres and about 20 million people suffered, mostly by destruction of property, livelihood and infrastructure; around 2,000 were reportedly dead.

An aid of US$460 million was initially asked by the UN Secretary-General for emergency relief, noting that the flood was the worst disaster he had ever seen. Only 20% of the relief funds requested were received till ending August 2010. The UN bodies were concerned because [as per WHO reports] ten million people were forced to drink unsafe water; extensive damage to infrastructure and crops were lost in addition - estimated to exceed US$4.5 billion both. Total economic impact was initially worked out to be of US$43 billion.

[*In response to Indus River floods in 1973 and 1976, Pakistan had created the Federal Flood Commission (FFC) in 1977 to operate under Ministry of Water and Power. It was made responsible for executing flood control projects and protecting lives and property of Pakistanis. The fact remains that since its inception, the FFC received Rs:87.8 billion (till 2010); certain projects were initiated and funded but all were mostly completed on papers only – hats off to the corruption made by successive leaderships.*]

During the floods of 2010, the power infrastructure of Pakistan also took a severe blow damaging about 10,000 transmission lines and transformers, feeders and power houses in different flood-hit areas; a power shortfall of 3.5 giga-watts was calculated when the water level went down. Lack of clean drinking water and sanitation posed a serious new risk of health of flood victims. In mid August, the first documented case of cholera emerged in Mingora town threatening millions of stranded flood victims, who were already suffering from gastroenteritis and diarrhoea.

As per UN documents, some 800,000 people were cut off by 2010's floods in Pakistan and at least 40 more helicopters were needed to ferry lifesaving aid to them. Many of those cut off were in the mountainous northwest, where roads and bridges were swept away. There were no official celebrations of Pakistan's 63rd Independence Day on 14th August, due to the calamity but the people were seen disappointed because President of the country, Mr Zardari, had left for France on holidays staying there for weeks whatsoever.

It is still available on record that 2010's floods had submerged 69,000 km² of Pakistan's most fertile crop land, killed about 200,000 livestock and washed away massive amounts of grain. A major concern was that farmers were unable to plant new seeds in 2010 implying a loss of food production in 2011, too. The agricultural damage reached more than $2.9 billion, had eaten up over 2,800 km^2 of cotton crops, 810 km^2 of sugar cane and 800 km^2 of rice, in addition to the loss of over 500,000 tonnes of stocked wheat, 1,200 km^2 of animal fodder and other stored grains.

As per International Labour Organization [ILO]'s report dated 7th *September 2010,* the floods had cost more than 5.3 million jobs in Pakistan. Other quarters told that the GDP growth rate of 4% prior to the floods was lost in vacuum; thus Pakistan was unable to meet the IMF's target budget deficit cap of 5.1% of GDP, and the then existing $55 billion of external debt caused alarms. Agricultural production dropped by more than 15%; nationwide car sales fell by 25% and milk supplies fell by 15%.

World Food Programme's report dated *24*[th] *September 2010* declared that about 70% of Pakistan's population, mostly in rural areas, did not have adequate access to proper nutrition. Already resurgent in the Federally Administered Tribal Areas [FATA] and Khyber PK province, agricultural devastation by floods left Pakistan in utter misery and loss. An estimated 3,916 km of highway and 5,646 km of railway tracks were affected and their repairs expenditure was expected at $158 million $131 million respectively. Public building damage was estimated at $1 billion while about 5,000 schools were either washed away or went in total deplorable conditions.

On 2nd *April 2011;* the PPP's government was caught red-handed protecting the rich and punishing the poor through an under the table deal, as the 15 percent flood tax, imposed through a presidential ordinance, was imposed on common taxpayers while the big businesses were exempted, costing a hefty Rs:10b loss to the exchequer.

Pakistan's Federal Board of Revenue [FBR] acknowledged that corporate entities were exempted through the language of the Flood Tax Ordinance. *"Yes, at this point, it [ordinance] is not applicable on corporate tax payers; however, an amendment in the ordinance will be made to include the corporate tax-payers."*

The fact that the rich companies including multinationals, banks and oil companies were not covered by the Flood Tax and some tax experts in Karachi opted to challenge it in the court as it was a discriminatory piece of legislation. The issue went unnoticed when President Zardari imposed this tax without consulting the parliament and on the same very night Pakistanis were mourning the release of American killer, Raymond Davis.

Few could notice this midnight robbery, unique by all means, as it was entirely discriminatory in the core with one section of the society, already crushed by poverty, taxed in contrast with the privileged elite running big businesses like multi-national companies, banks, insurance firms as well as oil and gas companies. The ordinance read as:

"4A Surcharge:-(1) Subject to this ordinance, a surcharge shall be payable by every taxpayer at the rate of fifteen percent of the income tax payable under this ordinance including the tax payable under Part V of Chapter X or Chapter XII, as the case may be, for the period commencing from the promulgation of this ordinance, till the 30th June, 2011.

(2) Surcharge shall be paid, collected, deducted and deposited at the same time and in the same manner as the tax is paid, collected deducted and deposited under this Ordinance including Chapter X or XII as the case may be: Provided that this surcharge shall not be payable for the tax year 2010 and prior tax years and shall be applicable, subject to the provisions of sub-section (1), for the tax year 2011 only."

As for as corporate tax is concerned, the amount under this head for 2011 was to be deposited by 31st December 2010, as all tax years are defined one year in advance. The presidential ordinance that was promulgated on 15th March, had to expire on 30th June 2011, hence covering only the individual tax payers, not the corporate giants whose tax year 2011 had already been closed on 31st December 2010.

Going into details: the fourth line of section 4A was worded as follows: *"under Part V of Chapter X or Chapter XII"*. Ironically there was no Part V of Chapter X or Chapter XII in the Income Tax Ordinance, 2001.

Also the word 'surcharge' had not been defined in the ordinance nor did it stand defined in Pakistan's Income tax Ordinance 2001. It should have been defined in section 2 (63) of Income Tax Ordinance. Also, the surcharge had not been included in sections 168 & 169 of Income Tax Ordinance 2001 which was a section dealing with "credit of tax collected or deposited" so even credit of the same could not be legally claimed.

These mistakes were considered deliberate and the officers of the Law Ministry and the FBR were in collusion with big businesses in exempting them from the Flood Tax thus saving them a cool Rs:10b; thus the said changes in ordinance were immediately challenged by one Shahid Orakzai in the Supreme Court of Pakistan terming it illegal and unjustified.

The petition stated that parliament was the sole authority to impose such taxes AND that the president had no power with regard to a money bill under Article 75 of the Constitution; he cannot return such a bill to parliament for reconsideration.

The SC issued several notices to the respondents but no one turned up to defend that ordinance. Ultimately, *on 8th November 2011*, that the life of an ordinance was 120 days, thus it died its own death.

FLOOD DONATIONS SAGA:

[As per *Fact-sheet published by Humanitarian Global Assistance on 17th August 2010*; *Pakistan's statistics were: Population – 173 million; GDP per capita in 2007 – US$2496 with Global Ranking of 132/184; UNDP's Human Development Index (HDI) – 0.572 with Global Ranking at 141/182; BUT with 60.3% of the population living on less than US$2 a day. The country was a major aid beneficiary receiving US$1.5 billion in Official Development Assistance (ODA) and ranking as the 14th largest global recipient of aid in 2008.*

In 2005 severe flooding affected seven million people in Pakistan's mainland and an additional five million were affected by an earthquake in Kashmir. For the Global Peace Index [regional and domestic instability] Pakistan ranked at 145 out of 149 in 2010. During War on Terror [WOT] activities in north-west Pakistan, more than two million people were displaced in year 2009 only. Pakistan also hosted one of the world's largest refugee populations, 1.7 million people from Afghanistan.]

Pakistan received US$576 million under flooding and Kashmir earthquake heads in 2005, and a further US$465 million in 2006 as humanitarian needs in Kashmir continued. In 2008 Pakistan was the 16th largest global recipient of humanitarian aid it received US$1.5 billion in ODA but was at its lowest level since 2003 and a 34% drop from the year 2007's US$2.3 billion.

Humanitarian aid contributions to Pakistan respond to natural disaster events. In 2005 Pakistan received substantial humanitarian aid, US$576 million (which made up 31% of ODA) in response to the earthquake and floods which affected 12 million people. Humanitarian aid to Pakistan declined between 2006 and 2008 but remained significantly higher than in any year preceding the 2005 peak.

In 2005 Turkey was the most charitable donor, reporting US$66 million to Pakistan, of which US$25 million was channelled bilaterally to the Pakistan government.

Between 2007 and 2008, Central Emergency Response Fund [CERF] contributions to Pakistan increased by 222% from US$5.8 million in 2007 to US$18.7 million in 2008. In 2008 Pakistan was the 5th largest recipient of CERF funds. In 2009 CERF contributions to Pakistan dropped to US$8.9 million ranking Pakistan 12th. In 2009 the UAE was the most generous donor donating US$30 million to Pakistan, the majority of which went through UN agencies.

Coming to 2010's flood catastrophe now:

In response to the appeal and subsequent visit of the UN Sec General, Ban Ki-Moon's personal visit to Pakistan, the following governments actually sent their donations, **mostly in cash**:

*"Afghanistan - $ 1 million; **Algeria** - €100,000; **Austria** - €5.6 million; Azerbaijan - $2 million; **Bahrain** - $6.9 million; **Belgium** - €150,000; Botswana - $ 103,040; **People's Liberation Army of China** - 10 million yuan; **The Chinese Red Cross** - US$50,000; Cyprus - €131,062; **Denmark** - 193 million DKK (33 million euro); **Estonia** - €64,000; The European Union - €80 million; Finland - €1.2 million [€600,000 channelled through the WHO & €400,000 through the UNHCR and €200,000 through Finn Church Aid]; **France** - €1.05 million and 35 tonnes of emergency supplies; **Georgia** - € 100,000; **Germany** - €25 million in direct help plus €43 million via contributions through international organisations with which it is associated. Greece - €100,000; **Hungary** - €50,000; **Iceland** - ISK 23 million (€190,000); India - $5 million; Ireland - €4.5 million [Ireland proved to be the most generous European country in donating aid to disastrous Pakistan at that moment]. Israel's aid was not answered by Pakistan; **Italy** - € 1.33 million; **Japan** - $ 230,000 for emergency relief goods AND an additional $3 million for rehabilitation process; **Kosovo** - €150,000; Kuwait - US $5 million; **Lithuania** - LTL 50,000; **Luxembourg** - € 2,364,621; **Malaysia** - $1 million; **Maldives** - MVR 10 million (US $1 million); **Malta** - €13,106; **Mauritius** - US$ 300,000; Monaco - €127,065; **Nepal** – Rs:10 million; **Netherlands** - €8.6*

*million; **Netherlands's population** -€17 million; **New Zealand** - NZ$4 million; **Nigeria** - US$ 1 million; **Norway** - NOK 30 million [NOK 9 million through UN Central Emergency Response Fund, and NOK 21 million through UNICEF]; **Oman** - US$ 500,000; **Poland** - €196,592; **Samoa** - US$20,000; **Saudi Arabia** - US $362 million + $105.29 million donated by the Saudi Government, US $14.7 million donated by the Saudi Fund for Development, and US $242 million collected through Saudi Public Fund Relief; US$5.3 million were handed over to National Disaster Management Authority [NDMA] in cash; **Singapore** – US$ 50000 cash, 800 water filters and 10,000 blankets; **Slovakia** - €170,380 cash plus power generators, water pumps and tents; **Slovenia** - €13,106; **Switzerland** - CHF 3 million; **Thailand** - $75,000; **Turkey** - $18million + other relief [details given separately]; **UAE** - $5million + other relief goods [details given separately]; **United Kingdom** - £134 million + £10 million for washed away bridges + £60 million from private donations + 400 metric tons of aid including tents, shelter kits, blankets, water containers and nutritional items; **Vietnam** – US$50,000; **World Bank** - US$ 1.3 million immediate cash + a loan of US$900 million for long term reconstruction [__Hillary Clinton personally donated $10 to encourage the Americans to donate, no matter how small the amount was__]; **Asian Development Bank [ADB]** offered a loan of $2 billion AND **Islamic Development Bank** offered a loan of $11 million US dollars for the reconstruction efforts."*

Besides the national governments, world known NGOs contributed towards the rehabilitation of 2010's floods victims, too, with an unprecedented history of their past. **The Islamic Turkish NGO [IHH]** sent 450 tonnes of supplies on a train and another on a cargo aeroplane; plus 3000 tonnes of medications, medical materials, textile products, tents, blankets, cleaning materials and kitchenware. IHH opened 10 water purification units to supply clean drinking water. The foundation also set up two tent camps of 70 tents each Nowshera & Islamabad; the camps included tents for schooling and for medical doctors.

To mention only few for instance, the UK based **Disasters Emergency Committee** raised over £60 million; **Oxfam** provided clean water and hot meals to over 180,000 people immediately and later reached around 900,000 people with clean water, sanitation kits and hygiene supplies; **Save the Children** used helicopters, donkeys and boats to deliver doctors and medical supplies to families cut off by the water. **CARE International** provided water purification tablets, tents, family hygiene kits, kitchen sets, tarpaulins and mosquito nets to 4,500 people; **Islamic Relief** distributed 3,570 family hygiene kits in Nowshera and Mardan districts benefiting 24,990 people, also distributed 2,850 household kits (containing mattresses, mosquito nets etc.) and 2,850 kitchen sets to benefit 19,950 people. **Concern** helped 24,500 people in Charsadda district, raised more than €1 million in public donations from the Irish public.

> *ERT Search and Rescue, Focus Humanitarian Assistance, Humanity First in collaboration with NCHD, Heritage Foundation (HF), MERCY Malaysia, ICNA Relief Canada, Muslim Charity, Trócaire of Ireland, Giving Children Hope, and Médecins Sans Frontières* can be named with golden words in addition.

Response by certain individuals was more encouraging in those hours of distress and misery. To name a few that the **Saudi King Abdullah bin Abdul Aziz** donated US$5.3 million from his private money; the **Saudi Crown Prince Sultan Abdullah bin Abdul Aziz** donated US$ 2.7 million; the **Saudi Interior Minister Nayef bin Abdul Aziz Al Saud** donated US$ 2 million; the **Governor of Tabuk** Province in Saudi Arabia donated US$1 million; the Chairman of Samba Financial Group of Saudi Arabia, **Eesa bin Mohammad al Eesa** donated US$2 million; **Her Highness Fatima bint Mubarak Al Ketbi**, the wife of the UAE's president donated AED 5 million.

The wife of Turkish PM **Emine Erdoğan** personally donated TL 100,000 and also her jewellery including a precious necklace, which was very memorable - given to her by her husband on their wedding. [*The Turkish people bought the necklace in an auction and gifted it back to her but she again donated it to the flood victims*] **Merve Tekinay**, a nine-year old Turkish girl donated her savings of $83.72 and her only doll.

The **Kuwait Finance House** donated $2 million; the **E-Q8 Petrochemicals of Kuwait** donated $100,000; the **Open Society Foundation** donated $5.5 million; the **Bill and Melinda Gates Foundation** donated $700,000. **Angelina Julie** donated $100,000; **Tim Beel** donated $500,000 AND the **Queen Elizabeth II** made a personal donation of an undisclosed amount. Most of the donations in this paragraph were sent through UN agency or via the British Red Cross.

There were countries like Argentina, Australia, Azerbaijan, Brazil, Canada, China, Indonesia, Iran, Jordon, Saudi Arabia, USA, UK, Sri Lanka, Sudan, Sweden, Spain, Syria, Turkey, Turkmenistan, UAE which frequently kept on sending the emergency relief items, medicines, mobile clinics with their doctors and staff, tents, clean water equipment and filters, water bottles, food packets etc through cargo planes and via shipping & trains. The material and stuff were of worth tens of million dollars. Some countries like USA and UAE had sent their helicopters to help the Pak-Army in relief activities.

WERE THE DONATIONS ACCOUNTED FOR:

HOWEVER, the Pakistani government was blamed for sluggish and disorganised response to the floods. The perceived disorganised and insufficient response led to riots, with looting of aid convoys by hunger-stricken people. In Sindh, the ruling PPP ministers were accused of using their influence to redirect floodwaters from their crops while risking densely populated areas leading Pakistani UN ambassador Abdullah Hussain Haroon to call for an inquiry. British Prime Minister David Cameron was accused by Pakistan of hampering international aid efforts after he claimed that Pakistan was responsible for promoting terrorism. *The Guardian* had cried that:

> 'There was a dire need of relief - six million [of the 14 million affected] are children and 3 million women of child-bearing age. This is a higher figure than in the 2004 Indian Ocean tsunami – but were they actually addressed.'

From all corners of the country and from all walks of life, there were dissident voices that the funds and donations received from the world community should have been accounted for. Till today no report has been published that what was the total collections and how they were spent for the welfare of the flood victims.

Many said that the corruption stories of 2005's earthquake in Kashmir were repeated by those who were at the helm of the affairs in 2010.

On 21ˢᵗ August 2011; PM Gilani told the media that Rs:1.98 billion were collected through the Prime Minister's Flood Relief Fund till then. As per his contention, the foreign aid was pouring in from abroad standing as a testimony to the fact that the world had started trusting Pakistan government. A proposal forwarded by PML[N]'s Nawaz Sharif, to form an independent commission for the collection of funds, was straightaway rejected by the PPP's prime minister. Even CM Punjab Shahbaz Sharif's advice of setting up an aid commission was thrown out.

The media pointed out that the international community's no confidence was evident from the official statistics of foreign assistance for 2010 flood victims with Prime Minister's Relief Fund getting peanuts; only $21m from world capitals; it was out of total $697m assistance committed by them.

The foreign countries and donors instead preferred to depend on international agencies and non-governmental organizations [NGOs] to ensure that the money donated would be properly utilised and was not corrupted by the government, which was rated by foreign agencies as one of the most corrupt regimes in the world.

The Finance Ministry's official website told **on 8**[th] **January 2011** that a total of $3.042b foreign assistance for the flood affectees was committed. Out of this amount $2.34b was committed to be spent through the United Nations or other international agencies and NGOs whereas the remaining $696m was to be spent through the Government of Pakistan. The total committed assistance included a soft loan of $243m too.

Amongst the major donors, the US committed $571m but opted to spend this entire amount through international agencies like USAID etc. Not even a single dollar was donated by Washington to PM's Relief Fund. Britain, which had pledged $216m, also did the same and did not contribute even a single penny to PM Gilani's account. The Turkish government committed $53m besides raising a total of $142m through a fundraiser but had contributed only $10m to PM's Relief Fund.

Japan committed a total of $519m but did not give any amount for the PM's Relief Fund. Iran too committed $100m but it too avoided to deposit any amount in the Prime Minister's Relief Fund. After Turkey [$10m], the Asian Development Bank was a major contributor with $3m amount. Afghanistan gave $2m for the PM's Relief Fund and emerged as the third largest foreign contributor.

Let us wait for the 'Accountability Day'.

Scenario 74

NICL SCAM OF 2010-11:

On 12th October 2010, the Supreme Court of Pakistan [SC] took a *Suo Moto* notice of a case concerning with the National Insurance Company Limited (NICL), and directed the Secretary Commerce, Government of Pakistan [GOP] to get registered a criminal case with FIA in respect of certain transactions allegedly embezzled. As a result whereof a case FIR No.24/2010 dated 12th October 2010 under sections 409, 420, 109 PPC read with 5(2) PCA was registered with FIA Circle, Lahore.

The background of the incident was that on 6th May 2010, a letter was sent to the, Chairman NICL [Ayaz Khan] from Transparency International Pakistan [TIP], having mention of the following allegations:

> Procurement of 804 kanal [a measurement of land equivalent to 1/8th of an acre] land in Lahore reportedly belonging to Ex-MNA Mr Habibullah Warraich, which had market value of Rs:0.3 million per Kanal, whereas NICL was buying it at Rs:2 million per kanal.

> 27000 sq ft office space in Dubai in Liberty Tower was purchased in July 2009 @ UAE Dirham 2,700 per sq ft against the market price of AED 1,200 per sq ft allegedly causing loss of Rs:900 million to the government exchequer.

> 10 Acre piece of land purchased in Korangi Deh Phihai, in August 2009 @ Rs:90 million per acre, against the maximum market price of Rs:20 million per acre.

> Award of Contracts of painting works and furniture to M/s Casa Bella Lahore; at Karachi for Rs:26.987 million and at Islamabad for Rs:9.31 million, who was not a licence holder of Pakistan Engineering Council. The tender for Karachi was for 6 floors but the Contractor was asked to paint only 4 floors.

> Land was purchased in Lahore in the year 2009 from Mr Mohsin Warraich for Rs:1.5 billion, of which market value was Rs:30 million only at that time.

On an earlier communication, the Chief Secretary Punjab, had sent his report on 4th March 2010 stating therein that NICL intended to purchase a piece of land for developing a housing colony at Lahore at exorbitant price to benefit a few persons, who were behind the deal. A similar report was received [on 2ⁿᵈ April 2010] from Secretary Board of Revenue [Punjab] Lahore, too.

On 26ᵗʰ April 2010, the matter was referred to Chairman NAB for conducting discreet inquiry and report. NAB office had sent their report in three parts confirming the embezzlement of huge amounts done in the above deals. NAB had also opined that such big amounts could not be misappropriated without the 'iron hand' behind the wrong doers.

In the *suo moto* notice, the SC directed the FIA to accelerate the proceedings; cause arrest of the accused, particularly the influential persons behind them; and to register cases regarding other related incidents.

On 9ᵗʰ December 2010, Zafar Ahmed Qureshi, the then Director FIA, informed the apex court that at Lahore, another FIR No: 29/2010 was registered against Ayaz Khan Niazi and others, whereas, in FIR No: 24/2010, one Habibullah Warraich was arrested and Rs:1.4 billion were recovered from him. In the meanwhile 'influential politicians' started interfering in the investigations and the whole issue was put on 'go slow' track.

Immediately after the FIA's heavy hand, the detained Chairman of the NICL, Ayaz Khan Niazi, blamed the top guns of TIP for offering him help to clear his name in corruption cases presently with the Supreme Court, if he signed a Memorandum of Understanding (MoU) to award all future contracts on their recommendations. An absconding NICL board member, Qasim Dada, wanted by the FIA in another Rs:4 billion land scam, tried to convince his colleagues to strike a deal with TIP representatives.

Dada's son was married to the daughter of Aqeel Dhedhi, an influential stock broker. The investigators believed that Dhedhi was using his political and financial clout to stop the investigation and also blocked attempts to smoke out Dada from his hiding place. TIP was alleged to volunteer for placing a *'fact-finding report'* before the SC establishing the innocence of NICL officials; **but it all proved to be hearsay.**

Meanwhile, Ayaz Khan Niazi was continued with interrogations by FIA's Zafar Qureshi at Lahore, after he was escorted from Karachi on the orders of the Chief Justice Iftikhar M Chaudhry.

The allegations against TIP were considered to be serious, as Niazi had given details of TIP officials' involvement in the alleged blackmail in his

30-page written statement to Zafar Qureshi [*later proved bogus*]. Niazi said that he and his colleagues had refused TIP's unconventional offer. He named three other board members who were present when Dada had offered him negotiations on TIP's behalf.

MOONIS ELAHI NAMED IN NICL CASE:

Abruptly, Mr Zafar Qureshi, Director FIA, was transferred to National Police Foundation [NPF] as Managing Director, after giving him promotion in Grade 21. The SC, however, compelled FIA to continue with the investigation of the said case. In the meanwhile, *on 24ᵗʰ January 2011*, Mr Qureshi was appointed as Additional Director General [ADG] FIA in addition to his original assignment as MD NPF, to supervise investigation of NICL case at Lahore.

FIA's findings first time revealed that FIA had collected incriminating evidence against Mohsin Warraich, Habibullah Warraich, Moonis Elahi [*son of PML(Q)'s Pervez Elahi, the former Chief Minister Punjab and the sitting member of Punjab Assembly*] and one Raja Muhammad Ali but expressed that during discharge of his official functions, he was threatened of dire consequences by some 'influential' persons.

Moonis Elahi was allegedly involved in facilitating the land deals of the NICL scam. The FIA had summoned Moonis after one of the arrested accused in the NICL corruption case had stated that the *al-Tahoor Company drew Rs:220 million* through fake bank accounts of Moonis Elahi's manager named Abdul Malick. According to Malick, this money was given to Moonis Elahi.

After this statement, the Supreme Court had ordered the FIA to probe into the matter energetically. A questionnaire was sent to Moonis Elahi to appear before the FIA on *27ᵗʰ January 2011* with answers of the given questions. The FIA also wrote to the Speaker Punjab Assembly to direct MPA Moonis Elahi to appear before the investigation team of the FIA.

Zafar Qureshi, the ADG FIA, got recorded his statement in open Court that in case of his unnatural death, Ch Shuja'at Hussain, Ch Pervez Elahi, Ch Wajahat Hussain, Moonis Elahi, Major Habibullah Warraich and Mohsin Habib Warraich, would be held responsible. It was a serious blow to the Chaudhries, the old time tested politicians of Punjab. Zafar Qureshi also compiled his interim investigation report and placed before the apex court on or around *17ᵗʰ February 2011.*

In response to this situation, Ch Shuja'at Hussain approached the apex court with a request that Mr Qureshi be proceeded against as he had made a false statement before the SC's bench. In the meanwhile, *on 21ˢᵗ March 2011, Mr Qureshi placed another report* before the apex court mentioning therein that in case FIR No.24/2010 with regard to 803 kanals of land, an amount of Rs:1.686 billion had also been recovered and *Challan* [investigation report] against the accused persons had been forwarded to the court of competent jurisdiction.

[*According to the FIR, Warraich's company, Messrs Privilege, sold an 803-kanal piece of land to NICL at Mauza Toor, Lahore, for Rs: 1.68 billion in February [2010], but without getting the land mutated in its favour. This was a serious breach of financial discipline and a major irregularity, the FIR held.*]

In case FIR No.29/2010 an amount of Rs:80 million was recovered and in FIRs No. 46/2010 and 05/2011, subsequently registered during investigation, the accused including Ch Moonis Elahi were arrested and interim *Challans* were submitted in the respective courts. However, Moonis Elahi agitated that he was being maligned unnecessarily in the media by some of the arrested persons. The Chaudhries moved the court for transfer of investigation from Mr Qureshi to some other officer.

During investigation of FIR No.29 of 2010 it surfaced that a commercial plot measuring 20 kanals at Airport Road Lahore was also purchased by NICL for an excessively inflated price Rs:1.06 billion which by all survey reports, was highly extravagant price. An amount of Rs:80.4 million was recovered and deposited in the bank account of NICL. For the balance amount of Rs:42 Million, post-dated cheques were deposited by one Akram Warraich [uncle of Mohsin Habib] before the Special Judge (Central) Lahore, to be paid in five years.

It was also available on SC's record that arrest of one Amin Qasim Dada, one of the directors of NICL, could not be sought because he was allegedly hiding himself in DG FIA's camp office at Karachi. Thus the apex court had to write a note on file that:

"*It seems that instead of allowing his Director to make progress in the case, he (DG FIA) is providing shelter to the accused persons*".

On 17ᵗʰ March 2011, the Lahore High Court had already rejected the bail plea of PML(Q)'s Moonis Elahi, after which the FIA arrested him from the premises. Zafar Qureshi had requested the court for time to recover Rs:260 million from Mr Elahi which he had allegedly embezzled in the scam. He was on interim bail till that day.

During investigation of the NICL cases, the FIA officials contacted the Serious Organized Crime Agency (SOCA) of UK for obtaining information regarding the foreign currency accounts of Moonis Elahi, accused in FIR No. 46/2010.

According to reports received then, Moonis Elahi had an account in EFG Private Bank UK having balance of £11,39,000. Another account in Barclays Bank in the name of Beenish Khan [wife of Mohsin Habib Warraich] had a balance of £102,307 which had been transferred from the account in EFG Private Bank Ltd; thereby indicating that the two persons were in joint business. The then DG FIA, Waseem Ahmed, kept the said information secret with him for weeks.

DG FIA CHARGED FOR CONTEMPT:

When the above information went open to media and the SC started enquiring about DG Waseem Ahmed's conduct, the later preferred to seek retirement; and Malik M Iqbal joined the FIA as new DG. Mr Malik, instead of facilitating Mr Qureshi in accomplishing the task assigned to him by the SC, sent a letter dated 15th April 2011 to the Ministry of Interior saying:

> '........ that the interim challans in NICL cases have been submitted in the Court of competent jurisdiction on 11-04-2011 and a report thereof has already been submitted in the honourable Supreme Court of Pakistan on 14-04-2011 by the said officer.'

The apparent intention of writing such letter was to seek guidance that 'what should be done further'. The reply and reaction was obvious. The Interior Ministry forwarded that letter to the Establishment Division which, in turn, issued a notification dated 18th April 2011, saying that:

> 'Capt (Retd) Zafar Ahmed Qureshi (BS-21) was posted as ADG FIA in addition to his present assignment as MD NPF, to supervise the investigation of NICL case ......

> .... that the recoveries have been made and the Challan submitted in the said case. Therefore, the additional charge of the officer as ADG FIA is hereby withdrawn with immediate effect.'

On those developments, the SC held the opinion in writing that:

> 'Malik M Iqbal, DG FIA by sending a letter dated 15th April created obstacles in investigation of the case being conducted by Mr Qureshi; thus disturbed, disobeyed and disregarded the order / direction of the apex court; and interfered with, the process of law and due course of judicial proceedings by getting the ADG FIA, disassociated from the investigation.'

Therefore, **vide order dated 10th May 2011**, Show Cause Notice [SCN] of contempt of Court was issued to him under Article 204 of the Constitution read with section 3 & 5 of the Contempt of Court Ordinance (Ordinance V) of 2003 to explain as to why he should not be proceeded against for interfering in the affairs of the SC.

Malik M Iqbal, DG FIA initially filed his explanation to the SCN, then filed a written reply to the same ending: **'I do not want to contest the charge. I humbly and respectfully seek mercy and clemency of the august Court and by way of extenuating circumstance I submit that I am superannuating on 14th July 2011 and I shall immediately proceed on leave and shall not continue my service.'**

In his reply he also mentioned that he had tried to convince the Interior Ministry that Mr Qureshi be allowed to continue as per apex court's directions but no one heard him. However, the SC termed the DG's reply untenable and unsound; so **on 3rd June 2011**, after having discussed the case at some length, charge was framed against Malik M Iqbal, DG FIA.

Another row between the superior judiciary and executive was there to be seen. Every other day, the officers of FIA, Interior Ministry and Establishment division were called in the proceedings; given sermons and sometimes harsh exchange of feelings; ultimately **Zafar Ahmad Qureshi was suspended by the government on 4th July 2011** and proceedings were initiated against him under the services discipline rules.

The superior court had done a good job by initiating *suo moto* proceedings in a case where the national exchequer was being plundered. But suddenly, their good job was turned into general hatred when the apex court degraded itself to a menial level by wasting its time and energy on passing harsh words and shouting on the officer class.

The SC knew that who were behind the curtain; see one media comment:

> '.... So, the interior ministry has pulled yet another stunt with Additional Director of the Federal Investigation Agency (FIA), Zafar Qureshi. We

can now officially say that the PML(Q) has started reaping the benefits of joining the Pakistan Peoples Party (PPP) led government coalition.'

The SC had known that which political figures had created that tense situation but instead of calling them in court, the officers of various departments were summoned and made them to take showers of the venom and desperation of the judiciary.

Two days later, **on 6th July 2011,** A Rauf Chaudhry, Secretary Establishment, opted to go on retirement because he had honoured the apex court's orders and had issued notification for the return of Zafar Qureshi to the FIA to take over NICL probe; but the sitting government of the PPP got annoyed with Secretary's conduct in obeyance of SC's directions.

Rauf Chaudhry had earlier moved a summary to the PM Gilani seeking his approval to reverse Qureshi's transfer out of the FIA but when directed by the SC he issued the required notification on 1st July without sending a fresh summary to the PM or waiting for his approval of the previous summary in that respect.

Rauf Chaudhry, who had a clear & shining service record, was reprimanded by the PM's office for issuing the notification; the poor career officer had no option except to say good-bye.

On 14th July 2011, DG FIA Malik M Iqbal, ended his 60 years glorious career in bitter tone; Abdul Rauf, Secretary Establishment opted to go on retirement in an un-ceremonial way and Zafar Qureshi, who had recovered billions of rupees from the rogues, was placed under suspension & faced enquiries AND what the SC got better out of this situation; nothing except utter disappointment and humiliation.

On 17th August 2011, the new incumbent DG FIA, Tehseen Anwar had also offered to proceed on retirement while attending the same bench of the SC and in the same NICL case, because he was being ordered by the apex court to work under the directions of Zafer Qureshi, his ADG much junior to him; how was it possible. Later, **on 1st October 2011,** Zafar Qureshi himself proceeded on retirement after submitting his last 100 pages report to the SC's bench hearing NICL Case. Notification of his retirement was issued two weeks earlier.

Another aspect of our judicial-executive apathy; both the pillars of state were bent upon pushing each other's head down into the knees of **NICL case.** For three months Supreme Court kept on passing orders for Zafar

Qureshi of FIA and every time executive was turning around their face by thrashing the court orders into waste basket on one pretext or the other.

The NICL proceedings was an eye-opening scenario for our independent judiciary which knew that who politicians were actually playing with the judicial norms and values but, hats off to our brave judiciary, they could never find courage to call those politicians in docks – four senior officers [with blameless record] were sent home in row.

It was shameful for the executive, too; but the political masters of PPP were on a mission of saving their coalition government through PML(Q), which was based mainly on NICL-exit relationship. Through NICL, the apex court was trying to catch Moonis Elahi; and what else [*who was otherwise freed soon after because all the witnesses had already been won over – salute to our 150 years old law & judicial gimmicks*].

PML(Q) + PPP – PAK POLITICAL CULTURE:

In the back drop of NICL Case, the PML(Q) aligned with the professionals of PPP and made sure that the corruption charges levelled against Moonis Elahi would never be translated into a conviction. The Chudhries were successful in their mission because soon after the witnesses were *'won over'* and the cases were fizzled out to the extent of Mr Elahi at least. Hats off to Pakistan's judicial system where UK's bank accounts confirmations did not carry weight as evidence, the oral statements of liars do.

As usual, cleansing Elahi's image required sacrifice from those who believed in principles; thus Ch Shuja'at had to come forward. ADG Zafar Qureshi had been in the line of fire ever since he linked the scam to Moonis, a potential candidate for the next 'chief ministry of Punjab'; how he dared to take him into custody for investigation. On the other end, the PML(Q) was not letting the future prospects of Moonis be tarnished by an actual conviction. Zafar Qureshi had not known that his record breaking recovery of Rs:1.686 billion in the NICL scam would not matter for Pakistan's ruling elite; AND as judicial evidence too.

A typical Pakistani politics drama ensued. The leading investigator was suddenly transferred to the NPF before the investigation finished. The SC, continuing its bid to go after all power houses, stepped in to ensure that he was reinstated at his position. Hard luck, that in another dramatic twist, court orders were immediately sterilized by the transfer of four key members of Zafar Qureshi's team in FIA to different provinces. ADG Zafar Qureshi's second suspension came in the wake of his request to restore back those four FIA officials at their original postings.

The SC stepped in again, summoned the Attorney General with complete record of the suspension but the government continued its blatant efforts to twist the investigation. The case was then *'made to take dramatic turns'* when the key witnesses changed their versions and had denied ever giving a statement to FIA or its ADG Zafar Qureshi.

After issuance of SC's orders regarding repatriation of Zafar Qureshi - later the suspended ADG of the FIA, the scenario started changing rapidly. Soon there prevailed an impression that even if ADG Qureshi returns as chief investigator of the NICL scam again, he would have to take a new start to establish allegations against Moonis Elahi as the case at hand had already been destroyed by the succeeding investigation team.

The retaliation of about a dozen prosecution witnesses and the declaration by FIA's I O that Moonis was innocent had destroyed the entire case. In his testimony before special banking offences court, the Director FIA, Basharat Shahzad, the new supervisor after Mr Qureshi, stated that Moonis Elahi was not directly involved in subsequent two fraud cases of Rs:320 million.

The available details revealed that on 25ᵗʰ May 2011, eight witnesses produced against Moonis Elahi by FIA retracted from their statements before the court; saying that they had never given any statement to the FIA. All the eight witnesses were the employees of Allied Bank Limited, the bank in which an account was traced by ADG Zafar Qureshi which appeared to be suspicious and the later was declared to be of Moonis Elahi's front man.

[*Most of the witnesses especially bank officials had categorically denied recording of their statements against Moonis Elahi with wording that FIA officials got their signatures on plain papers and prepared their fake statements – what a character of Pakistan's educated class, the bankers.*]

On 29ᵗʰ June, three more prosecution witnesses denied recording any statement before the FIA against Moonis Elahi. The prosecution witnesses named Safdar, Hafiz Junaid and Ma'roofur Rehman, employees of the Allied Bank Limited, Multan Road Branch Lahore were allegedly won over by the political elite involved.

Originally, the FIA had details that Moonis had opened bogus accounts in the name of his manager named Malick, and his wife for corruption in the NICL. Later, the agency lodged two FIRs against Moonis, alleging that his manger Malick had opened forged accounts in the Allied Bank Limited, New Airport, and Dubai Islamic Bank, Main Boulevard branch of Gulberg Lahore. Mohsin Warraich had deposited huge amount of money in both the accounts; the record revealed.

The first FIR was registered on 27th December 2010 while the second was lodged on 27th January 2011. The FIA alleged that the money was actually taken by Moonis Elahi. The FIA report further quoted Malick as saying that he had opened an account on the instruction of Moonis and an amount of Rs:320 million was allegedly transferred to the account. [*Mohsin Warraich had deposited Rs:320 million; Rs:220 million in the first account and Rs:100 million in second account.*]

Moonis Elahi denied receiving Rs:320 million from his manager Abdul Malick. Later Malick also denied giving that money to Moonis Elahi claiming that the FIA had tortured him to make a confession. The whole story was twisted by playing with the words wherein actually it was Mohsin who had deposited money in Malick's account *but for and on behalf of Moonis*. Interrogation with Malick had led to Moonis' arrest.

[Till that moment, it was available on SC's record that the FIA had recovered Rs:1.686 billion of misappropriated amount while a sum of Rs:42 million was still to be recovered (the accused had given post-dated cheques for that amount, as stated earlier).

Also that land measuring 20 kanal near the Lahore airport was purchased by the NICL for Rs:1.06 billion in 2009, whereas, its market value was only Rs:150 million. This caused a loss of Rs: 915.3 million to the national exchequer via NICL. 10 persons were identified in that deal; seven of them were arrested and three namely, Mohsin Habib Warraich, Javed Syed and Amin Qasim Dada, were declared proclaimed offenders.

During the hearing, Moonis Elahi's counsel, Waseem Sajjad, was not able to convince the bench about his client's innocence.

The FIA report was on file saying that *"accused Moonis Elahi remained on physical remand with the FIA till 1st April 2011, and during the course of interrogation, the accused failed to negate the allegations and could not produce a rebuttal to the evidence recorded by the agency".*]

The legal experts had held that the documentary evidence was there in the case which could not be changed but even then the case was so weakened by FIA in Zafar Qureshi's absence that twisting the investigation and facts later it was brought on file that *'prima facia there was no evidence available against Moonis Elahi on record'*.

The fact remains that the 2nd report of FIA's investigating officer was not binding on the court and any upright judicial officer could dig many things out of it even if ADG Zafar Qureshi was not there. But here the District Judges did not like to follow that track because Chaudhrys would have got angry – AND that is known as Pakistani justice.

For the ruling PPP and its allies, it was a test case for their endurance; the Chaudhry family had joined the government to save Moonis Elahi. Had the PPP failed to protect him, the PML(Q) would have withdrawn its support from the PPP which was likely to lose its majority in the National Assembly then. The PPP government had pulled a number of tricks out of their executive sleeve to stop FIA's ADG Zafar Qureshi from investigating the case.

After getting all his cards in order, Moonis Elahi, **on 19th August 2011,** filed in the Supreme Court a petition seeking review of its 8th August verdict which had quashed the suspension order of FIA's ADG Zafar Qureshi and had asked him to resume investigation into the scam.

This time, the former law minister Babar Awan was engaged for Moonis Elahi's petition, requesting the court to transfer the NICL probe to a fair, impartial and independent officer other than Zafar Qureshi who could investigate without *"bias or any pre-conceived and unfounded apprehension"*. Moonis Elahi, was under house-arrest then.

Through this petition, the SC was also reminded of Zafar Qureshi's statement dated 17th February 2011 before the apex court [*that he was being threatened with dire consequences and that if he met an unnatural death, PML(Q) Chief Ch Shujaat Hussain, Pervaiz Elahi, Moonis Elahi, Ch Wajahat, Maj (retd) Habibullah Warraich and Mohsin Habib Warraich would be responsible for that.*] indicating open bias of Zafar Qureshi against Moonis; thus request for change of I O had merits.

JUDGES THREATENED & PRICED, TOO:

Next step; Ch Shuja'at Hussain as PML(Q)'s Chief and Pervaiz Elahi as the Deputy PM had especially arranged additional portfolio and powers of Special Banking Court for Sessions Judge Mujahid Mustaqeem to start hearing the NICL case in the 2nd week of August 2011. The federal government had given approval of that bargain on the orders of the CJ Lahore High Court, Justice Ijaz Ahmad Chaudhry.

[It was *Judge Abdul Rasheed of Special Banking Offences Court* who had previously indicted Moonis Elahi in the NICL Case. Moonis was produced before the court by Zafar Qureshi's team of FIA from Nadra Rest House, a specially notified & declared sub-jail where Moonis was kept during his judicial remand.

Moonis Elahi's three counsels Amjad Parvez, Rai Bashir Ahmad and Misbahur Rehman had requested to show them the record of witnesses statements under 164 CrPC but the judge rejected their plea of providing copies of the statements, saying the precedents cited by them did not establish the argument that the court was bound to provide copies to the accused.

At this moment, one of Moonis's counsels, Rai Basheer, also quoted a Hadith, The Prophet (PBUH) said: *"Judges are of three types, one of whom will go to paradise and two to hell. The one who will go to paradise is a man who knows what is right and gives judgment accordingly; but a man who knows what is right and acts tyrannically in his judgment will go to hell; and a man who gives judgment for people when he is ignorant will also go to Hell."*

The atmosphere of the court got tense for a while; however, the judge framed charges against Moonis Elahi. Subsequently, the judge was threatened, some say was maltreated also; ultimately he was forced to say that *'I'll no more hear this case.'*

That was why the political elite got arranged another judge of their own choice, too.]

Referring to *'the Friday Times of 5-11 August 2011*; this high profile case had serious political consequences for the government and the Chaudhrys of Gujrat; though it made open to the whole world that what standards of accountability Pakistan used to keep. Moonis Elahi once claimed that ADG Zafar Qureshi was trying to settle old scores with him and his family, saying that:

"When my father was chief minister [Punjab], he had made Mr Qureshi an Officer on Special Duty (OSD) for his poor performance. He also had a grudge against us for not making his brother Ismail Qureshi the

chief secretary, and refusing a PML(Q) National Assembly ticket to his other brother Mazhar Qureshi."

Zafar Qureshi disagreed saying that:

"I was made an OSD after I refused to do a partial inquiry in the Sonia Naz Case. Ismail Qureshi had never been an aspirant for the slot of Punjab's chief secretary and Mazhar Qureshi had quit the Q-League after the assassination of Benazir Bhutto. I'll ensure transparent investigation into the case and would not yield to pressure."

Showing his colours and to prove his allegiance for the government, the judge Mr Mujahid, **on 26th September 2011,** turned down the FIA's plea for 15-day extension in investigation of the NICL Case. The Judge directed the FIA to be prepared to argue against Moonis Elahi's acquittal plea on the next hearing on 3rd October 2011 in case it failed to submit a complete *challan* by then. ADG FIA Zafar Qureshi was exempted from personal appearance on account of *'several death threats'.*

The proceedings continued on almost daily basis till **15th October 2011,** when the Session Court judge had concluded the hearing but kept reserved its verdict. A week later, the judgment was announced **on 22nd October 2011;** *Moonis Elahi was acquitted* and was released from Nadra Rest House which had been declared a sub-jail when FIA took him in its custody in May 2011, after cancellation of his pre-arrest bail in the same case by the LHC.

The acquittal order contained that:

'The golden principle laid down in celebrated precedents, referred supra, and the dictates of justice demand that the accused be acquitted / set at liberty. Accordingly, the application in hand is accepted and accused Moonis is acquitted u/s 249-A CrPC. Accused is under custody if he is not needed in any other case, be released forthwith.'

A large number of party workers and few MPAs were also present in the court and they chanted slogans in favour of Moonis Elahi & PML(Q).

On 16th November 2011, the SC appeared surprised when it was informed that the FIA had on its own unfrozen two bank accounts of Rs: 19.3 million which it had frozen on apprehensions of containing dirty money during the course of investigation into the NICL scam. These accounts pertained to M/S Agro Tractors (Pvt) Ltd in Al Baraka

Bank [Rs: 1.8 million] and Al-Tahoor in Allied Bank Limited [over Rs:17 million]. The Investigating Officer Zulfikar Ali had de-frozen the accounts after seeking approval from his Director FIA Lahore Waqar Haider.

"Surprisingly without any justification and knowing well in advance that the matter is pending before the court for adjudication, the amount was unfrozen," the CJP, heading a 3-member bench, had observed and asked the two officers to get back that money within three days. Director Legal FIA, however, tried to convince the apex court that under the FIA rules, the investigation officer could unfreeze the money; though CrPC should have prevailed upon FIA Act.

On 17th August 2012, the Supreme Court resumed the hearing in the NICL corruption case. A 3-judge bench of the apex court headed by CJP Iftikhar M Chaudhry [Justice Jawwad S Khawaja and Justice Khilji Arif Hussain were other two members] rejected the FIA's report pertaining to the recovery of Rs:320 million submitted before the bench a day earlier. Chief Justice Iftikhar M Chaudhry in his remarks said that the FIA had constantly been working in violation of court orders since the transfer of ADG Zafar Qureshi.

On 12th October 2012; the National Assembly Standing Committee on Commerce was informed that the monetary dispute in NICL had been resolved and they had recovered an outstanding amount of Rs:1.06 billion from the accused persons. Briefing the committee's meeting, held with Engineer MNA Khuram Dastgir in chair, ADG FIA Afzal Tariq Malik told that out of 17 accused, 13 were arrested and subsequently released on bail and the four offenders were still at large.

On 22nd December 2012, the kingpin in the NICL Case, ex-chairman of ICCL Ayaz Khan Niazi was released due to evidence 'not enough'. The media and intelligentsia raised their loud voices that *'Gilani's government has deliberately provided him facilities on the instance of their coalition partners; as had been earlier they got released Moonis Elahi'*. Reasons were cited that PM Gilani's own sons were involved in similar mega corruptions.

On 4th February 2013; a 3-member bench of the SC headed by Chief Justice Iftikhar M Chaudhry took up the case for hearing and remarked that *'NICL case is the case of national wealth and national interest. There is need that institutions discharge their respective obligations. Now the orders will have to be issued for return of public wealth'*.

The government's lawyer told the court that the entire amount involved with reference to NICL case had been recovered. The CJP wanted separate charts of all such cases in this respect with details of the money recovered and comments for court's record. Interior minister Rehman Malik, in his capacity of Federal Interior Minister and the top boss of the FIA, appeared before the apex court in person and told that he would ensure gearing up the pace of the case.

This case became another perfect example of *how justice is 'managed' and 'manoeuvred' in Pakistan's political circles.* Sadly, there was nothing new in this whole scenario; just new characters playing out the same old story at the stage of Pakistani political stage. See another media comment in an arena of frustration:

> *'Who says Pakistan doesn't have opportunities? The only thing you need is to be associated with the right people at the right time. So, forget principles and forget merit. Don't worry about making a fortune in a legal manner. Join a party, link yourself with the rich and the powerful, and your fortune, no matter how you've made it would be legalized – for that is the way of Pakistan.'*

On 5th March 2013, the Supreme Court's 3 member bench headed by Chief Justice Iftikhar M Chaudhry resumed the hearing of the said NICL Case and remarked that the money trail in NICL scandal led to the bank account of Mahkdoom Amin Fahim; also that the former NICL Chairman Ayaz Niazi was appointed at the behest of Mr Makhdoom.

Justice Gulzar Ahmed also remarked that in this scandalous money loop all the paper tails lead to Amin Fahim & his family members; and that why the two major accused named Amin Qasim Dada and Mohsin Warriach were still at large. The apex court was informed that the red warrants had been issued for the accused as they had fled the country.

On 1st April 2013, arrest warrants were issued for Pakistan People's Party [PPP] leader and former federal Commerce Minister Makhdoom Amin Fahim besides six others accused in the said corruption case. The arrest warrants were issued by the Federal Anti-Corruption Court over the suspects' failure to appear before court. Apart from Makhdoom Amin Fahim, other suspects in the case included former federal Commerce Secretary Salman Ghani, Qasim Dada, Khalid Anwar and Aamir Hussain.

Next day, Chief Justice Iftikhar M Chaudhry asked as to how a bail could be granted without presenting the suspects before the court.

Director Legal of the FIA informed the apex court that Amin Fahim and Mohsin Warriach had been granted bail by the Sindh High Court (SHC) and Islamabad High Court (IHC) respectively. The court was also appraised that Secretary Trade Salman Ghani had also been granted bail.

The known British *daily 'guardian' dated 4*th *April 2013* published crash details about Moonis Elahi's offshore company '**Olive Grove Assets Ltd**' saying:

> '*Details: Elahi is a politician from a prominent Punjab dynasty. He is the son of Pakistan's former deputy prime minister Ch Pervez Elahi, and runs a family textile business. The company was incorporated in the BVI in 2006, and the address listed in BVI records is the Chaudry's family residence in Lahore. Elahi was acquitted in a Pakistan court in 2011 of receiving payments in a corruption scandal.*'

Elahi said "I do not own" nor control the BVI Company but he did not state whether he had previously owned the firm.

Pakistan's *'the News' dated 5*th *April 2013* added that Moonis Elahi became the first Pakistani whose name was revealed as owner of an offshore company called Olive Grove Assets Ltd in British Virgin Island (BVI). A planned leak of 2.5 million secret bank accounts of companies and nationals in 170 countries by a Washington-based International Consortium of Investigative Journalists [ICIJ], in collaboration with the UK's Guardian and other international media had hit the off-shore investors worldwide.

The leak amounted to 260 gigabytes of data, or 162 times larger than the US State Department cables published by WikiLeaks in 2010.

Many Pakistanis have their offshore accounts but they pay a heavy price to maintain their secrecy; they have private bankers who manage their assets. During the trial of former Pakistani investments minister Senator Waqar Khan, it was astonishingly revealed that he owned more than £100 million worth of assets in London alone.

On 23rd **May 2013,** Aamir Hussain was arrested by the FIA in Karachi. FIA Sindh further told that the agency was in contact with the Interpol to arrest other absconders. Arrested accused Hussain was allegedly involved in irregularities in acquiring lands.

On 10th **July 2013,** the Supreme Court directed the Additional Attorney General [AAG] in NICL case to set the priorities first as how to run matters related to recoveries, land and appointment.

A 3-member bench, led by the CJP Iftikhar M Chaudhry held that the SC had not been apprised of proceedings initiated with reference to appointment of former Chairman NICL Ayyaz Niazi. Recoveries amounting to Rs: 420 million were yet to be made in Lahore land case.

Mohsin Warraich had long ago fled from the country and FIA initiated no proceedings to bring him back in the country nor was any action taken in connection with cancellation of bail.

Once more, the intelligentsia and the media had observed that the apex court was more interested in the contempt of court proceedings to be run rather to finish the said NICL Case which was on their list since about half a decade.

On 16th August 2013; an anti-corruption court, ATC – II Karachi, issued arrest warrants for Director Qasim Amin Dada in the said Case again while the appearing of Makhdoom Amin Fahim was condoned due to his parliamentary duties.

On 4th November 2013; the SC bench, headed by the CJP Iftikhar M Chaudhry, remarked that the FIA failed to recover the plundered money in the said NICL Case; adding that the looted money had gone in the pockets of the influential persons, who did not allow the investigative agency to make any progress. The CJP inquired from Shah Khawar [the AAG] whether the Secretary Commerce had taken action against those involved in the NICL scam. The contempt of court notices against three federal secretaries, including incumbent Chairman NAB Qamar Zaman Ch, Abdul Rauf Ch and Khushnood Lashari were also pending. The CJP observed with sorrow that when Zafar Qureshi was investigating the case, Rs:2.5 billion were recovered, but after his transfer no development there.

Scenario 75

HAJJ CORRUPTION CASE 2010-11:

In mid 2010, a *letter from HE Prince Bander Bin Khalid Bin Abdul Aziz al-Saud* was received by the Supreme Court of Pakistan Court alleging corruption and embezzlement in Hajj arrangements on the part of the officials responsible in hiring accommodation for the *Hujjaj* in regard to the buildings which were situated distantly from the *Haram* (Khana Ka'aba) on exorbitant rates in place of buildings available on much less rent which were nearer & closer to the *Haram*. Giving importance to this letter, the *SC on 29ᵗʰ October 2010 ordered* the Secretaries of Religious Affairs and Foreign Affairs to submit their comments.

Earlier, a Committee of the Parliamentarians comprising of Maulana Muhammad Qasim MNA, Chairman Standing Committee for Religious Affairs (National Assembly), Syed Muhammad Saleh Shah Senator, Chairman Standing Committee for Religious Affairs (Senate), Pirzada Syed Imran Ahmad Shah MNA, Mr Bilal Yaasin MNA and Dr Khalid Soomro was sent by the Prime Minister to Saudi Arabia so as to observe the Hajj arrangements.

On 1ˢᵗ September 2010, the said Committee reported to the Prime Minister Yousaf Raza Gilani that corruption and malpractices were committed by the officials of the Ministry of Religious Affairs in the Hajj arrangements in the hiring of buildings for the *Hujjaj*. A copy of that Committee Report was also sent to the Chief Justice of Pakistan.

The Parliamentarian Committee Report had further stated that the allegations of corruption were correct, because excessive rent was charged from the pilgrims for providing them cheap accommodation located at a distance of more than 3 KM from the *Haram* ostensibly at the high rate of SR:3600. This issue then became the hot cake for top print and electronic media, not only in Pakistan but abroad also.

A leading English daily *'Dawn' dated 7ᵗʰ November 2010* published the facts through an article titled *'Hajj Accommodation Scam'* wherein a Senator demanded a 'House Committee' to probe into the allegations contained in the letter of the Saudi Prince, addressed to the Chief Justice.

The daily *'Nawa e Waqt' dated 10ᵗʰ November 2010* published a report on *'Hajj Corruption'* alleging that the former DG Hajj Rao Shakeel Ahmed was appointed to the office in violation of the rules. The said DG had a tainted past with corruption cases pending against him in the Accountability Court Lahore.

During the Hajj, some of the *Hujjaj* had also submitted complaints to **Justice Khalil ur Rehman Ramday** who later forwarded the same to the CJP with the following remarks:

> *"A large number of persons came to me in Makkah Mukarramah and even in Mina complaining of grave mismanagement in the Hajj arrangements regarding the buildings hired in Makkah and Madina and the accommodation in Mina. The stories narrated were pathetic. Complaints were made even in writing.*
>
> *I appear to have misplaced those written complaints, but two of them are available with me, which I am placing before you for such action as may be deemed appropriate to eliminate the sufferings of thousands of Hajis who collect pennies all their lives to perform Hajj and this is how the money earned by them through their blood and sweat is wasted."*

On 22nd November 2010, the BBC termed it the *'country's biggest Hajj pilgrimage fraud'*. BBC further commented that:

> *'The housing provided to pilgrims was said to lack basic facilities, such as running water, proper sanitation and electricity; in some cases the buildings were still under construction.*
>
> *Each pilgrim was charged about Rs:230,000 (£1,700) by the govern-ment for transport and accommodation in Saudi Arabia during the Hajj. It takes a long time for most ordinary Pakistani Muslims to save up that much money.'*

Federal Minister Incharge, Hamid Saeed Kazmi, was banned to speak to the media, the BBC held. About 25,000 Pakistanis used the government service this year, bringing in around Rs:5.8bn in revenue.

SC STARTS JUDICIAL PROCEEDINGS:

On 2nd *December 2010* the CJP Iftikhar Chaudhry ordered to hear the matter on the judicial side.

On 8th December 2010, the Supreme Court started hearing petitions of the Hajj corruption case. On the first day Federal Minister of Science and Technology, Azam Khan Swati delivered a statement against the

PPP government and told the court that he had earlier warned the prime minister about the ongoing Hajj corruption in a cabinet meeting and that the Federal Minister of Religious Affairs, Hamid Saeed Kazmi was the king-pin.

Sitting on the bench, Justice Javed Iqbal was much disturbed over *'corruption in Hajj affairs'* saying that he hadn't seen corruption like this in his 28 years of professional life.

On the same day [of 8th December 2010] Raja Aftab, Joint Secretary Religious Affairs was arrested by FIA officials and taken to the 'drawing room' for further investigations. Earlier, the former Director General Hajj, Rao Shakeel was picked up in the first phase of investigations. JS Raja Aftab ul Islam had hired the residential buildings for the Hajj pilgrims, which were virtually inaccessible from the Haram. Subsequently the Pakistani pilgrims had to suffer on that count. In Mina, the tents provided to the pilgrims, lacked basic utilities as well.

[*Earlier, on 14th December 2010, Allama Kazmi was sacked from the Federal Minister's slot. The other Federal Minister named Azam Swati, who in fact was the complainant in that corruption case, was also discharged from his portfolio; it was done so by PM Gilani to teach the other coalition ministers 'not to fight mutually and not to point out corruption of their fellow members of the cabinet'.*]

On 19th December 2010, FIA arrested the brother-in-law of Hamid Saeed Kazmi, for his alleged involvement in the Hajj scam. Abdullah Mahmood Khokhar was arrested from his residence in Lahore and subsequently transferred to FIA HQ Islamabad. Mr Khokhar was facing charges of getting money from travel agents as commission in the name of Mr Kazmi, the former & fired off Federal Minister.

More revelations relating to the Hajj fiasco surfaced when the Senate Standing Committee on Religious Affairs was informed that the government had charged pilgrims an extra Rs:153 million in the name of 'royalty' to be paid to two airlines. Each of the 85,000 pilgrims under the government scheme paid $20 [*around Rs:1,800*] above the original cost.

Former Secretary Religious Affairs Agha Sarwar Qazilbash informed the committee that the money had gone to the PIA and the Saudi Airlines which were primarily responsible for transporting Pakistani pilgrims to Saudi Arabia. Under an agreement between the airlines, each of them had a 50% share in the pilgrimage to Jeddah and back.

In the event of one airline failing to fly its allotted quota of pilgrims, the other would be paid an additional $20 per pilgrim to do the job. Instead of penalising the failing airline, how come poor pilgrims were asked to foot the additional bill; an issue was raised in the Senate. The practice had been there since several years, the Senate was told but with no figures that how much average used to be paid in the previous years.

On 10ᵗʰ February 2011, the government conceded in the SC that officials in the Pakistani Hajj Directorate had approached operators in Saudi Arabia with a plan to rip off intending pilgrims. FIA's Additional Director General (ADG) Syed Javaid Ali told a seven-judge bench of the SC that:

> *'People related to Hajj operations in the kingdom have admitted that officials of the Pakistan Hajj operations requested them to overcharge pilgrims for a price, but they were not willing to give the statement in writing because the Saudi government would not allow them.'*

One Zain Sukhera was named as 'go in between' too, who was extensively known as PM Gilani's family friend; the media had found exclusive pictures of Sukhera taken with President Zardari and PM Gilani & his daughter etc. Mr Sukhera was appointed as a consultant in the ministry of Information Technology through PM's approval in January 2010.

Mr Sukhera was alleged [by an MNA Imran Shah] of passing over the money to the PM's son Ali Qadir Gilani, after getting it from the former DG Hajj Rao Shakil (who was under custody then). Meanwhile Ali Qadir Gilani told the media that he had done nothing wrong.

The matter of issuance of the diplomatic passports to Rao Shakil and his wife had also come under investigation, although both were included in the Exit Control List (ECL) in 2009. No clue surfaced ever that who had recommended for this favour and why; whether the illegal favour of having that facility had been used ever or not.

Mr Khushnood Akhtar Lashari, the then Secretary Establishment, placed [before the SC] summary of the appointment of Rao Shakeel Ahmed as DG Hajj wherein his name was considered along with two other officers by a Departmental Selection Committee [DSC] for the said appointment.

Astonishingly, it was categorically mentioned in the summary that two NAB cases were pending against Rao Shakeel Ahmed. However, the PM Gilani approved him to be appointed as Director General Hajj, Jeddah.

[Rao Shakeel had been facing criminal proceedings in Reference No: 76 of 2007 pending adjudication before the Accountability Court No. II, Lahore wherein evidence of 18 out of 32 witnesses was recorded.

The SC was further informed that investigation in a NAB case on the charge of 'assets beyond known sources of income' was pending against him since 2004.

Interestingly his name was appearing on the ECL at the time when he was selected out of a panel of three persons as DG Hajj. **Rao Shakeel himself had applied to Federal Minister for Interior Rehman Malik for deletion of his name from the ECL; and that on an SMS message by the Interior Minister, his name was removed from the ECL though cases were pending against him before the Accountability Court Lahore & NAB.]**

On the same day of **10ᵗʰ February 2011,** following more facts were revealed before the Supreme Court:

- *FIA's Director Legal Azam Khan told the apex court that the Federal Minister for Religious Affairs, Hamid Saeed Kazmi, operated one bank account with a balance amount of Rs:180,000 but he also operated other bank accounts, one with over Rs: 10 million deposit and another with £60,000 [UK currency].*

- *The FIA was also investigating the transfer of 66 kanals [one kanal comes equivalent to 1/8ᵗʰ acre] of land in his name during the same Hajj days.*

- *The FIA's ADG pointed out that Zain Sukhera [another accused and a friend of the prime minister's son Ali Qadir Gilani] had an LLM degree but he was appointed an information technology expert by former IT Secretary Najibullah, of course, on the direct instructions of the sitting PM.*

- *The issue of import of a bullet-proof armoured vehicle for Ali Qadir Gilani also surfaced during the proceedings; not declared from which source; was he entitled for a custome free vehicle of that type.*

- *All Pakistan Travel Agents told the court that the Minister Mr Kazmi was involved in overcharging pilgrims by over Rs:2 billion.*

- *Secretary Religious Affairs Shaukat Durrani told that only 1,142 of the 26,658 affected pilgrims were yet to be reimbursed 700 riyals per head [as per instructions of the SC] and 728 others would be paid 250 riyals given by the Saudi government.*

On 14th March 2011, Special Judge Central (SJC) Sohail Nasir rejected the bail of former Federal Minister Hamid Saeed Kazmi and a dejected looking scholar was immediately arrested by the FIA officers from the courtroom. Though the FIA had registered a case against him for corruption during the Hajj season of 2010 but the former minister was on interim bail since then.

During the bail confirmation hearing, the accused minister told the court that he was not nominated in the FIR and the two main accused of this corruption case had already recorded their statements in the court, in the light of which he was totally innocent. After becoming a member of the National Assembly, transaction in his bank account was made only twice; those amounts belonged to his relatives, he had urged before the court.

Khurram Latif Khosa, the lawyer of ex-Federal Minister Kazmi, argued that the FIA should have arrested Ahmed Faiz, the main accused in the case, who was absconding. However, AD (Legal) of the FIA, deposed before the court that the Government of Pakistan had to suffer a loss of Rs: 200 million due to the mismanagement of Hamid Saeed Kazmi in his capacity of in-charge federal minister.

[*The Ministry of Religious Affairs had appointed Ahmed Faiz as the 'Building Supervisor in Jeddah on 7th March 2010, who hired 11 buildings there.*]

The apex court knew that the former federal minister was getting Rs: 95,000 per month as salary, including all allowances, but his transactions from bank accounts were out of proportion. Record was there to prove that Allama Kazmi had:

- On 18th April 2009, made a transaction of Rs:1,000,000 in Muslim Commercial Bank (MCB), Nishtar Chowk, Multan;

- On 6th November 2009 transacted Rs:500,000;

- On 5th January 2010 he made a transaction of Rs:380,000

- On 5th August 2010 he made another transaction of Rs:500,000

- On 21st March 2009 he made a transaction of £9,008 and

- On 28th August 2009 transacted £7,000.

Till then more investigations were in hand and so the bail was cancelled despite that son of the Attorney General of Pakistan and later the Governor Punjab [Lateef Khosa] was contesting his case.

During the 3rd week of April 2011, the government of Saudi Arabia gave Rs:30 million to the Ministry of Religious Affairs & FIA in compensation for the hardships Pakistani pilgrims faced during previous year's Hajj.

Interestingly, the Saudi government's 'compensation money' was to be paid by the parliamentarians and journalists who had performed Hajj free of cost; perhaps the Federal Interior Minister Rehman Malik had requested the Saudi government for that. Earlier, Malik Riaz of Bahria Town, and former Deputy Speaker National Assembly Haji Nawaz Khokar had deposited Rs:3.3 million and Rs:2.2 million in the government exchequer respectively.

On 22nd April 2011, a six-member bench of the SC lead by the CJP Iftikhar M Chaudhry heard that Hajj corruption case and termed FIA's investigation report unsatisfactory saying that the evidence gathered was being wasted. The apex court was told that the owner of Bahria Town Malik Riaz, the private secretary of the Federal Interior Minister Raja Javed, the former joint secretary of the Ministry of Religious Affairs and former DG Hajj Rao Shakeel and Sultan Shar were involved in the Hajj corruption.

JUDICIARY vs EXECUTIVE ROW AGAIN:

The FIA's investigations and the apex court's proceedings were going on at normal pace. The PM Gilani's government, off course, was feeling much pressure from inside and also that his elder son was being named, connected and dragged into the scam. Suddenly, the investigation team was changed in the FIA; the main Investigation Officer Hussain Asghar was sent to Gilgit as IGP on the pretext of his career requirement. The SC got its concerns registered at once.

On 6th May 2011, the government informed the Supreme Court about quashing the transfers of FIA investigators who were handling the task of probing into Hajj corruption case, reinstating them back to their original positions. The FIA boss had told the apex court that the senior officers deputed to investigate the said case had, at their own, requested him in writing to take away the Hajj Case from them.

Senior Advocate Hafeez Pirzada submitted before a 4-member special bench headed by the Chief Justice Iftikhar M Chaudhry that a summary for notifying the repatriation of Javed Bukhari and Hussain Asgher to their previous positions had been sent to the PM Mr Gilani. The chief justice remarked that the government suffered a loss of Rs:460 million because of this corruption plus a stigma of corruption in *Hajj* affairs. *'The money belongs to the nation and it would be recovered at any cost,'* the chief justice had reiterated.

DG FIA Malik Iqbal was ordered to submit the record of applications of Hussain Ashger and Syed Javaid in which they had requested to detach them from the case, adding that if there were no such applications, why did he make this false statement before the apex court that they had requested the transfer themselves.

In Para 32 of its judgment, the SC observed that Mr Hussain Asghar was already working as Director in the FIA and in fact it was DG FIA, who assigned him investigation of the case ..... Malik M Iqbal, DG FIA, admitted his omission....... See the details:

'Hussain Asghar appeared and placed before the Court notification of his transfer to Gilgit-Baltistan as Inspector General of Police (IGP), therefore, explanation of Malik M Iqbal, DG FIA was sought. The SC observed that instead of ensuring to accelerate progress of the investigation in the right direction, the new DG FIA, Malik Iqbal, started hampering the investigation after taking over the charge and things had come to a stand still.

DG FIA was called upon to explain as to why in the mid of the investigation he relieved Hussain Asghar without bringing into the notice of this Court. The DG FIA had no objection if Hussain Asghar was re-posted to complete investigation and in this regard Malik Iqbal had sent a letter to the competent authority but got no response.

On 10th June 2011, the then Secretary Establishment and DG FIA both appeared in Court and sought time to enable them to approach the competent authority. The SC passed an order angrily because gimmicks were being played to block the investigation.

It was noted by the apex court that DG FIA Malik Iqbal had dishonestly gave the spare-ability report knowing well about Hussain Asghar's engagement.

Secretary Establishment obeyed the judicial order and issued the required Notification on 26th July 2011 for re-posting of Hussain

Asghar back in FIA, but another big hindrance, the Chief Minister Gilgit-Baltistan had declined to relieve his IGP Hussain Asghar without provision of replacement.

However, DG FIA gave an assurance to the apex court that as and when Hussain Asghar reported for duty in FIA, the investigation of Hajj Scam cases would be handed over to him and the investigation team, already working with him, would be re-attached with the officer.

On the same day of 26th July 2011, Sohail Ahmed, the Secretary Establishment, who issued notification of transfer of Hussain Asgar in compliance with SC's orders, was made OSD an hour later.'

DG FIA Malik Iqbal had also requested the court for more time to seek the prime minister's directions in this regard; *he got the time but suddenly opted to proceed on retirement.*

[However, the irony of fate was that Hussain Asghar never reported back to FIA; the gimmicks between Establishment Division, FIA, SC and CM Gilgit played its role. At last, the SC, **on 28th June 2012,** ordered the federal government to suspend IG Gilgit-Baltistan Police Hussain Asghar for not reporting back to the FIA HQ.

A 3-member bench headed by the Chief Justice Iftikhar M Chaudhry and comprising Justice Jawwad S Khawaja and Justice Khilji Arif Hussain was continuing with the said Hajj Case instead of 6-members in chairs.

Attorney General Irfan Qadir, during an earlier hearing, had informed the apex court that the federal government had issued a notification regarding cancellation of Hussain's transfer orders as IGP Gilgit-Baltistan and he was directed to report back to FIA HQ immediately but the officer did not come back despite being summoned several times.]

SC'S LANDMARK OBSERVATION AGAIN:

On 27th July 2011, the SC had taken notice of government's decision of making Sohail Ahmad [Secretary Establishment] an OSD after he issued a notification for placing Hussain Asghar to join back the FIA. The Secretary Establishment had issued the said notification in compliance with SC's order dated 25-26th July 2011. The apex court asked the Attorney General (AG) to meet the PM in person to convey the Court's concern. The AG was asked to ensure that notification of making Sohail Ahmed as OSD should be withdrawn. The CJP had observed that:

'There is no doubt that transfers and postings fall in the domain of the executive, but the executive should use these powers judiciously. If any authority makes a departure from any of its provisions, it is likely to lead to chaos in the country, which may lead to serious consequences.

The court cannot leave such officers at the mercy of the executive to deal with them in a manner they like. Once a judicial order is passed, it has a binding effect on the executive as well as judicial functionaries in terms of Articles 5 & 190 of the constitution.'

There had been harsh row between the Judiciary & the Executive over this issue. Certain law experts had taken it as un-necessary step on the part of SC as the judiciary had no authority to make investigation teams of their choice whatever be the circumstances. The judiciary should be sternly concerned with the outcome & results based on facts nothing beyond. That was why Sohail Ahmed's help by the SC could not bring any fruit except more frustration for all.

The apex court was right to point out that *'the executive should also use his powers and prerogatives judiciously'*. In Para 38, the judgment said that *'the discretionary powers vesting in an authority are to be exercised judiciously and in reasonable manner. In the case of **Tariq Aziz-ud-Din: in re (2010 SCMR 1301)**, it has been held that the authorities cannot be allowed to exercise discretion at their whims, sweet will or in an arbitrary manner; rather they are bound to act fairly, evenly and justly.'*

An FIR no: 3/11 dated 17th March 2011 was also registered against Joint Secretary S M Tahir of Ministry of Religious Affairs under sections 409/420/467/468/471/109 PPC r/w 5 (2) 1947 PCA [Anti-corruption Act]. S M Tahir was member of the selection committee who had appointed Rao Shakeel as Director General (DG) Hajj and certain irregularities were committed during the appointment procedure.

One FIA official informed the court about the statements of two Additional Secretaries and other officers accusing Ismail Qureshi of suppressing the information that Rao Shakeel did not deserve to become DG Hajj because he had tampered with his age column in the unsigned curriculum vitae and was involved in two corruption cases; one in the AC Court and other being investigated by the National Accountability Bureau (NAB).

The court noted that the additional secretary, who had prepared the working paper for the Special Selection Board [SSB] that approved the appointment, had not mentioned the two disqualifications. Joint Secretary Mr Tahir stated that Secretary Ismail Qureshi had asked him not to bring the information to the notice of the SSB.

Ahmed Faiz, another main accused in the Hajj scandal [*the middleman for hiring accommodation in Saudi Arabia but was living there illegally after his visa had expired*] was working on directions of S M Tahir and Minister Hamid Saeed Kazmi. S M Tahir had denied any contact with Ahmed Faiz but the investigators presented phone-calls record that showed frequent contacts made to Faiz from Tahir's mobile.

Ahmed Faiz was on the official roll of Directorate of Hajj and Rao Shakil had told the apex court on its first hearing [on 8th December 2010] that *'he dismissed an officer Ahmed Faiz upon corruption charges.'*

The FIA had checked 21 banking records of six persons including S M Tahir, Former Minister Hamid Saeed Kazmi, Shagufta Jumani, Secretary Religious Affairs Agha Qazilbash, Rao Shakeel's brothers in law Nadeem Khan, M Aleem Khan and M Waseem Khan.

JUSTICE SIDDIQUI'S INJUSTICE:

From the bank accounts record it was revealed that there were millions of rupees transferred during year 2009-2010 to the account of S M Tahir. The FIA arrested Tahir on 6th October 2011 from the court premises when Special Judge Central (SJC) Sohail Nasir had rejected his bail and after routine investigations, he was sent to judicial lockup four days later.

However, on **30th March 2012,** Justice Shaukat Aziz Siddiqui of the Islamabad High Court (IHC) quashed that FIR registered by the FIA against S M Tahir though there was ample evidence on the file, including details of huge transactions of money into his accounts; obviously unjustified.

There were allegations against S M Tahir including distortion of facts in appointing DG Hajj Rao Shakeel, frequent contacts on phone with other major accused Ahmed Faiz, illegal transactions of ill-gotten money shares into his bank and lot more *BUT EVEN THEN JUSTICE SHAUKAT AZIZ SIDDIQUI OF IHC issued the 'quash' orders.* FIA people termed this decision as unjustified, calling Justice Siddiqui as a *'friend of friends'* because, the FIA maintained, the offence was very much there and quite a serious one. One cannot hold tongue of the general public - especially of a bad policeman. Also available on FIA's files that:

'In 1995, two HMRC officers from UK visited FIA (HQ). They had come to Pakistan to trace high value stolen Mitsubishi Shogun Jeeps, taken out fraudulently from UK, on forged ownership & insurance documents and were plying frequently in Mirpur District of Azad Kashmir.

Those officers had traced some of them and told the FIA; FIA team recovered them, and most of the keepers admitted their guilt. They handed over the jeeps to FIA which were in turn to be given to those British Officers after legal formalities. Cases were registered against those keepers; jeeps were impounded in FIA yard.

Two of the keepers were 'friends' of Justice Nawaz Abbassi [then used to be in Lahore High Court at Rawalpindi Bench, subsequently elevated to the SC from where he was sent home in 2009 being a PCO judge with CJP Dogar], they approached him. Justice Nawaz Abbassi called the FIA people with record next day. FIRs were placed before the court along with forged documents.

Justice Abbassi smiled for a while and quashed the FIRs; FIA was not given any reason then. The British Officers 'gathered a nice impression of Pakistan's higher judiciary' and went back to UK in the same day flight.'

SC'S VERDICT – MONEY GIVEN BACK:

The *judgment on 'HAJJ SCAM' dated 29*th *July 2011* authored by the Chief Justice Iftikhar M Chaudhry contained that the then Minister for Religious Affairs, Hamid Saeed Kazmi was firmly involved in the Hajj Scam. It was a 6-members bench which heard the case and gave unanimous judgment. The other members on the bench were Justice MIAN SHAKIRULLAH JAN, Justice TARIQ PARVEZ, Justice KHILJI ARIF HUSSAIN, Justice M A SHAHID SIDDIQUI, and Justice AMIR HANI MUSLIM.

The judgment said that Allama Kazmi had appeared before the bench voluntarily along with his counsel. Since it was a high profile case relating to massive corruption, the Members of the Parliament and the Hujjaj also started appearing before the Court during proceedings and joint application signed by 122 Hujjaj was also filed before this Court raising painful voices, highlighting the miseries of the pilgrims.

To ensure above the board accountability of the wrongdoers responsible for massive corruption, the DG FIA was asked *'to appoint some senior officer in order to see that investigation is carried out transparently, in accordance with law without caring status of the accused.'*

The judgment observed that the Ministry of Hajj had charged SR:700 from each Haji for providing them suitable accommodation in *Haram & Mina* and admittedly they were not provided accommodation despite collecting the rent from them. Therefore, by Court's order dated 13th December 2010, the Secretary Religious Affairs was directed to refund the amount of SR:700 to the said pilgrims and submit certificate to this effect before the court. In pursuance of the aforesaid directions, the Government of Pakistan had reimbursed an amount of Rs:470 million to about 25000 Hujjaj, which amount was charged from them towards rent.

The SC had also declared that Secretary Ministry of Religious Affairs (MORA) was having no control on the affairs of the Directorate General of Hajj, Jeddah. DG Hajj had assumed unchecked authority in all administrative and financial matters. This reflected gross mismanagement and lost control on the part of Secretary MORA.

Hussain Asghar, Director FIA with the rank of DIG Police, was assigned [by the DG FIA] the task to head investigation in the Hajj Scam. He took over the charge and accelerated the investigation by collecting evidence. During the course of investigation, he also visited Saudi Arabia. One of the Federal Ministers [Mr Swati] was supporting the allegation of corruption against the other Federal Minister [Allama Kazmi].

When the investigation was in progress and sufficient incriminating evidence was collected by the FIA team headed by Hussain Asghar, Syed Jawaid Bokhari was posted as ADG FIA, and the officers earlier assigned investigation were disassociated without assigning reason. ADG Bokhari was assigned investigation but he soon disassociated himself [for reasons best known to him]. *The details are given in above paragraphs.*

The SC bench observed that *'the NAB had done nothing at all in the matter for almost TWO YEARS; who had remained only the silent spectators of this entire drama and had only witnessed the escape of the accused persons to foreign lands.'*

Interestingly, the former Federal Minister Mr Kazmi, declared 'kingpin' for that corrupt practice, was declared guilty by the Supreme Court's 6 member bench headed by the CJP himself. However, *on 22ⁿᵈ May 2012, an FIA team, in its completed investigation report of the said case, found him 'innocent'*, [how the millions of rupees & UK Pounds in his bank accounts were accounted for; from where the same money came during 2009-10 suddenly; where they had gone?].

As per FIA's comprehensive report, the FIA investigators found no evidence against Former Minister Mr Kazmi, whereas Rao Shakeel had hired expensive accommodation for pilgrims and JS Aftab Raja continued endorsing his (Rao's) decisions.

FIA had declared former Director Hajj Rao Shakeel as 'main accused' and former Joint Secretary (Hajj) Aftab ul Islam Raja as 'co-accused'; that was enough in those days. S M Tahir was let off by Justice Siddiqui through quashing an FIR against him. Ali Qadir Gilani was sitting PM's son and Zain Sukhera was their family friend – they could not be named or touched so FIA went silent about them.

Who bothers about *'such minor things'* in Pakistan?

As per final report, the accused paid 55 percent rents of the 87 acquired buildings in advance, while under the set procedure, it was to be paid at the rate of 15 percent. They hired some under-construction buildings also, which created more difficulties for Pakistani pilgrims in Saudi Arabia.

On 27ᵗʰ August 2012, Special Central Judge M Ahmad Farooqui of Rawalpindi bench accepted the bail plea of former Federal Minister Hamid Saeed Kazmi in Hajj corruption case and directed the authorities for his immediate release against two surety bonds of Rs:100,000 each. He was arrested on 15ᵗʰ March 2011, in the FIA's FIR under Sections 409/420/467/468/471/109 of the Pakistan Penal Code (PPC). The former federal minister had been imprisoned in Adiala Jail Rawalpindi, for about seventeen months.

FIA'S OLD TEAM COMES BACK:

On 26ᵗʰ September 2012 at last, the Supreme Court ordered for immediate re-instatement and posting in FIA of the suspended police officer Hussain Asghar, who earlier was investigating into the Hajj corruption scandal. The 3-member bench headed by the Chief Justice Iftikhar M Chaudhry was hearing the Hajj corruption scandal case.

It was on the apex court's record that former Gilgit Baltistan IG Hussain Asghar was suspended and a departmental action was underway against him, while a new Gilgit Baltistan IG had been posted. The apex court ordered Establishment Division to at once re-instate Hussain Asghar, post him in FIA and apprise the court about it.

The federal government, however, acted upon SC's orders this time.

On 25th October 2012, the 2-member bench of the Supreme Court, comprising Chief Justice Iftikhar M Chaudhry and Justice Jawwad S Khawaja, was informed that Saudi nationals were also involved in the said Hajj corruption scandal, therefore, the Saudi government was not willing to help in the investigation of the case. FIA's Hussain Asghar submitted that Saudi authorities had refused to hand over the proclaimed offender, Ahmad Faiz, who was otherwise residing in Saudi Arabia in an illegal way.

The FIA told the bench that majority of the people involved in corruption were Saudis and Ahmed Faiz was working as a middleman. Ahmad Faiz was the only person who knew about the exact amount of the 2010 Hajj corruption embezzled at Saudi's end. A parliamentary delegation led by Khalid Soomro had also visited Saudi Arabia earlier to investigate it.

Irony of fate was that till that day, the investigation into the appointments of Rao Shakeel as DG Hajj and of Zain Sukhera in IT Ministry as Consultant and later's association with Hajj matters in 2009-10 were not finalized by the FIA; a poor performance indeed. FIA's IO, Hussain Asghar, informed the apex court that Prime Minister's Secretariat, Establishment Division and MORA were not cooperating with the agency regarding the said two aspects; the reasons were obvious. Bahauddin Zakariya University Multan was also not providing the details of alleged fake degree of Zain Sukhera.

On 5th November 2012, FIA summoned Abdul Qadir Gilani son of the former PM Gilani and his friend Zain Sukhera for investigation. The investigations had taken a new start following the restoration of Hussain Asghar as investigation officer [IO] and a new investigation team got constituted to deal with the Hajj scam afresh.

The then Principal Secretary to the PM and the sitting Secretary for Water & Power Nargis Sethi was also called in FIA to record her statement. Details of assets in respect of the persons summoned were also collected. Nargis Sethi was investigated with regard to appointment of DG Hajj while Abdul Qadir Gilani was required to explain his conduct in matters related to Zain Sukhera.

On 25th **February 2013**, the Supreme Court (SC) passed orders for the federal law ministry to send legal opinion to the FIA on question of probing into the involvement of former PM Gilani in the Haj corruption case. A 3-member SC bench led by the CJP Iftikhar M Chaudhry was told that evidences from 44 witnesses had been recorded and six witnesses had been left, *while astonishingly adding that evidence was not available against Hamid Saeed Kazmi.*

The federal interior ministry did not allow the FIA's IO to file an application seeking rejection of Kazmi's bail which was earlier accepted on 27th August. Whereas Director (Legal) Azam Khan of the same organization [FIA] exactly maintained his view at 180 angle – saying that there was not enough evidence to get Kazami's bail cancelled. Hussain Asghar told the apex court that Kazmi had influenced the witnesses; therefore, the application was filed to seek cancellation of his bail.

During the discussion on the bail issue of Allama Kazmi, Justice Ejaz Afzal remarked *'if an accused misuses bail, then the Prosecutor General could move the court against him'*. The CJP observed, *'You need not approach the interior ministry in connection with the cancellation of bail'*. The apex court also admonished the federation's counsel for supporting Kazmi while saying that:

> *"You are a lawyer for the federation and not for the accused. You should review your attitude. You should oppose the accused but you are defending him. Time does not remain the same always."*

For another accused Ahmed Faiz, the CJP told the FIA's IO to get the accused's passport cancelled [which was already cancelled till then]; if the interior ministry would cooperate in that regard, then the Saudi government would also cooperate. It was mystery that why he was not being arrested.

It has been narrated earlier that the name of DG Hajj Rao Shakil had been removed from the ECL by the Federal Interior Minister Rehman Malik himself after Rao's appointment to that assignment. Rao Shakil had been placed on the ECL again, the apex court was told. He said the former establishment secretary had appointed Rao Shakil despite knowing that his name was on the ECL.

During the course of proceedings, the counsel for Rao Shakeel, the DG Jajj in FIA's custody, once prayed the Islamabad High Court that his client was imprisoned for the last two years so should be released on bail. The IHC, however, rejected the plea for bail **on 8th March 2013** because the court was told that trial could not be concluded due to delaying tactics by the accused.

FORMER PM CALLED IN HAJJ DOCKS:

On 10th April 2013, the SC summoned the former PM Mr Gilani to appear in person or through his counsel and submit a reply regarding his alleged involvement in this scandal but he refused to come, saying he was enjoying immunity as per constitution. The matter was referred to law ministry but no reply had been received by the apex court till then. FIA's IO Hussain Asghar had earlier told the court that the then PM Gilani was also involved with reference to Zain Sukhera as the former had appointed him as joint secretary and consultant in the PM's House.

A 3-member bench of the apex court, headed by the Chief Justice Iftikhar M Chaudhry, taking notice over the Law Ministry's opinion regarding the immunity of former premier, issued notice to the federal Law Secretary and Attorney General of Pakistan (AGP). The court also sought explanation from the Law Ministry about its legal opinion to the FIA, wherein it had approved Gilani's claim about his immunity under Article 248 of the constitution during the investigation of Hajj scandal, despite knowing that he was not occupying the prime minister's post anymore.

The SC also asked the Law Ministry to explain whether it had given this opinion on its own behalf or on the advice of the prime minister.

The court also directed the caretaker interior minister to consult his counterpart in Saudi Arabia for bringing back a Hajj scam accused, Ahmad Faiz. It also said that they should be told why another accused, former Establishment Secretary Ismail Qureshi had not been called in the said investigation.

On 20th April 2013, former Establishment Secretary, Ismael Qureshi, when called to join the investigation, who asserted his innocence in a statement made to the FIA saying that PM Gilani had simply ignored his advice against Rao Shakeel's appointment as Director Hajj and putting Zain Sukhaira as Information Technology advisor. [*Sukhaira was* *allegedly the front man for Abdul Qadir Gilani, the former premier's son*]

Ismael Qureshi was facing serious charges, such as the concealing of facts and making illegal appointments. He affirmed in his written statement that Rao Shakeel was facing a reference for a record tempering case with the NAB's Punjab office; thus his appointment as DG Hajj Affairs was not in line with appropriate rules and procedure. PM Gilani had ignored his written note on the summary and went ahead.

Moreover, Ismael Qureshi held PM Gilani responsible for appointing Sukhaira as the IT ministry's advisor despite his not having the required qualifications.

Contrarily, the other officials of the Establishment Division had given the written statements to the FIA that Ismael Qureshi had concealed essential facts in the summary moved for the appointments of Shakeel and Sukhaira. He had failed to mention that Shakeel was on the Exit Control List; he did not mention that Shakeel was facing trial for record tampering and many more facts.

About bringing back Ahmed Faiz, FIA informed the apex court that the ministries of interior and foreign affairs had written letters to their Saudi counterparts but till then no response from them. Ahmed Faiz was an agent who, on behalf of Pakistani authorities, had arranged buildings in Saudi Arabia. In fact, Saudi police were reluctant to raid the places they had pointed out to them.

On 21st June 2013; Pakistan's real estate tycoon Malik Riaz appeared before a Special Investigation Unit (SIU) of the FIA in Hajj corruption scam; Hussain Asghar, the director of FIA's SIU questioned Malik Riaz regarding the provision of accommodation to 448 Hujjaj who had performed Hajj on courtesy visas facilitated by the MORA and Interior Minister Rehman Malik during 2009 and 2010.

Malik Riaz, in his written statement said that in 2009 he had made a Rs:1,750,000 payment for air tickets of 200 pilgrims, including 32 employees of Bahria Town, through cheque No: 0191690 dated 4th November 2009; similarly, in 2010 he paid for the air tickets of 248 pilgrims including some journalists, and 56 employees of Bahria Town. He also paid Rs:1,69,400 for the air tickets in 2010 through cheque No: 0191720 and Rs:3,200,000 through cheque No: 0191722 to PIA. He said that courtesy visas of Hujjaj in 2009 and 2010 were facilitated by Raja Javed Iqbal, Personal Secretary to Rehman Malik.

Malik Riaz informed the FIA investigators that he later paid Rs:2,552,416 accommodation charges of his 32 employees who travelled for Hajj in 2009 through a cheque No: 0191738 AND Rs:64,40,000 accommodation charges of 56 employees who went for Hajj in 2010 through cheque No: 0191739.

When asked whether he paid the accommodation expanses of his employees following the direction of the SC, he said when he came to know that some amount was due against him he paid the same.

On 4th July 2013, the SC rejected an application seeking immunity for former PM Mr Gilani; the CJP Iftikhar M Chaudhry was heading the bench.

TRANSPARENCY INT'L REPORT [2012] SPEAKS:

Referring to *Transparency International Pakistan [TIP]'s report* published in all media *on 5th February 2012*, Pakistan lost more than Rs:8,500 billion (equivalent to US$94 billion then), in corruption, tax evasion and bad governance during the four years of Prime Minister Yusaf Raza Gilani's tenure.

The TIP advisor, Adil Gillani, told the media [and believed] that:

'Pakistan does not need even a single penny from the outside world if it effectively checks the menace of corruption and ensures good governance. During the four years of the PPP regime under Gilani has broken all past records of corruption and Pakistan started rising in the ranks of the most corrupt nations of the world.'

Adil Gillani explained that the TIP pointed out corruption of Rs:390 billion in 2008, Rs:450 billion in 2009, Rs:825 billion in 2010 and Rs:1,100 billion in 2011 [totaling Rs: 2765 billion] in identified cases, like that of Hajj Corruption Case, NICL Case etc running those days at high peak.

In addition to this, Adil Gilani explained the following:

'The PPP's Finance Minister himself confirmed corruption in FBR of over Rs:500 billon per year, which makes the total Rs:2,000 billion in four years; Auditor General of Pakistan pointed out Rs:315 billion corruption in 2010; Public Accounts Committee recovered Rs:115 billion in 30 months till 2011; circular debt is Rs:190 million; KESC

was given Rs:55 billion illegal benefits per annum since 2008; state-owned enterprises like PSO, PIA, Pakistan Steel, Railways, SSGC, SNGC are eating away Rs:150-300 billion per annum; tax to GDP ratio in 2008 was 11%, which in 2011 has reduced to 9.1% instead of being increased.'

Adil Gillani further added *that 'Pakistan's Gross Domestic Product [GDP] is worth US$175 billion and the drop of 1.9% in the tax GDP means annual loss of US$3.3 billion. This confirms that FBR is losing Rs:300 million per annum; thus annual additional loss since 2008 makes Rs:1,200 billon in four years.'*

It was not only the Transparency International but other international bodies including the World Bank and ADB had also been showing their concern over rising trend of corruption in Pakistan under PM Gilani's regime. It was that mounting corruption and extremely bad governance, which even dithered the outside world to offer cash to Pakistan during 2010 and 2011 floods.

Those were the days when corruption became a fashion in such a shameless manner that even the cabinet ministers started openly pointing fingers at each other and even at the highest levels including the prime minister. Some even approached the Supreme Court but despite all this, corruption remained the hallmark of the PPP regime under Gilani & Zardari, who always defended it in the name of democracy; Hajj Scam & NICL Case are referred in that context.

Scenario 76

BANK OF PUNJAB [BOP] SCAM:

On 27th September 2007, the National Accountability Bureau [NAB], Punjab, had filed a reference in an accountability court against 12 people, including six officials of the Bank of Punjab [BoP] and six other accused of Rs:9 billion fraud. The BoP had granted this amount to the Haris Steel Industries (HSI), Lahore, without fulfilling legal requirements and consequently the said business concern defaulted the loan.

When the investigations started, the scam surfaced worth far beyond the mentioned amount. One Law Minister was also implicated in the loan scandal and one Finance Secretary Salman Siddique popped up on the same count, too.

[Salman Siddique, then one of the two directors of the bank, approved unlawful credit proposals amounting to Rs:1.1 billion in July 2006. The actual corruption at the BoP went up to Rs:76.178 billion. While the bank shows profits from 2005 to 2008 on paper, it was actually running in loss.

Terming the BoP scam one of the largest swindles in the country's history, the bank was deprived of over Rs:11 billion in advances and mark up by one Haris Group alone. When the media scrutiny of the bank started on 21st June 2007, its very continuity came into question and its equity's market capitalisation declined by a whopping amount of around Rs:64 billion within a short time period.]

Current and the previous eras encompassed that scandal and then Gen Musharraf was also dragged in the dirty game. A significant development was achieved when a plea was filed pleading the competent court that one State Minister Raees Muneer of Gen Musharraf's rule borrowed Rs:120 million from the BoP.

On 18th November 2008, the Supreme Court [SC] of Pakistan ordered for the transfer of Bank of Punjab [BoP] cases, within fifteen days, against four people involved in a Rs:9 billion scam from the Lahore High Court (LHC) to the Islamabad High Court (IHC). The 3-members bench of the SC headed by the then Chief Justice Abdul Hameed Dogar [Justice Nasirul Mulk and Justice Ejaz Yousaf were other two members] gave the said ruling while hearing identical appeals against interim bails granted by the LHC to the accused bank employees. Attorney General (AG) Sardar Latif Khosa and Punjab's Advocate General Khwaja Haris had requested the court to transfer the appeals to the IHC.

On 15th July 2009, the SC [under the new judge's team of CJP Iftikhar M Chaudhry] directed the Director General [DG] of the Federal Investigation Agency (FIA) to expedite action against the accused who managed to flee the country despite having his name placed on the Exit Control List (ECL). The 3-member bench consisting of Chief Justice Iftikhar M Chaudhry, Justice M Sair Ali and Justice Jawwad S Khawaja asked the FIA to submit the explanation in that respect.

The BoP had granted the Rs:9 billion loan to Haris Steel Industries, Lahore without fulfilling legal requirements. After hearing the arguments, the court directed authorities to appear in court along with the complete address and passport numbers of the accused, President BoP Humesh Khan, who had fled the country to the United Kingdom.

On 11th September 2009, the SC ordered the arrest of Haris Steel Mills Chief Executive Sheikh Munir for not depositing Rs:500 million towards the total loss of Rs:9 billion Bank loan without fulfilling the legal requirements. The 3-member SC bench, then comprising Chief Justice Iftikhar M Chaudhry, Justice Ghulam Rabbani and Justice Jawwad S Khwaja heard the said case this time and observed that first the high officials had floated that huge loan with all hands in one glove and then filed petition against the Haris Steel Mills.

The apex court ordered the Bank to confiscate the property of Sheikh Afzal, the owner of Haris Steel, after duly publicising the same in newspapers. Once the court had directed Sheikh Munir, brother of Sheikh Afzal, to deposit Rs:500 million in BoP, besides surrendering property worth the same amount as a token of goodwill for resolving the case outside the court but they deposited Rs:200 million only.

At that point, the chief justice expressed displeasure over the attitude of the owners saying *'they have betrayed the court.'* The court also issued arrest warrants for Sheikh Munir, the owners of Prime Steel and Hyder Steel; Abid Raza and Naeem Siddiq, besides fourteen other accused in the case. The apex court was informed that Sheikh Afzal's family members had purchased properties in Dubai with the amounts drawn from the BoP.

The chief justice directed the BoP's counsel to present a list of such properties in court so that the matter could be taken up through the Foreign

Office. The bench expressed serious displeasure over the conduct of the National Accountability Bureau (NAB); the later was not interested in disposal of the case nor did they want to extradite the owners of Haris Steel back in Pakistan.

WHO ELSE NAKED IN BOP'S 'HAMAM':

On 21st December 2009; the SC's 3-members bench was told that Rs:7.5 billion, out of the Rs:9 billion bank loan in the said scam had been recovered from Sheikh Afzal, the Chief Executive of the Haris Steel, and his accomplices by seizing foreign and domestic assets owned by the accused.

This time the bench, comprising Chief Justice Iftikhar M Chaudhry, Justice Anwar Zaheer Jamali and Justice Khilji Arif Hussain, withdrew the protection the SC had granted earlier to Seth Nisar, one of Sheikh Afzal's brothers and co-accused in the scam, when it was informed that he was not cooperating with the NAB. [*On* 24th *November, the court had granted protection to Seth Nisar when he had shown willingness to clear all the liabilities*]

Meanwhile, Sheikh Afzal was brought back from Malaysia. He confessed in a statement recorded by the NAB that he had paid a lot of money to 'many concerned' out of fraudulently withdrawn funds to win undue favours for the said loan. He urged the court to recover that much amount of money from those persons, mostly belonging to the BoP and the political clout around.

According to Mr Afzal's written confessional statement, he had paid Rs:one million to Advocate Irfan Qadir for filing a petition against NAB proceedings in the LHC. When NAB officials raided his house, Irfan Qadir suggested him to engage a panel of prominent lawyers to influence the court. He then contacted advocates Wasim Sajjad and Sharifuddin Pirzada.

In June 2008, when the NAB seized his office, Sheikh Afzal claimed that Ali Wasim, Wasim Sajjad's son, contacted him and said: *'Mr Afzal, Insaaf Lainay Ke Liye Kuch Aur Bhi Karna Parta Hay* (Mr Afzal, if one wants to get justice, one has to do 'other' things) and offered to let his office vacated because he had a very close association with a son-in-law of a judge at LHC. Sh Afzal contended that he had paid Rs:7.5 million to Ali Wasim through Irfan Ali (manager of Haris Steel).

One Tony Shah, a cricket matches broker and mutual friend of Ali Wasim and Sheikh Afzal, also told the NAB that after failing to do the job Ali Wasim did not pay back the money he had obtained from Sh Afzal, but said he would pay only half the amount because he had partially succeeded in getting the promised results.

When the case was fixed before the LHC in mid 2008, Sh Afzal said he paid Rs:3.5 million to one journalist Mohsin Naqvi when he offered to get the case 'quashed' because *'he enjoyed good relations with the LHC judge'*. Allegedly the said amount of Rs:3.5m was paid to Malik Qayyum [the former judge] who had perhaps spoken to relevant LHC judges on telephone in presence of his lawyer and assured him that he would get relief.

Later, when the case was transferred to the Supreme Court, Advocate Malik Qayyum told Sh Afzal that he and Advocate Sharifuddin Prizada had held a number of meetings with a judge of the apex court. Sheikh Afzal alleged that, apart from legal fees, he had paid Mr Pirzada Rs:10 million during July-August last year [2008]. The amount, he claimed, was given in return for orders obtained in July because he [Mr Pirzada] had attributed the success to his relations with a judge of the apex court.

Sh Afzal also alleged that Malik Qayyum had told him that his counsel had paid Rs:1million to Advocate Ibrahim Satti (private counsel representing NAB in the apex court) in the same days through him [Malik Qayyum] and Mr Pirzada and in September 2008 Rs:1.5 million to former Attorney-General Sardar Latif Khan Khosa.

According to Sh Afzal's confessional statement, Malik Qayyum, who was then Attorney-General, had visited him in Malaysia in mid 2008 and stayed at Shangri La Hotel in Kuala Lumpur arranged by him [Sh Afzal]. During the dinner, Malik Qayyum had even called a judge of the Supreme Court and promised to get the case settled in 10 days. Sh Afzal added that:

'Later we got a favourable order from the Supreme Court which ordered restoration of the position of investigation as it existed in June 2008. Advocate Malik Qayyum called me to claim credit for the verdict.'

Sh Afzal alleged that Malik Qayyum had visited him thrice along with his wife when he was in UAE in August - September 2008 and assured him that he had paid officials concerned to get the case 'quashed', either by the apex court or the high court. He said at that time he was paid 300,000 UAE Dirhams.

Sh Afzal maintained that Malik Qayyum had also introduced him to Sarfraz Merchant, a Karachi based businessman, in July 2008 last year and told him that he had good ties with a judge of the Supreme Court. In July the same year, Malik Qayyum told him that Senator Babar Awan, who 'commanded great influence' was his friend and that it was necessary to *'pay him over and above the agreed amount of Rs:50 million'*. Mr Awan then arrived in Dubai in Ramzan of 2008 where the balance amount was paid in addition to 50,000 UAE Dirhams for shopping.

During the proceedings, Director Law of the FIA, Azam Khan, informed the Supreme Court about former Chief Commissioner Islamabad, Fazeel Asghar's alleged role in helping Sheikh Afzal's flee from the country despite his name being on the Exit Control List (ECL). Although Mr Asghar refuted the allegations, he agreed to submit a detailed report on a questionnaire by the FIA within a week.

Director FIA Azam Khan told the apex court that after paying Rs:6 million, Mr Asghar had introduced Sh Afzal to Gohar Sarfraz, an Assistant Director in the Airport Security Force (ASF), for immigration clearance. As Gohar Sarfraz was on a 'long leave' then, therefore, despite repeated raids on his house, he could not be arrested. However, one Hafiz Mohammad Tariq, the helping Immigration Officer at the airport, was duly arrested.

Meanwhile, BoP's lawyer Khwaja Haris, informed the apex court about Sh Afzal's version that Rs:1.2 billion out of total loan had been given to Seth Yaqoob, Mr Afzal's brother, but he was not able to repay the money in less than three years. The CJP Iftikhar M Chaudhry ordered to negotiate with Seth Yaqoob for an amicable and out-of-court settlement and directed the authorities not to arrest Seth Yaqoob till 11th January 2010.

One thing was clear that Sh Afzal and his son's arrest from Malaysia was only possible due to SC's strong stance. The judges on the bench had kept away all the twisting arguments of many heavy weight and high profiled advocates who were engaged by these forged and tainted billionaires. The same lawyers had been representing them in Dogar's courts and coming out wavering triumphant flags. Some lawyers were alleged for openly bargaining with their rich clients on behalf of SC assuring them of winning any sentence they wanted to hear.

On 22nd February 2010, a 3-member bench of the SC comprising Chief Justice Iftikhar M Chaudhry, Justice Ch Ijaz Ahmed and Justice Ghulam

Rabbani, was told by the NAB that two sons of Seth Yaqoob were released after he deposited Rs:510 million as the first instalment of the total outstanding dues of Rs:1.5 billion claimed against him. Rest of the money was to be paid in monthly instalments of Rs:100 million each.

The apex court was told that the NAB had approved a plea bargain with 18 prime suspects in the scam, and the plea-bargain agreement had been filed with the court. The main suspect in the scam – Hamesh Khan, former BoP president – and Seth Nisar were not included in the plea bargain. NAB had taken into custody the property, vehicles, gold and other valuables owned by the suspects till they return the money.

Referring to 'the News' dated 26th May 2010:

'Hamesh Khan's stunning revelations before the NAB investigators have taken the lid off a unique scandal of the banking history in which the Bank of Punjab offered loans worth billions of rupees to the business concerns of its directors.

These directors were associated with the Bank of Punjab during Pervez Elahi's tenure as Chief Minister Punjab. Besides Salman Siddique, [then MD BoP & later the Federal Secretary Finance in PPP regime], four other directors of the Board availed loans from the BoP while they were sitting members; under the rules they were not permitted.

One of these directors had purchased the Phalia Sugar Mills from the Chaudhrys of Gujrat. The BoP record confirmed that five directors of the BoP and their relatives were recipient of huge BoP loans in violation of the bank's policy.'

Under Section 19.4 of the Bank of Punjab Act 1988 *'the bank shall not grant any person who has been elected or appointed as a director and for so long as he continues to hold that office any advances, loan, credit limit, guarantee or other facilities, or alter to his advantage, loan, credit limit, guarantee or other facility granted before his election or appointment as a director.'*

In most of the BoP's meetings of Board of Directors, the top item discussed was the *'re-scheduling & accepting other bank's loans'*. Each director used to keep names of some parties in his pocket to be announced at 'appropriate' time under which the loans taken by certain high profile people from other private banks were accepted by the BoP, paid off each penny of those private banks and release 'much simple' terms from BoP in lieu of those accepted loans. That *'fayyazi'* [generousness] brought admiration, appreciations and praises for Gen Musharraf and his provincial teams widely spread in many media articles and programs; especially concocted, the apex court believed.

Being Director & Acting Chairman of the BoP, Salman Siddique's father was offered a loan of Rs:40 million; the said loan was returned in 2008. However, the case of other four ex-directors of the BoP [named Gohar Ejaz, Khurram Iftikhar, Fareed Mughees Sheikh and Mian Muhammad Latif] went serious as in their cases not only the amount involved was big it was yet to be re-paid [till 2010 at least].

Gohar Ejaz [BoD member: June 2003 - April 2008] obtained loans worth Rs:974 million in the name of his companies Ejaz Spinning Mills Ltd and Ejaz Textile Mills Limited; Gohar Ejaz categorically denied this later.

Khurram Iftikhar [BoD member: March 2007 – April 2008] borrowed loans of Rs:5.6 billion in name of his companies titled Amfort (Pvt) Ltd, Amtex Limited, and Shama Exports (Pvt) Ltd. However, the said companies were shown running as normal.

Fareed Mughees Sheikh [CEO Colony Group] was appointed Director BoP in March 2007. Colony Group took loans worth Rs:10 billion, later labelled as non-prudent loans and needed rescheduling. This Group, as revealed by Hamesh Khan, purchased the Phalia Sugar Mills belonging to Ch Pervaiz Elahi in 2007, through loans taken out from the BoP during BoD incumbency of Mr Fareed.

> [*The major item on agenda was the sugar mill of Mr Elahi's family, Phalia Sugar Mills. It was sold on the asked price and the buyers were those who also happen to be on Board of Directors; the needed money was 100 % funded by the BoP; thus both buyers and sellers were too much delighted though the bank was the ultimate casualty.*]

Mian Muhammad Latif of Chenab Limited [Popularly known as Chen-One] remained Director of BoP from October 2002 till April 2008 and allegedly got loan worth Rs:1.24 billion from BoP.

The absconder Humesh Khan was a dummy president of the BoP; but he was intelligent enough to keep Moonis Elahi happy and thus was also the beneficiary of the whole-some decisions of loot and plunder. The businesses which were not able to earn million a year were given loans of one hundred million straightaway and the people who did not know the alphabets of business were declared industrialist over night.

It is worth mentioning that it was the BOD, which had approved rescheduling of the Harris Steel fraudulent loan. A 3-member SC's bench **on 28th May 2010** directed the constitution of an investigation team, headed by former DG FIA Tariq Khosa, to probe into that Rs:9 billion loan scam and see the possibility of the BoP's criminal involvement.

The bench comprising Chief Justice Iftikhar M Chaudhry, Justice Ghulam Rabbani and Justice Khalilur Rehman Ramday issued the directives while examining progress into the scam case. The orders contained that:

> "We direct the NAB chairman to send a requisition to the establishment secretary to appoint a head of the investigation team to probe criminal cases in the BoP case and the authority is required to issue a notification today for the appointment of Tariq Khosa to this post in addition to his duties as the Anti-Narcotics Division Secretary."

HAMESH KHAN'S HOUSING SOCIETY:

Hamesh Khan, being the president of the Bank of Punjab (BoP), allegedly in collusion with Moonis Elahi, the son of the then CM Punjab Pervaiz Elahi in year 2004, launched a housing society for the employees of the BoP having the name Bankers Avenue Cooperative Housing Society (BACHS) on Baidian Road Lahore. Naeemuddin, President of the BoP, while talking to media, once said that:

> 'In fact making a society was not the domain of a bank and thus the State Bank of Pakistan had made serious objections to it. It was made for doing corruption.'

As per report published in **'the News' of 14th June 2010**, the corruption in BACHS had been investigated by the Registrar Cooperative Societies and by the NAB too. Moonis Elahi remained involved in the purchase of land, through a BoP employee named Mr Raja, from the poor farmers of the area by using his influence. There were wide ranging protests by local people from whom land was purchased by using un-ethical means and forcefully on cheap rates and was later sold to the bank on high prices. Allegedly, the land was purchased at Rs:3 million per acre while it was sold to the BACHS for Rs:6 million per acre.

In another dubious move, when this land was registered with Registrar of Cooperative Societies, Government of Punjab, Hamesh Khan had shown its worth at Rs:2 million per acre, in order to save stamp duty to the provincial exchequer. The development job of the BACHS was awarded to the husband of a lady MPA of PML(Q) who was also the real sister of the then GM of BoP, Haroon Aziz, a major accused in the BoP scam after Hamesh Khan, subsequently remained in jail for a long time on this account.

A report from the Registrar of Cooperative Societies Lahore placed before the SC bench on 9th June 2010 had verified the above facts confirming an embezzlement of Rs:412.3 million. [A letter from the Registrar CS HRC No 21278-P/2009 dated 27th May 2010 is referred in this regard]

Earlier, the Punjab Cooperative Department had conducted an inquiry under section 44-A of the Cooperative Societies Act 1925 of BACHSL Lahore, in February 2010. The inspection report had confirmed that the managing committee was involved in misappropriation and embezzlement of funds to the tune of Rs 412,316,950/. The BoP, after purchase of land, asked its employees to make initial payments, which was set too high. Thus, all the employees were offered loans from the bank [BOP]. The price of a plot was fixed at Rs:1.8 million in which loan of Rs:270,000/ was given by the bank for payment of booking while the rest Rs:1.53 million was to be given by the House Building Finance Corporation.

The employees made investment of their life-long savings but got nothing. As not only the society funds disappeared, after passage of five years, the employees who had been paying major portion of their salaries to the ghost society even did not know where their plots were located; there were no rules of the society on record till then at least.

JIT's REPORT ON BOP SCAM:

On 21st April 2011, the Punjab government had also placed a report before the SC on that BoP scam and revealed that former CM Punjab, Ch Pervaiz Elahi, had siphoned out Rs:5.4 billion from the bank while Chairman Federal Board of Revenue (FBR), Salman Siddique, had approved unlawful credit proposals of Rs:1.1 billion in July 2006 for them.

The 5000 pages report was prepared by Punjab's Additional Inspector General Police, Aftab Sultan [later DG IB], who headed a joint investigation team set up by the SC in June 2010 to look into irregularities in the BoP. The SC had set up the investigation team because it was not satisfied with investigations conducted by the National Accountability Bureau (NAB). During the course of investigations, 61 persons were examined.

During the hearing of the BoP loan scam, a 3-member SC's bench comprising Chief Justice Iftikhar M Chaudhry, Justice Muhammad Sair Ali and Justice Ghulam Rabbani was told that:

'Former Punjab CM secured a huge loan of Rs:5.4 billion from the bank in the name of Phalia Sugar Mills while the amount was later spent on a new project, 'Colony Sugar Mills'. Another source disclosed that the said loan was spent on buying the property.

The then Chief Secretary Punjab, Kamran Rasool, took long leave from his government service and during the leave period worked in Pervaiz Elahi's mills while remaining Chairman of the Board of Directors at BoP. During this period, Kamran Rasool interacted with the then president of the BoP, Hamesh Khan.

The FBR Chairman, then one of the two directors of the bank, approved, on behalf of the board of directors of BoP, unlawful credit proposals amounting to Rs:1.1 billion in July 2006. The actual corruption at the BoP amounts to Rs:76.178 billion.

The bank shows profits from 2005 to 2008 on paper, it was actually running in loss.'

[After this report, the influential gurus got restructured their loans worth Rs:38 billion immediately on terms suitable to them.]

The report said that the bank's liabilities had been increasing everyday but both the State Bank and the Punjab government had no clue what was going on; Hamesh Khan, with the help of board members, had issued loans to bank defaulters.

Terming the BoP scam one of the largest swindles in the country's history, the report said the bank was deprived of over Rs:11 billion in advances and mark up by one Harris Group alone. The media scrutiny of the bank started on 21st June 2007 with small breaking news initially; its very continuity came into question when its equity's market capitalisation declined by a whopping amount of around Rs:64 billion within a short period.

The report regretted that millions of rupees had been doled out from the BoP, against negligible securities and without any collateral, to non-existent clients like Harris Group, the main beneficiary of the scam [*later became one of the petitioners*]. Despite having no businesses, Harris Group opened accounts in the BoP by using fake identities and documents while the funds were sanctioned to them at their discretion. In 95% cases the sanctioned funds were withdrawn within a day after approval.

It was then conclusively established that properties placed as security with the bank were heavily over-valued; such over-valuations were the result of active connivance with the valuators; it was obvious.

The court directed the Advocate General Punjab to make the report public and accessible to all citizens interested in seeing a copy, subject to rules and regulation. The court also directed the NAB authorities to obtain a copy of the report and consider it in respect of the cases and references already pending. NAB was also asked to get benefit of the report and collect evidences in its light; however, the NAB once again avoided filing the references on one pretext or the other.

The court also held that none of the accused be allowed to enter into a plea bargain and that the principal amount, along with full mark-up at penal rates, be recovered from the main accused, Sheikh Afzal, and his accomplices.

The JIT's report said the references and complaints pending with NAB were testimony to the criminal and negligent behaviour of the bank's management while Hamesh Khan was at the helm of affairs. The bank's survival was vital for more than 5,000 families who depended on the bank for their livlihood. '*More than any body else, the depositors would be the greatest losers if the bank goes bankrupt,*' the report added.

It was suggested that NAB should move for the cancellation of bails of the accused so that the money and valuables illegally obtained by them could be recovered. NAB was desired to file a separate reference against four directors, including Farid Mughis Sheikh, Khurram Iftikhar, Ijaz Gohar and Mian M Latif, who obtained credit facilities for their industrial groups in contravention of the Bank of Punjab Act.

The Punjab government could have amended the bank's by-laws and allowed the Punjab Assembly's Public Accounts Committee [PAC] to review all appointments to the Board of Directors so that, in future, the rogues like those 19 accused mentioned in the said report, and who had inflicted huge losses to the bank, could be kept away from the bank premises; but who bothers for the public money in Pakistan.

Astonishingly, Board of Directors of the BoP had formed fake companies and obtained loans of over Rs:6 billion. Expressing alarm over this state of affairs, the CJ asked: *"How is it possible that bank directors allowed loans to themselves; massive corruption has been committed in the Bank of Punjab."* The court was informed that the bank's Board of Directors comprised persons nominated by the then president Hamesh Khan. The apex court was also told that a sum of Rs:90 million was swallowed in the name of bonuses only.

The JIT's said report on BoP also suggested that Hamesh Khan, the BoP President, had shown the door to the then Acting Chairman Shahzad Malik after the later was alarmed by the BoP - Harris Steel loan deal. However, the documentary evidence later revealed that it was the then Chief Minister Punjab Pervaiz Elahi, who being the competent authority, had removed Malik, might be on the recommendations of Hamesh Khan.

The investigations further revealed that:

"Hamesh Khan, in his capacity as the President of the Bank, reduced this sleepy Board to a mere rubber stamp. In its 95th meeting of 27-28th June 2003, the Board agreed to Hamesh Khan's desire to allow Board's business to be conducted in circulation by two directors and the Chairman. This change deprived the Bank of the collective wisdom of its directors and also made it much easier for Hamesh Khan to manipulate the Board's business.

If the Chairman or a director refused to toe the line, he was shown the outer door, as happened with Shahzad Ali Malik, who was first replaced as Chairman and then removed from the Board altogether in July 2007. He had raised a factual objection that the minutes of Board meetings were not recorded accurately and that the Bank's President Mr Hamesh Khan and his GM Azizul Hameed, who was Secretary to Board also, manipulated them to their advantage."

As per record, the competent authority for the appointment of the Chairman and directors was the Chief Minister, who was the authority for appointment of "accused" directors and five chairmen who had **"exercised poor oversight and were grossly negligent"** but still recommended to be spared from any action.

Another plunder; the Colony Group was given over Rs:5 billion loan by the BoP to buy Phalia Sugar Mill, belonging Chaudhries of Gujrat, but it strangely ignored certain important procedural formalities.

Independent experts were of the opinion that fair price of the Phalia Sugar was around Rs:1.5 billion whereas through BoP loan money it was bought for Rs:2.2 billion by one of the BoP Directors who also happened to be from the CM's family.

The investigation reports later revealed the fact that some businessmen like Jehangir Tareen were approached by Hamesh Khan to buy the Chaudhrys' sugar mill with the BoP money; Jehangir Tareen had himself revealed it to the media. Another MNA from Rahim Yar Khan was also approached by the BoP President Hamesh Khan but he had declined too.

The investigating team for BoP, though talked of the huge swindle, had not reflected on the reported Rs:2 billion default of Gas Natural, owned by son-in-law of Gen Khalid Maqbool, former Governor of the Punjab. The report did not mention the details of a BoP loan that was taken for a real estate project by the son of a senior bureaucrat and director of the bank.

BOP DIRECTORS SUMMONED IN SC:

On 10th June 2011, the SC summoned four former directors of the BoP Board; Gohar Ijaz, Farid Mughees, Farrukh Iftikhar and Mian Latif, for representing different industrial groups and borrowing approximately Rs: 20 billion in violation of section 19(4) of BoP Act 1909.

The SC bench, headed by the CJP Iftikhar M Chaudhry, was told that Rs: 1.5 billion had been recovered from 31 defaulters during year 2010; criminal cases were registered against few of them while for some others going under process. 'Hamesh Khan was extradited from USA, so why can't these defaulters be arrested', Chief Justice remarked.

The BoP Counsel told the apex court that the size of corruption in the Bank scam was touching Rs:80 billion in total till then whereas according to Aftab Sultan's investigation report the scam was of about Rs:76 billion.

NAB on that day also confirmed the fact unearthed in Aftab Sultan's Report that as per NAB's investigations, one of the directors Farid Mughees borrowed Rs:5 billion for a textile mill but gave the money to the former CM Ch Pervez Elahi for the purchase of his Phalia Sugar Mill. Governor Punjab, Sardar Latif Khosa's statement dated 9th April 2011 was discussed that why he had not opposed the Harris Steel Mill case as

Attorney General in Supreme Court. [*The Governor had categorically denied the charge of getting Rs:1.5 million bribe from Sheikh Afzal for that role.*]

Chief Justice had, however, remarked on the Governor's statement that these accusations were of serious nature.

On 19th August 2011, the SC ordered Sh Afzal to submit a written apology for writing a contemptuous letter to former SC judge Syed Jamshed Ali who was heading the committee formed to recover misappropriated money by selling their assets. The letter, described by the court as obnoxious, had accused the committee's chairman of discriminating against Sh Afzal by favouring the lawyers appearing against him because of their role in the Black Coat Movement for restoration of the judges in 2007-09. It was also alleged that the salvage committee was allegedly selling their properties at throwaway prices.

A 3-judge bench comprising Chief Justice Iftikhar M Chaudhry, Justice Amir Hani Muslim and Justice Ghulam Rabbani asked Punjab's Advocate General Khwaja Haris, and Kh Tariq Raheem, the counsel for Sh Afzal, to sit together and settle the entire accounts by determining the outstanding amount, without prejudice to the current proceedings then going on before the court or the salvage committee. Sh Afzal was in jail those days.

The apex court was informed that Sh Afzal and his family had agreed to clear the entire outstanding amount of BoP, but the amount to be paid was yet to be determined. It was also complained that the bank wanted cash, and no property, to settle the dispute. Till then it had been sorted out that the total plundered money stood at Rs:8.403 billion while the value of properties surrendered by Sh Afzal to the bank amounted to Rs: 5.58 billion only.

The court observed that Sh Afzal had not disclosed ALL the assets and properties owned by him and his family members. A representative of the bank had also resigned after receiving threats from the accused side. Sh Afzal had managed to approach the apex court for bail, in the meantime, on the plea that he had returned Rs:3.67 billion cash and 600-tola gold to the bank.

Sh Afzal then moved another petition in the apex court, pleading for a fair trial as envisaged in Article 10-A of the Constitution. He contended that the said proceedings in the case were neither *suo moto* nor covered by Article 184(3) of the constitution, thus the appeal was an inherent right.

The accused contended that more than three-fourth of the outstanding principal amount had been settled as per Aftab Sultan's Report, and yet he was languishing in jail, whereas as per practice for plea bargaining, 34 percent of the total outstanding amount was required to be paid in cash and rest of the payment was allowed to be paid in instalments, with the release of the accused.

On 23rd March 2012, the NAB rejected a plea bargain offer of Rs:3.077 billion made by Sh Afzal in the said scam. *'[NAB] decided to re-determine the plea bargain amount as the principal amount borrowed by them [Afzal and his family] from the Bank is Rs:8.404 billion,'* NAB Chairman Admiral (retd) Fasih Bokhari told after holding a meeting in that regard. The meeting also considered that Justice (retd) Malik Qayyum had voluntarily agreed to return Rs:98 million to the aggrieved parties in the Aglam Global Links Private Ltd (Qasr-e-Zauk) Case.

The executive board of the bureau approved the 'voluntary return' by Malik Qayyum who was an illegal beneficiary in this case; he had obtained money in the shape of 63 plots, depriving the remaining claimants of their shares.

NAB's board meeting also approved a 'voluntary return' for Rs:70 million submitted by World Automobiles as per rules for misappropriation of public funds in the supply of cars to the Canadian International Development Agency funded education project in Sindh. NAB, on that day, also authorized an inquiry against CEO Sohail Ahmed and Islam Akhtar Khan, Project Director of Gujranwala Tool Dies & Moulds Centre, (GTDMC) for corruption and misappropriation of public funds.

On 12th April 2012; the Accountability Court at Lahore indicted Hamesh Khan, Sheikh Afzal and Seth Nisar in BoP's Rs:9 billion scam; all of them had refused to accept charges levelled against them by NAB. The NAB of Punjab had filed a reference in that Accountability Court in September 2007 against 12 people including six officials of BoP and six others. The accused persons, in connivance with Hamesh Khan, had opened 23 fictitious accounts by their fake and forged national identity cards to obtain loans of the said amount. The NAB accused Hamesh of misuse of power and sanctioning illegal loans while Seth Nisar was accused of committing wilful default of Rs:930 million he borrowed from BoP.

On 22nd October 2012, the SC expressed its discontentment over the "go-slow" policy adopted by the NAB officials in recovery process. A 3-member bench headed by Chief Justice Iftikhar M Chaudhry was informed that the plea bargain process with the NAB had almost been completed and half of the amount had been paid back to the NAB.

Sh Afzal complained that some of his property in Dubai was 'secretly' sold for Rs:1.5 billion – at half the actual price – and pleaded that the court should order the NAB to investigate the matter. Responding to the complaint, the chief justice remarked that assets could not be sold without the owner's consent; NAB was asked to submit details within three days.

The SC bench headed by Chief Justice Iftikhar M Chaudhry, during the regular hearing on that day [ultimately] said that former BoP President Hamesh Khan, the principal accused and Sheikh Afzal, and one more main character in the scam, could not be kept in jail indefinitely. The bench expressed displeasure over NAB for not sorting out the issue of property with respect to debt recovery in the reconciliation committee.

The apex court also held that *'no one trusts the state institutions now and how NAB can be sent abroad to fix the issues when they are unable to do it here'.*

> [*There was much roar in media at those orders; many questions were raised. How the huge loan-money of BoP was allowed to fly to Dubai for investment. Definitely BoP had not loaned the money for that. The SC should have ordered to register a criminal case against the party; Sh Afzal & others.*]

NAB's performance was also termed dubious; how could NAB be expected to investigate matters abroad when it had failed to carry out investigations within the country.

THE CASE PUT ON GO-SLOW MAT:

Referring to various media reports *dated 13th April 2013;* Amir Shahzad Chaudhry, assistant vice president of the BoP, who helped unearth corruption of Rs:9 billion, in one of the biggest scams in the banking history of Pakistan, was made to run from pillar to post to get back his job after termination by the bank administration for *'forwarding indecent mails to colleagues'.* In fact he was victimised for exposing mega corruption scandals like the Harris Steel Mills case and BoP Housing scheme corruption, involving billions of rupees.

Mr Chaudhry had to approach the Supreme Court seeking his reinstatement on the previous position. He had been facing the wrath of the Bank management since June 2007, when he first exposed the then BOP President Hamish Khan and was charged with conspiracy against the bank management.

Immediately after the scandal broke out, Amir Shahzad was transferred to Quetta as punishment by Hamesh Khan. He approached the Labour Court Lahore which granted him stay order against his transfer, but the management did not allow him to resume duty till August 2008 when the interim management took over the Bank and allowed him to occupy his desk.

However, when the next President of BoP, Naeemuddin Khan, took over, Amir Shahzad again came under the management's fire. He filed a writ petition in the Lahore High Court (LHC) against unlawful termination of his 20-year service, but for three years there was no decision. Ultimately, he had to knock at the doors of the SC for justice. Naeemuddin told the media that:

"We would like to bring to your attention that Mr Amir was involved in serious misconduct in that he was forwarding indecent material to female staff of the bank. His services were, therefore, terminated from the bank. He filed an appeal to the appellate authority, considering the heinous / immoral nature of his offence, the appeal was turned down. At present his case is subjudice before the Lahore High Court."

The media persons could not resist their high laughs; concocted allegations of *'forwarding indecent material to the fellow employees was considered more serious offence than eating up Rs:9 billions collectively with all hands in glove'*.

At last, **on 22nd May 2013**, the BoP management in compliance with the SC's orders referred 83 cases of loan defaults to the State Bank of Pakistan (SBP) and the NAB. Out of this lot, 41 cases of defaults worth over Rs:38.50 billion were sent to NAB and 42 cases worth of Rs:18.79 billion to SBP under section 31-D of National Accountability Ordinance (NAO) 1999.

Already, the BoP had referred 66 loan default cases to the central bank for referral to NAB. Out of those SBP could forward only 24 loan default cases involving Rs:8.25 billion to NAB till ending May 2013; the rest of the cases were *'kept under scrutiny'* [thus for bargain] due to undue political pressures. Despite numerous reminders, the NAB deliberately avoided to proceed against the mighty son-in-law of former governor of Punjab Gen Khalid Maqbool and some other influentials.

In most cases the loan defaulters had acquired stay orders from the Lahore High Court [*in Pakistan, there prevails a general impression that one can get stay order from most civil judges for Rs:500, equivalent to £3.25 only, which can run valid for decades*].

The NAB was also reluctant to initiate any legal action against the directors of six companies of a leading textile group who had fraudulently and dishonestly caused loss worth of Rs:7.320 billion to the bank. The new management had also requested the NAB for initiating inquiry against ex-directors of her own BoP who had obtained loans worth Rs:18.4 billion during their tenure.

A 3-member bench of the SC headed by the CJP Iftikhar M Chaudhry, was told that Rs:31 billion on account of non-performing loans had been recovered since 2009 due to SC's timely action.

On 27th May 2013; the SC hinted at day-to-day proceedings in the BOP Case and sought a list of those people who got Rs:38 billion loans rescheduled. A 3-judges bench led by Chief Justice Iftikhar M Chaudhry was informed that the profit of the bank was recorded to Rs:11.30 billion after the recovery of default loans.

Submitting a report pertaining to the details of recoveries and action taken against defaulters in pursuance of the court's orders, the bank's counsel, Anwar Mansoor, told the apex court that during the financial year 2008-09 the bank's loss was recorded to Rs:10 billion. To which, the bench observed that it had nothing to do with the bank's profit; the bench just wanted to know the legality behind all the compromises and rescheduled loans.

QASR E ZAUK AFFAIRS:

On 23rd December 2010; a 3-member bench of the Supreme Court of Pakistan [SC] ordered the National Accountability Bureau [NAB] to retrieve a property named Qasr e Zauk, worth Rs:1.38 billion, conduct a thorough investigation and arrest all [most influential] culprits involved in the scam, without any fear. The bench, headed by Chief Justice Iftikhar M Chaudhry, and comprising Justice Jawwad S Khwaja and Justice Khalilur Rehman Ramday, also directed DG NAB Punjab Rana Zahid to probe defective investigation, earlier conducted by their Deputy Director Ziaullah Khan.

The court was informed that Justice (Rtd) Malik Qayyum, former IGP Azhar Hassan Nadeem, uncle of former LHC judge Sheikh Rasheed, Senator Gulzar Ahmed Khan, his sons Senator Waqar Ahmed Khan and Senator Ammar Ahmed Khan, former Minister Iqbal Tikka and his relative DSP Mukhtar Tikka were involved in the land scam and got transferred the said property in their names after kidnapping the owners - Sheikh Ayub and his son Mohsin Ayub.

Justice Jawwad also noted that over the last two-and-a-half years, the said property had been running as a marriage hall, earning millions thus far. He asked the NAB authorities whether the money was accounted for by any means when the property was frozen and declared non-transferable; the money should have been deposited with NAB. NAB's previous IO had declared the senator innocent and held others responsible to which the SC objected. The bench was hearing the bail petition of Mohsin Ayub, who had been in NAB custody over the last four years.

The facts were that Qasr e Zauq at Liberty Market Lahore was sold out and transferred to M/S Asian Gas of Senator Ammar by NAB. Appearing before the court, Sh Ayub submitted that a plea bargain of Rs:600 million took place between him and the investors in presence of Justice (Rtd) Malik Qayyum, the senators and the former IGP, who were also investors at that time in the property. Justice (Rtd) Malik Qayyum invested Rs:30 million which were returned to him, but with malafide intentions they managed to make a NAB reference against him. A retired Brigadier, an ally of these big guns, had taken possession of his house at Nicholson Road, Lahore, too.

The SC bench was told that the said property was valued at Rs:1.2 billion, but Justice Qayyum and others sold it for only Rs:600 million. Counsel for Mohsin Ayub argued that his client entertained investments of the people, but was allegedly trapped by the influential who abducted him and first took him to the residence of Iqbal Tikka in Johar Town Lahore and then to Faisalabad. They took into possession the power of attorney in respect of the investors and got signed some papers in their favour during this course, he alleged.

Qasr e Zauk was purchased by the petitioner from one Ashfaq Sheikh; he then invited investors, including the above mentioned influential big guns, who later managed to rob him of the property, setting the claimants after him to ultimately take the matter to NAB for unfair probe. That the NAB court had ordered freezing of the property and a stay about its transfer was also passed by the LHC but NAB, despite all that, sold and transferred the same to Asian Gas of Senator Ammar Ahmed.

On 30th December 2010, NAB Punjab recorded the statements of 13 persons, including Senators Waqar Ahmad and his brother Ammar Ahmad, in connection with the above said property in pursuance of the SC orders. The notables were former Minister Tikka Muhammad Iqbal, DSP Mukhtar Tikka, Sh Ayub, Hammad Tikka, Haseeb Azhar, former IGP Azhar Hassan Nadeem and Senators Waqar Ahmad and Aammar Ahmad amongst others. Justice (Rtd) Qayyum and Senator Gulzar Ahmed Khan could not afford to join the probe then.

On 15th March 2011; the NAB arrested Adil Saleem Tikka, son-in-law of former Minister Iqbal Tikka, just after he withdrew his pre-arrest bail application from the LHC; he was accused of embezzling millions of rupees in the Qasr e Zauq property scam which they had got transferred in their names after kidnapping the owners Sh Ayub and his son Mohsin Ayub. The investigation continued with NAB remands and judicial custody of the accused persons. Negotiations between the two parties to reach an amicable solution, however, continued. Ex-Senator Ammar Khan and former IGP Azhar Nadeem continued attending the NAB office for investigations.

On 18th May 2012, Justice (rtd) Malik Qayyum deposited Rs:98 million as a Voluntary Return in the said case; he was alleged to be an illegal beneficiary in this case who obtained money in the shape of 63 plots, depriving the remaining claimants of their share. The SC had already directed NAB to retrieve money from the illegal beneficiaries of the Rs:1.38 billion Qasr e Zauq property for refunding the genuine affectees of M/s Aglam Global Links (Pvt) Ltd; a forex exchange company which had arranged finance from the people through fraud. Qasr e Zauq property was owned by M/s Aglam Global Links (Pvt) Ltd, and it was purchased by Gulzar family—Senator Waqar Ali Khan and ex-Senator Ammar Khan—at around Rs:480 million. Allegedly the market value of that property was around Rs:1.38 billion; the company had not paid back its 400 affectees.

On 7th April 2013; the NAB finally arrested former minister and PPP's candidate for NA-166 and PP-230 Tikka Muhammad Iqbal in connection with the Qasr e Zauq scandal. It was portrayed an election move from PML(N) then because the elections were ahead for 11th May 2013. Though Tikka Iqbal and his accomplices had expressed a desire to return the remaining amount, both before NAB and the Supreme Court but they could not manage to do so. NAB subsequently summoned all the actors named by Ayub and recovered Rs:618 million from Ayub, his son and Adil Saleem on account of plea bargains; Justice (Rtd) Malik Qayyum's deposit of Rs:98 million was already lying with NAB as a 'voluntary return'.

No doubt it was a private deal; a small fry in Pakistan's chequered history. However, the event has been noted here with certain questions. From where the Justice (Rtd) Malik Qayyum had sourced his share in so expensive property and from where he had taken out Rs:98 million to make that 'voluntary return'. Were the contributions made by the other shareholders, senior police officers, politicians, former ministers etc were 'tax paid' money – properly accounted for in documents. Was Capital Gain Tax paid on the transactions made over that property? Were they all not *living beyond means* while on government assignments including that defamed Judge of the LHC?

In Pakistan, the estate and property business [since decades] is so lucrative that big moneys associated with all sorts of corruption, kickbacks and commissions are easily and invariably covered with knowledge-full over-sight of TAXMEN.

Scenario 77

NAB & ACCOUNTABILITY – HIGH DRAMA:

PPP's [Drama] ACCOUNTABILITY COMMISSION:

On 15th April 2009, Parliamentary Affairs Minister Babar Awan tabled *'the Holder of Public Office (Accountability) Act, 2009'* in the National Assembly. Among the major proposals was the removal of the immunity enjoyed by members of the armed forces, the judiciary and parliamentarians by re-defining public office given in Article 260 of the Constitution of Pakistan; it was generally termed as draft of the National Accountability Commission [NAC] Act.

Perhaps first time, all the political parties had reached a consensus that besides politicians and civil bureaucrats, members of the armed forces and judiciary should also be made accountable.

The PML(N) had forwarded about five dozen proposals which were not accepted by the working committee. The body had been operational on the bill since April 2009. PML(N)'s one major proposal, which was not accepted was that the NAC should be headed by a sitting judge of the Supreme Court. The committee, however, decided that the post should be held either by a sitting or retired judge or any person qualified to be a judge of the Supreme Court.

The Committee's head, Mr Fatiana told the media that NAB would be dissolved after the new law comes into effect and its assets and employees would be transferred to the NAC. All cases being pursued by NAB would also be transferred to the NAC. However, the NAC would not carry out investigations against any accused who might had been named having committed fraud before 1985.

As per NAC's draft the prime minister would not have discretionary powers to appoint the head of the NAC, to be appointed for three years, and his nominee would require the approval of an eight-member parliamentary committee having equal representation of the treasury and opposition benches.

The draft suggested that an official found guilty of corruption by a court after hearing a reference moved by the NAC would stand dismissed. Any elected representative or other public office-holder would be disqualified for contesting elections after conviction till five years after completion of his sentence.

The speaker and deputy speaker of the National Assembly and the chairman and deputy chairman of the Senate were also made accountable through another clause of the proposed law. PML(N) alleged that the PPP government had in the past changed some approved drafts at the last moment.

Later Prime Minister Yousuf Raza Gilani announced that the government would bring the accountability bill before the parliament after consulting all political parties. A copy of the draft bill was sent to the PML(N), which suggested more than 50 amendments. PM Gilani had consulted Nawaz Sharif on the draft law in January 2010 and asked the committee to expedite the process of reviewing it.

The PML(N), however, raised objections on the language and provisions in the draft and refused to accept it; *till the end of their governments, of the PPP & the PML(N) on 16*th *March 2013, that NAC Bill could not be passed.*

Coming back; the said proposed ACT of 2009 of Babar Awan could not go through because the opposition parties raised many objections on it and demanded amendments in it. Then an exercise of recasting the said bill, in its generic name of *National Accountability Commission* [NAC] started; dozens of meetings of the Parliamentary Committee held, tens of mutual discussions amongst the PPP & PML(N) members took place during the four years but of no avail.

Till the end of their governments on 16th March 2013, the proposed improvements in NAB or its controlling NAO / NAC changed many shapes and faces. In November 2012 at last, the PPP government made a serious try to bring forward the National Accountability Commission Bill (NACB) of 2012 but timely shouts of one Anusha Rehman saved the nation from a **'calculated legal disaster'** in the history of Pakistan.

To transform NAB into the National Accountability Commission [NAC], the proposed Bill was [mildly; may be off the record now] tabled in the National Assembly to seek a simple majority vote to make it an Act. The salient features, as noted by a freelance columnist [Referring to qaisarrashid@yahoo.com], were:

• It laid down a broad consultation mechanism to seek the consent of the leader of the opposition to nominate the Chairman of the NAC.

- Consultation with the Chief Justice of High Court concerned was made mandatory to nominate a judge for the accountability court.

- It made a mandatory provision that the chairman NAC should be a retired judge of the Supreme Court (SC) or a retired grade-22 federal government officer.

- Provisions were included that both judges and army Generals would also be held accountable for their misdeeds.

- A National Accountability Investigation Agency (NAIA) would be formed to investigate any alleged affair.

- Once appointed, the chairman of the NAC would stay in the office till completion of his four-year tenure.

- The powers of the chairman to seek mutual legal assistance, where the jurisdiction would be foreign, was reduced. **The question:** *Why did the PPP government wanted the scope of mutual legal assistance reduced unilaterally? Why should those Pakistanis who siphoned off the wealth of this country and escaped abroad not be apprehended and the booty recovered?*

- The powers of the chairman to procure banking information about an alleged person was made subject to prior permission granted by a court. **The question:** *Why should the chairman not be independent to procure any banking information without letting the accused know that an investigation was being carried out against him? Why was it important to put in place a mechanism to alert an accused person so that he could shift his money through telephone or internet banking?*

- The scope of the NAC would be limited only to public office holders (politicians or government servants) while the people falling under the definition of '**other persons**' would be spared. **The question:** *how many front men used by the corrupt public office holders would also be termed pubic office holders? What would be the mechanism for apprehending the front men to unearth the trail leading to the actual face indulging in corruption?*

- The powers of the investigation agency (NAIA) would be short of arresting a public office holder if he cooperated with the NAIA even if there was available solid evidence of corruption against him. **The question:** *Good messages - indulge in corruption but cooperate with the NAIA to avoid arrest if the scam was exposed; in the meantime,* *flee from the country, save your skin and enjoy the fruits of the booty. Do corruption but be careful to give any clue; you are free to plunder and if caught unluckily then cooperate.*

- The accountability courts of the NAC would not punish a culprit for more than seven years imprisonment (instead of 14 years) in case corruption was proved against him but the looted money not recovered. **The question:** *In such a scenario, should the duration of punishment be decreased or increased? For such a hardened criminal, why not the limit be extended to 20 years?*

- The accountability courts of the NAC would not punish a culprit at all in case corruption was proved against him but he returned the looted money before the judgement of the court or his plea bargain was accepted by the NAC. **The question:** *Why should there be a soft corner for a proven corrupt public office holder; this clause was an encouragement for plundering process in fact – loot the country but go careful to be caught – if caught, return the money immediately and try the next move.*

- Any act of corruption would be condoned if done 'in good faith'. **The question:** *who will define the clause and at which stage that faith would be disclosed.*

- The *'benami'* accounts and property of a culprit would not fall in the ambit of the NAC. **Very cogent message:** *you will be a fool of the first order if you would keep the looted money or property in your own name.*

The above said points especially in an arena of reduction in powers of the chairman to seek mutual foreign legal assistance and reduction in the scope of the NAC only to bureaucrats and politicians would hardly help Pakistanis in reducing corruption. Unless the corrupt people's bank accounts would be checked without alerting him; including all members of the society like parliamentarians, ministers, judges and army officers from Major ranks and above in the net; why should any wrongdoer chiselling out money from the poorest or governments on one pretext or another get off scot-free?

The questions; *why should the cooperation of a corrupt public office holder be a guarantee against his arrest? Why should not he fall from grace if he was corrupt? Why should the arrest not act as a deterrent against corruption? Had such immunities offered to a corrupt public office holder, then no need of having any anti-corruption body?*

In nut shell, the PPP government wanted to encourage and institutionalize corruption at all levels of the government under the protection of the said National Accountability Commission. The high class elite were being given an LCP [*License to Corrupt Practices*].

Even then if a bureaucrat or politician would not do corruption [*in the light of above provisions of law*] he should straightaway be disqualified to hold an office or be sent to a mental hospital.

Were the courts ready to take cognizance of such loot & plunder?

APG BASEER QURESHI's PLEA:

On 1st February 2010, Additional Prosecutor General [APG] of the NAB Abdul Baseer Qureshi moved an application in the Supreme Court requesting to expunge adverse observations made against him in its verdict on the NRO.

> [*A 17-judge bench of the court in a short order, issued on 16th December 2009, had expressed displeasure over the conduct and lack of proper and honest assistance and cooperation to the court by NAB's Chairman, Prosecutor General and Additional Prosecutor General.*
>
> *The apex court had suggested the government to replace them with persons possessing high degree of competence and impeccable integrity in terms of Section 6 of the NAB Ordinance as also in terms of the observations made by the apex court in the Asfandyar Wali Khan case.*
>
> *The SC full bench had regretted that the conduct of the top NAB executives made it impossible for the court to trust them with proper and diligent pursuit of cases falling within their spheres of operation.*]

The Chairman, the Additional Prosecutor General of NAB, former Attorney General Justice (Rtd) Malik Qayyum and the federal government had filed review petitions against the apex court's order.

After the release of the detailed judgment, Baseer Qureshi filed additional grounds requesting the court to remove the adverse remarks passed against him in the judgment so that he could concentrate on his work which he said was his only source of income. Mr Qureshi told the court that '*he was nearing 70 years of age and is not interested to continue working in the NAB.*' It was contended that he was once granted a special certificate of appreciation and a cash reward of Rs:100,000 for his extra-ordinary dedication and devotion to duty while appearing against Mr Zardari in Steel Mills and BMW References.

The apex court, however, was not inclined to give any relief to Qureshi.

JUSTICE DEEDAR H SHAH AS NAB's CHIEF:

In the **first week of October 2010**, the federal government appointed Justice (Rtd) Deedar Hussain Shah as Chairman NAB while PML(N) had rejected the move mainly because he had been an MPA from Ratodero (Larkana) twice in 1990s on the PPP ticket when he was picked up as judge of the Sindh High Court in 1994 and then later elevated to the Supreme Court.

Justice (Rtd) Deedar Shah was appointed NAB's Chief after his predecessor Nawid Ahsan was removed under a 16th December 2009's ruling of the Supreme Court that held the controversial National Reconciliation Ordinance (NRO) as unconstitutional.

Then it was ordered that the government should revive all cases withdrawn under the ordinance and expressed displeasure over the perceived lack of proper and honest assistance and had also suggested the appointment of a new chairman.

Justice (Rtd) Syed Deedar Hussain Shah was appointed as Chairman National Accountability Bureau [NAB] by President Zardari vide Notification no: F.8.(17)/2010-A.I dated 8th October 2010 with the wording:

'The President of Islamic Republic of Pakistan has been pleased to appoint Mr Justice (Retd) Syed Deedar Hussain Shah as Chairman, National Accountability Bureau in terms of Section 6(b)(i) of the National Accountability Ordinance 1999, with immediate effect.'

Justice Shah took over the charge immediately and started the routine functions. Within one week of that Notification the said appointment was challenged in the Supreme Court of Pakistan. While the proceedings were going on in the apex court, the original notification was taken back or withdrawn and on 9th **February 2011** another notification was issued with details below:

'No.F.8.(17) / 2010-A.I The President of Islamic Republic of Pakistan has been pleased to withdraw/recall his order dated 07.10.2010,

appointing Mr Justice (R) Syed Deedar Hussain Shah as Chairman, National Accountability Bureau (NAB). Consequently, notification No.F.8(17)/2010-A.I dated 08.10.2010 is hereby rescinded / cancelled.

2. Further, the President of Islamic Republic of Pakistan has also been pleased to appoint Mr. Justice (R) Syed Deedar Hussain Shah as Chairman, National Accountability Bureau (NAB), in terms of Section 6(b)(i) of the National Accountability Ordinance, 1999 with immediate effect.'

Abdul Hafeez Pirzada, the counsel for the federal government, was asked to explain 7th October's presidential summary before the court especially in the context that PM Gilani had, on 10th October 2010, disowned the whole issue declaring it as President's exclusive domain.

Mr Pirzada submitted the 10-page summary to establish that it was prepared by the law ministry and sent to the PM Secretariat for onward approval. The summary suggested that PM Gilani had talked to Ch Nisar Ali Khan [*the then Leader of the Opposition in the National Assembly*] on the matter and even discussed objections raised by the latter. Under Section 6 of the National Accountability Ordinance (NAO) such appointments, though finally approved by the President, but were to be made on the advice of the prime minister.

However, it was found on record that few days before appointment of Justice Shah, probably on 22nd September 2010, PM Gilani had informed the Opposition Leader Ch Nisar Ali Khan on telephone that Justice (Rtd) Mukhtar Junejo was being considered for the post of NAB's chairman but in October a different summary was sent and got approved. Ch Nisar had serious reservations over the proposal and he had communicated them to the prime minister in writing, but the very next day the name of Justice Deedar Shah was communicated to him by PM Gilani without any reference to his earlier letter.

On 10th March 2011, the Supreme Court of Pakistan, on two petitions filed by one Shahid Orakzai and Ch Nisar Ali Khan MNA [No: 60 & 61 of 2010], challenging the appointment of Justice (Rtd) S Deedar Hussain Shah as Chairman NAB, declared that the appointment was illegal. The 33-page ruling was authored by Supreme Court's Justice Asif Saeed Khosa in which it was ordered that Justice (Rtd) Shah should immediately relinquish the office.

The verdict by a three-judge bench headed by Justice Javed Iqbal [Justice Raja Fayyaz Ahmed & Justice Asif Saeed Khan Khosa were others two judges] required Justice Shah, a former judge of the Supreme Court, to immediately leave the office he assumed five months ago after a legal row in which the apex court had ordered the removal of his predecessor.

Justice Shah left the office immediately; however, the PPP government filed review petition against the decision on 9th April 2011, but of no avail.

On 11th March 2011 during mid-night, the President Zardari again proposed the reappointment of Justice (Rtd) Deedar H Shah as Chairman of the NAB while he had been removed from the office by the Supreme Court only a day earlier. The president proposed Justice Shah in two separate letters addressed to PM Mr Gilani and Leader of the Opposition Ch Nisar Ali Khan to meet the mandatory consultative process.

Both letters were sent to Mr Gilani who was asked to forward one to Ch Nisar. The president's letter had described Justice (Rtd) Shah as a 'man of integrity' recalling his services in superior judiciary. The president had taken note of the earlier objections on Justice Shah's name, including the criticism that he had *'political affiliation with the ruling political party'*.

The President's letter had also quoted the 1996's Supreme Court judgment in Al-Jehad Trust case that had settled the issue of political affiliation of a candidate for a judicial post by concluding that political affiliation alone might not disqualify a candidate. The PML(N) was not convinced and rejected this proposal by saying that *'we believe that the transparent process of accountability cannot take place if a controversial man is appointed as the NAB's Chairman.'*

The position of NAB's chairman always remained controversial during Nawaz Sharif's rule and more in Gen Musharraf's regimes since he could 'selectively' pursue accountability cases against the opposition. Partly to address this controversy, the 18th Constitutional Amendment required the prime minister to consult the opposition before making the appointment.

However, PML(N)'s stance on Deedar Shah was unchanged. The PPP held that Nawaz Sharif had in 2000 expressed full confidence in Justice (rtd) Shah. Rauf Klasra had [referring to *'the News of 9th October 2010'*] described the facts as:

- The 10 years official record of the Sindh High Court (SHC) revealed that PML(N)'s Nawaz Sharif, when he was a high profile detainee of Gen Musharraf, during his trial on the hijacking charges punishable with death penalty, had not only shown confidence but also praised professionalism of the then CJ of the Sindh High Court J Deedar H Shah.

- With the elevation of the then CJ SHC J Shah to the Supreme Court on 28th April 2000, detainee Nawaz Sharif had suddenly found himself in big trouble at the hands of the new CJ of the SHC, who had constituted a full bench to hear the hijacking case on daily basis. It created panic in the ranks of Nawaz Sharif's legal team.

- Contrarily, CJ SHC Deedar Hussain Shah had actually appointed a 3-member bench comprising Justice A Hameed Dogar, Justice Rabbani and another judge, to hear Nawaz Sharif's case and the later was quite satisfied with this bench and its proceedings. It was quite obvious that CJ Deedar Shah was sent to the Supreme Court because Gen Musharraf was unhappy with him during the trial of Nawaz Sharif.

- Nawaz's legal team had praised CJ Shah in their petition no. 43(172) / 2000 dated 27th June 2000 which was filed to challenge the speedy trial and formation of a full bench by the new CJ SHC. Nawaz Sharif's lawyer had also complained in writing then to the SHC that the role of secret agencies had suddenly become important in proceedings that had greatly disturbed Nawaz Sharif and brought inconveniences for him.

- However, 10 years later, the PML(N) leaders came out to attack the same judge and challenged his appointment as the NAB Chairman on grounds that once he was a PPP worker and had contested elections on its tickets. Nawaz Sharif's companions did not question him or his past political affiliation when they had found him a professional judge who did not allow secret agencies to disturb his Court's decorum. J Deedar Shah had also worked with the CJP Iftikhar M Chaudhary and had retired without any complaint against him.

SC's judgment against Justice Shah was based on facts because his appointment was not made by taking due precautions; the given procedure [of consultation] was not followed.

It is on record that the whole Sindh protested the SC's judgment against Justice Shah; the PPP passed a resolution condemning the decision and later its MPAs marched towards the Sindh High Court to register their protest. At the same time, the PPP in Islamabad loudly hinted about the reappointment of Deedar Shah as the NAB Chairman again.

The fingers were pointed out on why he should be re-appointed. Justice (Rtd) Tariq Mehmood, a legal expert, had cogently raised the question as to whether or not an individual could be made NAB Chairman for the second term because the second appointment of former Prosecutor General Irfan Qadir was challenged in the apex court on the same grounds. Mr Qadir was sent home under the court orders.

[*That is another story that how the PPP retaliated Irfan Qadir's quit; he was brought back in the same SC at Attorney General's slot.*]

Gen Musharraf had made the NAB controversial because he had brought five army Generals, serving & retired, to 'selectively' pursue accountability cases against the opposition. Partly to address this controversy, the 18th Constitutional Amendment required the prime minister to consult the Opposition Leader before making the appointment, but the rifts have always been there.

Indeed, it was the government's failure to consult Ch Nisar Ali that led to the removal of the NAB Chairman Justice (Rtd) Deedar Hussain Shah. *J Deedar Shah was widely regarded as a PPP loyalist and not a 'person of impartial character'* for the said post, the PML(N) had contested.

On 22nd March 2011, the SC issued detailed judgment over the appointment issue of NAB's Chairman and held that *'Justice (r) Deedar Hussain Shah stands disqualified to be appointed to that office again on account of the Section 6(b)(i) of the National Accountability Ordinance (NAO) 1999'*; and the matter of appointing Mr Shah as NAB's Chairman had been handled by the Law Ministry in a manner depicting shallow and perfunctory understanding of the constitution and the relevant law.

The apex court in its 33-page detailed judgement written by Justice Asif Saeed Khosa pointed out that because of his two appointments to that office, both botched and messed up by the Law Ministry's wrong legal advice to the relevant quarters and that he stood disqualified to be appointed to that office again on account of the provision regarding "non-extendable period" contained in section 6(b)(i) of the NAO, 1999.

Justice Khosa had also observed that:

'..... *Anybody interested in making an honest appointment of NAB's chairman would not feel shy of consulting the Chief Justice of Pakistan.'*

It concluded that the appointment of Justice Shah as NAB's Chairman by President Asif Ali Zardari on 9th February 2011 was *ultra vires* and against the spirit of section 6(b)(i) of the NAO, 1999 and through such illegal appointment, the fundamental rights of the people of the country, including their right to life, right to liberty, due process of law, fair trial and access to justice, were adversely affected.

Senior ASC Akram Sheikh argued that appointing NAB's Chairman was not a discretionary power of the president [Mr Zardari] and in making such an appointment, the president was, in terms of Article 48(1) of the constitution, bound to act on the advice of Prime Minister [Yousaf Raza Gilani]; but for Justice Shah's first appointment dated 7th October 2010 the prime minister had not tendered such advice to the president.

Justice Khosa after discussing at length the importance of office of NAB Chairman and its functions said that it was perceived as an institution which was possibly being misused for covering up corruption at high places through appointment of its hand-picked chairman, therefore, consultation with the chief justice of Pakistan and the leader of opposition was necessary.

It was in that backdrop that in the case of *'Dr Mobashir Hassan and others vs Federation of Pakistan and others'*, the SC had suggested consultation with the chief justice of Pakistan in the matter of appointment of NAB chairman. That suggestion was once again repeated by the apex court in the case of *'The Bank of Punjab vs Haris Steel Industries (Pvt) Ltd.'* saying that consultations with the leader of opposition in the NA and with the CJP were essentially meant for noble and laudable purposes to achieve the very objects for which NAB was established.

2 NEW CONTEMPT NOTICES AGAIN:

The general populace of Sindh protested against the SC's judgment; the PPP in the provincial assembly passed a resolution condemning the SC's decision and later its members marched towards the Sindh High Court to register their protest. The Federal Law Minister Babar Awan had told the media outside SC building just after the short order announced by the apex court [on 11th March 2011] that *'we are thinking about the reappointment of J Deedar Shah as the NAB Chairman; the office of NAB should not be left vacant even for a day.'*

Babar Awan had known the law better but was compelled by his party policy thus an ambiguity prevailed because an individual could not be appointed as NAB's Chairman for the second term; rejection of second appointment of former Prosecutor General Irfan Qadir was in sight. It was on record that Mr Qadir was sent home under the similar court orders.

On 11th March 2011, all over the Sindh province, the PPP workers held strikes, seized processions and raised slogans against the apex Court's verdict. The Supreme Court had taken a serious view of this violence-ridden strike, issued contempt of court notices to the two organizers and asked them to submit their replies.

On 26th March 2011, the Supreme Court of Pakistan issued contempt notices to PPP leaders Taj Haider and Sharjeel Memon for criticising, ridiculing and instigating the people against the apex court's verdict of disqualifying the Chairman NAB Justice (Rtd) Deedar Hussain Shah. The two leaders had shown their utmost resentment and made an open public call to their party workers to come out on roads in protest.

Both of them appeared in the Supreme Court accompanied by hundreds of PPP office bearers and politicians from Sindh who had flown to Islamabad on poor people's expenses just to make out a show, to demonstrate their strength and to pressurize the judiciary. Amidst all this show of political force, it was claimed by the PPP that the proceedings against Justice Shah were held in the open court, in presence of media persons – thus the people already knew it and there was not an air of confrontation.

On 25th April 2011, a 3-member bench of the Supreme Court headed by Chief Justice Iftikhar M Chaudhry adjourned the hearing of contempt of court case against the two PPP leaders till the 27th May. During the hearing, Taj Haider submitted his reply whereas Sharjeel Memon sought time on the plea that his counsel Abdul Hafeez Pirzada was not available in country and secondly that they were busy in making the new budget.

The apex court knew that Mr Sharjeel was not the finance minister of Sindh and also that *he was actually made the Information Minister only when the SC had issued him contempt of court notice.* Admittedly the said gesture was posed on the orders of the Presidency just to place another note of confrontation on record muffled with utter humiliation. The chief justice had remarked that *'after fighting with the judiciary you have become minister in the Sindh.'*

During the first week of July 2011, Information Minister of Sindh Sharjeel Memon, while submitting his reply urged that a wrong and negative perception was taken by the people of Sindh about the disqualification of

Justice Deedar H Shah and a timely call for strike was given to avoid any potential uncontrollable situation.

In his reply, Memon submitted that while making the statement, he had no intention to ridicule the court and it was a *'fair and healthy comment on the decision'* of the apex court. He urged that his statement, unfortunately, had been misconstrued as no judge was ridiculed nor scandalized.

As the matter was dragged into controversy, the apex court was likely to face another humiliation at the hands of the ruling PPP. To a question about unconditional apology, Sharjeel Memon said:

> *'I did not commit any contempt of court and there is no question of apology. It was a call for peaceful strike and that was our right. ......*
> *(About killing of citizens during the strike, he added) that target killing of six or seven persons has become a routine in Karachi which must be stopped and same happened during the strike call. It is my request that do not attribute it with the strike call. PPP has sacrificed its precious lives for the restoration of the judiciary and we are committed for its independence.'*

While serving the contempt notices to Haider and Memon, the SC had quoted a statement by Haider that legislators would take out a rally from the Sindh Assembly building to the Sindh High Court to lodge a protest against what he called a *'politically-motivated decision of the superior judiciary'* and that there would be a general strike across Sindh against the *'interference of the judiciary in administrative affairs'*.

It remained a point to ponder that NAB was a federal organization, based in Islamabad, working previously under the direct control of Gen Musharraf and then under PM Gilani, both times in the capacity of 'Chief Executive'. Even in the previous regime it remained under Nawaz Sharif as the PM. As such reaction to the SC's verdict, if at all it was necessary, should have come at central command level of the PPP. The move was given a start from Sindh and the strikes remained confined within Sindh because the defunct chairman Justice Shah belonged to Sindh.

AND nothing happened to Sharjeel Memon & Taj Haider in subsequent proceedings for not admitting their guilt and for not tendering un-conditional apologies. See another page of our history.

CONTEMPT LAW IN PERSPECTIVE:

Considering the history of contempt of court cases in Pakistan in those days, the said law was running out of control. It was Sajjad Ali Shah's decision to charge-sheet Nawaz Sharif for contempt of court after the later made a remark criticising him that led directly to storming of the Supreme Court by a mob in November 1997, dismissal of three heads of the premier instituteions – CJ Sajjad Ali Shah, COAS Jehangir Karamat and President Farooq Leghari which in turn contributed to the over-concentration of powers in PM Nawaz Sharif's hands and eventually his own dismissal.

In developed countries like United States, to charge someone with contempt of court for criticising a judge or a court is totally unheard of, largely because of their longstanding commitment to freedom of speech. *A US Supreme Court's decision in 1941 dismissively mentioned the concept of "scandalising the court" and pointed out that "Such foolishness has long since been disavowed in England and has never found lodgement here".*

The other inheritors of English common law; Canada, Australia and New Zealand have generally refrained from using this charge, though it remains on the books there. An Australian trade unionist was convicted under contempt in 1982. However, his conviction caused a huge outcry and spurred calls for the reform of the relevant laws.

Thus, while *"contempt of court"* remains a valid and widely used principle in Anglo-American law, used to prevent interference with or obstruction of the administration of justice, such as by ignoring court orders, disrupting court proceedings, or interfering with witnesses, the specific variety that has run out of control in Pakistan and nobody takes notice of them.

The issuance of charge-sheet against [late] Mr Cowasjee, a veteran columnist, was condemned all over for his quite reasonable remarks about the Pakistani judges and courts. Reference can be made towards judges like Molvi Mushtaq Hussain and CJP Anwar ul Haq in Z A Bhutto's hanging case; J Malik Qayyum and CJ Rashid Aziz in Benazir Bhutto and Zardari's conviction cases and CJP Hameed Dogar' team upholding the 3rd November 2007's Emergency and more.

Once, *on 26th October 1999,* Ardsher Cowasjee, Pakistan's popular columnist attached with Dawn of Karachi, while standing before the

Supreme Court of Pakistan, pleaded not guilty to charges of contempt of court arising from critical remarks he made about the Pakistan's judiciary on a TV program. He was charged with 'scandalising the court'. Mr Ardeshir Cowasjee had said:

> *"Today Judiciary has no respect. The judiciary has killed itself. The Judiciary is corrupt. The Government made it corrupt. The Government has got a book on all the Judges. The people looked down on the Judges. The higher the Judge, the lower he is looked down upon....."*

> *"Judiciary can never demand respect. I mean these guys can threaten us that we will take you to court and charge you with contempt case. But it's all nonsense. They should command respect [through their judgments] and that will take a long time to come, every thing is corrupt."*

The Court had observed that these remarks *"scandalized the Superior Courts of this country and the Judges comprising such courts and tended to bring them into hatred, ridicule and contempt"*.

Mr Cowasjee was also charged earlier, four years ago in 1995, for essentially the same offence of "scandalising the court" for writing a column in 1994 questioning certain appointments in the Supreme Court.

Subsequently, Chief Justice Sajjad Ali Shah was made to quit his office in 1997 to prevent Nawaz Sharif from being tried for contempt of court and subsequent storming event.

> [*The fact remained that the legal landscape surrounding the doctrine of "contempt of court" had changed significantly in Pakistan since the Nawaz Sharif government repealed the Contempt of Court Act 1976, and replaced it with the Contempt of Court Ordinance 1998.*]

After all, Mr Cowasjee was among the bitterest critics of Sharifs unabashedly changing this law solely to protect himself from prosecution; and then Mr Cowasjee could also benefit from the same Ordinance which was meant for those charged with such contempt. Some people had opined that Mr Cowasjee and Nawaz Sharif were both fellow "scandalizers" of the judiciary of those times.

JUSTICE SHAH's HONESTY IN QUESTION?

It may not be out of place to mention that Justice (Rtd) Deedar Shah was known as an upright and honest judge throughout his previous career and Nawaz Sharif of PML(N) had himself admired him, at least once on record, when he was given relief by a full bench of the Sindh HC in Cr Appeal no: 43/2000 dated 27th June 2000. Then Nawaz Sharif had reposed full confidence in Justice (Rtd) Shah who was the Chief Justice of Sindh HC then.

At the same time it was also very strange to be noted that so honest justice (Rtd) Deedar Shah had been enjoying official perks and privileges till late being NAB's former chairman despite his removal from the office. (*Ref: Daily 'Dawn' of 25*th *June 2011*) Despite receiving several letters from NAB HQ, Justice Shah had not returned his two official vehicles and kept on occupying official residence.

- *During his posting as the Chairman, Justice Shah was not able to control his DG for Rawalpindi and Lahore, Zahid Mehmood, who was using six official vehicles even though he was entitled to only one 1300CC car. Mr Mehmood had also taken away Rs:500,000 special funds from NAB's pooled money; Rs:300,000 from Rawalpindi region and Rs:200,000 from Lahore region. The NAB HQ was also charged a bill of Rs:55,000 as accommodation rent in federal lodge Islamabad because Mr Mehmood kept on living in a suit in the lodges.*

- *Mr Mehmood was appointed as Director General NAB Rawalpindi for one year on 21st April 2010 and later he was also given the additional charge of NAB Lahore DG. He retired from NAB on 21st April 2011, but continued to hold the two offices. Finally, he was removed from the bureau on the Supreme Court's orders.*

Similarly, NAB's former Prosecutor General Irfan Qadir continued using an official car and his official residence in Islamabad. Justice Shah failed to boast power over him even. Mr Qadir, whose appointment as the PG, was declared illegal by the Supreme Court on 1st September 2010, continued occupying his official residence near Kohsar Market in F - 6/3 area Islamabad along with chauffeur-driven car and official security guards.

(Part of this essay was published at
*www.Pakspectator.com on 11*th *July 2011)*

[The above referred essay of 11th July 2011 contained a mention of respectable Ardsher Cowasjee. When it reached him he was kind enough to send his comments to the author - reproduced below:

"Thank you for a good essay.
You have covered everything.

My case is still alive and has been called on 3 occasions.
But due to ill health I have not been able to go to the Court.
Like all else in this country, the judiciary remains a mess and is
largely helpless.
Best
AC"

{But alas! We lost Honourable Cowasjee last year; he is no more with us}

In March 2011, when NAB's Chairman Justice Deedar H Shah was sent home under the Supreme Court's orders, the National Accountability Bureau [NAB] was pushed into the process of a painful slow death when its key investigators, who were handling high profile corruption cases including NRO, were made to leave the organization.

More importantly, the official record and critical evidence of corruption, including the Swiss-cartons brought back from Geneva in 2010, were passing into 'nominated political' hands. The old guys were to leave NAB because of the non-renewal of their contracts, which under the NAB law was the authority of NAB's Chairman only and Justice (R) Deedar Shah had left NAB.

In the 2nd week of October 2011, the federal government pleaded before the Supreme Court that it wanted an early hearing of its pending review petition challenging the 10th March verdict (judgment was released on 22nd March) which had declared the appointment of Justice (Rtd) Deedar Hussain Shah illegal and unconstitutional as NAB Chairman.

Additional Attorney General K.K. Agha had urged before a four-judge special bench [*comprising Justice Tassaduq Hussain Jillani, Justice Nasirul Mulk, Justice Asif Saeed Khan Khosa and Justice Amir Hani Muslim*] to constitute a larger bench to hear the matter.

The matter earned significance since the apex court itself had been continuously asking the government to immediately appoint the new NAB Chairman and had even dismissed a different review petition of the government seeking time for the appointment, but had lost sight that the review petition of 9th April 2011 was lying pending with them for the last seven months.

[*On 14th October 2011; the 4-judge bench of the SC referred the matter to the CJP back to form an appropriate bench to hear the government's two applications seeking a stay on the verdict and a larger bench to hear the review plea. A 5-judges bench was formed to deal with that*

*review petition which ultimately disposed it off on 28th May 2013
keeping the old judgment intact.*

*The obvious reason for so much delay might be that the said review
petition had lost its utility as President Leghari had notified another
person, Adml Bokhari, as the new Chairman of NAB.]*

ADML BOKHARI AS NEW CHAIRMAN NAB:

On 16th **October 2011,** President Zardari appointed Admiral (Rtd) Fasih
Bokhari as new Chairman of the NAB and a notification to that effect
was issued by the Federal Ministry of Law, Justice and Parliamentary
Affairs. The appointment was made under Section 6(b) of the National
Accountability Ordinance 1999 on the advice of the prime minister and
after consultation with leaders of the House and the Opposition in the
National Assembly.

The Section 6(b) of the NAO 1999 reads:

*'A person shall not be appointed as chairman NAB unless he (i) is a
retired chief justice or judge of the Supreme Court, or a chief justice of
a high court; or (ii) is a retired officer of the armed forces of Pakistan
equivalent to the rank of a lieutenant general; or (iii) is a retired federal
government officer in BPS-22 or equivalent.'*

Admiral Fasih Bokhari, had served as the 14th Chief of Naval Staff
(CNS) of Pakistan Navy from 1997 to 1999. He had resigned, in protest,
from his post on 6th October 1999 after being superseded by much junior
and newly promoted Gen Musharraf, when he was appointed as
Chairman of the Joint Chiefs of Staff Committee in addition to his being
Chief of Army Staff of the Pakistan Army.

This historical mistake was done by the Prime Minister Nawaz Sharif
and he had immediately paid for it because just after six days the PM was
sent home by the same Army Chief.

Pakistan Navy [and for that matter the PAF also] was not taken into
confidence when Gen Musharraf, had launched the Kargil Operation.
After retirement, Fasih Bokhari along with former Air Chief Marshal
Parvaiz Mehdi Qureshi, who were leading their respective forces during
Kargil War, had demanded a commission of inquiry to probe the Kargil
operation and had agreed to appear before it to give their version of the
events surrounding the Kargil episode.

The PML(N) initially rejected Adml Fasih Bokhari's name, too [*but mildly*] as the Chairman NAB though he was the person who had repeatedly called for court-martial of Gen Musharraf urging that the later had violated the Constitution, and had illegally overthrown the democratically elected government of Nawaz Sharif in 1999. According to him, he was fully aware of Gen Musharraf's intentions when he became the Chairman of the Joint Chiefs of Staff Committee.

Why the nomination of Admiral Fasih Bokhari was opposed then? As per PML(N)'s version, he was allegedly involved in different questionable deals, was accused of not proceeding against those submariners who had received kickbacks from Agosta Submarine scandal when he assumed the charge as Naval Chief despite knowing all the facts. Additionally a case ['**Brooks and Garcia Spares Case**'], allegedly involving Adml Bokhari, was also being heard by Ch Nisar Ali Khan's Public Accounts Committee in earlier months of 2011.

> *[Details of 'Augusta Sub-marines Kickbacks' have already been discussed in Vol-II of this book]*

In '**Brooks and Garcia Spares Case**' Admiral Bokhari was alleged to have favoured one of his close friend Commander (R) Naeem Sarfraz. He was also accused of taking a luxurious plot which in fact existed in the category reserved for 'widows of martyrs' by changing the category of plot in his capacity as Naval Chief.

Former senior Navy officer Rear Admiral (R) Tanveer Ahmad once told the media that even if Fasih Bokhari was not directly involved in Agosta Submarine scandal, he as a submariner let all those submariners who were involved, off the hook, and instead gave them promotions after becoming Naval Chief.

Shireen Mazari's column '**Reciprocity: A costly omission**' appeared in '*the News' of 6*th *February 2008* reads:

> *"What's with the admirals of the Pakistan Navy? When Admiral Fasih Bokhari was Chief of the Naval Staff (CNS), soon after Pakistan's nuclear tests in May 1998, I was surprised to be asked for a meeting with him but was then horrified to find him questioning why I had supported Pakistan's nuclear testing. He declared that Pakistan had made a big mistake at which point I asked him why as naval chief he had not given his view officially.*
>
> *Anyhow, it was not at all astonishing to find Admiral Bokhari, after retirement, declaring at an IISS meeting in the Gulf, that Quaid-i-Azam*

had made a mistake in seeking the creation of Pakistan. It appears Admiral Bokhari got away with a mild rebuke when his peculiar view became known to the military leadership."

Justice (Rtd) Wajihuddin Ahmad commented on Adml Fasih Bokhari's nomination that:

'It is in fact a mindset to make controversial decisions .... to which one's own interest is attached; to keep on creating controversies in high-profile corruption cases..... when your objective is to create controversies and confusion, you always appoint your close aides or friends on such positions which otherwise needs people with completely spotless career and impeccable integrity.'

However, some media people kept the opinion that **'Bokhari is an honest and respectable person'**. Adml Bokhari had been a known supporter of peace with India and even adversaries had recognized it. Indian Navy Admiral (rtd) JG Nadkarni recently wrote that:

'Pakistan had sensible mariners in decision-making positions who were keen to have agreements with the Indian Navy. Admiral Fasih Bokhari, Pakistan's Naval Chief from 1997 to 1999, was a great supporter of maritime co-operation with India, and believed that it would benefit both countries'.

Coming back to Admiral Fasih Bokhari's appointment, the PML(N) indicated that it might challenge the appointment in the Supreme Court on the basis that **'thorough consultations with opposition'** had not been done. The PML(N) was hoping to get success again in the back drop of general public perception that the superior judiciary, especially the CJP Iftikhar M Chaudhry, always had soft corners for the Sharif family and the PML(N).

Mr Bokhari was the fifth NAB Chairman belonging to the armed forces. Earlier, NAB Chiefs from the military were Lt Gen Amjad Hussain, Lt Gen Khalid Maqbool, Lt Gen Munir Hafiez and Lt Gen Shahid Aziz. The two civilian heads of the bureau were Nawid Ahsan and Justice (Rtd) Deedar Hussain Shah.

President Zardari had sent a letter to Ch Nisar Ali on 9th October 2011 seeking his consent for the said appointment as he was required to do so under the 18th Amendment to the constitution [the fate of Justice Deedar Shah is also referred]. Ch Nisar Ali replied after a week raising objections to the appointment on technical grounds. He asked the government to prepare a list of possible candidates for the office of NAB's Chairman saying that:

> 'Mr President, if the objective of the entire exercise is to select a nominee with impeccable reputation, integrity and credibility and unquestionable impartiality, there is no reason whatsoever for hesitation on the part of the government to engage with the opposition in a thorough, concrete and meaningful consultation.'

The President thanked Ch Nisar Ali of PML(N) 'for taking part in the consultative process as mandated by the law' in the nomination of Adml Bokhari as NAB Chairman but at the same time held that:

> 'The sense of various judgments of superior courts is that the consultation shall be meaningful and for this purpose there is no necessity of sending a panel of nominees. Therefore, meaningful consultation can be done even on a single person and for that purpose you are taken on board quite candidly.
>
> Sending of a panel for consultation does not have any legal cover as well, there being no legal requirement as such. I have consulted the Leader of the House in the National Assembly on the subject who has concurred to the proposal.'

Mr Zardari also made clear to Ch Nisar Ali that:

> 'The name of Fasih Bokhari had been proposed in accordance with the provisions of the National Accountability Ordinance 1999, which was the 'existing law at the point of time'. Also that the opposition leader had offered no comments on the profile and integrity of the nominee, which in fact is the material aspect of the consultation'.

Referring to the implementation of superior court's verdicts mentioned in the letter of the opposition leader, the president said a bill was already pending in the parliament since nearly [then] thirty months; also related to the qualification of appointment of a chairman of the proposed National Accountability Commission. PML(N)'s view was that the chairman should be a serving judge of the Supreme Court. However, it remained a fact that the PPP government had proposed the appointment of a person who was not a judge nor qualified to be a judge.

The office of the Chairman NAB was lying vacant since the removal of Justice (Rtd) Deedar Hussain Shah in March that year [2011]. The top accountability institution in the country had been ineffective and without a Chief for seven months. It was also evident that the PPP government had no intention to pass the new accountability law.

PML(N)'s Secretary Information Senator Mushahidullah Khan told at a live program of ARY NEWS during the 2nd week of October 2011:

> *'I wonder why President Zardari cannot find someone with undisputed character. If Bokhari is not directly involved, he is linked in some way to the Agosta submarines corruption of a $520 million deal for French submarines. The government intended to appoint Bokhari in order to receive clearance from the NAB in cases against them. It reflects nothing but cronyism.*
>
> *The government should consider the PML(N)'s request that a former judge of the Supreme Court be appointed, rather than someone who would face resistance from the entire opposition'.*

But Mushahidullah Khan's voice was considered hollow as he could not bring forward any reference proving Adml Bokhari's weakness in Agosta Submarine Deal. However, despite such unproved allegations, the employees of the NAB and Accountability Courts had welcomed the appointment of Admiral (r) Fasih Bokhari as their Chairman calling him the *"right man for the right job"* because several NAB prosecutors whose contracts were expiring during the next two months and a chairman was required to extend their contracts.

The NAB employees considered the new nominee fair enough who could act impartially without absorbing political pressure; new references were in the queue to be filed with NAB. In 2010, NAB-Punjab had filed 44 new references whereas in 2011, the bureau could entertain only 13 references till then.

Now the tail piece:

On 19th September 2011: [BERN] Director Swiss Bank said:

> *'Pakistanis are poor but Pakistan isn't a poor country; that 97 billion dollars of Pakistan is deposited in respective bank and if this money would be utilized for the welfare of Pakistan and its people then Pakistan can make tax-less budget for 30 years, can create 60 million jobs, can carpet four lanes road from any village to Islamabad, endless power supply to five hundred social projects, every citizen can get 20000 rupees salary for the next 60 years and there is no need to see IMF and any World Bank for loans.'*

Referring to the *daily 'Nation' dated 11ᵗʰ July 2013*; yet another survey by Transparency International bemoaned the unpalatable reality about corruption in Pakistan. In the report, facts only corroborate what everybody already knew; that the land revenue department was top of the list followed by police. The holy judiciary was at number six since its underbelly, the lower courts, remained place ordinary citizens avoided like the plague. Unscrupulous lawyers and their court clerks were generally seen boasting *'they have judges and judicial officers in their pockets'*.

In Pakistan, there was no body to bother that how the average cases were dragged for years, even decades despite with all the autonomy and freedom the NAB used to enjoy. It was not even planned to be so because the will of the people and their representatives in the assemblies had seemingly run dry.

{*Part of this essay was published at*
www.pakspectators.com *on 11ᵗʰ July 2011*}

Scenario 78

PAKISTAN RUNS UNDER US GOVERNANCE:

Once in December 2010, the Lahore High Court dismissed a petition registered by one Arif Gondal seeking a ban on the WikiLeaks website. In his petition Mr Gondal had termed the leakage of secret information by WikiLeaks a conspiracy to create a rift among Pakistan, Saudi Arabia, Iran like Muslim countries and the Western world. Requesting the court to issue orders for imposing a ban on the website, the petitioner argued that since Pakistan had good bilateral relations with a number of countries, particularly Saudi Arabia and Iran, the leakage of secret information would adversely affect these ties.

LHC's Justice Sh Azmat Saeed dismissed the petition, calling it non-maintainable. The Court passed the remarks that *'we must bear the truth, no matter how harmful it is'.*

Earlier on 29th November 2010, Pakistan's Foreign Office spokesman Abdul Basit had told the media that they were taking stock of the revelations concerning Pakistan. Officially Pakistan had termed uncovering of sensitive documents by WikiLeaks as irresponsible behavior declaring it as *'condemnable, misleading, contrary to facts and extremely negative'.*

The *Daily Dawn of 3rd December 2010* expressed about *WikiLeaks* in the editorial lines that:

> *'....... the sheer scale of the revelations is staggering. The world has perhaps never before been provided with such a large volume of evidence about the wheels within wheels and the shady deals and negotiations that lurk in the shadows of inter-state diplomacy.*
>
> *State relations and governance across the world have historically been conducted on the assumption that certain information should and can be kept out of the public domain. It is unsurprising, then, that governments and political players have on different occasions succumbed to the temptation of resorting to means that are hardly considered acceptable.'*

One of the most important lessons to be learnt from the *'WikiLeaks'* disclosures was that states and governments should not assume that their secrets would forever remain under their control. Transparency is required to win the people's trust both by political and military circles. The meanness of many national leaders had been exposed by their sayings they were quoted in the leaked cables. More depressing, perhaps, was how most of the Pakistan's civilian and military leaders appeared to consider the US envoy as some sort of viceroy who was urged (better to say begged) for help in gaining power to govern Pakistan after achieving certificates of loyalty from America.

US CONTROLLED PAK - PRESIDENCY:

Ironically, the people of Pakistan had always been fooled both by 'Pakistan and US officials' through long-repeated denials about the US military presence on Pakistani soils. Later it was revealed that the US Special Operations Forces have been conducting joint operations with Pakistan's military forces further proving that Pakistan's leaders had quietly approved the drone attacks inside its Federally Administered Tribal Areas [FATA]. All blatant lies from PM Gilani and the Pakistan's Foreign Office before the general populace - but they continued to raise verbal demands for *'no more drone attacks'*.

WikiLeaks, whatever be the truth or background, had then attracted the whole attention of media and intelligentsia all over. Various opinions popped up from anchors of the TV talk shows, from opinion makers of leading newspapers, from spokesmen and front-persons of all political parties and even from so-called first grade leaders themselves.

Most of them tried to convince the people that *'WikiLeaks are designed to sour our relationship with the Islamic world and to malign our army'*. Some opined that *'Julian Assange (who controlled the WikiLeaks internet site), deserves a Nobel Peace prize for upholding the freedom of information and advocating transparency in the functioning of democracy.'*

On the other hand, for some people *WikiLeaks's* revelations were shocking. Especially quoting Afghanistan and Saudi Arabia's remarks about Pakistani leadership, headlines as:

• 'President Zardari being the great hurdle in the progress of Pakistan';

• 'U.S. trying to remove enriched uranium from the soil of Pakistan';

• 'Pakistan being the most bullied US ally',

- 'Gen Kayani's intended threat to intervene for ending the lawyer's long march',

- 'Gen Kayani informed US envoy in Islamabad of his intention to dethrone Zardari and replacing him with NAP's Asfandyar Wali Khan';

- President Zardari's apprehension of being assassinated and proposing his sister to succeed him.

And much more like this have really shaken people's confidence in the democracy and political wisdom of their heroes. See a little details of American concern in the aftermath of emergency of 3rd November 2007.

According to a US Embassy in Kabul dispatch, released by **WikiLeaks** the United States had expressed 'dissatisfaction' over the imposition of emergency and promulgation of the Provisional Constitutional Order (PCO) by Gen Musharraf on 3rd November 2007.

Just three days after the sweeping steps taken by Gen Musharraf, Secretary of Defence for Policy Eric Edelman told Afghan President Hamid Karzai that US-Pakistan Defence Consultative Group (DCG) talks were postponed to mark the US dissatisfaction with the imposition of the PCO; whether Pakistani interlocutors would be able to focus on the DCG agenda, given the current political turmoil.

Another cable: Gen Musharraf recognised that *'if and when [Benazir] Bhutto takes power, he will be out, and he may not be ready yet to take that step.'* Pakistani authorities should move against terrorist sanctuaries and the Taliban's Quetta Shura; arresting lawyers will not help in this regard. The White House had said that:

> *"We are urging Musharraf to focus on keeping to the election schedule, completing the deal with Bhutto, and taking off his uniform. Although there are special interests that are seeking to extend the period for martial law, it must be kept short. If not, Musharraf's interests and those of the Pakistani Army may begin to diverge."*

However, the Afghan president expressed hope that Gen Musharraf's extra-constitutional approach would work, but Karzai was not sure that Gen Musharraf was ready to fulfil the deal with Benazir Bhutto. He emphasised that the issue of Taliban sanctuary in Pakistan had to be solved, noting with dismay that the Taliban flag had been raised in three districts in FATA of Pakistan. *'Musharraf must be sincere because he has no further room for more games'*, Karzai held.

More details of **WikiLeaks** revealed that Mr Zardari had met Anne Patterson, the US Ambassador in Islamabad, *on 25th January 2008,* and said that *'the US was their 'safety blanket'* and recalled how Benazir Bhutto had returned despite threats against her, because of support and 'clearance' from the US.

PAK – POLITICS INTERFERED:

See another *'episode'* that how the PPP government was *advised* by the US aides in early 2008:

On 15th February 2008, National Security Advisor [NSA] Tariq Aziz met twice with Zardari, who asked him for "advice" on *'who should be prime minister if the PPP is asked to form a government,* [the PPP won elections on 18th instant].' Director ISI Nadeem Taj and Tariq Aziz had urged Zardari not to pursue the premiership for himself, as it would split the party and reduce PPP's national influence. Zardari had raised the idea of becoming Prime Minister with Tariq Aziz a day before.

In series of meetings immediately before and after elections, Tariq Aziz had encouraged Mr Zardari to support Amin Faheem for PM's slot. Zardari complained that Faheem was a poor administrator who lacks the skills needed to run the government. Aziz admitted that this was true; when Amin Faheem was Minister of Communications he spent much of his time at his home in Karachi. Though Tariq Aziz had tried to convince Zardari that Faheem's shortcomings could be mitigated by appointing a strong staff, but Zardari continued to stick to his point that Faheem was too weak to be the next prime minister.

Tariq Aziz had also told Asif Zardari that after being elected as a prime minister, Shah Mahmood Qureshi could challenge his authority, as Zardari was considering Qureshi as a PPP candidate for prime minister.

NSA Tariq Aziz had conveyed the whole conversation to the US Ambassador the same evening. She was also told by Aziz that Saudi Arabia had provided heavy funds to Nawaz Sharif for his election campaign in order to defeat Pakistan Peoples Party [PPP]. He had also told Anne Patterson that ISI Director Nadeem Taj had met with the Saudi Ambassador to request Saudi Arabia to stop funding Nawaz Sharif.

US Ambassador Anne Patterson sent comments to the White House:

'Mr Aziz was clearly depressed and pessimistic about the possibility that Gen Musharraf could remain in the power corridors any more; we

*see Zardari's continuing contacts with the government's key figures as a sign that he will **deal with Musharraf** soon.'*

On 25th July 2008, a cable from the then US Ambassador in Pakistan, Anne Patterson, was sent to Washington that Gen Musharraf was planning after just six months of February 2008 elections to send the National Assembly home and replace the PPP government with technocrats.

Gen Musharraf, the then President of Pakistan was, most probably, thinking so in view of weakening relations between Nawaz Sharif and Asif Zardari. If the two would part ways, Mr Zardari would need new allies to keep his majority from falling and under the circumstances; the PML(Q) could come forward. That was the reason - the PM Gilani and Mr Zardari wanted to raise a voice during their visit to the US apprehending that they could be at political disadvantage by working with Gen Musharraf.

Another leaked document revealed that President Zardari had dismissed a suggestion by the then US Ambassador Anne Patterson that the Tehrik-e-Taliban Pakistan (TTP)'s Chief Baitullah Mahsud was the only person responsible for Benazir Bhutto's death, saying he was 'just a pawn' in the process. *Mr Zardari was not very much interested in knowing that who the sniper was or exactly how Benazir was killed. This was not as important as finding out who financed the killing, and which were the 'hands behind' it.*

As per another **WikiLeaks** exposure, President Zardari had said that:

'He doesn't like the MQM's aggressive behaviour. MQM was gerrymandering in Karachi, by ensuring alterations in the electorate boundaries according to their suitability, to make sure its rule; while the Muslim League (N) also resorted to the same tactics in the Punjab'.

Another leaked document revealed that the United States Embassy in Islamabad believed there were some officers in the ISI who were out of control (working against the US interests) and Gen Musharraf and Chief of Army Staff (COAS) Gen Kayani had shown reluctance to remove ISI's Gen Nadeem Taj from the slot.

The cable of **25th July 2008** had stated that the Pakistan Army and ISI could take action against the extremists at Pak-Afghan borders but they followed the old policy of giving offers, secret action, divide and conquer instead of fighting in the battlefield. The government was concerned that military operation would lead to an uncontrollable war in the tribal areas. The analysis was communicated that *'the government had failed and it was losing writ in the tribal belt daily'*.

On 19th August 2009, Afghanistan's Minister of Interior Hanif Atmar lodged a formal complaint to the US that public claims by his Pakistani counterpart Rehman Malik [*that Afghanistan admitted to hosting Anti-Pakistan terrorist training camps*] was an outright lie and an attempt to please the ISI.

Atmar said that Pakistani Interior Minister Rehman Malik raised this issue when he visited Afghanistan last month as a special emissary of President Asif Ali Zardari; but, contrary to Malik's claims to the Pakistani media [*Geo News was named*], he had presented neither details nor evidence to support this assertion. Also that Malik was trying to please the ISI by showing that he was brave enough to say these things to President Karzai.

Though Afghan MOI was disappointed by several other factually incorrect comments of Mr Malik but he [Hanif Atmar] had accepted that *there was a refugee camp in Kandahar serving 400 to 500 Balochi and Sindhi separatists who fled Pakistan following former President Musharaff's crackdown on their separatist movements* – adding that *"Neither the Afghan Government nor UNHCR run official refugee camps in Kandahar."*

Hanif Atmar had also taken note of Mr Malik's statement that 90 percent of terrorists arrested in Pakistan were of Afghan origin.

US & UK RUN PAKISTAN AS JOINT VENTURE:

WikiLeaks revealed another affair in one of the cables sent by former US Ambassador Anne W Patterson to her government *on 9th February 2009* saying that:

> *'President Asif Ali Zardari wanted judiciary of his own choice, and believed that the Supreme Court will declare PML-N Chief Nawaz Sharif disqualified.*
>
> *Anne Patterson had called on President Zardari prior to the visit of US Special representative for Pakistan and Afghanistan Richard Holbrooke. The same was proved to be correct on 25th February.*
>
> *President Zardari also explained his plan to halt restoration of CJP Iftikhar M Chaudhary'.*

The cable further revealed that *'the President was confident that the Chief Justice would not be reinstated. The US government was also against the restoration of CJ.'*

This cable also highlighted the role of PCO judges, saying that:

- The judges under the leadership of Justice Hameed Dogar, worked on the directives of the rulers.

- The President wanted constitutional amendment for extending the retirement age of the judges.

- President Zardari was also prepared for a deal with Shahbaz Sharif, the Chief Minister of Punjab, but the latter was seen reluctant.

President Zardari also informed the US envoy that Shahbaz Sharif was preparing against Nawaz Sharif as PML(N) Chief and had chalked out a plan to bring nuclear scientist Abdul Qadir Khan in his party.

WikiLeaks had also made open a cable from the US Embassy in London dated **21ˢᵗ October 2008** saying that:

> *'During a meeting with a high-level US delegation, British Chief of the Defence Staff Jock Stirrup claimed that the British government had urged Zardari and civilian leadership to get control over the ISI but* **"when we put pressure on the Pakistanis they rearrange the furniture."**
>
> *Stirrup asserted that Gen Ahmed Pasha's recent appointment as head of the ISI by the Pakistani Army Chief Ashfaq Kayani (former ISI head) reflects Kayani's efforts to get control of the ISI and make sure that Zardari won't control the ISI.*
>
> *Britain's Permanent Under Secretary for Security Affairs Peter Ricketts described* **Pasha as "Kayani's man";** *also noted that during his recent trip to Pakistan "everyone spoke highly" of Pasha'.*

The same **WikiLeak** communication revealed that the Foreign and Security Adviser to the British Prime Minister Simon McDonald acknowledged US concerns about former Premier Nawaz Sharif, including ties to Islamists, but asserted that:

> *'He has indicated he is willing to change and some in the system believe he has already done that. Although Sharif's moment may not come for a couple of years, he is in line to be Pakistan's next president. Ricketts*

observed, however, that many members of the opposition are publicly irresponsible although some, like Sharif, are reasonable in private'.

It is worth mentioning here that the UK government was pessimistic and cynical about Pakistan those days, especially in the light of President Zardari's alleged poor leadership and the bad economy. However, UK had liked Zardari's efforts to cooperate with Afghan President Hamid Karzai.

The British PM wanted to "encourage communications" between Zardari and Karzai. Ricketts, who had just returned from visit to Pakistan, praised Zardari's efforts to reach out to Karzai. *Stirrup concurred that the Pakistani leadership was not at all troubled by US drone strikes* that killed "Arabs" and Taliban, although Stirrup cautioned that such attitudes could change any time.

While discussing Afghanistan's military capabilities, Cabinet's Deputy Head of the Foreign and Defence Policy Secretariat Margaret Aldred wondered whether one solution might be ***to follow Pakistan's model and "give the army some sort of economic benefit"***.

ON PAK – INDIA [ODD] RELATIONSHIP:

The leaked cable of *3rd January 2009,* sent from US Ambassador in Pakistan, Anne Patterson had also revealed that just a month after the Mumbai attacks episode, the **US had brokered a secret agreement between Pakistan and India** on information sharing.

Anne Patterson had informed her [US] government that:

> *'The ISI Chief Ahmad Shuja Pasha had just approved the sharing of tear line information on Pakistan's investigation (into the Mumbai attacks) with Indian intelligence, after assurances from the CIA that information would be held in intelligence channels only'.*

Anne Patterson wanted Washington to ask India not to release information about their investigation into the Mumbai attacks, which might jeopardise the new information-sharing arrangement. She said if Lt Gen Pasha was *'embarrassed by what is essentially public dissemination without the Indians providing the results of their own investigation to Pakistan, it will undercut Pakistan's ability to pursue its investigation, generate a public backlash in Pakistan and could undermine Pasha personally'.*

Two days after this cable, India handed over material related to the Mumbai investigation to the Pakistani High Commissioner in New Delhi. Information about the attacks was shared subsequently with other countries. To prevent another potential attack, Pakistan needed to keep channels of co-operation and information sharing open...the goal was not only to bring the perpetrators of this attack to justice, but also to begin a dialogue that was likely to reduce tensions between India and Pakistan.

The tension between the two neighbouring countries was escalating those days. It went up so high that in ending June 2009 the then Indian Army Chief Gen Deepak Kapoor had alleged that *'there are 43 terrorist camps in Pakistan, 22 of which are located in Pakistani administered Kashmir'*. Gen Kapoor had said this during a meeting between senior US officials including the then US National Security Advisor James Jones and Indian officials including Defense Minister A.K. Anthony.

'Although the Pakistanis raided some camps in the wake of Mumbai attacks of November 2008 but some camps have reinitiated operations,' Gen Kapoor had asserted. Gen Kapoor told James John that Pakistani military's statements regarding the Indian threat on its eastern border were wholly without merit.

According to another **Wikileaks** cable sent *on 16th February 2010* by US Ambassador in India Tim Roemer to the US State Department Washington saying that:

> *'The Indian Army's Cold Start Doctrine is a mixture of myth and reality. It has never been and may never be put to use on a battlefield because of substantial and serious resource constraints, but it is a developed operational attack plan announced in 2004 and intended to be taken off the shelf and implemented within 72-hour period during a crisis.*
>
> *Cold Start is not a plan for comprehensive invasion and occupation of Pakistan. Instead, it calls for a rapid, time and distance limited penetration into Pakistani territory with the goal of quickly punishing Pakistan, possibly in response to a Pakistan linked terrorist attack in India, without threatening the survival of the Pakistani state or provoking a nuclear response.*
>
> *It was announced by the BJP-led government in 2004, but the government of Prime Minister Manmohan Singh has not publicly embraced Cold Start and GOI uncertainty over Pakistani nuclear restraint may inhibit future implementation by any government. If*

the GOI were to implement Cold Start given present Indian military capabilities, it is the collective judgment of the Mission that India would encounter mixed results.'

FORGOTTEN PAGE OF PAK – HISTORY:

WikiLeaks, in one of his documents has, however, revealed an unturned page of forgotten history saying that:

'Russia assesses that Islamists are not only seeking power in Pakistan but are also trying to get their hands on nuclear materials. Russia is aware that Pakistani authorities, with help from the US, have created a well-structured system of security for protecting nuclear facilities, which includes physical protection.

There are 120,000-130,000 people directly involved in Pakistan's nuclear and missile programs, working in these facilities and protecting them. However, regardless of the clearance process for these people, there is no way to guarantee that all are 100% loyal and reliable.'

One can recall the Western propaganda of those days that Pakistan had hired people to protect nuclear facilities who had strict religious beliefs. And that the extremist organisations had more opportunities to recruit people working in the nuclear and missile programs. This thinking was developed then because at times, the extremists had attacked vehicles that carried staff to and from Kahuta facilities; some were killed and some were abducted with no trace of them.

It is worth-mentioning here that the COAS Gen Kayani told the former US Ambassador Anne Patterson in a meeting in March 2009 that *'he did not want to see PML(N) Chief Nawaz Sharif rule the country and had made it clear that regardless of how much he disliked Zardari, he distrusted Nawaz even more.'*

When the above feeling appeared in media, the DG ISPR had to dispel it in a briefing to the media conveying that *'the COAS Gen Kayani holds all national leaders, including the PML(N) Chief Nawaz Sharif, in high esteem. The armed forces give preference to national interests in dealing with the challenges confronting Pakistan.'*

It remains a fact that to repair the damage and to off-set the embarrassment caused to Pak-Army and the Presidency those days, US Secretary of State Hillary Clinton called President Zardari and reportedly regretted the leaks and assured him that the leaks would not affect bilateral relations between the two countries.

However, the point to ponder was that *at nowhere the Secretary had challenged the authenticity of the leaked material.* The cogent widespread opinion was that:

> 'These WikiLeaks have proved that terrorism is not the only threat which the people of this country are confronted with, but the biggest threat for Pakistan is its insincere political leadership who stands totally exposed before the world now'.

Let Pakistanis wait for the time when their leadership would start giving priority to the national interest, start behaving responsibly, start considering people as partners in government, start trusting their own voters and start respecting their own words which they uttered while reading oath.

One more evidence of *US 'GUIDANCE' on Baluchistan*:

Solecki, an American, was kidnapped *on 2ⁿᵈ February 2009* from Quetta where he was working as head of the local office of the UN refugee agency UNHCR. US Ambassador Anne Patterson and UN Resident Representative in Islamabad Akcura met Pakistan's Interior Minister on 19ᵗʰ February 2009 as follow up on the Solecki kidnapping case.

The *WikiLeaks* disclosed that:

> '[Rehman] Malik continued to insist that Brahamdagh Bugti was primarily responsible for [Solecki's] kidnapping. He also suggested that the Bugtis and the Marris, although rivals, were in fact colluding in this case and that their accusations against each other were only stalling tactics.
>
> In the end Rehman Malik agreed to send his brother to reach out to Mir Gazin Marri (aka Kaiaga Marri) in Dubai to talk about the release of kidnapped UN official John Solecki. He proposed efforts to split them by telling each side the other was privately accusing it of kidnapping Solecki.
>
> Mr Malik also urged that the US (through intermediaries) begin to threaten [Brahamdagh] Bugti with extradition to Pakistan in the event something happened to Solecki. The ambassador said in that case Bugti would be extradited to the US to be tried for allegedly murdering a US citizen'.

Mr Malik confirmed that the Balochistan Frontier Corps had cordoned off an area in which they believed Solecki was located near Quetta. They were surveilling an individual connected to kidnappers; this individual reported the abductee was in failing health and referred to his moving into Afghanistan. Malik expected to hear additional information from this individual next day but the interior ministry did not have geo-coordinates on the individual.

Mr Malik asked the US Ambassador for guidance on whether the interior ministry should facilitate or block the kidnappers' movement across the border. He was concerned that the kidnappers' failure to steal an ambulance and Solecki's deteriorating health meant that time was of the essence and clearly did not want the GOP to be blamed for failing to rescue Solecki.

Solecki had been working for the United Nations refugee agency for several years before he was seized on 2nd February 2009 while on his way to work. His driver was a 17-year employee of UNHCR who was killed in the ambush. **On 4th April 2009** Solecki was thrown away with his hands and feet bound, otherwise unharmed, along a dirt road at Pak-Afghan border.

A previously unknown group, the *Baluchistan Liberation United Front,* claimed responsibility for his abduction, threatening to behead him on 13th February 2009 amidst issuing a grainy video of a blindfolded Solecki pleading for help. The said group renewed the threats in March, demanding the release of hundreds of people from alleged detention by Pakistani security agencies.

As per American media reports dated **8th *April 2009,*** John Solecki returned home and in good spirits. He was sent back from Pakistan on a special medical flight after spending one night in a military hospital in Quetta.

Scenario 79

PAKISTAN UNDER US ATTACK:

PAK – AFGHAN RELATIONS IN WOT:

On 18ᵗʰ July 2010, a *Transit Trade Agreement* was signed by Afghanistan and Pakistan to open up multibillion-dollar Asian markets and build trust between the two countries at a key juncture allegedly under US efforts. Its main aim was to allow Afghans to transit goods through Pakistan to markets in India – seen as vital to ending the Taliban insurgency and allowing US and NATO forces to leave Afghanistan.

That most significant bilateral economic treaty was signed in Islamabad, watched by the US Secretary of State Hillary Clinton ahead of a conference in Kabul looking to steer the country to peace and independent leadership. Pakistan called the agreement an "important milestone" in economic relations which was likely to increase trade between the two countries from $1.5 b to $5 billion a year by 2015.

Almost 50 percent of Afghanistan's trade traditionally goes with its five neighbours — Pakistan, Iran, Tajikistan, Turkmenistan and Uzbekistan. The deal was expected to create jobs in trucking, shipping, freight forwarding, brokerage services and banking, and cut trading delays. However, Islamabad had refused to let Indian trucks cross Pakistan into Afghanistan. Kabul was left holding out for future amendments as the Afghan Commerce Ministry wanted to bring Indian goods via Pakistan to Afghanistan.

Under the US pressure Pakistan later agreed to provide transit trade between Afghanistan and India through its air space. The Pakistani populace resented taking it as *'damaging to Pakistan's security as well as its economy'*. India had successfully attained Pakistani air space for trade with Afghanistan by coaxing the US to put pressure on Pakistan. Most Pakistanis got agitated that why the US was interested so much in promoting India's cause and interest.

[*Transit rights to India for trade with Afghanistan were already available under the Pak-Afghan Transit Trade Agreement of 1965, which was in force then. The need for negotiation of a new transit trade agreement was not understandable. The problem might be of 'effective implementation' of the agreement on the part of Pakistan.*]

It was pertinent to note that *India for security reasons had never allowed transit facilities to Pakistan's exports to Nepal and Bhutan* through its land routes. It was also a fact that Afghanistan was recommended to be included in the SAARC to justify India's designs to extend its domain beyond Afghanistan.

The ruling PPP government of Pakistan was widely criticized for taking an important decision overnight by approving and signing the deal **without consulting the parliament.** What was the difference between a dictator and a democratic government then? It was said that Afghanistan would facilitate Pakistan a transit trade route to Central Asian States – which Pakistan never asked for because of China at its north always ready to extend all related facilities need for trade.

One cogent reason for involvement of the US in the business interests of this region, perhaps, was that the USA's oil was depleting fast; it was likely to knock it off as a global leader. The Taliban government in Afghanistan was never an enemy of the USA. Its removal from Afghanistan was decided much before 9/11 of 2001. It fell out of favour because it had put terms and conditions on the pipelines that the USA's oil giants then planned to run through the Afghan territory.

AFGHAN WAR DIARY OF SIX YEARS:

On one side Pakistan had signed pact with Afghanistan to facilitate India and to please America but just a week after, **on 25th July 2010,** Wikileaks released 75000 pages on Pak-Afghan War with eye-opening treatise; see details:

The Afghan War documents consisted of 91,731 documents, covering the period between January 2004 and December 2009 out of which only 75,000 were released to the public. It was considered to be one of the largest break in the US military to dig out information on the deaths of civilians, increased Taliban attacks, and involvement of Pakistan and Iran in Afghan War. Leaked data was directly sent to three outlets in advance namely The New York Times, The Guardian, and Der Spiegel.

'The New York Times' dated 25th July 2010 described the said exposure as *"an unvarnished and grim picture of the Afghan war"* AND concluded that:

> *"Pakistan allows representatives of its spy service [ISI] to meet directly with the Taliban in secret strategy sessions to organize networks of*

militant groups that fight against American soldiers in Afghanistan, and even hatch plots to assassinate Afghan leaders."

An article on ISI's role published in *The NYT* on the same day provided a wide range of information focusing on coalition successes, and at the same time excerpting sections that highlighted coalition failures - mostly illustrating American frustration quoting that *"glimpses of what appear to be Pakistani skullduggery contrast sharply with the frequently rosy public pronouncements of Pakistan as an ally by American officials."*

In an interview with the *UK's Channel 4 in June 2010*, Wikileaks founder Julian Assange said that:

"..... other journalists try to verify sources; we verify documents. We don't care where it came from.

We don't have a view about whether the war should continue or stop – we do have a view that it should be prosecuted as humanely as possible."

The *Toronto Sun* wrote that *"this material shines light on the everyday brutality and squalor of war."*

According to *Der Spiegel*, *"the documents clearly show that the Pakistani intelligence agency ISI is the most important accomplice the Taliban has outside of Afghanistan."*

The Guardian dated 25th July 2010, however, *"..... did not think there was a convincing smoking gun for complicity between Pakistan intelligence services and the Taliban".*

The said newspaper called the material *"... a devastating portrait of the failing war in Afghanistan, revealing how coalition forces have killed hundreds of civilians in unreported incidents, Taliban attacks have soared and NATO commanders fear neighbouring Pakistan and Iran are fuelling the insurgency".*

On the same aspect *'the Guardian'* of the same day [referring to Declan Walsh] stated:

'But for all their eye-popping details, the intelligence files, which are mostly collated by junior officers relying on informants and Afghan officials, fail to provide a convincing smoking gun for ISI complicity. Most of the reports are vague, filled with incongruent detail, or crudely fabricated.

The same characters – famous Taliban commanders, well-known ISI officials – and scenarios repeatedly pop up. And few of the events predicted in the reports subsequently occurred.

A retired senior American officer said ground-level reports were considered to be a mixture of "rumours, bullshit and second-hand information" and were weeded out as they passed up the chain of command.'

Issues that Iran had also been providing extensive assistance to the Taliban were discussed at length in Wikileaks documents. Afghan spies and paid informants tried to justify their work by alleging that Iranian involvement in Afghanistan steadily widened from 2004 onwards and constituted armaments, money, and physical deployment of anti-NATO militants; Iran, however, denied supporting the militants and condemned the American pointing fingers towards them.

Once a *journalist Jeff Stein of the Washington Post*, during the same days stated that Hezb e Islami [HI]'s leader Gulbuddin Hekmatyar and Amin al-Haq, allegedly the financial advisor of Osama Bin Laden, both flew to North Korea on 19th November 2005, and purchased remote controlled rockets to be used against American and coalition aircraft. Subsequently, no corroborating report or evidence ever surfaced from any intelligence agency or the media showing North Korean involvement in armaments dealing with Taliban.

Blake Hounshell wrote in **Foreign Policy** that, after reading leaked documents, he believed that there was less new information in the documents than leading newspapers had already disclosed. Commenting on the significance of the documents:

'I'd say that so far the documents confirm what we already know about the war: It's going badly; Pakistan is not the world's greatest ally and is probably playing a double game; coalition forces have been responsible for far too many civilian casualties; and the United States doesn't have very reliable intelligence in Afghanistan.'

Pakistan's President Asif Ali Zardari announced that allegations about ISI's involvement had been heard and analyzed which represented low-level intelligence reports and did not represent a convincing picture; there was no convincing evidence. The documents circulated by Wikileaks did not reflect the WHOLESOME on-ground realities.

Politicians and defence analysts critically commented on leaks and that why the western media tried to malign the ISI more while NOT highlighting most of the civilian casualties resulting from bombing of NATO forces like how US special forces dropped six 2000 lb bombs on a compound where they believed a *'high-value individual'* was hiding, after *"ensuring there were no innocent Afghans in the surrounding area"*. In fact, 300 civilians had died in those attacks.

On 28th July 2010, Britain announced that it would launch two new inquiries into the country's role in the war; the launching of the inquiries had nothing to do with the Wikileaks documents.

White House National Security Advisor James Jones issued a statement to the media reporters that the leaks were *'irresponsible and would not impact US strategy in Afghanistan and Pakistan'*. However, the Democrat Representative Dennis Kucinich of Ohio said:

> *"These documents provide a fuller picture of what we have long known about Afghanistan: The war is going badly. We have to show the ability to respond to what's right in front of our face: This war is no longer justifiable under any circumstances."*

Chairman of the US Senate Foreign Relations Committee Senator John Kerry had to admit:

> *"However illegally these documents came to light, they raise serious questions about the reality of America's policy toward Pakistan and Afghanistan. Those policies are at a critical stage and these documents may very well underscore the stakes and make the calibrations needed to get the policy right. All of us [are] concerned that after nine years of war ... the Taliban appear to be as strong as they have been."*

Taliban spokesperson, Zabihullah Mujahid *[actually belonging to Haqqani group – later killed in Islamabad during ist week of November 2013]*, had replied the above comments that:

> *'They are inspecting the leaked documents which contain the names, tribes, and family information of Afghan informants who were helping the US. We know about the spies and people who collaborate with US forces. We will investigate through our own secret sources whether the people mentioned are really spies working for the US. If found correct, then we know how to punish them.'*

Later the Afghanistan Independent Human Rights Commission [AIHRC] published figures showing that during the first seven months of 2010, 197 persons, who supported the Afghan government, or their family members, or who might have come into contact with the US or NATO, were brutally killed by the Taliban.

On 12ᵗʰ August 2010, the international press watchdog *Reporters Without Borders* (RWB) accused WikiLeaks of 'incredible irresponsibility' because their release to open media went highly dangerous, particularly when it named Afghan informants.

AFGHAN CONTRACTOR'S SAGA:

The **US Senate Report of October 2010** clearly stated that *'US funds for private security contractors in Afghanistan have flowed to warlords and Taliban insurgents, undermining the war effort and fuelling corruption'*. The investigations done by the Senate Armed Services Committee found that the government had failed to vet or manage those hired to provide security under contracts worth billions of dollars, with disastrous results and set back.

Carl Levin, Chairman of the Senate Armed Services Committee, worriedly mentioned that:

> "Our reliance on private security contractors in Afghanistan has too often empowered local warlords and powerbrokers who operate outside the Afghan government's control and act against coalition interests. This situation threatens the security of our troops and puts the success of our mission at risk.
>
> One US Air Force subcontract for an Afghan air base Armour Group [under the British firm G4S] recruited security guards including 'Taliban supporters'. One of the warlords was killed in a US-Afghan military raid 'during a Taliban meeting being held at his house'."

The US Defence Secretary Robert Gates had acknowledged the problem in a letter addressed to Levin, the Committee's Chairman.

But there prevailed another viewpoint in US-Afghan policy related circles that the US itself allowed subcontractors to pay the Taliban protection money to avoid a higher degree of risk of attacks. The Karzai government, in August 2010, had condemned the role of private security contractors and finally formally banned eight foreign firms, including the controversial company called BLACKWATER; giving four months to cease operations in Afghanistan.

However, the historians believed that the corruption within the Afghan administrative departments had become the hallmark since President Karzai had taken over; might be the Karzai's officers continued to mint money more than the Taliban contractors while going in between.

Commenting upon the then British PM Mr Blair's efforts to win back the lost hearts and minds of Pakistan & Afghanistan, the *'Independent'* of *20th November 2006* had said:

> 'Five years after the Taliban were toppled [in 2001], the infrastructure in many places [of **Afghanistan**] **is still in ruins, the opium poppy is back and corruption is endemic.** The rights of women are being steadily diminished, while popular dissatisfaction with the Karzai government is high.
>
> **The distressing truth is that, having helped oust the Taliban, Britain did precisely what it promised not to do: we "walked away" from Afghanistan and chose to fight a war in Iraq.** The situation in the region now is too reminiscent of six years ago for anyone's comfort. Until this truth is acknowledged, we fear the deterioration in security will only continue.'

CONSPIRACY THEORIES [2010 - 12]:

Despite the whole set of conspiracy theories; every Pakistani seriously believed two things during 2010-12. **Firstly,** that the America would quit Afghanistan till 2014 and **secondly** that America needed Pakistan for its safe exit. Both issues got hot debates as the Pakistanis mostly kept wishful thinking based on the opinions of their beloved columnists and not on factual analysis of their own.

A very cogent question remained that would America militarily attack Pakistan as its next target. Many people believed it was not the case; based on America's invasion history during the past decade; it launched the military attacks on countries where the 'take over' was otherwise not possible. Pakistan was already in US pockets through its successive Generals and politician rulers.

Iraq was a case study in that respect: Saddam Hussain's later years of dictatorial rule had bare minimum relationship with America. Iraq was supplying oil to the whole world but having no business with the US. No American was allowed to enter Iraq even as the tourist or media correspondent. If some American was given visa under compulsions, he had been constantly kept under disguised security check till he left its borders. If some Iraqi exchanged good wish with that American, he was brought to the interrogation centre the same evening. Even diplomatic meetings with Americans were secretly supervised by 'three tier' control strategies.

Iraq did not need dollars from them; it had sufficient resources for Iraqi public. There was no influx of religious terrorists, saboteurs, secret agents in Iraqi lands nor could any dollar aid be floated or offered. So when America wished to take over Iraq in 2003, it had no other option except to attack directly on the pretext of *'weapons of mass destruction [WMD]'*.

Consider Afghanistan: It was a devastated, internally wrecked and tribally torn out land with no economic or administrative pedestal. There was no social cohesion so there was no chance of conspiracy. There was no industry or monetary structure to which America could influence or penetrate in. Extremists from all corners of the world were having their group bases there in the name of Islamic renaissance and revitalization. Those groups could only be equipped with mortars, automatic rifles and ammunitions plus some dollars for their daily needs; but all without any auditable returns.

So when America wished to establish base in Afghanistan for its future **'New World Order'** designs in 2001, it had no option except to directly attack it militarily in the name of *'eliminating Al Qaeda'*.

However in Libya, the US applied opposite strategy - when Col Qaddafi decided to end embargo on the Americans and tried to earn their favours, he re-established the business relationship with Washington. Americans got free access into the Libya and quickly recruited the local desperate youth as their secret agents. All the people who were once pushed out of Libyan borders as 'rebels' by Col Qaddafi were managed to come in side. When the two factions; secretly paid American agents and rebel opponents of Col Qaddafi, were made to join hands, uproar cropped up.

Thus when America wished to change leadership in Libya, it asked NATO bombing planes to help the rebel opponents in the name of *'ending tyrannical rule'*. Col Qaddafi's armed strength was directly attacked till he was killed by his own junta and dragged through the streets of Tripoli.

Consider Pakistan having another scenario - most of the intelligentsia kept an opinion that:

'If America would wish to conquer this country, it does not need to attack it directly as had been done in Iraq; nor does it need to send NATO planes to level the Pakistanis down. In fact the US has already done its work; has taken over the country to the extent it needed.'

Necessary home work had already been done through:

- CIA's secret agents by getting 4000 visas issued for Americans in one day; recall 2010.

- CIA's viceroys in Pakistan; recall dubious actions of Gen Musharraf, Rehman Malik & Hussain Haqqani and others alike. Consider Mr Zardari's certain acts too.

- Influencing Pakistan's monetary policy by allowing India's imports open and barring Pakistan to trade for Iran's oil, gas, & electricity.

- Creating insurgency in Balochistan through terrorist attacks on Shias and Punjabis by their paid Raymond Davis like agents & kidnapping Balochis through their paid elements in the Pakistan Army and intelligence units.

- Compelling Pakistan Army to launch direct attacks in Northern Wazirastan to keep Pakistan in a state of constant war with its own people; forget colossal losses by drone attacks.

- Helping India in getting civil nuclear technology but refusing Pakistan to avail any such facility so that shortage of power could ruin its industrial and commercial infrastructure.

Many more sub-heads could be added to this list but the cogent question remained that did Pakistani rulers, civil & military, really love Pakistan. What was their priority: devastated Pakistan, killings, and arsons through religious extremism or American interests?

Historians would remember 2nd May 2011's US attack on Abbotabad; the Pak-US relations started taking negative turn. At a news conference held at the White House during early October 2011 to mark the 10th anniversary of the US invasion of Afghanistan, President Obama claimed having *'pushed the Taliban out of its key strongholds'* and also pointed a finger at Pakistan for complicating Washington's war strategy. It was quite contrary to the reality on ground in Afghanistan.

President Obama's views also included that:

- *'Despite possessing the required might, the Americans were ending the wars in Afghanistan and Iraq in a responsible manner;*

- *The US proved the point that it was not fighting against Islam anywhere in the world.*

- *Raymond Davis had diplomatic status.'*

The international community present there was much surprised at the utter falsehood of Mr Obama's dubious remarks. The reality was otherwise which made the US uneasy and that Obama wanted to hide. In addition to an admission of failure made by the German Gen Harald Kujat [the man who planned the Bundeswehr's mission in Afghanistan], the US own former in-charge of the war Gen McChrystal said:

> *'Most of us – me included – had a very superficial understanding of the country and history.'*

The conclusion was obvious.

During the same days [of May 2011], Pakistan's corps commanders meeting at GHQ firmly held that, *'no more [US] operations'*, the political leadership wholeheartedly sided with the armed forces. A meeting of the Troika – President Zardari, Prime Minister Gilani and the COAS Gen Kayani – insisted that they would implement the all parties' conference [*held in PM House on 30th September 2011*] decisions. Time had revealed the chicanery of the superpower and the truth behind its words. Under no circumstances, Pakistan could compromise its own interests for the sake of maintaining such a fake friendship; *but the metaphor lasted hardly for six months.*

What happened with those myths and aspirations after the then on-going Raza Rabbani's gimmicks? *'Some Pakistanis cannot live without dollars'*, the Americans knew it well. [*A LEAD story published at www. pakspectator.com on 3rd April 2012 is referred*]

In a joint report prepared by the Sherry Rehman-led Jinnah Institute in Pakistan and the US Institute for Peace (USIP), titled as *'Pakistan, the US and the End-game in Afghanistan'*, published *in October 2011*, it was wrongly projected that a genocide process of the Pakhtuns was on cards since three decades. Basically, the report was aimed at justifying Pakistani establishment's long-standing Afghan policy which brought nothing but created religious bigotry in Pakistan. They perhaps used the name of the Pakhtun nation to camouflage the Taliban terrorists. The report was basically a 'liberal' cover-up of an essentially fundamentalist state policy of Pakistan.

The question, therefore, remained that could there be Taliban without Talibanisation, especially when they continuously emerged from the conflict as 'victors'? What about the thousands of Pakhtun killed by the Taliban? In the above report, the composers expressed anti-Pakhtun, pro-establishment and Talibanian views and then assembled their voices in one chorus and tried to float the American future plans from various angles but leading to the same convergence.

WESTERN MEDIA ATTACKED ISI:

Under the title 'Secret Pakistan', BBC2 released a documentary on 26th October & 2nd November 2011 on how Pakistan's ISI trained and armed Taliban. The two episodes [Double Cross (part 1) & Back-lash (part 2)], tried to reflect the alleged role of Pakistan's ISI in training Islamo-fascist terrorists (TTP, LeJ, SSP, JeM etc) for attacks in Afghanistan. The whole script was apparently written by India's secret service RAW to apprise the world that 'Pakistan's ISI provides weapons and training to Taliban insurgents fighting US and British troops in Afghanistan'.

Through this documentary, the UK in fact openly conveyed the message of US intelligence to the whole world alleging that Pakistan had been playing a double game, acting as America's ally in public while secretly training and arming its enemy in Afghanistan.

The whole story was fabricated in a prison cell near Kabul, where the Afghan Intelligence Service was holding a young man who was shown recruited by Pakistan's ISI, then trained to be a suicide bomber in the Taliban's intensifying military campaign against the Western coalition forces – and preparations for his mission were supervised by an ISI officer in a camp in Pakistan. After 15 days training he was sent into Afghanistan but he changed his mind at the last minute and was later captured by the Afghan intelligence service.

As per documentary, the Americ's suspicions started as early as 2002, just only a few months after formal inauguration of War on Terror in September 2001, when the Taliban began launching attacks across the border from their bases in Pakistan, but they became more widely held after 2006 when the Taliban's assault increased in its ferocity against the British forces in Helmand.

The final turning point in American policy was the 26th November 2008's alleged attack on Mumbai when 10 gunmen rampaged through the Indian city, killing 170 people. Despite Pakistan's claims of playing no part in the said attack, the CIA was convinced that the ISI were directly involved in training the participating gunmen in that massacre.

It was the moment when President Obama had ordered a review of all intelligence on the South Asian region by a veteran CIA officer, Bruce Riedel, who later reported that:

> *"Our own intelligence was unequivocal. In Afghanistan we saw an insurgency that was not only getting passive support from the Pakistani army and the Pakistani intelligence service, the ISI, but getting active support."*

Pakistan repeatedly denied the claims but the BBC's media team had spoken to a number of middle-ranking – and active – Taliban commanders who provided detailed evidence of how the Pakistan's ISI had rebuilt, trained and supported the Taliban throughout the War on Terror [WOT]. One Taliban commander named Mullah Qaseem was shown telling that:

> *"For a fighter there are two important things – supplies and a place to hide; Pakistan provided both. First they support us by providing a place to hide and then they provide us weapons."*

Another commander, Najib was shown saying:

> *"Because Obama put more troops into Afghanistan and increased operations here, so Pakistan's support for us increased as well. His militia received a supply truck with 500 landmines with remote controls, 20 rocket-propelled grenade launchers with 2000 to 3000 grenades... AK-47 machine-guns and rockets."*

Bruce Riedel [*a former CIA analyst and counter-terrorism expert, served in the Agency for 29 years until his retirement in 2006, later joined White House's National Security team*] in his 2009's papers alleged that **'***insurgents are allowed [by the Pak-Army] to cross the Pak-Afghan borders at will***'** but his home work was so weak – he did not know that 2200 miles long Pak-Afghan border was never manned by any, not even by Afghan Army since centuries, due to tribal and hilly terrains all over and the tribes around were always free to move in either country.

Bruce Riedel's report of March 2012 went disturbing, of course, when he reported that:

'....the US had to make the recent drone attacks in Pakistan more effective as intelligence has been withheld from the Pakistanis.

At the beginning of the drone operations, we gave Pakistan an advance tip-off of where we were going, and every single time the target wasn't there anymore. You didn't have to be Sherlock Holmes to put the dots together.

Osama Bin Laden's capture and killing followed this same model – the Americans acting on their own, to the humiliation of Pakistan. Trust between the two supposed allies has never been lower.'

Earlier, in **February 2010,** Mullah Baradar, the Taliban's second-in-command, was captured by the ISI from Karachi because he had secretly made contact with the Afghan government to discuss a deal that would end that Afghan war. He had allegedly done so without the ISI's permission thus was detained *'to bring him back under control'*. On 21st September 2013, Mulla Baradar was unconditionally released by Pakistan government without any investigation, charge or trial.

In ending 2011, one Hawa Nooristani, a member of Afghanistan's High Peace Council, was called to a secret meeting with a commander of the Haqqani network; to her astonishment Haqqani's rep wanted peace talks. Hawa also held that:

"He [the commander] said that Pakistan's intelligence knew nothing of the meeting - so not to disclose it because Pakistan does not want peace with Afghanistan and even now they are training new Taliban units. He was also scared that the Pakistanis will arrest him because he lives in Pakistan."

Allegedly the whole peace process, talks with the Taliban, collapsed after its chief negotiator, former President Rabbani, was killed by a suicide bomber purporting to be a Taliban envoy. The American policy advisers like Bruce Riedel had got the clear message that *'the ISI did not want to bring Taliban to the negotiating table; they could certainly spoil any negotiations process – AND perhaps Pakistan was not interested in a political deal.'*

General Athar Abbas, chief spokesman for Pak-Army had denied links to the Taliban and insisted that Pakistan was doing no more than what any country would do in similar circumstances; while adding that *'we cannot disregard our long term interest because this is our own area.'*

This was the moment when US Secretary of State Hillary Clinton had to say during her visit to Pakistan: *"The Pakistanis have a role to play; they can either be helpful, indifferent or harmful."*

Bruce Riedel had also concluded then: *'there is probably no worse nightmare, for America, for Europe, for the world, in the 21st Century than if Pakistan gets out of control under the influence of extremist Islamic forces, armed with nuclear weapons...The stakes here are huge.'*

2010-US TOLD TO QUIT HONOURABLY:

Various cogent deliberations from American think-tanks like Benjamin Barber and Melissa Roddy [*Director of CONFLICT OF INTEREST, a documentary film focused on unreported issues regarding Afghanistan and Pakistan*], had been appearing in western media in which their intelligentsia had framed and forwarded tens of reasons to the White House urging that '**the US cannot win war in Afghanistan**'.

For instance '*The Public Record' dated 21*st *May 2010*, pointed out some "jingoistic reasons", the summary of which is placed below:

1. *'Afghanistan is not a country but only an amorphous collection of warring tribes, factions and clans.'* The country was organized as a nation-state in 1747, more than 30 years before the American colonies won their independence from Great Britain; and 200 years prior to Pakistan into being.

    Afghanistan came into being when a group of elders from around the country got together in *'jirga'* [council] and chose a king from among the group. At that time, the Indian subcontinent was under the colonial control of Britain which, over the following 150 years, exerted constant military pressure on India's western boundary but could gain nothing except humiliation.

    Finally, in 1893, Sir Mortimer Durand negotiated a treaty with the Afghan ruler, establishing what was later known as the **Durand Line** – a line so arbitrarily drawn that it not only divided large swaths of Pashtun and Baloch ethnic regions, it actually ran through the middle of towns and even properties. When the British were leaving India in 1947, the Afghans eagerly asserted that it was time for reunification of their country. Instead, Pakistan got the major chunks.

    Since many of Pakistan's Pashtun were inclined towards reunification with their brethren in Afghanistan, the Pak-Army and its ISI believed for the last six decades that it must keep Afghanistan either unstable or under Pakistani control.

2. Afghanistan's successive governments went deeply corrupt and unable to control its own divided country. Much of the leaders, including President Hamid Karzai, were virtually controlled by ISI for various reasons. Afghan leaders, who did not avail themselves of Pakistan's influence, got threatened and were mostly assassinated. Unfortunately, the US and NATO did not comprehend this dynamic until fairly recently.

Most of the Afghan tribal leaders were based in Pakistan during the 1980s war against the Soviet Union thus could never go free from ISI influence any time. This was evidenced in 1988, when Sayed Majroo, Director of the Afghan Information Service, published a survey taken among Afghans in the refugee camps in Pakistan.

3. President Karzai, the US ally, on whose behalf the US got agitated, would prefer that the Americans should leave the soil at the earliest. He was unduly influenced by Pakistan which country always kept the policy that Afghanistan must be kept weak and unstable. The policy was misleadingly known as "strategic depth." It was misleading; the strategic depth was actually aimed at Karzai's reputed desire for the US and NATO to withdraw from the Afghan soil to please the ISI.

4. Since President Karzai was, for all practical purposes, little more than the Mayor of Kabul – the statement was not the whole truth. It described a complex situation influenced by not only Pakistan and the corrupt Afghan warlords it controlled, but also Karzai's own ability, to the extent he was interested, to effect change and nurture development in his country. What's more, the US owed this support to the Afghans, because the Americans enabled Pakistan's demolition during the 1980s and 90s.

One could see the candid remarks of a veteran journalist Selig Harrison and former UN Special Envoy Diego Cordovez in that respect:

> *"The Soviet Union began expressing its desire to withdraw from Afghanistan as early as 1981. It was American support for the Islamic fundamentalist militias [in CIA & Pentagon's documents they were called 'freedom fighters'] organized by Pakistan, which prevented them from doing so."*

5. The only thing that united those non-state Afghan fractious tribes who despised one another, hate foreigners even more. It was Pakistani propaganda to convince the world that *'Afghanistan is not much of a country, and Afghans would be better off under Pakistani dominion'*

whereas the most deeply scorned foreigners in Afghanistan were the Taliban from Pakistan.

6. Foreign forces, whatever be their intentions, would always be seen as occupiers and hence, the enemy.

    In the autumn of 2009, a group of US women, organized by the well-known anti-war group - Code Pink, travelled to Afghanistan. Simply put, every Afghan woman with whom they met expressed the firm belief that the US / NATO forces were the only thing standing between them and the abject misery of life under the Taliban. Much to their astonishment, the women on that Code Pink trip came home with a very different perspective than what they had anticipated.

    Many believed that a premature exit of US and NATO forces from Afghanistan was not likely to bring peace for the Afghan people - it would result in a repeat of the horrors of the 1990s. It boggled the planners that people who generally took pride in their sense of compassion, had not only succumbed to memory loss, but also seem completely immune to the vivid reminders of that period as demonstrated by the Taliban upon the people of Swat Valley in ending months of 2007.

7. The British and the Russians all tried to 'win' in Afghanistan, and they failed; it would be an exaggeration to say their futile attempts brought down three empires. Afghanistan had not been conquered in the near past centuries though earlier paraded through the Greeks under Alexander; by the Persians, the Mongols, and the Tartars.

    [*Ghengis Khan conquered Afghanistan, which remained part of the Mongol Empire for about 150 years. The British could claim a partial success through the Durand Treaty of 1893, however, the US apparently tried to 'win' or conquer Afghanistan in the name of reconstruction. Later, the US started propaganda that they would be leaving Afghanistan strong enough to defend itself against the ongoing threat from its neighbor, Pakistan.*]

8. The US should have remembered the age's old and tested slogan that *'you can't win wars when you're killing civilians'*; and in Afghanistan the boundary between combatants and civilians was positively blurred. Many catastrophic mistakes were committed by the US and NATO allies; world media reports published many tragic confessions made by the fighters themselves, still available on record.

Since 2001 [till mid 2010], about 16,000 civilians were killed on record but the figure should be high as many events might have gone un-reported. Upon taking command in the summer of 2009, Gen Stanley McChrystal issued new rules by which US and NATO soldiers were ordered to hold fire if pursuit of the enemy put civilians at risk; the fresh policy brought the toll of civilian deaths 28% less till the end of that year.

The western press, however, continued to propagate that *'there were no Afghani Taliban at all; the Taliban is a Pakistani paramilitary force. They come from Pakistan and go back to Pakistan after fighting events'*. [Melissa Roddy's observations of **21st May 2010** are quoted below verbatim:]

> *'Since 2003, the Taliban has assassinated hundreds of Pashtun tribal leaders in Pakistan and destroyed hundreds of schools in the Khyber PK, so that families have no choice but to send their sons to JUI madrassahs, i.e., Taliban training centers.*
>
> *In the past year, they have blown up bazaars in the region and even the UN Food Program. This is a direct assault on Pashtun women and children; no one makes friends with a group that targets their children.'*

9. The places, where Muslims live and where they die at the hands of US & NATO forces, would always be seen as a war against Islam rather than a war against terrorism. That was why the majority of the Afghan populace [and the residents of tribal regions of Pakistan] viewed the Americans as conquerors and not as defenders or their allies.

10. Absolute power can't make people free at the barrel of gun; a historical truth it remained.

11. *'There was no better way to create terrorism than to make war on Muslims in the name of fighting wars against terrorism.'* However, the western press continued to blow their trumpets that the US and NATO were not creating the terrorists - Pakistan and Saudi Arabia were doing that; the Saudis provided funds and Pakistan provided trained manpower.

12. America was mistakenly confident that it could save the world; such risky steps had proved the US policies wrong in the past. Jumping into other's affairs without analyzing the historical facts of that region normally ends in disasters as the US & the NATO forces were facing [in Afghanistan].

13. The US & NATO's military forces and overwhelming firepower applied in Pak-Afghan regions patently undermined the development of democracies in Afghanistan and Pakistan - totally an opposite theory what the western super powers usually propagate amongst their own societies.

14. The White House and other US establishments knew well that Al Qaeda was not ruling Afghanistan and it was not the Taliban either; it was a militant NGO aimed at winning Afghanistan. Defeating the Taliban might not be able to vanquish al Qaeda whatsoever. Though Afghanistan at that moment was a safe haven for Al Qaeda but the menace of global terrorism, if at all it was spread by Al Qaeda, was not being controlled from Afghan soils at least.

15. The American taxpayers were not supposed to pay for questionable wars abroad while suffering from social injustice and economic downfalls at home. It was widely propagated that the cash, weapons and training provided by the US to Pakistan in the Afghan War with Russians during the 1980s were utilized elsewhere. The American people held that in the first decade of 2001, it was not at all required for the White House to extend the same treatment to Afghanistan itself in the name of fighting terrorism.

The above 15 points concluded from Benjamin Barber and Melissa Roddy's documentary *'CONFLICT OF INTEREST'* was enough to open the eyes of American public and of White House, too. Though the main theme of 2009-11's media stories was that the ISI had twisted the Afghan situation but the US was timely warned to *'make no mistake'*.

Barber and Melissa's last message was also clear that staying there or partial withdrawal of US and NATO forces from Afghanistan was not supposed to fetch peace for the Afghan people. It would result in a repeat of horrors of the 1990s, when, according to Human Rights Watch, over 400,000 Afghans were killed.

THE ENDING TALK:

While the western media remained busy in attacking Pakistan's ISI, labelling them for sponsoring the Taliban or at least terming them the major handling tool in the milieu of Pak - Afghan War, the Pak - Army itself was upset by certain odd trends developed in its own ranks and files. See one major news item in that context:

Five Pakistan Army officers were convicted for links with a banned religious outfit after the Field General Court Martial (FGCM) completed its proceedings; an *ISPR press release issued on 3rd August 2012* is **referred**. The officers court - martialled included Brig Ali Khan, Maj Inayat Aziz, Maj Iftikhar, Maj Sohail Akbar and Maj Jawad Baseer. The FGCM awarded five-year rigorous imprisonment (RI) to Brig Ali Khan while Maj Sohail Akbar was handed a three-year RI and Maj Jawad Baseer sentenced to two-year RI. The remaining two officers were awarded one-year and six-month RI respectively.

> *'This was the first time that senior army officers were convicted and jailed over associations with banned religious organisations in Pakistan on the frontline of the US-led war on al-Qaeda and fighting Taliban insurgency. The officers were having contacts with Hizb ut Tahrir. Brigadier Khan was detained days after the US Navy SEALS found and killed Osama bin Laden in Abbottabad on 2nd May 2011.*
>
> *Hizb-ut-Tahrir is not banned in Britain, but has been outlawed in Pakistan and lies on the fringes of Western concerns about links between the military and terror groups.'*

In short; whether you blame the ISI or President Karzai or the Afghan history, the Americans do admit that it was their fault to step into this region especially when they had 200 years Afghan history in sight. President Obama had been rightly advised within his initial years of statesmanship that *'America cannot win this [Afghan] war....'*; and Mr President himself was convinced with that conclusion.

Reference of *'Washington Post' & 'NYT' dated 2nd December 2009* may be considered relevant here [while quoting President Obama's speech of a day before at the US Military Academy West Point, New York and comments there upon] which wrote:

> *'........ President Asif Ali Zardari, who is so weak that his government seems near collapse...... Zardari's political weakness is an additional hazard for a new bilateral relationship ..... [but even then] we can't succeed without Pakistan; you have to differentiate between public statements and reality...... Changing the nature of US-Pakistan relations in a new direction, <u>you're not going to win in Afghanistan ...... and that will make Afghanistan look like child's play......</u>*
>
> *Everyone understands this is a complex, nuanced, critical relationship.'*

The rest is the truthful history we all have witnessed.

Scenario 80

SAGA OF MISSING PERSONS:

Referring to **AS Ghazali's** essay titled *'The Issue of 10,000 Disappeared Persons....'* dated 9ᵗʰ *January 2010*, appeared on internet media:

> *'Perhaps the issue of missing persons and the NRO's legality were the main causes behind the US and Mr Zardari's reluctance to reinstate the CJP Iftikhar M Chaudhry. However, under intensive public pressure and massive pro-Chief Justice Demonstrations, President Zardari and Washington agreed to his restoration in March 2009.*

> *Now the nightmare is coming true.*

> *On January 7, 2010, the Supreme Court has opened another front [besides NRO's Pindora box] against the Zardari government with the resumption of hearings on the case of thousands of disappeared or missing persons apparently kidnapped by the intelligence agencies and many of whom have been handed over to the United States.'*

As per Ghazali's research - the term *'disappearance'* was created during the 1960s at the School of Americans, an institute set up by the US military at Fort Guilick in Panama, which ran there till 1984. 45,000 Latin American officers were trained in counter insurgency there. Along with anti - guerrilla tactics, they were taught how to torture, and how to 'manage' prisoners. As soon as the officers left for their home countries, they applied what they had learned with *'disappearances'* taking place in a large number of South American nations through the 1960s and 1970s. Four decades on, the families of the 'disappeared', in Argentina, in Chile, in Venezuela and in other countries were [still] pursuing the matter and were gaining at least some justice.

A generation ago, officials from Argentina's Naval Mechanics School, known by its Spanish acronym, ESMA, secretly loaded drugged prisoners into aircraft and threw them out over the brown and frosty waters. As many as 5,000 people were "disappeared" at the hands of ESMA, perhaps the most horrifying symbol of South American repression in the 1970s.

In December 2009, almost 40 years after these crimes were committed, 19 officials from ESMA, who were previously given amnesty by the government, finally appeared in court. Not surprisingly, similar methods were [till recent past at least] adopted by the Pakistani intelligence agencies in their cooperation with Washington's *war on terror* [WOT].

Nobody knows the exact number of the people who had been picked up by the Pakistani intelligence agencies during the last few years, particularly after 9/11. According to the Human Rights NGOs of Pakistan, about 10,000 people disappeared while a government list provided in 2010 to the Supreme Court mentioned 1390 people only. Baluchistan province's government said that 922 Baluchis were missing. In his book *'In the line of fire'*, Gen Musharraf had acknowledged at page 237 that:

'We have captured 689 [persons] and handed over 369 to the United States. Various people have earned bounties totaling millions of dollars.'

In 2003, Dr Aafia Siddiqui [*a Pakistani neuroscientist*] and her three children disappeared while on their way to Karachi airport to get a flight to Islamabad. In August 2008, US officials claimed she had been in their custody in Afghanistan only since July 2008, even though she had disappeared five years earlier. She was shifted to the US then tried in court on charges of firing at American soldiers in Afghanistan and was sentenced for 84 years imprisonment; the US slogan of humanity – HURRAY.

START OF THIS MENACE IN 1990s:

The fact remains that one of the cogent reasons that why CJP Iftikhar M Chaudhry was sent home on 9th March 2007 was that he had rendered a number of alarming and disturbing decisions challenging the then Establishment's policies. One of them was regarding 'the missing persons' for which one Amna Masood Janjua had started open street protests in Islamabad which was gaining momentum day by day pointing towards ISI, IB and FIA directly. By demanding accountability for the missing persons, the Supreme Court had refused to reduce constitutional rights and liberties to the military cum political regime then in power.

After comeback in March 2009, CJP Iftikhar M Chaudhry continued to hold the Establishment accountable on that count. The hearing of missing persons case continued but, regretfully saying, that till mid 2013 at least, the case could not give actual desired relief except few recoveries out of 256 as stated by the Human right activists. No sensible government on globe, military or democratic, normally opt to commit torture, engage in extra-judicial killings, and allow foreign agents to abduct persons with or without the connivance of domestic intelligence agencies. Deportations and extraditions of so called 'terrorists', were mostly exercised to balance personal scores, abundantly deceiving due process of law.

Most of the people think that Gen Musharraf's regime had made a pact with the Bush administration to institute a faceless [and lawless too] 'war on terror'. The constitutional rights and freedom of Pakistani citizens were severely compromised. Hundreds of Pakistanis had disappeared with no trace, no FIR, no entry in any police or army record which was otherwise a criminal act on behalf of the state. It was a ruthless and brutal violation of human rights charter in which domestic and foreign intelligence agencies were jointly involved in hunting down real and imagined terrorists.

The actual game had secretly taken start much earlier. In fact these illegal, unauthorized and under-hand deportations had started in the days of Rehman Malik's tenure in FIA in 1995-96 when Aamil Kansi was [*first such offence on police record*] handed over to Americans for personal reward. For him it was a way of minting [rewards] money overnight starting from $25000 per person.

Only one of his officers named Sajjad Hyder had knowledge of Mr Malik's extra-judicial activities and once in 1996 they both were called in the President House, by the then President Farooq Leghari, where they were awarded and decorated with medals sponsored and sent by the CIA. Since then Rehman Malik, later became Senator and Federal Interior Minister, is being considered on CIA's pay roll.

The Supreme Court has never questioned this background of missing persons. The lists of wanted persons were used to be prepared by the Americans in association with other western powers secret agents in Afghanistan and Pakistan since 1992-93 when Rehman Malik was holding a key post of FIA in the then NWFP and FATA. These lists, after due clearance from the CIA HQ, were usually given to Mr Malik for onward operations sometimes without knowledge or approval of the then Interior Ministry or high command of FIA.

When Nawaz Sharif took over reigns of the government in early 1997, the task of picking up persons on the secret lists went dormant. One officer of Intelligence Bureau named Maj (Rtd) Mulazim Hussain Bhatti, posted in K Block Islamabad, tried to help the Americans but due to his limited mobility and lack of professional skills in this field, he was soon shunted out from the *'influential helping people list'* and he was not considered for even a part of his first case of $25000 reward for CIA's wanted person.

When Nawaz Sharif's government was rolled back by Gen Musharraf in October 1999, this role of abducting persons wanted by the US agencies was allocated to the military agencies. The operation remained under military control till July 2007 when Rehman Malik openly joined Gen Musharraf in the garb of *'secret negotiator for restoration of democracy'* on behalf of Benazir Bhutto. After come back of democracy in Pakistan Mr Malik continued as Advisor to Gen Musharraf on the instance of US decision makers. CIA was successful in launching their agent deep into the Presidency allocating him a key post concerning with the internal security of Pakistan at highest decision making level.

Illegal deportations and extraditions of innocent people got sudden momentum in late 2007 and 2008 because then the military secret agencies had also got full ancillary support from the FIA and the IB through their boss, the then Advisor on Interior affairs, Mr Malik. The higher courts, however, failed to establish a clear principle that no foreign hand or agency should interfere in due constitutional process or fundamental rights of Pakistani people. Perhaps the judiciary had no powers or will to hold the military brass accountable so the case remained pending [till ending 2013 at least] since 2006.

The history would also remember two ugly episodes of 2008-09 when twice official notifications were issued by the Cabinet Secretariat Islamabad for placement of ISI, the top military establishment dealing with internal and external intelligence operations since 1975, under the Advisor / Minister for Interior. The reaction from GHQ based military echelons in this respect was so strong and immediate that the notifications were withdrawn by the government within next six hours leaving a black scar on the face of Interior Ministry both ways. {*An essay published at Pak Spectator's internet site on 22*nd *September 2013 is referred*}

AMRIT SINGH REPORT ON PAKISTAN:

Referring to a Washington based group report outlined in the 'Dawn' dated 6th February 2013, *'Pakistan extended full cooperation to the CIA in tracing suspected terrorists and provided secret detention and interrogation facilities to the US intelligence agency. Pakistan captured, detained, interrogated, tortured, and abused hundreds of individuals, including about a dozen key Al Qaeda leaders, for the CIA.'*

The report documented **participation of 54 foreign governments** in CIA's operations against terrorists and was first published by The *New York Times* a day earlier and Indian Prime Minister Manmohan Singh's daughter Amrit Singh was one of the principal writers of the report. The chapter on Pakistan described that:

'Pakistan also permitted its airspace and airports to be used for flights operated by Jeppesen Dataplan that were associated with CIA's extraordinary operations.'

The report mentioned the US court records as showing that in 2003, Pakistan allowed use of its airports and air space for at least one flight flown by the private charter company *Richmor Aviation*, which operated flights for the CIA's rendition programme. This flight was registered as N85VM and stopped over in Islamabad during the first week of March 2003. Pakistan allowed their airports to be used frequently for refuelling while moving prisoners around the world.

Furthermore, a 2010 UN report observed that from December 2001 until the summer of 2002, Pakistan operated a secret detention programme under which detainees were initially kept in custody in Pakistan before being transferred to Afghanistan and / or to Guantanamo Bay. Former President Gen Musharraf's admissions in his book are referred again for more details.

Detention facilities in which detainees were held at the behest of the CIA included the ISI detention facility in Karachi, which was allegedly used as an initial detention and interrogation point before detainees were transferred to other prisons. Although it was controlled by the ISI, but the detainees were generally interviewed by both US and British intelligence officials.

There had been kept no official investigation or interrogation record in Pakistan by the ISI or their American counterpart CIA and the disappeared ones went through the mill like Aafia Siddiqui, Masood Janjua, Binyam Mohammed and others. While many habeas corpus petitions were filed in Pakistani courts on behalf of disappeared individuals, the vast majority of these petitions were dismissed because Pakistani police and military agencies denied arresting or holding the individuals in question.

In 2005-06's media record, these cases of disappearance brought to light the inadequacies of the judiciary and their shallow process because the superior courts could offer no relief if the agency or force named as respondents denied the arrest or detention of the missing persons.

The Amrit Singh report identified 136 people who were held or transferred by the CIA and described what was known about when and where they were held. It added new detail about the handling of both, Al Qaeda operatives and innocent people, caught up in the global arena of counter-terrorism. Many prisoners were subjected to extraordinary rendition — transferred from one country to another without any legal process — and sent to countries where torture was a standard practice.

Such operations remained the subject of fierce debate, with former Bush administration officials asserting that such intimidations were valid to keep the country safe and critics saying the brutal interrogation techniques were illegal and ineffective. The debate was renewed later with the release of the movie *'Zero Dark Thirty'*, which portrayed the use of torture in the hunt for Osama bin Laden, though intelligence officials denied that was the case. When he took office in 2009, Mr Obama rejected calls for a national commission to investigate such practices, saying he wanted to look forward and not back.

The US Senate Intelligence Committee once completed a 6,000-page study of the CIA detention and interrogation program, but it remained classified. Amrit Singh, the author of the *Open Society report, 'Globalising Torture'*, said she had found evidence that 25 countries in Europe, 14 in Asia and 13 in Africa lent some sort of assistance to the CIA, in addition to Canada and Australia. They included Thailand, Romania, Poland and Lithuania, where prisoners were held, but also Denmark, which facilitated CIA air operations, and Gambia, which arrested and turned over a prisoner to the agency. The report held that:

"The moral cost of these programs was borne not just by the US but by the 54 other countries it recruited to help".

Michael V. Hayden, the former CIA Director, held that few voices had called for restraint in the panicky aftermath of 9/11 but we were often and bitterly accused of not doing enough to defend America when people felt endangered; and then as soon as they made people feel safe again, they were accused of doing too much. However, Amrit Singh said in the report that the United States had flagrantly violated domestic and international laws and that its efforts to avoid accountability were beginning to break down.

In December 2012, the European Court of Human Rights found the CIA responsible for the torture of Khalid el-Masri, a German citizen abducted by the agency and taken to Afghanistan in a case of mistaken identification. About two months later, an Italian Appalant Court convicted a CIA Station Chief and two other Americans for kidnapping of a radical cleric taken from the streets of Milan in 2003 and sent to Egypt; twenty three [23] Americans had previously been convicted in such cases.

CRISIS IN PAK-JUDICIARY [US REPORT]:

Referring to a report titled as *'Crisis in Pakistan's Judiciary'* released by the *US Library of Congress*, in 2006, the Human Rights Commission of Pakistan (HRCP) issued a 340 page report stating that a large number of persons, and growing at an 'alarming rate' had been picked up by intelligence agencies and taken to be detained in secret locations. Some of them were handed over to the CIA and flown to Bagram, Afghanistan and later shipped off to Guantanemo Bay.

Through this report *the Americans openly admitted* that the cases of forced abductions by the Pakistani state first began arising in 2001, in the aftermath of the United States invasion of Afghanistan and the commencement of the US-led War on Terror. Many of the missing persons were activists associated with the secular and nationalist movements going on in Balochistan and Khyber PK provinces allegedly financed & guided by the western powers through Indian secret agency RAW. Gen Musharraf, the military ruler of Pakistan [1999-2008] went on record to suggest that the *'jihadis'* and not the intelligence agencies were responsible for their disappearances.

Justin Huggler, the *Asia Correspondent*, while commenting on Gen Musharraf's staunch speech at one British Government's official night dinner, told in his essay titled *'President's boast undermined by human rights violations'* published *on 30th September 2006*, that:

'*In a derogatory report into reality of the situation in Pakistan......
several cases in which Pakistani security forces detained innocent people and sold them to the US as suspected "terrorists" for cash rewards are detailed, as are their subsequent flights to US detention centre at Guantanamo.*

The US typically offers $5,000 for a captured "terrorist". Children, as young as 10, are sent from Pakistan to Guantanamo where they face torture and other forms of abuse.

Moazzam Baig, a British citizen who was abducted from his home in the Pakistani capital, Islamabad, at gunpoint in January 2002 by Pakistani and American forces, was handcuffed and a hood was put over his head. He was thrown in the back of a vehicle and driven to a private house where he was interrogated by Americans. After some time he was taken to Guantanamo where he was tortured. He was released without charge last year.'

It was not just the rate of 'disappearance' from Pakistan that worried human rights groups, the actual hard luck was that most of the people handed over to the US authorities were not terrorists at all. They were captured by the agencies, civil and military, just to get cash prizes for each by drafting bogus charge sheets.

Americans might know the truth but the money was paid against those innocent people so had to go through the mill at Guantanamo. Time would tell that whether the whole game was played by the ISI as had been alleged or other law enforcing agencies were also involved and to what extent. No one knows that how many of them were picked up under personal rivalaries, family feuds, business compromises and so on.

The Asian Human Rights Commission on Pakistan, too, backed it stating that *'some 600 persons are believed to have disappeared during this year [2006] following their arrests by the law enforcement agencies.'* The HRCP Chairman, Asma Jahangir, filed a petition on behalf of the families of missing persons in the Supreme Court of Pakistan. The Supreme Court, which maintained subdued silence in the past in such cases, took up the missing persons case when the CJP constituted a bench for hearing and sent notices to the Attorney General and the Ministry of Interior for filing detailed replies; both did not take it seriously. Finally, at the hearing **on 10th April 2007**, the DAG in frustration stated before the Court that:

'It's a very sensitive case and I am completely helpless. All I can do is to contact Interior Ministry and that I did. But they didn't give me any information about the whereabouts of those missing people.'

After five hearings since December 2006, no clue as to the whereabouts of the missing persons was given to the DAG. The apex court held that crisis in the country was due to the non-enforcement of the Constitution. *'I have sentiments, too, being a father, a brother and a husband and feel the difficulties of the families of the missing persons'*, the Deputy Attorney General conceded.

Referring to the 'Asian Human Rights Commission Report' of February 2008, the veteran senior lawyer Munir Malik was once asked that 'the Supreme Court was getting in its way of fighting terrorism. We all know that the problem of terrorism is there and that the executive needs certain powers or a certain space to deal with this extraordinary issue. How should we fight terrorism, and how can the judiciary contribute?'

Mr Malik had urged that the executive should not shift the entire onus to the judiciary. He conceded that citizens' rights could be balanced against the interest of state security; but where the balance line be drawn and who would draw it? It could only be drawn by the parliament, and then the executive would implement the law. To decide whether the executive transgressed the law would be the judiciary's function. Malik added that:

'In England they had been the same problem, but their parliament enacted a law, they had adopted specific regulations after 7/7. Pakistanis, on the other hand, haven't been able to define terrorism yet. What is terrorism & what is a terrorist act? Al-Qaeda is a state within a state and it has to be dealt with.

In state terrorism, the state uses its coercive power to repress its citizens. Supposing the state picks you up on a charge of national security, your family have a right to know that they have you in their custody? The state must account for persons........'

Referring to 'the News' of 16th September 2008, Pak-Army's former Chief of General Staff [CGS] Gen Shahid Aziz had made open the whole scenario of the 'missing persons' at the hands of ISI or other military establishments. He told that:

"In my capacity as CGS, ... I was aware of the Pakistanis which were handed over by us to the US; I could only respond that the militant prisoners taken by the Army were handed over to the ISI for interrogation. Beyond that is not in my knowledge.

It was much later that one read of Pakistani prisoners in Guantanamo Bay, and yes we all felt very bad about it. However, if ISI was involved in their handing over, it was certainly in violation of the government policy. A team led by an Army colonel visited Guantanamo to find out if any Pakistanis were imprisoned there and to arrange for their release and return to their homes.

Likewise, the cooperation with the CIA, through the ISI, did provide the Army useful information regarding the presence of foreigners in FATA; it also included drones flown over FATA for intelligence purposes."

THE COURTS CONTINUED CRYING:

Referring to the *'Dawn' dated* 6th *January 2010,* a Supreme Court judge held that *'the missing persons issue is more serious than NRO.'*

During the missing persons case hearing that day when Advocate Hashmat Habib requested the apex court to summon heads of the Military Intelligence [MI] and the Inter-Services Intelligence [ISI], Justice Javed Iqbal said that last time when *'we tried to summon them we were sent home for almost 16 months'.* Moving scenes were witnessed in the courtroom when Mrs Amina Masood Janjua regretted that there was silence despite the fact that witnesses were ready to help locate her husband, Masood Janjua.

Justice Javed Iqbal remarked that individuals taken by intelligence agencies were considered as missing persons and the military's role was in their view. The esteemed judges added that:

'There is always a mention of brigadiers and majors; who have given them power? Frontier Corps has no rights to arrest and detain any person. There is a Gestapo-like reign of terror...anyone can come into a house, where is the enforcement of law?

Incidents involving hundreds of missing persons have been reported to this court in the past four years. Relatives of the missing allege they were picked up by intelligence agencies.'

However, the apex court's voice again lost in vacuum.

In the 3rd week of February 2010, a bench of the Supreme Court of Pakistan [comprising Justice Javed Iqbal, Justice Sair Ali and Justice Tariq Pervez] held that it would not examine evidence against intelligence agencies in the missing persons' case; further saying that evidence and allegations of involvement of intelligence agencies in abducting people would be examined by an *'appropriate forum at the relevant time.'*

The four-page order noted that police officials had expressed their inability to make further probes in certain cases regarding the missing persons' due to alleged involvement of various intelligence agencies.

Extracts from a report appeared in *'the Independent' of UK dated 18*th *March 2010* is being placed below to reflect an image of a senseless country named Pakistan:

'Up to 8,000 of Pakistan's missing citizens, men, were mostly seized from their homes by cops and soldiers on the orders of spies and intelligence agents and Americans since Nine Eleven 2001. In Lahore alone, there are 120 "torture houses" just for the missing of the Punjab. Their shrieks of pain from the basements could be heard by residents [around].

.... "They" is the Inter-Services Intelligence. "They" is military intelligence. "They" are the Americans – according to the few "disappeared" who have been released during torture sessions. [Around them] US soldiers are observed in Pakistani uniforms – sometimes female American soldiers dressed in the uniforms of Pakistani military paramedics.

So far, the Supreme Court and the Lahore High Court have squeezed around 200 detainees out of the maw of the country's security apparatus – those, that is, who were still in Pakistan. Many are known to have been freighted off to the tender mercies of the Americans at Bagram in Afghanistan, where Arab detainees have long ago testified to being beaten and sodomised with broom sticks. There have been prisoner murders, too, in Bagram, the jail that President Barack Obama refuses to close.

All of the 200 got released had been tortured. Initially, it was very ruthless – they were not allowed to sleep; there were beatings and thrashings; they were hanged upside down. There were actual torture rooms where the things were done to them.

The questions they were asked were repetitive; where are the guns? Where are the weapons? Where is Mullah Omar? Sometimes taken for questioning to Islamabad; .... Interrogated by foreigners – they were English-speaking; not sure they were Americans or British.

The DHRP files show that there are 1,700 missing from Balochistan alone. At least 4,000 appear to be in the hands of the Pakistani interior ministry, while 750 of the missing Pakistanis were believably taken by the Americans – illegally, of course – to Bagram, the Policharki prison outside Kabul, or to Herat in western Afghanistan.'

During May 2010, families of the missing persons gathered before the Parliament to lodge a protest collectively against the government, army and the higher judiciary. *In this protest, the then Opposition Leader Ch Nisar Ali Khan and Dr Firdaus Ashiq Awan, a Federal Minister, were also sitting with the families to show their solidarity with the aggrieved ones.* In this sit-in, one media member named Shakil Turabi raised issue of his own lost son. The Chief Justice of the SC took *suo moto* notice of Mr Turabi's missing son next day.

Some anchors and columnists then named Hamid Mir in the abduction & murder of Ex-ISI officer named Khwaja Khalid and dragged him in the criminal case through an audio tape in which Hamid Mir was purportedly talking with two 'kidnapers'. A petition was moved in the Police HQ from Khalid Khwaja's son pleading that his dad was kidnapped and sent to North Wazirastan by Hamid Mir, the anchor & journalist.

One section of media, however, maintained that Khwaja Khalid had himself gone to North Wazirastan in March 2010 along with one Col Imam of the ISI and an English journalist named Asad Qureshi; he was murdered there in April 2010. Six minutes video of Col Imam's killing by Taliban Commander Hakeemullah Mehsud is available on internet media and the experts have termed it *'genuine'* by all means.

UMAR CHEEMA 'NICELY BRIEFED':

Referring to the *'New York Times' dated 25*[th] *September 2010*, Umar Cheema, the staff reporter of 'the News' since 2007, was on his way home from dinner *on 4*[th] *September 2010* when men in black commando garb stopped his car, blindfolded him and drove him to a house on the outskirts of town. There he was beaten and stripped naked. His head and eyebrows were shaved, and he was videotaped in humiliating positions by assailants who he and other journalists believe were affiliated with Pakistan's powerful spy agency.

At one point, while Umar Cheema was laid face down on the floor with his hands cuffed behind him, his captors made clear why he had been singled out for punishment: for writing against the government. *'If you can't avoid rape, enjoy it,'* one taunted him. His ordeal was not uncommon for a journalist or politician who crossed the interests of the military and intelligence agencies in Pakistan. What makes his case different was that Mr Cheema had spoken out about it, describing in graphic detail what happened with him, something rare in a country where victims often choose, out of fear, to keep quiet.

'I have suspicions and every journalist has suspicions that all fingers point to the ISI,' Mr Cheema told. In response to an e-mail for comments, the official stance of the ISI came, *'they are nothing but allegations with no substance or truth.'* [then what; the tone expressed]

[*Some of his fellow journalists kept the view that Mr Cheema was targeted not as a normal journalist only but being a 'suspected American pin' as he had won a Daniel Pearl Journalism Fellowship in 2007 and had worked in 'The New York Times' newsroom for six months.*]

Mr Cheema had written till then about 50 articles in 2010 that questioned various aspects of Pak-Army's conduct and of the government, including corruption accusations against President Zardari, however, three articles in particular, made the military angry. One reported article was on the sensitive issue of the courts-martial of two SSG-elite commando squad who had refused to obey orders and joined the assault on Red-Mosque Islamabad event in July 2007.

In an article of early August 2010, Mr Cheema described how Army House, the residence of the Army Chief, was protected by 400 city police officers and not by the army soldiers, as required by law. In another article, he wrote that the suspects in a major terrorist attack against a bus carrying ISI employees [*perhaps referring to RA Bazar RWP's incident*] were acquitted because of the 'mishandling' of the court case by the ISI.

[*Apparently ISI was not at fault. In Pakistan, not even a single case of suicide bombing or terrorist attack has met with success during the last 13 years because the police could never investigate any case sincerely & professionally; and where some case was worked out, the coward judges never punished any culprit; lack of evidence has invariably been used as an excuse by all courts.*]

Punjab's Law Minister, Rana Sanullah Khan, said that in 2003, when he was an opposition politician and had criticized the army during Gen Musharraf's rule, he was kidnapped and brutalized in a similar manner.

In January 2010, in Islamabad, the home of one Azaz Syed, a reporter for daily the 'Dawn', was attacked by unknown assailants days after he was threatened by some spy agents over an investigative article he was researching related to the military.

Kamran Shafi, a leading columnist and himself a former army officer who writes critically of the military, was harassed and his house was attacked in December 2009 by *'elements linked to the security establishment,'* according to his own account.

Whether a plus point or not, Pakistan has developed a vibrant news media spearheaded by round the clock television news channels in the last decade. The military and the ISI, however, were always treated with respect invariably by all TV anchors and by print media reporters who admired the Pak-Army in battling the Taliban; but the black sheep are everywhere.

Also one reason for such reverence and respect was that the agency kept most of the anchors and journalists on its payroll. Unspoken rules prevailed amongst both sides. A journalist who trespassed over the given line was 'told & briefed' to behave. Earlier that year [of 2010], Mr Cheema was initially called to a coffee shop in Islamabad by an ISI officer and was 'properly briefed', but he did not 'behave nicely' thus suffered.

During the 2nd week of April 2011, while hearing the 'missing persons' case, Justice Javed Iqbal reiterated it was government's responsibility to recover these people. Till then 222 missing persons had been traced due to the apex court's efforts. Justice Raja Fayyaz asked why this issue had not been raised in the parliament till then and also that complete details of the dead bodies found so far should have been submitted there too.

The apex court apparently went impotent on this issue but, just to satisfy its ego, it directed that home ministers of all the four provinces and federation to appear before the court on the next hearing. What the home ministers [in-charge of respective poor local police] had to reply or explain before the apex court except for coming, going and sitting on benches outside the court room while adding millions of travelling expenses to the public expenditure. What else the apex court could do – by the way; it has been the routine practice of the 'independent judiciary' of Pakistan since about a decade.

On 29th June 2011, the Supreme Court was informed that missing persons — Masood Janjua and Faisal Faraz– had been killed by the al Qaeda six years back.

[*Masood Janjua was 44 when he "disappeared" on 30th July 2005. He ran an IT college and a travel agency, father of three then; he just never came home. Nobody saw what happened but his wife, Amina Janjua still believes, and has cogent evidence, that he is still alive.*]

Allegedly Masood Janjua ..... was inside a cell at 111 Brigade barracks. There was evidence that those "disappeared" were moved around, between barracks and interrogation centres and underground torture facilities in different towns and cities. Amina Janjua was determined to get her husband back so she turned to the *'only brave institution still fighting in Pakistan: the lawyers and the judges and the courts'* as the *daily 'Independent' of UK* cited above had observed.

On 29th June 2011, the Additional AG KK Agha told the 3-member bench headed by Justice Javed Iqbal that the data gathered from laptops in possession of Janjua and Faraz showed their links with al Qaeda. Amina Masood Janjua [*an intelligent painter and interior designer belonging to middle class*], wife of Masood Janjua and chairperson Defence of Human Rights, had demanded that *'their [the two mentioned above – Masood & Faraz] graves should be identified'* and DNA tests be carried out to determine their identity, if they were really dead.

The government was found lingering on action against those FC personnel who had been identified by six of the missing persons' families, accusing them of taking away their loved ones; no action was taken against the FC personnel till then. The apex court went more disturbed to hear that one MNA Fazal Rab Pirzada had gone missing few years back but no clue since ever.

During the first week of August 2011, the Supreme Court bench comprising Justice Shakirullah Jan, Justice Jawwad S. Khwaja and Justice Sarmad Jalal Osmany, heard more complaints about forced disappearances, and asked the government to complete the composition of the Commission of Inquiry on Enforced Disappearances within one week; the post of its chairman was vacant since its former head Fazalur Rehman from Balochistan had relinquished the post after becoming member of the Election Commission of Pakistan.

Justice Khwaja asked the Additional AG that *'what should the court do if someone from intelligence agencies appeared before the court but did not admit about picking up a certain person. The judge observed that it was the main concern of the court to sit here with a clean slate. Even picking up a man by police is a big issue for us.'*

The additional AG informed the court that [till that day] out of 392 cases, 104 people had been traced while 96 did not fall under the category of missing persons and 138 people, including 10 chronic cases, were still untraced.

On 19th August 2011, a UN delegation, under Rupert Colville of UNHCHR approached the government of Pakistan with a concern to investigate numerous killings and abductions, particularly of journalists.

The UN had come there with reports on the killing of one journalist Munir Shakir in Balochistan on 14th August 2011, and the disappearance of another journalist Rehmatullah Daparkhel on 11th August from North Waziristan. The HRCP held that in almost all cases of violence against journalists in the last few years, those responsible were never identified.

Shakir was shot dead after covering a protest organized by a Baloch separatist organization. Irshad Mastoi, the Bureau Chief for the *Online News Network* where Shakir worked, told that the killing was linked to professional journalistic job and nothing beyond. The whereabouts of Daparkhel, kidnapped on 11th August, went unknown though, as it is widely believed, that *'local journalists have to do the job of the police and investigate on their own using their contacts.'*

At least 48 journalists have been killed in Pakistan in last ten years and 35 of them were deliberately targeted and murdered because of their work. In 2012 alone, six journalists were killed in the country. Of the 48 journalists killed in the line of duty during these 11 years, 14 were from Khyber PK, 12 from Balochistan, 9 from Sindh, 8 from Federally Administrated Tribal Agencies (FATA), 3 from Punjab and 2 from the federal capital, Islamabad. Of 48 journalists killed, 25 were shot and 9 abducted before murder.

ISI ADMITTED 4 DEAD OUT OF 11:

On **31st January 2012,** The Supreme Court came down hard on the ISI and MI Chiefs and ordered immediate production of 11 suspects picked up by intelligence agencies for their alleged involvement in the October 2009 attacks at GHQ and ISI's Hamza Camp in Rawalpindi.

The 11 prisoners 'disappeared' from outside Rawalpindi's Adiala Jail the day they were acquitted of terrorism charges on 8th April 2010. The two spy agencies had conceded before the court that the prisoners were in their custody, claiming that they were recovered from terror camps. Four of the prisoners were later found dead in mysterious circumstances outside the Lady Reading Hospital in Peshawar.

At a hearing during ending 2012, the spy agencies' counsel told the court that four of the prisoners had died but the others were no longer in the custody of intelligence agencies and had been handed over to the Khyber PK government.

The apex court inquired that how four of the prisoners were killed and left by a roadside; certainly not enough for the spy agencies to reject as 'wild allegations'. Especially since — given the confirmation that four of the prisoners were dead — there appeared to be a breach of Articles 9 (security of person), 10 (safeguards as to arrest and detention) and 10A (right to fair trial) of the Constitution.

During the last hearing on 22nd January 2013, a 3-member bench of the apex court, headed by the CJP Iftikhar M Chaudhry, ISI's counsel Raja Irshad could not forward any cogent reason for keeping the remaining seven persons in illegal custody. However, the whole case remained confined to the academic discussions.

In Pakistan, the issues pertaining to 'missing persons' always remained significant. It concerns not only the rights of the missing persons themselves but also of their families who are in agony because of the inexplicable disappearances of their loved ones. The SC has been hearing cases on missing persons since 2006; the matter has been taken up by several national and international human rights bodies and has also received extensive media coverage; but of no avail.

Despite this, there were incidents where dumped bodies were found and there was no one to answer for what really happened. Instead, the spy agencies' counsel suggested that the court could appoint private commission to meet the prisoners in the hospital because they could not be produced before the court.

Another parallel case was being heard in Peshawar High Court [PHC] on the same issue of 'missing persons' but the point to ponder was that if the *persons all over Pakistan were only picked up by the two military spy agencies* and no other political faction, religious extremist groups, IB or Special Branch of Police, Pakistani or Afghan Taliban, criminal mafias for ransom, Black-water or XE workers or Indian RAW agents in-filtered in border areas of Khyber PK and Balochistan provinces were not involved; *why putting the guns on Pak-Army's shoulders only*. However, again this aspect had to be looked into by the two military agencies seriously to clear their position.

On 1st February 2012, the CJ Peshawar High Court (PHC) Justice Dost Muhammad Khan warned that criminal cases would be registered against the heads and officers of intelligence agencies if forced disappearance of citizens weren't halted and legal procedures not adopted for detained missing persons. He issued the warning in the case of two missing students when the Judge Advocate General [JAG] of the Pakistan Army, Colonel Noor Muhammad, and Deputy AG, Iqbal Mohmand, expressed ignorance about the whereabouts of the students.

At the previous hearing, the agency education officer and principal of the school had submitted to the court on oath that the students were indeed taken away by the security agencies. Said Nazeem and Ajaz, students of Grade IV and V respectively, were *picked up from Government Primary School*, Lali Jan Killay in Bara Tehsil on 1st January 2010.

Earlier, on **13th October, 2011** another bench of the Peshawar high court had passed an order in the said missing students' case and had directed the respondents, including security agencies, to produce the students before the court within 15 days. The CJ PHC had observed:

'This is too much. …. this attitude will force the court to order registration of cases under Sections 365 (kidnapping) & 342 of PPC (Pakistan Penal Code) against the ISI, MI and IG FC. Don't force the people to come out on the streets against you as it will be dangerous for you and the country as well.

I have ordered sub-ordinate judges not to go internment centres [of army] for granting custody of the prisoners. It is a fact that security forces have rendered sacrifices in the war on terror, but their excesses are not tolerable.'

In routine, under-trial prisoners arrested on terror charges used to be handed over to the army while thousands were already languishing in illegal detention. The Frontier Corps had submitted before the court that no missing student was in the custody of any security agency under FC.

In another missing person's case the PHC bench directed SP Peshawar Cantt Mian M Saeed and ASP Cantt Faisal Shehzad to produce the missing person within 14 days or face registration of FIR under Section 365 PPC.

RADICALIZATION IN PAK-FORCES:

One Major (Rtd) Osaid Zahidi had served in the Military Intelligence [MI] for almost nine years, got retirement in 2008 but then went missing since 15th October 2010. The media claimed that some eye witnesses had seen uniformed men chasing him in Gulshan Chawrangi Karachi. His family doubted that he had been picked up by intelligence agencies.

Osaid's elder brother, Junaid Zahidi, a former Union Council Nazim from Jamaat e Islami [JI], started looking for him and learnt that his brother was in 'safe house' of the country's security agencies in the Malir Cantonment. Junaid moved a bit further to collect evidence in that regard but, six months later, his [Junaid's] body was found in the limits of the same Malir Cantonment. Junaid's friends later revealed that he had received threats to back off from finding his brother. The Zahidi family lost two men and their 11 children were robbed off their future.

Osaid's wife Adeela could only get her husband's name included in a petition on missing people filed at the Supreme Court. Adeela described her husband not as an 'extremist' but one who opposed *'US intervention and interference'* in Pakistan.

The appearance of seven victims of enforced disappearances in the Supreme Court in early February [2012] afforded the Karachites some hope, but their condition – described as being sick, emaciated and bewildered – depressed them. One victim's mother suffered a heart attack after witnessing her son's appearance.

In Pakistan's way of fighting terrorism, the danger of radicalisation is exposed across all sections of the society. Major Zahidi was perhaps persuaded by the militants to help them during his counterterrorism assignment. Here, only a scientific probe could lead to determine what motivated state functionaries to join the cause of the militants, if at all, it was the case.

Referring to *the 'Dawn' dated 26*th *February 2012:*

> *'The phenomenon of radicals penetrating the security apparatus has caused jitters. The detention [later conviction] of Brig Ali Khan for suspected links with the banned Hizbut Tahrir was also seen as an example of the growing influence of the radicals.*
>
> *Gen Musharraf had also once stated in 2004 that some junior army and Pakistan Air Force (PAF) personnel had links with terrorist organisations. Later, 57 PAF personnel were arrested in connection with an attempt on Musharraf's life; some of them were convicted too.*
>
> *Dr Usman [known in militant's circles as Dr otherwise not], the mastermind of the October 2009 attack on military headquarters [GHQ] in Rawalpindi, was a deserter from the army's medical corps. In Lahore a policeman who had established links with Al Qaeda was assigned VVIP duty with Punjab's Governor Salmaan Taseer who ultimately killed him in January 2011.'*

A study by the Pakistan Institute for Peace Studies (PIPS), an Islamabad-based think tank, on detained militants to identify what motivated and inspired them, is hereby quoted here as reference.

The murder of a Sindhi nationalist leader Muzaffar Bhutto in mid-May 2012, one of the prominent victims of enforced disappearance in Sindh, [*and the brazen attack on a peaceful political rally in Karachi on 22nd May 2012 that claimed at least 16 lives*] once again manifested the violent suppression of political debate pushing Sindh into Balochistan-style mayhem. Muzaffar Bhutto, Secretary General of Jeay Sindh Muttahida Mahaz (JSMM), had gone missing since February 2011 and then his dead body was found near Hyderabad with a shot-wound in the head and torture marks on the body. The family alleged involvement of state agencies as Mr Bhutto was neither a terrorist nor a criminal.

The HRCP had till then verified about 41 cases of enforced disappearance in 'interior Sindh' since November 2010; 26 people were traced out and released but 15 remained missing; these missing individuals were mainly the political activists from Badin. The courts were not able to take note of the disappearances nor the police bothered to record statements of those who had come back from captivity with a view to bring the perpetrators to justice.

COMMISSIONS & COMMITTEES – NO RELIEF:

On 5th June 2012, Pakistan's human rights activist Asma Jahangir claimed that the country's top security agency [ISI] plotted to murder her. In an exclusive interview with Shamil Shams of DW, Asma J told that:

'I am a very responsible person, and I do not usually make these kinds of allegations. My sources are extremely reliable. It is true that I have been critical of them [Army & ISI] but I am critical of their policies, which I do not agree with. As a lawyer in the missing people's cases I hoped that there would be a change in the mindset of the establishment, which unfortunately doesn't appear to have happened.'

Replying a question [*that do you think the ISI and other security agencies could kill an internationally renowned person like you*], Asma quoted history of Pakistan when prominent people were killed; the difference between Pakistan and other countries was that in Pakistan nobody ever knew who was responsible for those murders. She sent a very clear message to the PPP government that *'they are the ones who are responsible for my protection'.* Some protection was provided but not sufficient.

There was an attack on her in 1995 too when some persons tried to kill Asma Jahangir inside her house. Subsequently, some people were arrested and there was a trial. She said before the court that *'there is a nexus; the agencies may not have connections with all groups, but they used a lot of these groups'.*

On 2ⁿᵈ October 2012, the SC - appointed commission on missing persons disclosed that 80 more cases of disappearance had been reported to it during the past three months. The announcement contrasted sharply with a claim government made a month earlier during their meetings with UN mission on enforced disappearances that the number of such incidents had dropped over recent months.

At the end of their 10-day official visit to Pakistan a month earlier, members of the *United Nations Working Group on Enforced or Involuntary Disappearances* talked about 'serious challenges' and said in a news conference that:

> *'There is acknowledgement that enforced disappearances have occurred and still occur in the country. We note that cases continue to be reported to the national authorities. But there are controversies both on the figures and on the nature of the practice of enforced disappearances.'*

The latest figures released by the two-member Commission of Inquiry on Enforced Disappearances, headed by Justice (retd) Javed Iqbal, show that 539 cases of missing persons were under investigation before 30ᵗʰ September 2012. On 1ˢᵗ January 2011, there were 138 cases pending before the Commission and had received 714 new cases during the past 21 months, increasing the total number to 852. By 30ᵗʰ June 2012 the total pendency with the Commission was 772 and 80 cases were added during the previous three months.

The said Commission set up under the Supreme Court's new directives had disposed of 313 cases till then; it had succeeded in tracing 27 persons during one month of September when it held its proceedings in Islamabad but the government remained silent about the places from where they were found and the identity of their captors.

Speaking at a news conference in June in Quetta, Justice (retd) Javed Iqbal had held foreign intelligence agencies responsible for the deteriorating situation in Balochistan, claiming that there was concrete evidence against them. He had also expressed regrets over the baseless propaganda about the actual number of missing persons in the country.

On 8th January 2013, the Parliamentary Committee on National Security (PCNS), headed by PPP's Senator Raza Rabbani, which had taken up the lingering issue of the enforced disappearances about four months earlier, issued 15 recommendations.

It was all an exercise in futile as the recommendations made were of advisory type, mainly the 'dos & do nots' already available in editorials and columns of all newspapers AND mainly the same concerns & instructions had repeatedly been conveyed by the higher courts in all their hearings since six years. For example, the recommendations were like:

- *'strict action should be taken against the officers or agencies doing wrong';*

- *'that all training institutes of the army, intelligence agencies and police should be administered in accordance with the law';*

- *'the government to announce immediate prison reforms';*

- *'to take measures to provide knowledge of fundamental rights to its police trainees';*

- *'that no action be taken against officials who present the missing persons in court within the stipulated time';*

- *'a person's arrest by any agency or department must be in accordance with Article 10 of the Constitution';*

- *'that activities of intelligence agencies must be regulated';*

- *'that the chief justices of the Supreme Court and High Courts form special benches in their respective courts to hear the cases of missing persons';*

- *'that the government should enter the names of those arrested in a computerised register within 24 hours of the arrest';*

- *'that the arrested individual should be informed about the sections used against him or her within 24 hours of the arrest.*

- *'That strict action in accordance with the law be taken against officers who detain people illegally'.*

In nut shell Raza Rabbani's Report was all an exercise to make fool of the poor nation once again; the report was not considered by the parliament, by any agency, by any department and not even by the media to be commented upon.

GIMMICKS STILL ON:

The question remains that how many persons are actually missing. The law enforcement agencies and intelligence services held that the true figure of the missing persons was much less than had been propagated at different levels. The main plea was that from the given list of missing persons:

- How many individuals joined a particular cult or *Jihadi groups* or national movements and did not return home?

- How many of them had preferred to become suicide bombers.

- How many victims of bomb attacks whose bodies could not be recognized were included in the missing persons' list?

- What about those who died far from their homes and information of their death is not known to their kins or family?

- Are some proclaimed offenders and people running away because of family disputes and shifting to other cities without informing their kins also included in the list?

- What about those who kept links with different terrorist organizations and were working for them in far-flung areas of FATA or the Khyber-PK?

- Some of the missing persons could have gone abroad and living there on fake names because of their asylum problems.

- Many of the terrorists if killed in action by law-enforcement agencies are normally buried secretly by their accomplices and since their families do not know anything about it.

Referring to *'the News' dated 9*th *March 2012;* no NGO has ever claimed that they worked on the above lines to reach a factual list of missing persons. *In the year 2008, during the initial hype of this issue, some 2,390 persons were propagated as missing whereas through detailed* _scrutiny, the actual figures came down to 392 persons_. Cases of those 392 missing persons were handed over to the first Judicial Commission, which by the end of year 2010, had traced 134 missing persons.

The second judicial commission was formed in March 2011 and 445 cases (including 138 in balance) were given to it. Out of these cases, 142 missing persons were traced out till March 2012. The stakeholders could have worked together to identify the true number of actually missing persons at the hands of agencies, as it has been blamed since years.

Contrarily, the missing people's case, lingering on since seven years is still alive in Supreme Court's record with no cogent progress in fact. The SC was informed **on 16**th **July 2013** that the United Nations Working Group on Enforced Disappearances in Islamabad would extend cooperation to the Pakistani police regarding the investigation in a case of enforced disappearance.

The apex court on that day had discussed the case of a missing person, Mudasir Iqbal, which was registered by the Commission of Inquiry on Enforced Disappearances (CIED) on the initiative of a UN team. According to the UN team, several people had seen Mudasir Iqbal detained at a secret detention centre.

During proceedings it was objected that how the police could be allowed to proceed against army officers as no law existed in this regard. Chief Justice Iftikhar M Chaudhry, heading a 3-member bench, observed [once more] that it was high time to probe why the allegations were being levelled against spy agencies.

The MI's counsel contended that no FIR could be registered against armed forces officials; they are dealt under Army Act 1952.

> [_In this case, the Attorney General of Pakistan (AGP), while appearing on 12_th _July, had stated that there was no provision in the Army Act, Criminal Procedure Court and Pakistan Penal Code that bars initiating legal proceedings against the serving army officers. He also said that there was no immunity to armed forces in matters related to the fundamental rights._
>
> _Justice Jawwad S Khwaja, member of the bench, affirmed that the AGP was right as the apex court had already decided this point of law._]

On next hearing **on 23**rd **July 2013**, the SC's same bench sought from the federation a comprehensive, meaningful and viable policy regarding missing persons within 10 days.

In nutshell, the governments continued to think on policy formulations and the superior courts kept on crying but – nothing concrete result appeared. The case has already taken seven years – no end; let us salute to Pakistan's marvelous judicial system and its judges.

Lastly, **on 27th August 2013**, the Supreme Court of Pakistan [once again] gave Frontier Corps (FC), police and other intelligence agencies two week's time for the recovery of missing persons. A 3-member bench, headed by the CJP Iftikhar M Chaudhry, heard the case pertaining to unrest in Balochistan at SC's Quetta registry. During the hearing, the bench remarked that there was no progress in the recovery of missing persons during the past three years. Till that day there were records of at least 506 people in custody of government agencies, the bench quoted.

Scenario 81

ON JUDICIAL ACTIVISM IN PAKISTAN:

On 7ᵗʰ *April 2009*, the Supreme Court (SC) of Pakistan ordered for an independent commission headed by former SC judge Rana Bhagwandas for an inquiry into the soaring prices of petroleum products and profits earned by the oil companies. The identical constitutional petitions moved by PPP Senator Rukhsana Zuberi, PML(N)'s Zafar Iqbal Jhagra and others were earlier taken up by a 3-member bench of the apex court headed by the CJP Iftikhar M Chaudhry on 30th March instant. The Court opined that ten (10) questions pertaining to the misuse of authority and objectionable regulatory provisions should be answered by the Commission.

Chief Justice Iftikhar M Chaudhry ordered investigations into cases of "forced disappearances" arising as part of the 'war on terror' in which the Pakistan military and ISI, as discussed in the previous chapter, were allegedly stated to have imprisoned hundreds of persons without due process. Many of those who had "disappeared" were allegedly from Balochistan where an insurgency was continuing. CJP's efforts resulted in the return of some of the missing persons but the frustration prevailed.

Since the birth of the independent judiciary in Pakistan during March 2009, various populist rulings by the CJP Iftikhar M Chaudhry against the executive displayed a type of judicial activism considered to be unsettling for the [PPP's] government. Under him, the Supreme Court took action on its own initiative to question the government on the role of the military, its intelligence wings and their policy decisions in Khyber PK, Balochistan and FATA affairs, financial malpractices and social injustices etc.

The SC's *verdict of 16ᵗʰ December 2009* in the NRO case followed by its pledge to come down on mega loan defaulters [referring to SC's thunderous announcements dated 22ⁿᵈ December 2009] had shaken some politicians but soon the people started divulging their resentment because not even a single date was proposed for serious proceeding in that loan eater's case. While heading a Supreme Court bench on *suo motu* notice of last written off dubious loans worth Rs:54 billion sanctioned by the State Bank, the Chief Justice Iftikhar M Chaudhry had observed:

> 'For [the] nation's sake, we are ready to accept blame for our involvement in the loan write-off matter, but across the board action will be taken

after providing opportunity to the bankers and the defaulters to pay back the outstanding money. We are making it clear that the Supreme Court intends to pursue cases of corruption and graft vigorously and indiscriminately.'

A group of influential lawyers, who had allegedly joined hands with the loan eaters and had got their shares in the name of 'fees & pleading charges' conveyed threats to the bench that the proceedings in loan cases would not be so easy-going for the 'bench and bar' on collective basis. Some circles did not even spare the higher judiciary labelling it as a stooge in the hands of one section of PML(N). It was apparent because some big politicians were shrewd enough to dictate NRO decision to the judges but opening up the 'Loan Cases' was not acceptable to them so termed it as beyond the apex court's constitutional role.

The prominent lawyers had thus turned their back to a basic principle that the real, meaningful, fair and principled justice ought never to worry about 'being blamed'. Those who have done wrong in the eyes of law were meant to be punished by the judiciary that is, after all, one of the primary purposes of the institution. Those **rich lawyers wanted the judicial activism in the name of 'independent judiciary'** but were simply dictating the benches for the fields of their peculiar choices. If the judiciary went contrary to their wish and choices, they raised flags against the whole process of judicial activism terming it 'victimization'.

HISTORY OF JUDICIAL ACTIVISM:

What is judicial activism? The former Chief Justice Sajjad Ali Shah, in his essay published in the daily *'Dawn' of 26*[th] *September 2006* has given its background details. According to him:

'Before partition, the judicial system in the subcontinent was provided by the British government that did not interfere with the personal laws of its subjects. Muslims were governed by their laws of inheritance, matrimonial affairs, custody of children, pre-emption in purchase and sale of land, etc, as rooted in their religion. Likewise, Hindus, Parsis and Christians were governed by their own personal laws.

The British gave us a system of courts, procedural laws and some substantive laws in codified form. For their own use, they have codified laws made by the parliament in Britain and rigidly followed conventions and precedent judgments.

The British are conservative by nature, but whenever their laws are silent and provide no remedy in a particular set of circumstances, they invoke equity, which means the use of good conscience and principles of natural justice and fair play. In fact, equity lays down the foundations of judicial activism so that courts do not feel helpless if the law does not allow remedy for any particular reason.'

When the British left in 1947, the emerging countries of India and Pakistan were allowed to follow the British legal order in the shape of the Government of India Act 1935 to be read with the Indian Independence Act 1947 until both countries drafted their own constitutions. The first case in court that demonstrated judicial activism in Pakistan was that of *Maulvi Tamizuddin Khan* (**PLD 1955 Sindh 96**).

The Chief Court of Sindh interpreted the words 'assent' and 'dominion' in a broader and more liberal manner and used judicial activism. It gave a landmark judgment to the effect that the Governor - General had no powers to dismiss the constituent assembly, which was duty-bound to prepare a constitution for the country.

[It is available on record that the executive were not allowing Maulvi Tameezuddin Khan to approach the Chief Court of Sindh to file a writ petition against the Governor General Ghulam Mohammad. Even so, his advocate (Sharifuddin Pirzada)'s car was hit on his way to the court.

To avoid executive's pressures, Maulvi Khan managed to get a lady 'burqa' to disguise himself as a woman, got cycle rickshaw and reached Registrar's office. There he got services of one other advocate named Manzar Alam. The Registrar was former CJP Sajjad Ali Shah's father in those days. When the two were in Registrar's office, the information reached Chief Commissioner Karachi (either Hashim Raza or A T Naqvi) who immediately phoned the Registrar to refuse the petition. The Registrar did not heed to the Chief Commissioner's instructions.

Angrily, the Registrar was 'ordered' to come to Commissioner's office with that petition, which was also turned down. The Registrar, in the meantime, took the petition, entered it in diary register and immediately placed it before the CJ Sindh Chief Court, Mr Constantine.

Afterwards, a five member's bench had announced relief for Maulvi Khan declaring Governor General's orders void. The government went in appeal before the Federal Court where Justice Ch Munir had given that 'stinking' decision in favour of GG Ghulam Mohammad while setting aside the verdict of Sindh Chief Court.]

In the contemporary legal history of Pakistan, the first argument against uncomfortable kind of judicial activism was brought forward in the name of 'principle of tri-chotomy' of powers and sovereignty of parliament as contained in the constitution of Pakistan under which the Apex Court had to respect the Parliament and the executive. The fact remains that the Parliament can dilute the powers and functions of the judiciary by amending the constitution but such amendments themselves are open to judicial review. They forget that to fill the vacuum resulting from any legislative-executive mal-functioning, the judiciary has to assert itself by providing relief to the sufferers of tyranny and by interpreting the respective laws.

Normally judicial activism is being exercised by the Supreme Court under Article 184, which is its original jurisdiction and the actions are initiated as *suo moto*. It empowers the court to make an order if it 'considers' that a question of public importance is involved or the fundamental rights are violated. It is for the apex court to decide whether the matter is important enough or not. The real power of activism comes with Articles 187 and 190 by virtue of which the Supreme Court issues all such directions, orders and decrees and can secure the attendance of any person, call for any document, any executive or judicial authority to reach a just decision.

In Pakistan's recent judicial activism history, one can mention the case of *Darshan Masih v The State* in 1990, where the Supreme Court had converted a telegram sent by bonded labourers into a writ petition. Then the Supreme Court rapidly started using its prerogative taking up cases on the basis of letters and media reports. Earlier in 1988 when the Supreme Court decided Benazir Bhutto v Federation of Pakistan (**PLD 1988 SC 416**), these broad constitutional powers were 'discovered' to provide justice to the people in public interest litigations.

Though judicial activism continued to be exercised since early years and CJP Sajjad Ali Shah was considered pioneer to give the term a meaningful interpretation but CJP Iftikhar M Chaudhry is the judge who has been using its jurisdiction at optimum level.

CJP Iftikhar M Chaudhry could not prove him bold enough during his earlier days of being Chief Justice; reference can be made towards **bail of Javaid Hashmi, who was refused justice** during days of Gen Musharraf and spent five years in jail on charges of false 'mutiny'. It was shameful for that time's judiciary. But later, CJP Chaudhry started taking *suo moto* actions on large scale giving weight to the public complaints, of course, without much annoying the military rule of Gen Musharraf barring one or two cases like of Pakistan Steel Mills.

Chief Justice Saeeduzzaman Siddiqui personally was against any kind of judicial activism. In his view the *Court should not speak itself unless moved by some one to speak*; Supreme Court's duty is to work under the Constitution and to uphold rule of law but some one have to come to the court with his grievances. CJP Siddiqui held the opinion that 'judicial activism' indirectly means that the court is going beyond its limits and thus 'judicial restraints' should be the real goal.

In the Code of Conduct for superior judges, it is clearly written that judges should avoid earning 'fame' and judicial activism has always been used in Pakistan by judges who wanted to go for 'instant fame' by picking up mostly non-issues. See below:

[*On 5*th *June 2011, Atiqa Odho, a well known TV & film actress, was caught at Islamabad Airport for possessing two bottles of imported liquor while travelling to Karachi from Islamabad by PK-319 flight. She was allowed to go by the officials concerned without taking any action apparently due to 'many' influences.*

*CJP J Iftikhar M Chaudhry took suo moto notice of the incident and the case was taken up for hearing on 8*th *June 2011. Officials of the Federal Board of Revenue and Airport Security Force submitted their explanations to a bench headed by the CJP himself. They said the matter was settled without informing the police as the value of recovered liquor was very little.*

Despite suo moto, Miss Odho remained blessed – no action.]

During CJP Sajjad Ali Shah's time, the media had taken it as 'judicial terrorism' when certain Articles of the Constitution, freshly passed by the then Parliament, were suspended by the Supreme Court. How could a court do that; there was very thin line difference between the two.

First time in the judicial history of Pakistan, a special cell was created in the Supreme Court by the CJP Iftikhar M Chaudhry, in which media reports were examined, analyzed and judicial actions recommended there upon. 21,000 media reports and complaints were taken up for *suo moto* action and 6,000 were finalized within three months. This new wave of activism created disturbance among the police because in 90% cases senior police officers were called and bullied in the apex Court.

On the other hand, when SC's instructions were acted upon, the executive authorities got furious thus the officer class could not go happy with CJP Iftikhar Ch. In *famous Monnu Bhel case*, one DIG Saleemullah Khan appeared before the SC and was harassed by his seniors and the Sindh Government. He went back to Sindh and acted upon the instructions of the SC. The Then Chief Minister Arbab Ghulam Rahim got angrier and placed him under suspension. The CJP could not save the senior police officer nor could speak against the CM. How brave our judiciary was then; many officers like Saleemullah Khan had lost their jobs [of course coupled with grace] during such *'dispensation of justice'*.

A fundamental equivalence of this issue, which is universally accepted too, is that an act of parliament is considered valid only if it does not conflict with the main spirit of the prevailing constitution. If a dispute arises as to the validity of an act of parliament, as was seen in the 18th Constitutional Amendment; or of an executive order, as was seen in *'out of turn promotions' of the secretaries by PM Gilani in 2010*; it is for the superior judiciary to interpret but this interpretation should be within the limits laid down by the constitution itself.

Similarly, the courts cannot assume the power of amending the constitution. The Supreme Court had held in **State vs Ziaur Rahman and others** that:

> *'In the case of a Government set up under a written Constitution, the functions of the State are distributed among the various State functionaries and their respective powers defined by the Constitution.... It cannot, therefore, be said that a Legislature, under a written Constitution possesses the same powers of 'omnipotence' as the British Parliament. Its powers have necessarily to be derived from, and to be circumscribed within the four corners of the written Constitution.'*
> (PLD 1973 SC 49)

JUDICIAL ACTIVISM IN RECENT TIMES:

In the contemporary judicial history of Pakistan, the year 2006 was probably a year of judicial activism as numerous high-profile cases with political, social, economic, constitutional and several human rights cases were taken up by the Supreme Court under its *suo moto* jurisdiction. The Chief Justice:

- Saved the Pakistan Steel Mills by striking down its illegal sell-off though political mins keep many reservations [*though subsequently the same PSM became a huge burden on Pakistan's economy – a real parasite*].

- Activated state machinery against the flow of counterfeit and bogus drugs.

- Cancelled the conversion of public parks into commercial ventures (like McDonald's outlet in F-9 National Park Islamabad; ***though it is still there***).

- Imposed ban on kite flying (referred to a case in the Punjab province) but here the people did not show any respect for the SC.

- Gave ruling against the notorious custom of *vanni* to stop the marriages of compensation.

- Stopped a number of projects which were proven hazardous to the environment.

- Ordered the authorities to recover the missing persons (specially pointing towards selling off certain people to the US by Gen Musharraf).

- Directed for closure of substandard private institutions & medical colleges (Baqai Medical College Islamabad was one of them).

- And above all, decided a number of human rights cases of abduction, elopement, marriages out of free will, detention, torture and murder etc.

Once in 2005, Gen Musharraf, in the capacity of President, had filed a reference against the **Hasba Bill**, which was passed by the NWFP Assembly, seeking opinion of the Supreme Court. A five-member bench of the apex court had directed the NWFP governor not to sign the bill.

Similarly, after an earthquake of 8th October 2005 the residents of a collapsed 10-storeyed Margalla Towers in Islamabad had filed a petition against the CDA and the building contractors, alleging that the respondents had failed to protect their fundamental rights of life, liberty and property. The Supreme Court had taken cognizance and ordered the CDA to provide accommodation to the displaced families of the Margalla Towers by acquiring residences of almost equal size.

To adjudicate maximum number of cases for clearance of the huge backlog, two additional judges were inducted on ad hoc basis. At the start of 2006 there were 19,000 cases pending in higher judiciary which, despite institution of fresh cases, were reduced to 13,876 cases till the last day of December that year.

A Human Rights Cell was established in the Supreme Court, which received hundreds of applications and complaints. An International Judicial Conference was also held in Islamabad in August 2006 in which about 75 delegates from 35 countries of all the continents participated.

During the year 2006, the Supreme Court had cancelled the lease deal of a CDA Public Park for its subsequent conversion into mini golf club, being contrary to fundamental rights of the general public. In another case, the Supreme Court on 15th December 2006 had ordered the private medical colleges to comply with the criteria of Pakistan Medical and Dental Council (PMDC) and ruled that after 14th August 2007 no substandard institution would be allowed to function in the country. The court, in a *suo moto* notice had also directed the Ministry of Health & authorities concerned to implement ban on smoking at public places.

Once the apex court was moved for abolishing the custom of *'vanni'* and *'swara'* (a mode of dispute settlement in which under aged girls of offenders family are given in marriage to the family of victim as a compensation for the crime committed by male members of the family), prevalent in some rural areas of the country. The Court directed the inspectors-general of police of the four provinces and the Northern Areas to protect women from being given in marriage as ransom being an un-Islamic and un-human custom. Though practically, this cruel custom is still there but at least the Court had taken notice of it and a law is there to curb this trend.

In nut shell, judicial activism is the last refuge against an arbitrary and irresponsible government. A vigilant but upright judiciary upholds the constitution, confining the legislative and executive to their constitutional spheres. However, if judicial activism is hijacked by individuals for personal exaggerations and not for the common man, then it can play havoc, disorder and disaster [as like cases of a girl's abduction or *karokaree* case in southern Punjab]. Theoretically, it must act as a check against the privileged power abusers of the society like the crime and drug mafias, corrupt parliamentarians and the influential law twisters [like in Steel Mills & Bank of Punjab cases].

More importantly, in ending 2007, before the expiration of five year term of Gen Musharraf as President, petitions were filed in the Supreme Court of Pakistan opposing his eligibility to contest the presidential election while also being the COAS. Just days before the pronouncement of court decision on these petitions, on 3rd November 2007, Gen Musharraf suddenly issued a Proclamation of Emergency (POE) and the Constitution was suspended. The international community was at a loss to understand the cause and course of the General's action amidst hearing of election petitions against him.

Gen Musharraf stated that *the action became imperative to end judicial activism and the hurdles which the Supreme Court was creating in the Government effort to return to complete civil rule.* Quoting President Abraham Lincoln in support of his action the General declared that:

'He, too, '*broke laws and usurped the rights of the people to preserve the Constitution. On one hand, Pakistan's sovereignty has been seriously challenged by terrorists and on the other the country's system is semi-paralyzed due to judicial activism.*'

In the back drop of 'judicial activism', the view of police beating the lawyers in public was a sight never seen before in Pakistan. Thousands of protesting lawyers were clubbed and tear gased. In Multan, two judges had fled the court on being threatened by the lawyers.

Some times the courts themselves provide a chance for the people to think adversely. As mentioned in earlier pages, it is on record that loans worth billions of rupees were waived off by commercial banks for political reasons. The Parliament have never taken cognizance of the matter but despite its own remarks of 22nd December 2009, the apex court never tried to touch the issue seriously; thus conveying a message to the people of Pakistan that the higher courts in poor countries are also meant for the rich and influential classes only; poor people's savings are eaten up, then what.

JUDICIAL ACTIVISM vs EXECUTIVE:

The problem comes that if the courts remain silent on the questionable or unjust acts of the government and do not exercise their constitutional jurisdiction; they are accused of being docile and subservient to the rulers. And if they do, they are charged with having a political agenda and are labelled with judicial activism. It is argued that judicial activism would undermine the authority of the parliament and the executive and thus weaken democracy. Speaking truly, such judicial activism is the effect rather than cause of ineffective role of both parliament and the executive.

Soon after his appointment as the Chief Justice of Pakistan (CJP) in 2005, Iftikhar M Chaudhry opted to exercise the court's *suo moto* powers. Many of these cases involved abuse of police powers, manipulation of legal processes by rural landed elites and corruption in the bureaucracy. These cases won the CJP & the SC increasing popularity amongst the populace as well as grudging respect amid the legal fraternity.

For instance, the Supreme Court set aside privatization of Pakistan Steel Mills which ruffled feathers of the Government and caused annoyance, especially for the Prime Minister who was responsible for making the order; the Government got wary of the CJP's style of judicial activism. The SC questioned freely high Government officials and threatened action against them in case they failed to show the legality of their actions; such exercise of judicial independence had upset the military regime.

Another issue; PM Nawaz Sharif was deposed in a bloodless coup by Gen Musharraf, he was charged and convicted on charges of tax evasion and treason. Instead of suffering imprisonment, by mutual agreement, Nawaz Sharif opted to go abroad on 10-year exile in December 2000. The 10-year exile term was brought to an end **on 23rd August 2007**, when the Supreme Court allowed his return to Pakistan. However, his return to Pakistan on 10th September 2007 proved even shorter when the police within hours of his landing at Islamabad Airport ordered him to board another flight for Saudi Arabia.

On 11th September 2007, Nawaz Sharif filed a contempt petition against the Government of Pakistan for refuting SC orders which was admitted. *On 17th October 2007* there was seen confrontation between Gen Musharraf and the judiciary when the CJP sought to pin point the official responsible for deportation of Nawaz Sharif in violation of its order.

The said tussle went on till *30th October 2007* when it was ascertained that PM Shaukat Aziz was ultimately responsible for that deportation. The Attorney General conceded government's guilt and promptly requested an adjournment to enable him to discuss the issue at the high-est level. The court granted it until *8th November 2007* but it became obvious that the CJP would issue a notice of contempt to the Prime Minister.

This escalated judicial activism was another reason to proclaim emergency on 3rd November 2007 because the military ruler took it as a revengeful behaviour on the part of CJP in the back drop of March 2007 events in which J Iftikhar M Chaudhry was sent home.

However, the intelligentsia and sane minds were of the view that the CJP should not have granted favour to Nawaz Sharif on 23rd August 2007 as it was an un-called for injunction. There was ample documentary evidence that Nawaz Sharif had willingly maneuvered that 10 year exile through their Saudi Royal guarantors. Its full details have already been mentioned in an earlier chapter but only to supplement it; the CJP had chosen that way at its own by calling Nawaz Sharif before time just to flare up the sentiments of Gen Musharraf and to fight him jointly.

In November 2007, Gen Musharraf announced he would introduce a constitutional amendment to withdraw the Supreme Court's *suo moto* powers under the authority of his Provisional Constitutional Order (PCO) but refrained due to timely advice of his legal advisors.

As per Daily *'Dawn' of 24*th *December 2009*:

> *'Given the broken system of governance in many areas, judicial intervention is probably necessary in many instances. But there is a thin line between wanted judicial intervention and unwanted judicial activism that encroaches on domains of the other institutions of the state.*

> *Clearly, the constitution has made the judiciary the guarantor of the fundamental rights of the people and given the superior judiciary wide-ranging suo motu powers. However, the judges must pay heed to the fact that along with duties to the people, they also have a responsibility to fashion a stronger democratic and constitutional system.'*

In Pakistan's contemporary history, its parliament remained silent over subversion of the constitution and dismissal of the judges by Gen Musharraf on 3rd November 2007. The Supreme Court had to invalidate and reverse those acts the same day. Similarly, when the NRO came up for hearing in the Supreme Court in December 2009, the court could either validate or invalidate it. Validation of the NRO was not possible because the sitting PPP government could not get it through its own elected Parliament; but targeting one person [Mr Zardari] leaving aside the whole lot of 8041 beneficiaries was also questionable.

*On 13*th *February 2010,* the CJP Iftikhar Chaudhry had rejected President Zardari's decision to elevate two judges of the Lahore High Court, including the Chief Justice of Punjab by taking *suo moto* notice of the presidential action. This move had shaken certain heads on two counts. Firstly, this move from the President House should have been resolved in a mutual official meeting or through correspondence and *suo-moto* could have been avoided.

Secondly, the CJ of the LHC Justice Kh Sharif was kept there because PML(N) wanted him there. It was thus considered as if the CJP Mr Chaudhry was trying to impose *'judicial dictatorship'* in the country. It was alleged that elevation of a junior judge of the LHC to the Supreme Court while retaining a senior judge, Kh Sharif, as Chief Justice of Lahore High Court was in itself a violation of the apex court's own verdicts of 1996 & 2002 which had set out the principle of seniority for appointment and elevation of the superior court judges.

By stretch of legal discussion, one may opine that verdicts of 1996 & 2002 have no explicit direction or connotation in the above maxim but one thing was quite obvious that *Kh Sharif was not being kept in the LHC Punjab on merit; he was Sharif family's judge and they wanted to see him there.*

[The long march of 16th March 2009, coupled with smart political intents of Nawaz Sharif brought Justice Iftikhar M Chaudhry's team back in saddles but subsequent behaviour of some of them raised serious questions about independence of judiciary. The name of Kh Sharif, Chief Justice of the Lahore High Court [LHC], was one which had spoiled the basic spirit of whole Lawyer's Movement (2007-09) when he openly sided with the ruling PML(N). Most of the bar members were disappointed while saying that *'the current judiciary is no different than its predecessors'* because the requirements of due process were not observed and the neutrality of the judges was not at all visible.

The assertions by CJ LHC, Kh Sharif were absolutely deplorable. Making statements regarding a defendant, Rehman Malik, in a case because of being associated with the PPP was taken as absolutely contrary to the judicial responsibility required of judges.

On this particular issue, certain bar councils and NGOs had asked for the CJP's resignation due to his inability to maintain the independence and impartiality of Pakistan's judiciary. Due to the fact that the movement in which he was restored was *NOT AT ALL political but a [Black Coat] Lawyer's Movement joined by the civil society,* all its supporters and enemies who were expected to be tried in the

Supreme Court required the CJP Mr Chaudhry to reclaim himself as an independent entity.]

The **US Report** on *'Pakistan's Rule of Law Assessment'* of **November 2008** had mentioned that the superior courts have the power to review legislation, over executive action and enforcement of fundamental rights set out in the Constitution. The power of the Chief Justices to initiate 'public interest litigation' is OK, however, the principle of judicial independence has been strong in rhetoric but weak in implementation. The Report categorically stated that:

'Pakistan's superior courts have been reluctant to challenge the executive to enforce fundamental rights, and have not invalidated any major legislation on account of inconformity with fundamental rights provisions. The dominance of the executive over the judicial branch has been apparent at all levels, with judges from the lower courts to the higher courts often succumbing to political pressure throughout Pakistan's history.

The lack of clarity and transparency in processes for the appointment and removal of judges has played a central role in enabling the executive to influence the judiciary. Articles 177 & 193 of the Constitution stand witness to it that the President and the Governors have 'much say' into the judges appointments [now the situation stands changed after 18th Constitutional Amendment].

Though 1996's 'Judges Case' is in vogue to regulate the judicial appointments but in practice, these principles have rarely been applied, and the selection process has largely been a product of back-room manoeuvring by various interests rather than an open process. There have been several incidents available in this regard.'

Thus, looking into the case from judiciary's viewpoint, one may like to approve Supreme Court's activism. In the famous 'Judges Case' of March 1996, the then Chief Justice Sajjad Ali Shah had declared that the CJP would have primacy in the appointment of judges to the superior judiciary. The 'consultation' with him by the executive regarding the appointment of judges, would have to be *'purposive, meaningful and consensual'*. This case had effectively put an end to the executive practice of appointment of judges to the higher judiciary by over-riding the advice of the Chief Justice of Pakistan.

Due credit should be given to the CJP Sajjad Ali Shah who was the first Chief Justice to introduce a meaningful judicial activism or who had brought a *'one man judicial revolution'* in the country. Chief Justices

Committee was also formed to take notice of excesses of the executive side where needed though the public could not see any tangible cognizance on that count. It was CJP Sajjad Ali Shah who in 1996 had forced the PPP government to promulgate the Legal Reforms Ordinance 1996, which separated the judiciary from the executive at the lower level.

Coming back, the fact remained that Nawaz Sharif of the PML(N) had decided to openly side with the judiciary in the aforesaid battle on the issue of raising two LHC judges to the Supreme Court between the two giants. The PPP had claimed that the Chief Justice was consulted in that regard but his recommendation was rejected by the president as he was the final authority to appoint and elevate judges of the superior courts. Contrarily, the CJP was contemplating to initiate contempt of court proceedings against President Zardari and PM Gilani for overlooking his recommendations for elevation of the two judges; one of them was consistently close to the Sharif brothers.

Contempt of Court proceedings in such administrative matters were not called for in fact but the judiciary had [always] opted to threat so. PPP's version was that as per constitutional provisions, the Chief Justice was only a consultee, and it was the President who had the ultimate authority to take a final decision. However, the CJP's action of suspending the presidential orders within three hours of their issuance was described by the PPP circles as a *'judicial martial law'*, as opined by Ayaz Amir in his article published on *15*th *February 2010* in *'the News'*.

Waseem A Qureshi, in his article available at internet rightly said that:

'Judicial activism has never been a feature of Pakistan's polity. Instead, our judicial history is replete with landmark decisions which legitimized executive arbitrariness and extra-constitutional adventures. Our higher judiciary has condoned, at various times, the dissolution of the first Constituent Assembly and the proclamation of martial laws in 1958, 1969 and 1977.

It would be short-sighted to put all the blame for the above on the judiciary alone. A free and assertive judiciary does not grow in vacuum. It needs a free and democratic dispensation to nurture it.'

There are no two opinions that the Supreme Court of Pakistan wanted to inject spirit of judicial activism by describing *'The Court wants that political institutions, elected representatives and government officials should perform their duties in a befitting manner which was very critical for good governance, socio-economic development and political development'*.

To an extent it meant that the judiciary could even make law and implement when the other branches fail to do so. The idea was probably imported from India where it was upheld by various Supreme Court judgments (*Vishaka v. State of Rajasthan, Vineet Narain v. Union of India*).

However, we preferred to move a step further. In India, the Supreme Court had held that questions of policy would not be interfered with and were the specific domain of the executive. In 2009, Pakistani higher judiciary interfered in the executive domain to determine an appropriate price of sugar which was not their prerogative; apparently leading to a conflict between the executive's and judiciary's realm of working and power. Even in India there was lot of criticism on such judicial verdicts.

Hussain Zaidi, in his essay published in the *'Dawn' of 3*rd *January 2010,* rightly opined that:

> '.... *while parliament can rename the Supreme Court as the Federal Court or fix the number of judges, it cannot abolish the court itself. The former will be a change within the basic framework of the constitution and hence an amendment; however, the later will not qualify as an amendment to the constitution.*'

Wise judicial minds avoid such clashes in the name of judicial activism sometimes taken as interference by many.

OPPOSITE SCHOOL OF THOUGHT:

One school of thought, of *CJ Saeeduzzaman Siddiqui*, keeps the opinion that excessive judicial activism undermines the independence of judiciary. The more a judiciary reacts to popular sentiment, the more prone it will become to deciding cases on the basis of what the public opinion wants and not on the basis of what the law says and justice commands.

Also, by allowing itself to be influenced by popular opinion, the judiciary permits outside interference in its affairs as well as lack of independence in dispensing justice. The *cases of sugar price fixing & Petrol pricing* can be cited again in that context.

In 2009, the LHC took suo *motu notice* of rising sugar prices and suddenly fixed the price of sugar at Rs:40 per kilogram when its market price was 50-60 rupees. The producers appealed to the SC, which upheld the LHC decision. This only made matters worse, leading to the sudden disappearance of sugar from the market and an increase in its price to almost double of what it was before the high court intervention. When sugar came in the market again, its price started from Rs: 70 per kg.

In this regard *'The Friday Times' of 19*th *March 2010* is referred which had held that:

> *'Unlike elected governments who are subject to recall by the masses, there is no equivalent mechanism for correction by the public when it comes to judges.*

> *If the judiciary becomes overly fond of the spotlight, there will come a time when the same forces of public passion that today shout slogans in favour of judicial independence will instead riot in opposition. It would be better for all concerned if that day never came.'*

When the higher judiciary becomes controversial, its reputation is damaged and public confidence in its impartiality suffers. Dissenting opinions are often seen as a barometer of how independent a judiciary is.

Since 64 years our judiciary could not earn the name of neutrality, fairness and fearlessness; it always compromised with the rulers, whether civil or military, on one pretext or the other. A very few judges could be termed as respectable in the chequered history of Pakistan while the main lot never realized that a judge is remembered by his decisions not by face or tenure.

PPP vs JUDICIARY ROW IN 2008 -13:

When the two PPP stalwarts, Sharjeel Memon and Taj Haider, were issued contempt notices for organizing public protests and processions of PPP workers in all over Sindh, some PPP worker *circulated on 29*th *March 2011*, the history [up till then] in the media, of the alleged mis-judgments, often referring to the sayings of Maula Bux Chandio, a parliamentarian of the PPP and later Federal Law Minister of Pakistan. Here are the scripts:

- ..... Contrarily, NRO case taken up. The case was not an issue; the government, over the signals of dismay however, decided to maintain good relations with apex court and submitted in the court room that the Ordinance may be declared void ab-initio, but the court decided to prolong the process and go into nitty-gritty.

- Even a person like Justice (rtd) Fakhruddin G Ebrahim was angry on the proceedings. *'There is no point to prolong the proceedings when the government was willing to declare the Ordinance void-ab initio'*, he commented when court started detailed hearing of NRO case later.

- Justice Ramday went to the extent of very personal remarks [during hearing of NRO Case] like *"apnay client (Asif Zardari) se kaho k Swiss banks main deposited 60 million dollars return karay; apni bhi jan churai aur hamari bhi choray"*. (Tell your client, Asif Zardari, to return 60 million dollars deposited with Swiss banks & get himself off the hook and also save us from undue bother).

- Further moving in the same direction, an action was ordered against Justice [rtd] Qayyum, the former Attorney General who had written letter to Swiss authorities for withdrawal of cases against Mr Zardari on the verbal instruction of the then President Gen Musharraf but without formal approval of the federal cabinet.

- No action was however, directed against former **Attorney General Ch Farooq** who himself wrote letter to Swiss authorities for legal assistance in the same cases without any order or formal approval of the cabinet of Mian Nawaz Sharif. He *happened to be elder brother of Justice Ramday and this was the point of major favour or clash*.

- Subsequently the statements of Khwaja Sharif, other remarks of Justice Ramday and CJP, and other brother judges further fuelled the fire.

- The onslaught did not stop there. The apex court and Lahore High Court at a very high pace took certain cases against the federal government and adverse judgments were passed, but there was no follow up *in Punjab Bank case which was under hearing and an anti Shahbaz Sharif statement was recorded by Hamesh Khan*, the former president of the Bank.

- In these circumstances, Justice Ramday's appointment and pressure exerted for appointments of judges in High Courts on which PPP government had serious reservations had increased the tensions. The issue was resolved with the intervention of Ch Aitzaz, but later he was kept out of the circle close to CJP and Hamid Khan, Akram Ch and Qazi Anwar filled his place.

- Moreover, 18th amendment case was decided in a particular manner and then the decision of parliamentary committee on judges appointment was turned down.

- Certain contract appointments, extension in services etc were terminated by the Supreme Court while the same principle was not applied on Justice Ramday. CJP recommended his name again for appointment as adhoc judge, though Supreme Court Bar Association had strongly objected.

• This principle was also not applied on Registrar Supreme Court who was on a two years extension then.

• ....and in this scenario a decision against Syed Deedar Hussain Shah triggered volcano in Sindh and a complete strike was observed on PPP Sindh chapter's call. The court moved rapidly and contempt notices were issued while *no suo moto notice was taken against the reaction on court decision in Raymond Davis case.*

• Taj Haider and Sharjeel Memon were summoned to appear before the apex court on 1st April; PPP considered the court decision and all steps part of a game believing that *the superior judiciary sided with rival PML(N);* this was an alarming situation.

What judicial norms Pakistan's SC built that way, only time would tell?

The apex court knew that Sharjeel Memon was just an MPA and was not holding any portfolio in Sindh but when contempt notice was issued to him, he was made Sindh's Information Minister.

[*He was actually made the Information Minister only when the SC had issued him contempt of court notice.*]

Admittedly the said gesture was posed on the orders of the Presidency just to place another note of confrontation on record muffled with utter humiliation. As earlier stated that when Sharjeel Memon attended the apex court after many weeks, the CJP Iftikhar M Chaudry remarked that:

'*After fighting with the judiciary you have become minister in the Sindh – [good luck].*'

OATH OF AGP AKHTAR B RANA:

On 27th **August 2011,** the Chief Justice Iftikhar M Chaudhry took oath from Akhtar Buland Rana, the new Auditor General of Pakistan [AGP] in his chambers in pursuance of notification dated 23rd August 2011 from the Presidency. The CJP, in performance of administrative functions under Article 168(2) of the Constitution, was required to administer the oath.

In the instant case, however, before administering oath, the CJP sent a letter to the President based on reports of the ISI, FIA and comments received from the former AGP in response to a notice issued on an anonymous application received in the Human Rights Cell of the apex court. The CJP wrote to the President Zardari:

> "It is to be noted that once a person is appointed Auditor General and administered oath of office by the Chief Justice, he enjoys the status of holder of a constitutional office. His removal is only possible by adhering to the procedure prescribed for removal of Judges of the Superior Courts before the Supreme Judicial Council [SJC] in terms of Article 209 of the Constitution.
>
> Being the Chief Justice and Chairman of the SJC, while discharging my duties and performing my functions, I honestly consider it necessary to bring it into the notice of the competent authority about the credentials of Mr M Akhtar Buland Rana, which, I believe, perhaps were not in the notice of the office, which processed his case.
>
> However, if, on having taken into consideration the .... facts, the competent authority still desires that he should be administered the oath, I may be informed accordingly."

The response of the President was received along with communication from the Prime Minister's Secretariat. The president wrote back to the CJP, saying that:

> 'Mr Rana is appropriate for the post and accusations against him were never proven right. He is the senior most officer of the audit department and according to service rules, his dual nationality can not be considered a hamper while the accusation of holding fake national identity card was also proved wrong.'

President Zardari also rejected the sexual harassment allegation against Rana saying that the investigation into the matter proved it false.

While accepting the president's response, the chief justice decided to hold the oath taking ceremony on 27th August 2011 afternoon.

However, the appointment of the new AGP became a simmering point of contention for the government; being lambasted by National Assembly Opposition Leader Ch Nisar Ali Khan, who also was the Chief of the Public Accounts Committee (PAC). PM Gilani had appointed Mr Rana as new AGP replacing Tanvir Ali Agha, who had earlier resigned amidst a controversy.

Tanvir Ali Agha was forced to leave AGP's office prematurely due to multiple factors including upcoming audit reports on multi-billion scams of NICL and the Hajj Scandal in which AGP Agha's cooperation with the Public Accounts Committee [PAC] had embarrassed the government. Secondly, Agha was sworn in as the 16th AGP for five years on 20th July 2007. According to the Constitution, he could remain in office for five years or until he attained 65 years of age. His 5-year term was ending in July 2012 but on 14th November 2011 he was going 65; thus Agha had lost only three months, nothing else.

Mr Rana, reportedly a close friend of the premier's younger brother Mujtaba Gilani, was promoted to grade-22 a few weeks earlier along with other seven bureaucrats. The government insisted that the appointment of any person to the key post was the sole prerogative of the prime minister.

PM Gilani defended his decision over Akhtar Buland Rana's appointment, saying that the official was a *"person of integrity and the senior-most officer in the Auditor General's office."* Nisar opposed Rana's appointment and dissolved the sub-committees of PAC in protest. The media had trumpeted against Mr Rana that he kept a Canadian nationality also without seeking prior permission from the government and travelled abroad on three Pakistani passports and two NI cards.

The CJP had written the letter to President Zardari after the ISI and the FIA had sent their reports on Rana's credentials. However, the fact remained that the CJP had no prerogative to ask for such reports at their own from the ISI or the FIA because there was no FORMAL petition before the SC challenging Mr Rana's promotion to grade 22 or his appointment as AGP.

The SC Registrar said the CJP had sought report on an anonymous application sent to the HR cell of the Supreme Court. The intelligentsia opined that the SC should not have done so; even though the SC or the CJP could take appropriate action in any matter simply by stretching their jurisdiction under 'human rights' or equality or fairness etc available in the Constitution. Where the state affairs would end then?

Scenario 82

BLOW TO JUDICIAL HIERARCHY:

AG ANWAR MANSOOR RESIGNS:

On 3rd **April 2010,** Attorney General [AG] Anwar Mansoor Khan tendered his resignation citing Law Minister Babar Awan as well as the law ministry's discretion as reasons. He submitted his resignation to Prime Minister Gilani adding *'whether it is accepted or not, I'm not joining.'*

AG Mansoor needed some documents in connection with NRO proceedings against President Zardari which the Law Ministry were not providing him. In fact neither the president nor the prime minister ever showed their confidence in him. A week earlier, AG Mansoor had stunned the 7 -judges SC bench by saying that:

> *'He was facing non cooperative attitude on part of the law minister for not handing over to him necessary information and communications to complete legal process of sending letters to the Swiss authorities for re-opening $60 million graft cases involving President Asif Ali Zardari.'*

AG Mansoor's resignation was an utter embarrassment for the government. Allegedly, when the AG asked the Law Minister to hand over the Swiss record, the later responded: *"Over my dead body"*. Years back the law ministry had opposed a proposal by Farooq Naek, the then counsel for Mr Zardari, for withdrawing the cases from Swiss courts.

"The law ministry or the law minister," inquired the shocked bench. "The law minister," AG Mansoor had replied calmly. The bench comprised Chief Justice Iftikhar M Chaudhry, Justice Mian Shakirullah Jan, Justice Tassaduq Hussain Jillani, Justice Chaudhry Ijaz Ahmed, Justice Tariq Parvez, Justice Asif Saeed Khan Khosa and Justice Khalil-ur-Rehman Ramday.

> [*The irony of fate was that Presiden Zardari and the PPP did not acknoledge the faithfulness, devotion, sacrifices and loyalty of that Law Minister Babar Awan when he was sidelined a year after quite unceremonially.*]

The AG urged the bench that, as per Federal Law Secretary's version, it was the federal government's decision and that he had no further explanation to offer. The Law Secretary, when summoned by the SC, told that he had received three sealed envelopes from the foreign office last night. He opened the one addressed to him as the other letters were addressed to the Swiss and other foreign authorities, no one had touched them. Also that he had to seek instructions from the prime minister.

JUDICIAL CRISIS IN AJK:

On 10th May 2009, one Ibrahim Zia moved a petition on behalf of Justice Manzoor H Gilani to the Supreme Court of Pakistan urging the CJP that:

> '......You have perhaps not noticed or ignored the brewing injustices in AJK [Azad Jammu & Kashmir], particularly in the appointments in the superior judiciary made during the era of Gen Musharaff and PM Shaukat Aziz, which are still continuing despite all resentments against it for the last three years. Judiciary in Pakistan is restored but AJK is put in dustbin, perhaps not deemed responsibility of Pakistan, which is grossest mistake.
>
> We are sending herewith a petition filed by a senior judge of AJK Supreme Court, in the Supreme Court of Pakistan, Justice Manzoor Hussain Gilani, who is a victim of grave injustice, judiciary of AJK is paralyzed and people of the state are dejected.
>
> Please .... get it rectified before it is too late. Another petition is also in offing by another senior judge of the AJK HC, Sardar M Nawaz khan who is also made a victim.'

The above mentioned gross injustice was referred to one **Justice Riaz Akhtar Chaudhry** who was first appointed as judge of AJK's Supreme Court on 24th September 2006 and then elevated as its Chief Justice within 25 days [*on 20th October 2006*] of his appointment by superseding the senior-most judge of the Supreme Court of AJK Justice Manzoor Hussain Gilani. Justice Gillani was senior to him by six years in judicial service, by more than two years in the Supreme Court. Justice Gilani had knocked the doors of the Supreme Court of Pakistan to seek justice.

Interestingly, a summary bearing number Law-3/3/2002-AJKC (Pt) dated 25th June 2008 was sent to the prime minister of Pakistan but it remained pending due to CJP Iftikhar M Chaudhry's own status in doldrums as he himself was deposed then.

On 24th March 2010, the Supreme Court of Azad Jummu and Kashmir [AJK] pushed constitutional experts in a state of shock when it came at loggerheads with the Supreme Court of Pakistan over an issue of *'unconstitutional appointment'* of the AJK's chief justice.

The incumbent Chief Justice of AJK, Riaz Akhtar Chaudhry, while heading a 3-member bench *on 15th March 2010,* passed an order barring Prime Minister of Pakistan to pass any notification regarding the Chief Justice of AJK. He also restrained the Federal Ministry of Law from issuing any fresh notification and the President of the AJK from administering oath to any judge for the office of the new AJK Chief Justice.

The issue was that the AJK CJ was hearing a case which directly involved his own person and the CJ himself was heading the bench with an ad hoc judge. The ad hoc judge Muhammad Azam Khan's appointment was at the pleasure of the CJ as long as he required him. The Article-IV of the Code of Conduct for Judges says: *"A judge must decline resolutely to act in a case involving his own interests, including those of persons whom he regards and treats as near relatives or close friends."*

[*The Chief Justice of Pakistan Iftikhar M Chaudhry, while hearing a petition challenging the AJK CJ's appointment, had passed remarks about the odd appointment of Justice Riaz Akhtar Chaudhry as the AJK CJ.*]

The order passed by AJK's CJ Riaz Akhtar Chaudhry contained that:

"The Supreme Court of Pakistan has no jurisdiction to entertain any petition regarding appointment of judges of superior courts of AJK. Such kind of petition does not come within the jurisdiction and sphere of Supreme Court of Pakistan.

The Supreme Court of Pakistan has no authority to extend its jurisdiction to the area of Azad Jummu and Kashmir because the territories of Pakistan have been defined in Article 1 of the Constitution of Islamic Republic of Pakistan."

Constitutional experts kept the opinion that the AJK SC was an appellate forum and could not entertain any writ petition and such an order of the AJK CJ was misconduct. Barrister Akram Sheikh was of opinion that *'the status of AJK is like a province and no court of a province could infringe in the jurisdiction of Supreme Court of Pakistan.'*

On 3rd **April 2010**, however, senior judge Manzoor Hussain Gilani took oath as the Chief Justice of AJK Supreme Court. The oath ceremony was held at Muzaffarabad presidency, where the acting President Shah Ghulam Qadir administered oath to Justice Gilani.

The ceremony was attended by PM Raja Farooq, CJ High Court Ghulam Mustafa, a large number of lawyers and other dignitaries. Meanwhile, AJK's PM Raja Farooq Haider sent a reference against CJ Riaz Akhtar Chaudhry to the Supreme Judicial Council.

On 7th **April 2010**, AJK President Raja Zulqarnain reinstated the deposed CJ AJK Riaz Akhtar Chaudhry after consulting legal experts, while AJK Prime Minister Raja Farooq Haider termed the president's decision unconstitutional – it was incumbent upon the president to act upon his advice as per 1974's Constitution of the AJK.

AJK's PM Farooq Haider said in a media conference at Islamabad that Justice Riaz had been ousted on the recommendation of the Supreme Judicial Council and could only be reinstated on the advice of the PM or the SJC. Meanwhile, AJK Legislative Assembly Speaker Shah Ghulam Qadir held that President Zulqarnain had violated Article 7 of the 1974's Constitution of the AJK.

[*In a move to clean up the dirt of Gen Musharraf era, the AJK government in its reference had levelled serious allegations against the CJ AJK Riaz Akhtar, including blasphemy, personal gains by using his office and acting beyond jurisdiction of the Supreme Court to bring it in direct conflict with the Supreme Court of Pakistan.*]

Two days later the AJK's CJ Riaz Akhtar was restricted from functioning by a 3-member bench of Supreme Judicial Council after a reference was filed against him as detailed earlier. Thus the senior most judge of AJK SC, Justice Manzoor Hussain Gilani took oath as chief justice of AJK.

The reference against Justice Chaudhry also included the formation of an unconstitutional monitoring cell and later using it for personal gains; that monitoring cell was declared as unconstitutional in October 2009. Meanwhile, AJK President Zulqarnain called on Pakistan's Prime Minister Gilani, who was the Chairman of the Kashmir Council, to discuss the constitutional cum judicial crisis in AJK; who, however, refused to play a role or interfere in the matter. The background details were:

Justice Gilani was fighting his case since 20th October 2006 when on intervention of the then Director General Military Intelligence [DG MI]

Gen Ijaz Nadeem the judiciary was ruined in AJK and a judge with only 25 days of service in SC was made the Chief Justice – one of the hall marks of Gen Musharraf's governance.

During the 3rd week of April 2010, AJK President Raja Zulqarnain, ruling Muslim Conference's Sardar Atiq Khan and the Federal Minister for Kashmir Affairs Mian Manzoor Watto allegedly tried to influence PM Gilani to avoid approving the SJC recommendations and NOT to sack AJK deposed CJ AJK Justice Riaz Akhtar Chaudhry. The three top minds were eager to allow the incumbent Acting CJ Justice Manzoor Gillani to continue till his superannuation i.e. 7th June 2010 when the deposed CJ could be brought back to take charge of the office of the CJ AJK.

AJK Prime Minister Raja Farooq Haider, however, advised PM Yousaf Raza Gilani that *'the AJK Constitution binds him to approve the SJC recommendations, which has already unanimously sought the sacking of AJK CJ Riaz Akhtar Chaudhry'*.

It is available on record that certain elements in the ISI were also trying to save the AJK's CJ Justice Chaudhry, who was rewarded by Gen Musharraf regime for his "services" rendered in his capacity as Chief Election Commissioner during the general elections of 2006 in AJK as a result of which Muslim Conference had come into power. As mentioned earlier, on 15th March 2010, the Supreme Court of Pakistan sought from the AJK Council the record of AJK CJ appointment but the Acting CJ AJK Justice Riaz Chaudhry, very next day, passed that questionable interim order barring the PM of Pakistan from issuing any order regarding judges appointment in the AJK.

Pakistan's Kashmir Affairs Ministry proposed that Justice Riaz Akhtar would be asked to proceed on leave till the retirement of the incumbent Acting Chief Justice Manzoor Gilani as a way out. However, the PM of AJK, speaker legislative assembly, substantial members of the AJK Muslim Conference and almost all bar councils of AJK were not prepared to show any leniency for the condemned CJ AJK. It is believed that had PM Yousaf Raza Gilani acceded to the advice of his Kashmir ministry, it would have lead to an agitation in favour of independent judiciary in the AJK. Not only the PML(N) Chief Nawaz Sharif but also the President Supreme Court Bar Association Qazi Anwar had supported the PM AJK Raja Farooq Haider's stance for rule of law.

However, such gimmicks also used to be played in Pakistan in the past. See the two episodes from Pakistan's judicial history:

President Rafiq Tarar once availed the audacity to meet the then CJP Justice Ajmal Mian [1998-99] in his chamber at Supreme Court and asked him not to appoint Justice Falak Sher as acting chief justice of Lahore High Court [LHC] as the PML(N) government did not like him. The CJP declined but government went ahead and nominated a junior justice Allah Nawaz as acting chief justice.

During her second term, PM Benazir Bhutto had appointed Justice Sajjad Ali Shah as the CJP by-passing three senior justices. She thought that Justice Shah would return the favour. About two years later, when tensions escalated between the two over appointment of some judges, the Bhutto government decided to strike back.

- Firstly, former Sindh CM Qaim Ali Shah spilled the beans in media claiming that he had persuaded Benazir Bhutto during her first term to elevate Justice Sajjad to the post of CJ of Sindh High Court [SHC].

- In the second term, Benazir didn't want to elevate Justice Sajjad as the CJ of the Supreme Court but he, along with Sindh's CM Abdullah Shah and Federal Defense Minister Aftab Shaban Mirani, persuaded Benzair Bhutto to appoint Sajjad A Shah as CJP.

In the judge's case of March 1996, the SC headed by CJP Sajjad A Shah had ruled that the senior most judge should be considered for appointment *'if there is no valid negative element against him'*. Benazir Bhutto decided to beat CJP Shah with his own stick and filed a review petition asking the apex court whether the rule of seniority was applied to the CJP himself also [*referring to Shah's elevation against the rule of seniority*].

CJP Sajjad A Shah could not be beaten in Benazir Bhutto's era but the CJP had to leave CJP's slot uncremonially in PM Nawaz Sharif's rule on the basis of the same principle he had coined.

TRANSPARENCY IN SELECTION OF JUDGES:

Hussain Zaidi, in daily *'Dawn' of 2nd January 2011* pointed out a very peculiar aspect of this exercise. In his opinion Pakistan has parliamentary system yet key appointments are normally not subject to parliamentary approval. No parliamentary confirmation is needed for the appointment of ministers, Governor State Bank of Pakistan, Chairman of the Federal Public Service Commission, or the AGP etc; then why should judicial appointments be subjected to parliamentary confirmation? Considered opinion was that just to keep the CJP in limits, the authors of the 18th Amendment had pushed the principle of checks & balances in the appointment of judges too far.

Appointment of judges has been a burning issue amongst the CJP and political executives at least since Benazir Bhutto's time. Once, as has been cited elsewhere in detail, the CJP Sajjad Ali Shah had flatly refused to accept any of 'her nominees', neither male nor ladies, during a high level meeting at Governor House Lahore.

The present cause of 2010, however, surfaced after SC's judgment of 31st July 2009 through which about one hundred judges were sent home, though most of them had taken oath under the 1973 Constitution but were punished because they were appointed by Justice A Hameed Dogar, subsequently termed as unconstitutional CJP.

Political intelligentsia could not consume this argument and the CJP Iftikhar M Chaudhry ultimately lost the whole prerogative and power which remained with the CJs even during Gen Musharraf's military rule. The cases of the above referred judges should have been reconsidered by a committee of senior judges on individual basis. They could have been referred to the Supreme Judicial Council under Article 209 of the Constitution and a sane judge in that place could have avoided to be labelled as cunning and revenge scoring Chief Justice in the judicial history of Pakistan whatsoever.

No doubt, due to CJP Iftikhar M Chaudhry's score balancing attitude, the whole superior judiciary lost its esteem, honour and respect. Contrarily, the CJP got an unprecedented unanimous resolution passed by all the judges of the SC that Justice Khalil Ramday and Justice Rehmat H Jaffery be retained as ad hoc judges [*after their retirements in due course*] only because the CJP Iftikhar Chaudhry wanted them.

Justice (retd) Tariq Mehmood had raised a thunderous voice in that connection but of no avail. The whole lawyer's community knew that appointment of a retired SC judge as an ad hoc judge was in violation of Article 182 of the Constitution and the spirit of al-Jihad Trust case both but the CJP Iftikhar M Chaudhry's impulse prevailed.

It was a serious blow to the cause of *'independence of judiciary';* the media and the general populace reacted strongly. Row between the

CJP and President Zardari on an issue of elevation of two judges of the LHC to the SC had also brought humiliations for the apex Court during those days. There are series of examples which can be quoted that independence of the judiciary came into play only to the extent of the PPP's involvement as government or as party starting from the decision on NRO on 16th December 2009. The people also knew that Justice Ramday was a close associate of the CJP, often seen at CJP's bench with another ad hoc judge Ghulam Rabbani.

'Dissenting opinions are often seen as a barometer of how independent a judiciary is', rightly observed **Asad Jamal** in the **Dawn of 21st March 2011.** The media record is available to show that how humiliating attitude Justice Ramday had continuously been showing towards those lawyers arguing against the challenges to the amendment while often and repeatedly describing it as *'an attack on the person of the sitting chief justice'.*

In early 2010, promotions of certain senior civil servants were declared illegal by the SC and also termed extensions of some retired civil servants illegal on the grounds, among others, that *'this promotes nepotism and becomes a barrier in the promotion of other in-service civil servants'*. A fair question was raised that if the judiciary had applied the same principle to itself in J Ramday and J Rehmat H jaffery's cases.

This tendency to create exceptions was not new to the judiciary. In 2009, Justice (retd) Rana Bhagwandas was given a slot of the Chairman Federal Public Service Commission despite the fact that only months before he occupied that chair, the National Judicial Policy (2009) had announced that *'no retired judge of the superior courts shall accept an appointment that is beneath his status or dignity'.*

Another area of concern for the people was the excessive *suo moto* notices that brought the independence and credibility of the Superior Courts at stake. Once more referring to **the Friday Times' dated 19th March 2010** that *'if the judiciary becomes overly fond of the spotlight, there will come a time when the same forces of public passion that today shout slogans in favour of judicial independence will instead riot in opposition. It would be better for all if that day never came'.*

One can see if our superior judiciary was passing through the same phase those days; it should not have gone controversial at least.

Universally acknowledged that judiciary's independence depends on so many other factors like the level of transparency, accountability in the mechanisms used to appoint & remove judges, degree of independence enjoyed by a court's individual judges and protection from the pressure of their peers. In the post 2008 era of Pakistan's judicial history, one year of CJP Abdul Hameed Dogar and three years of CJP Iftikhar M Chaudhry, independence of the Pakistan's judiciary had been seriously compromised on all counts; reasons were manifold.

Referring to the *'Dawn' of 19th May 2011,* Asma Jahangir, president of the Supreme Court Bar Association (SCBA) in 2011, had refused to recommend lawyers for appointment as judges because it was the sitting judges' responsibility to find candidates and evaluate their ability because lawyers appeared in cases before them. It remained a fact that the courts in Malakand Division of Khyber PK were not being made functional for want of judges; no judge was there to hear even appeals.

Also that once in the Sindh High Court, a woman and a minority community judge was shown the exit door on flimsy grounds; the woman judge was relieved on a complaint by her stenographer. Seniors could have been tolerant launching a proper enquiry into the facts.

A paragraph from the Supreme Court of Pakistan's website:

> *"The President of Pakistan appoints Judges to the Supreme Court from amongst the persons recommended by the Chief Justice of Pakistan on the basis of their knowledge and expertise in the different fields of law. The recommendation of Chief Justice is binding on the President and is accepted except for reasons to be recorded by President, which are justifiable."*

The Pakistan Bar Council's [PBC] executive body, in February 2012, unanimously expressed dissatisfaction over the appointment of superior courts' judges by the Judicial Commission of Pakistan (JCP) and declared the process non-transparent. Coming from the PBC, this was quite a serious criticism. The reasons the PBC raised the issue of non-transparency were of the JCP's in-camera proceedings and the judiciary's controversial veto power; thus becoming an institution free of all restraints, constraints and necessary checks and balance mechanism.

Ever since the judiciary was restored in March 2009, it opened itself as pioneering 'pick and choose' justice. Albeit; for appointment of judges, the PBC did not challenge the new procedure muffled in the 18th Amendment but then, at last, opted to become a party to the case. In appointment of judges, the judiciary could earn more credibility by opening its doors to other stake holders too; that would have been the judiciary's true independence.

'Judges must only be appointed on merit and this can only be ensured if the process is transparent', the PBC held.

BRUTUS, YOU TOO [JUDGES SOLD OUT]:

On 16th January 2010, Pakistan's Federal Minister for Housing Rehmatullah Kakar submitted, in reply to a question on record, a list in the Senate containing the names of 53 former judges, including ex-chief justices of the Supreme Court and High Courts, 65 former bureaucrats, 59 journalists and 36 politicians who were given residential plots [*pieces of land distributed by the governments virtually free of cost*] during 1985 - 2001.

The general populace of Pakistan always expected names of journalists, politicians, bureaucrats etc but were not able to grasp that judges would also appear in the list of 'illegal beneficiaries or plunderers' of the national wealth. Judges are supposed to be the individuals meant for taking care of basic provisions of fairness, equality and equal opportunities for all citizens given in the constitution but in Pakistan; *Brutus, you too.*

The said plots were given by the Federal Government Employees Housing Foundation [FGEHF], the Ministry of Housing and Works. The majority of the politicians and the bureaucrats were known to get residential plots allotted in their names from Gen Ziaul Haq to PMs Junejo, Benazir Bhutto to Nawaz Sharif by the Capital Development Authority [CDA] in successive periods of their rule but judges' inclusion was a surprise for all.

The journalists were given plots under the government quota of 2%, but only for those journalists who did not have any house or plot in their names in Islamabad.

Nine former judges of the Supreme Court were part of that list while rest of the judges who got plots belonged to the four provincial higher courts. Former Chief Justice of Pakistan Saeeduzzaman Siddiqui, Justice (retd) Bhagwandas, Justice (retd) Malik Qayyum and former LHC Chief Justice Ch Iftikhar Hussain were among the judges who got plots in Islamabad. Majority of the judges got residential plots in Islamabad while they were serving in the higher and superior judiciary but in other regions of the country.

Following were the names of some more honourable judges who got plots: Justice (retd) Mir Hazar Khan Khoso, Justice Saad Saud Jan, Justice Mukhtar Ahmed Junejo, Justice M Bashir Jahangiri, Justice Abdul Karim Khan Kundi, Justice Mohammad Aqil Mirza, Justice Qazi Mohammad Farooq, Justice Munir A Sheikh, Justice Nazim Hussain Siddiqi, Justice Rashid Aziz Khan, Justice Munwar Ahmed Mirza (BHC), Justice Nawaz Khan Gandapur (PHC), Justice Nawaz Abbasi (LHC), Justice Falaksher, Justice Abdul Hameed Dogar, Justice Khailur Rehman Ramday, Justice Amirul Mulk Mengal and many more.

On 27th November 2010, the allotment of plots to the higher judiciary took a new turn after it was disclosed before the Public Accounts Committee (PAC) that residential plots worth millions of rupees were allotted to three top judges apparently without completing mandatory legal formalities. As the official files of the FGEHF did not contain the dates of birth of the judges, the question of allotments on verbal orders, as opposed to proper procedure, came under discussion.

The set criteria required an applicant to fill out an official form and to give an affidavit that he or she did not own any other plot or house in the city but the three judges, former Chief Justice of Pakistan Sh Riaz Ahmed and LHC judges Faqeer M Khokar and Mumtaz Ali Mirza were allotted a one-kanal plot each on 17th November 2002 in Sector G-14. This playing with rules raised several questions over the allotment process and its transparency especially observed for the honourable judges.

The members of the PAC said that missing records meant that those judges had not filled out the proper official forms and, instead the orders were verbally given and immediately obeyed by the [allotment] authorities. Their dates of birth and joining the judiciary, the basic information required, were altogether missing. Some members passed sarcastic remarks that *'the three judges might have got the second plots'*.

In PAC it was also talked that important documents from Justice Sardar Raza Khan's file were also missing. In Justice Raza's case, the process of balloting was scrapped and he was given a multimillion-rupee corner plot of his choice. The then FGEHF Director General Arshad Mirza, a DMG officer but known to be a relative of Justice Raza, was accused of tampering with Justice Raza's records to enable him to acquire a second plot. These reports were never challenged.

After reading media reports about this case, PAC Chairperson Ch Nisar Ali Khan had ordered an inquiry against Arshad Mirza, a report of which was also pending before the PAC. Amid this scam, Mirza was, however, removed from the office.

On 8th July 2011, a Division Bench of the LHC resumed hearing of an appeal, *filed some 15 years ago*, to question **allotment, made in 1993,** of plots in **Lahore's Johar Town Scheme to some 28 judges by the then Nawaz Sharif government.**

The Bench, comprising Justice Khalid Mahmood Khan and Justice Syed Kazim Raza Shamsi, deferred the proceedings because no body attended the court; the case lingered on till all the judges in question were retired. A fresh appeal was moved against the single order, inter alia, contending that the allotments to senior judges were, being against the procedure laid down for allotment of plots in the Johar Town Housing Scheme and allotted by a judge who himself was a beneficiary, thus unlawful.

It was also unconstitutional, as the judges had submitted only a certificate and not an affidavit that whether they previously owned a plot in Lahore or not.

JUDGES PLOTS - 2ND SPILL:

In the first week of July 2012, all leading media papers published another chapter of such plots *quietly* showered on the judges of superior judiciary. Various papers mentioned that 21 [serving & retired] judges of the Supreme Court of Pakistan and around 56 bureaucrats were given residential plots [in G-12 & G-13 sectors of Islamabad] worth millions of rupees each in Islamabad's expensive sectors over the last two years [2008-2010] on the direct orders of the Prime Minister's Secretariat under a scheme somewhat incredulously called the *"Prime Minister's Assistance Package"*.

14 judges of the Supreme Court — both sitting and retired – and all the 56 bureaucrats mentioned therein were given two plots each by the government in violation of official policy, which restricts such allotments to only one plot per person, and that too if they do not already have a plot in the capital.

A list of the names of the beneficiaries, which also included the name of ad hoc judge Khalilur Rehman Ramday, was submitted to the PAC by the federal ministry of Housing. The plots were allotted by the FGEHF after it received official letters containing the names of 16 judges from the PM's Secretariat along with a list of about 100 judges from the four High Courts also.

However, no details ever surfaced that what prompted PM Gilani to float such a scheme, meant exclusively for the Supreme Court judges. Chairman PAC Nadeem Afzal Gondal had presided over the meeting of the PAC held in parliament house who had termed it injustice with poor citizens of the country.

Moreover, the judges of superior courts were allotted plots even though they were not serving in Islamabad – *a logical requirement for such allotments. The exception in the updated list of judges, who were allotted plots, was the name of CJP Iftikhar M Chaudhry.* Otherwise, a quick look at official files sent to the PAC revealed that almost all judges who served in the higher judiciary were given plots.

LHC Chief Justice *Khwaja Sharif* also *'accepted a plot'* in Islamabad although he was serving in Lahore. Justice Khalilur Rehman Ramday, who retired on 12th January 2010 and was given a new contract, however took two plots from the government. The then newly appointed Chairman NAB Justice Deedar Hussain Shah also got a plot in 2004 when he was a judge of the SC. Attorney General Moulvi Anwarul Haq also got a plot when he was a judge.

The names of *judges who acquired more than one residential plots* included Justice (Rtd) Mansoor Ahmed, Justice M Nawaz Abbasi, Justice Faqir M Khokhar, Justice M Javed Buttar, Justice Syed Ash'had, former Chief Justice Abdul Hameed Dogar, justice Sardar M Raza khan, Justice Mian Shakir Ullah Jan, Justice Tasadduq Hussain Jilani, Justice Javed Iqbal, Justice Falk Sher, Justice Nasirul Mulk, Justice Raja Fayyaz Ahmed, Justice Syed Jamshed Ali, Justice Ghulam Rabbani, Justice Ch Ijaz Ahmed, Justice M Sair Ali, Justice Anwar Zaheer and Justice Khilji Arif Hussain.

Justice Syed Zahid Hussain, however, made clear to the media that he had not accepted the said plot.

The Chairman PAC termed the issue *another NRO,* in which judges of the superior and higher judiciary were all included as party and beneficiaries. The committee was also informed that some of these senior government employees had changed their plots from one sector to another. Former PM Shaukat Aziz had introduced a scheme for allotting one residential plot each to bureaucrats in Grade 22. The PA committee was also provided a list of 214 top bureaucrats of Grade 22, both serving and retired, who were allotted two plots each.

On 6th **March 2013**, the Public Accounts Committee (PAC) recommended that there should be no special quota for allotment of plots for judges and journalists and for allotment of agricultural land to military officers except the disabled, widows, and families of martyrs.

The PAC's Chairman Nadeem Afzal Gondal submitted a report in the Parliament with above recommendations. It was resolved that the FGEHF and Pakistan Housing Authority (PHA) would not allot plots to anybody in contravention of an original and already approved scheme; transfer of allotted plots from one sector to the other under the Prime Minister's special assistance package or under the age-wise seniority scheme, were to be cancelled too.

On 14th **March 2013**, just a week after the PAC had placed its report before the house with much judicious recommendations, the event brought immediate fruit. Mighty bureaucrats, the AGP, two retired and two serving judges of the Supreme Court (SC) were at the top of a list of 102 Grade-22 officers who were considered by the PM Raja Pervaiz Ashraf for approval of plots on the last day of PPP's government.

PM Raja Pervaiz Ashraf did not hesitate to follow the discriminately state policy to award plots to only the elites of the society in violation of the PAC's recommendations to abolish special scheme of allotting one-kanal plots to Grade-22 officers whether he had got a plot earlier from governments or not.

The list compiled by the Federal Government Employees Housing Foundation (FGEHF) included the names of Establishment Secretary Taimoor Azmat Usman, Chairman PEMRA Ch Rasheed, Justice (retd) Tariq Pervaiz, Justice Mian Saqib Nisar, Justice (retd) MA Shahid Siddiqui, Akhtar Buland Rana the AGP, the Interior Secretary Khawaja Siddique Akbar, Information Secretary Agha Nadeem and many more.

After the federal secretaries were allowed two residential plots in the federal capital, the government decided to extend this facility to the judges of the Supreme Court as well despite the fact that the incumbent CJP Iftikhar M Chaudhry had taken *suo moto* notice of the two-plots policy for federal secretaries before Gen Musharraf's emergency of 3rd November 2007.

Later, the new CJP Justice Hameed Dogar had dismissed that *suo moto* case but all PCO judges of that time accepted the offer of two plots. The controversial policy continued till late though the re-born CJP Iftikhar

M Chaudhry himself had refused in 2009 the offer of a second plot. However, some judges of the post-March 2009 judiciary accepted the offer.

> [*In Islamabad, the government offered residential plots on throwaway prices to the journalists of Rawalpindi and Islamabad; while some of whom had also been allotted residential plots by the Punjab government in Rawalpindi. In military, the number of plots increased with the level of promotions and Generals got agriculture lands and commercial plots besides residential plots.*]

The poor populace in Pakistan were just to ponder and see that who else was there in the Q to ransack and plunder their beloved country.

Scenario 83

JUSTICE [MOSTLY NOT] FOR ALL:

In *Dr Shahid's live TV program* on a Pakistani channel *dated 14ᵗʰ December 2009*, former Chairman Ehtesab Saifur Rehman was taken on line who admitted that there were certain judges in the superior judiciary who were on the pay roll of the PPP [taking names of Justice Irshad Hasan Khan & Justice Sh Riaz] and were extending loss to the judicial cause so 'had to be monitored'. It might be a sprawl or a revengeful lie because Justice Irshad H Khan had upheld the military coup of Gen Musharraf in 2000 in famous Zafar Ali Shah judgment.

Justice Irshad Hasan was more criticised for giving Gen Musharraf three years in addition, to implement his 'program'; a relief by the apex court which was not even asked by the military government. Saifur Rehman was going one sided because when Dr Shahid asked him to comment upon the conduct of Justice Malik Qayyum in 'audio tape' context [*because Malik Qayyum had suffered just due to Saif's undue pressure*] Saifur Rehman had no words to answer.

What kind of judicial stuff Pakistan got; referring to another *Live TV program 'Frontline' dated 1ˢᵗ May 2010,* in a remarkable performance, PPP Senator Faisal Raza Abidi shocked the hell out of anchor Kamran Shahid as he questioned the "<u>independence of judiciary</u>" in Pakistan live on TV. From the two books in hand, Senator Abidi read that:

> *'Lahore High Court's Chief Justice Khwaja Sharif admits having close ties with Sharifs family, staying with them, going to dinners with and being offered money from Punjab's Chief Minister Shahbaz Sharif while on tour to London; in blatant violation of the Code of Conduct for judges. Kh Sharif ……..'*

Being the CJ of the Lahore High Court [LHC] later, Kh Sharif had not touched any case filed in or coming pending in the LHC which was related in any way with PML(N)'s office bearers especially of Sharif family or their friends. Senator Abidi stepped out to say on air that a case about disqualification of Kh Sa'ad Rafiq, then an MNA of PML(N) later Federal Minister of Railways in 2013, was kept pending since 2006 ignoring alleged assets and properties of millions disproportionate of his income. The main charge was that every year Kh Sa'ad Rafiq had 'legalised' his allegedly ill-gotten money by showing tens of prize bonds having millions in prizes on them. The High Court could not find it as a hilarious 'coincidence'.

QUESTIONING JUSTICE:

The Supreme Court of Pakistan had once narrated, in Constitutional Petition No: 60/96 [*Mahmood Khan Achakzai v. President of Pakistan*], that a constitution should be kept alive in line with the pace of progress, aspiration, will, needs and demands of the people. Constitution cannot be made static and there should be provisions for amendments.

Provisions may restrict the power of amendment specifically as provided in France and Germany but where an unrestricted power is given to the Legislature then the highest court would see whether an amendment to the existing constitution was duly proposed, adopted and assented in the manner required by the constitution so as to become a part thereof. The superior judiciary held that:

> '*However there are factors which restrict the power of the Legislature to amend the Constitution. It is the moral or political sentiment and more the pressure of public opinion which restricts and resists the unlimited power to amend the Constitution.*'

In Pakistan although Article 239 confers unlimited powers to the Legislature, yet it cannot, by sheer force of morality, convert democratic form in completely undemocratic one and similarly by amendment courts cannot be abolished. The basic theory would prevail that even if the constitution is suspended or abrogated, the judiciary continues to hold its position to impart justice and protect the rights of the people which are violated by authorities even which saddle themselves by unconstitutional means.

While considering the above sermons one should also analyze the hard facts of judicial history of Pakistan that the Supreme Court has frequently supported military and civilian dictators, allowing or tolerating deviations in the constitution and extending all possible legitimacy to the powerful Establishment. The Court's uncertain and doubtful history had been providing a basis for an unprincipled jurisprudence of expediency.

Contrary to its own derogatory traditions, the Supreme Court had started raising slogans of representing judicial independence and constitutional boldness in the name of '*holding the Establishment accountable*' under the control and instructions of re-instated Chief

Justice Iftikhar M Chaudhry in March 2009 who had earlier behaved quite differently.

For instance, as mentioned else where in the preceding pages, *on 12th May 2000*, Pakistan's 12-members Supreme Court had unanimously validated the October 1999 coup and granted Gen Musharraf executive and legislative authority for 3 years from the coup date. Justice Iftikhar M Chaudhry was one of the judges who had validated it. *On 7th October 2002*, the 5-member bench of the Supreme Court validated LFO and amendments made in the constitution by the military regime. Justice Iftikhar M Chaudhry was one of judges who had AGAIN validated it.

The PML(Q) government passed a constitutional amendment in National Assembly with two third majority, also approved by the Senate, that allowed Gen Musharraf to hold dual offices against the basic spirit of the Constitution. *On 13th April 2005*, a 5-member bench of the Supreme Court gave judgment in favour of 17th amendment and President's uniform. Justice Chaudhry was one of the judges who had validated it.

On 28th September 2007, the Supreme Court cleared the way for Gen Musharraf to seek another five-year term, when he stood for Presidential elections, when six of the nine judges, rejected a tangle of petitions against him and threw out a major legal challenge to his re-election plans. On that strength, Gen Musharraf was elected President of Pakistan, *on 6th October 2007*, by a combined electoral of the Senate, National Assembly and the four Provincial Assembles.

Gen Musharraf declared emergency on 3rd November 2007 using his (wrongly interpreted) prerogative as per Article 232 of the constitution and immediately after a 10-member bench of [CJ Dogar's] Supreme Court, *on 24th November 2007*, directed the Chief Election Commissioner and the government to declare Gen Musharraf president for a second term.

Same day the Pakistan Election Commission had confirmed Gen Musharraf's re-election as President on the basis of 58% votes. J Abdul Hameed Dogar was made the Chief Justice of Pakistan; brought forward by Gen Musharraf after the said emergency of 3rd November.

Every government organ was declared suspended in 3rd November's Emergency but Parliament's joint session's vote casting activity remained intact and the EC was there to receive SC's orders to notify Gen Musharraf as President for the next five years. The intelligentsia believed that the apex Court should have given verdict either on merit or at least as per general precedents outlined in Achakzai's case referred above.

As per *Ali Khan (professor of law, Washburn University Kansas):*

'It is not for the Supreme Court to shape the power structure of the federal government. Even the popular tune of Parliamentary Sovereignty must not tempt the Court to hear political disputes.

The Court is less free and is viewed as politicized when it aligns itself with one political ideology against the other or with one branch of the government against the other.

The Court must avoid any tilt towards or against the President or Governors, the Prime Minister or Chief Ministers, or Parliament or leaders of certain political party.

While maintaining its constitution-based neutrality towards other branches of the government, **the Court must nonetheless fix its own house, that is, the judiciary itself.'**

The Supreme Court, under the leadership of an able Chief Justice, should have found ways to provide affordable justice to the poor people of Pakistan. *Overly complicated procedures inherited from the nineteenth century common law needed massive revisions. Rules of evidence needed changes for a more efficient litigation.* The apex court could set in motion a process that would fix the decades old inefficient, even dysfunctional, litigation model.

An extract of *'Global Corruption Report 2007 by Transparency International'* is placed below:

'Perceptions of judicial corruption vary greatly across the [Asian] region. According to TI's Global Corruption Report 2006, Hong Kong and Singapore have low perceived levels of judicial corruption while India and Pakistan fare badly, with 77 percent and 55 percent of poll respondents respectively describing the judicial system as corrupt.

The main problem in the region is the lack of resources to solve the huge backlogs of court cases. It would take 350 years for India's 670 judges to clear present backlogs.

The official judicial system is also perceived as being weighted against the people; in Pakistan for instance, English is the judiciary's official language, although only 2% of the population can understand it.'

Let us move forward as a nation - leaving the score balancing games behind; let us look upwards.

SC CORRECTS THE EXECUTIVE:

On *1ˢᵗ August 2011* the Prime Minister Yousaf Raza Gilani made a blistering speech in the National Assembly accusing the Supreme Court of Pakistan for undue interference in the executive's domain on the issue of handling postings & transfers of officers. PM admitted that it was his prerogative to *'play with his officer's fates'*. Feeling much satisfied from inside, he was flogging punches & blows to the opposition desks saying that the apex court had finally accepted government's viewpoint.

The PM was referring to Supreme Court's order dated *30ᵗʰ July 2011* on FIA's Hussain Asghar and Secretary Establishment Sohail Ahmad. Though the officers could not receive that much relief which was expected or portrayed by the media but, as has been mentioned in earlier pages, the apex court had passed an observation on that count.

The *SC's 37-page order of 30ᵗʰ July 2011* highlighted that it was the parliamentarians and public at large who had complained to the judiciary regarding poor arrangements for *Hajis in Saudi Arabia* that year. Quite heartening to observe that even the worthy Parliamentarians had to approach the apex Court, like in the case of Rental Power Projects where one of the sitting Ministers namely Faisal Saleh Hayat was the complainant along with one MNA Khwaja Asif [*later, given to him the same federal ministry of Water & Power in PML(N) government in May 2013 but the situation got worsened*].

Similarly in the matter of Breach of embankments of rivers in floods causing damages, it was Marvi Memon MNA who approached the Supreme Court. Khwaja Asif MNA brought the case of OGDCL too. Matters of the steel Mills, LPG Case, National Police Foundation, NICL, unhuman Hajj arrangements and Bank of Punjab cases where millions of rupees got recovered under stern efforts of the apex court could be cited as more important instances.

[*Intelligentsia, however, observed that in not a single case quoted above, the SC could find courage to give the final decision. It was not the job of the superior courts to reduce itself to 'the recovery agency' – it was below dignity for judges to keep on shouting in courts for 'returning money'. Had the court issued verdicts, the NAB or FIA could have made better recoveries in the said cases, might be coupled with punishments for some.*]

Though the apex Court's decision could not do much about the Hajj and NICL cases which were originally suggested to be handled or investigated by Hussain Asghar and Zafar Qureshi respectively [both senior officers of FIA] but the people of Pakistan were at the same time expecting more from PM Gilani. As PM Gilani's son was also named in the Hajj Corruption case alleging to be the major beneficiary, the PM should have voluntarily announced that the said investigation be carried out by any officer; Hussain Asghar or some other, but entirely up to the court's satisfaction.

Similarly, as the names of Moonus Elahi and Makhdoom Amin Fahim were involved in NICL case; the same transparency was expected through Zafar Qureshi or some other officer. It was essential so that the credibility of the Prime Minister and the PPP's government could have been established while setting the best norms of rule of law.

On the same day of 30th **July 2011** at another occasion, Chief Justice Iftikhar M Chaudhry asked judges to make all-out efforts for the provision of inexpensive and expeditious justice to all without any fear or favour. He said so while presiding over a meeting of the National Judicial Policy Making Committee (NJPMC) adding that Pakistan's constitution discouraged all types of discrimination among persons / parties on the basis of their status. He also quoted that:

'Islam tells us that justice should be done without caring how the influential parties are and justice should not be compromised to accommodate any influential person so the independence of judiciary and its impartiality must be fully adhered to.'

However, it all proved to be academic cermons and nothing beyond.

Earlier, *on* 7th *February 2011*, while delivering his keynote address at the 17th Commonwealth Law Conference at the Hyderabad International Convention Centre, Chief Justice Iftikhar M Chaudhry had told the gathering of about 800 eminent jurists from across 53 Commonwealth countries that Pakistan's Judiciary remained under tremendous pressures but succeeded to survive through adverse circumstances. He said that:

'The Pakistan's judiciary has passed through different phases but has ensured its independence under all the circumstances. This is because the judiciary is of the opinion that when there is a Constitution and the rule of law, it always guarantees a democratic system in the country instead of the military rule.'

With all due respects to the higher courts, a lay man was bound to ponder if the Supreme Court was really doing justice to all or it passed the judicial verdicts simply to gain sympathies of the general populace through media breaking news. Media persons and able anchors conducting vibrant live discussions on top TV channels were mostly betrayed and they in turn made fool of innocent Pakistanis by calling political representatives from stake-holding parties and encountering them with embarrassing questions. The leading question remained that why the PPP government was not inclined to implement the Supreme Court's decisions.

Analyse the events of that era. For weeks the Supreme Court had been conducting regular hearings for two cases of NICL and Hajj Corruption and kept on urging that why the particular officers in each case were not allowed to continue with the investigations. The executive did not comply with the orders of the apex court. *It was an awful, dreadful and shocking precedent for all times to come.*

It was alleged that in both cases the apex court had stepped out of its shoes putting aside the required decorum of the highest judiciary. The respectable judges knew that allocating investigations to some particular officers was the prerogative of the concerned department and thus was the jurisdiction of the 'executive' but the executive had failed in delivering the good governance to the people. That was why the judiciary had to step in to get results.

Correctly, no court had ever held that a particular investigation should have been done by that particular officer. Shouting at the officers in the court brought neither good result in the under-investigation cases nor the required respect for the judges and judiciary. Of curse, the apex court should have concentrated on factual and speedy investigations in any case before it; how it was possible, no body knew in fact.

Apparently the Supreme Court was misguided by the prosecutors meant to assist the court on certain basic issues. Two week's regular hearings were aimed at only one 'out of context' thing that why the Secretary Establishment [Sohail Ahmed] was made OSD by the Prime Minister. See the 'threats' apex court had conveyed:

- *'We can call the PM here',*

- *'do not force us to take the extreme step',*

- *'no disgrace would be accepted this time for apex judiciary',*

- *'take explicit orders from the PM',*

- *'ask the PM to send us reply in writing',*

- *'we can call PM in contempt',*

- *'why officers not re-instated yet'.*

So many other phrases the nation kept on hearing and reading over the media pages. Pakistani judiciary's media friends left no stone unturned in making suggestions like that:

- *'Army would be called to get decisions implemented',*

- *'PM will go home now',*

- *'who would be the new PM then',*

- *'PPP government would wind up now'*

And many others but what happened at last........ **Tain Tain Fissh.** The same as expected. Corruption kept standing there; rather 'improved'.

POLICE & ARMY SHOUTED AT:

Sometimes it appeared that Pakistanis were not living in a civilized world. Not even in fool's paradise; perhaps living in 'fool's hell'. The country became a contemporary *colossium* of Italy where, centuries back, the 'un-liked' were pushed into the ring to fight the hungry lions. Imagine the fate of those poor fighters and recall the cheeky shoutings of the ruler families watching the show. Pakistan was going through the same replica where the people always kept waiting to raise enchanting slogans on events when an officer of army or police was disgraced or sacked or being shouted at with hate or humour because of being 'a **person in uniform**'.

Whether that officer, with ranks on, suffered at the hands of his own executive or by the judiciary or lawyers or from an angry mob when his uniform was torn in pieces and cap was volleyed in air - he was a symbol of authority. Most of the equivalent members of the society were jealous with (some of) his powers perhaps.

In most cases, the higher courts were party to it. Those uniformed people belonged to the same social fabric, rising from the same mud and yeast, hailed from equally dignified families, used to be students of the same respectable institutions, appeared in the same like Competitive Examinations and were ground in the same mills of administrative Civil or Military Service Academies but, when they came out in uniform, they were treated like 'bad boys', anti-ethics and some times enemies. Strange and astonishing! Let us peep into the awful past scenario that:

> 'In November 1997 when PML workers headed by their MsNA & MsPA ransacked the Supreme Court Islamabad, who got punished out of the whole mess. No MNA or MPA, no worker of PML, no CSP officer either Commissioner, DC or AC of Islamabad but IG Saleem Tariq Lone, SSP Altaf Ahmed, one DSP & an Inspector.

> In 2007 when the Chief Justice was allegedly mis-handled by Gen Musharraf's team then who was ultimately at loss. Neither Gen Musharraf nor any of his General, or Secretary Interior or Commissioner Islamabad; those were again IG Iftikhar Ahmed and his team comprising the SSP, DSP and Inspector who were declared guilty of 'contempt of court.'

> In 2011, thrice the IG Punjab Tariq Saleem Dogar was called in court for bullshit; one DG FIA Waseem Ahmed Khan was un-ceremonially sent home, DG FIA Malik Iqbal was forced to quit his post and his successor Anwar Tehseen was blessed with sarcasmtic remarks & shouts and ultimately made to leave the organization.'

Contrarily, during the last four years, the higher judiciary never called Secretary Water & Power or the Chairman WAPDA in court responsible for load shedding up to 18 hours; or Secretary Industries for NIL production and creating gross unemployment. In Pakistan 0.6 million people annually were added in 'Narcotics Addicts List' (**Ref: UN Office on Drugs & Crimes Report of June 2011**), no court ever called Secretary Narcotics to come up with policy papers to check the menace.

Secretary Oil & Gas was never called to explain about countrywide Gas shortage and Secretary FBR or Secretary Finance was never asked for loss of 14,000 containers through Afghan Transit Trade loophole. Secretary Commerce was never called in court to explain that in NICL case **how an amount of Rs:40 million had reached into Amin Fahim's accounts** which fact was admitted by worthy Federal Minister himself but no remorse or call up. No *suo-moto* or alike.

In those days when the apex court took *suo-moto* notice of Sialkot's killing or *Karo-kary* of DG Khan, or miss-handling of Hajj or NICL case, the IGs of Police or DGs of FIA were asked to come and reply. It was all aimed to get salute for the court, what else, at the cost of public expenses. Why not called the concerned secretaries, directors or chair persons in the above quoted few examples because the Superior Courts always stand by the administrative officers thus creating a cogent example of injustice. Had they never done wrong; their subordinates were not at all angels and only *'thaneydars'* were corrupt; not at all, but the courts felt shy or scared.

Suppose for a moment that the army Generals were guilty of desecrating and violating the Constitution of Pakistan and the police were corrupt but the question remained that if those two classes were the only corrupt in the country. The apex court never thought about the lower judiciary's lethargic attitudes, issuing stay orders for money equivalent to £5 only, doing away the bail matters in private chambers and so on. As per Transparency International figures the score of *public approval for Pakistani judiciary remained at 55% since a decade at least – but never a session judge, judicial magistrate, civil judge, or Tehsildar was called in the court to be shouted at.*

Take the politics; hundreds of instances could be quoted to prove that Pakistan's superior courts had blown their trumpet for only those cases where they were sure that the sitting PPP government could be harassed. The judiciary achieved praise by putting cannons of their 'false anger' on the shoulders of police officers making the sad & passive people happy for a while – what a mockery of justice it was.

Nowhere in the world, the judges were supposed to shout but in Pakistan it has been a normal practice for judges hoping that it would bring headlines for leading newspapers amidst waves of *'strong judiciary syndrome'*. In all societies, the judges do not but their decisions speak; but in Pakistan the judges speak loud but their decisions *'thuss'*.

[*See Saifullah's case and the FIA officer's reposting or Secretary Sohail Ahmed's cases during those days.*]

Similarly all higher courts kept friendly relations or 'soft corners' for media people. The newspapers and electronic media never, invariably never, wrote or spoke anything against unjust or partial decisions, unlikely behaviour of some judges, wilful and managed delays in justice, sarcastic remarks of courts etc because sword of contempt of court was always hanging on their heads. The owners of media organs kept a strict

policy of 'Not saying or writing' anything against judges and judiciary.
Thus to avoid 'scandalizing charges' the reporters and anchors were
always found writing in praise of judiciary and cursing the successive
governments; military or civil.

In SC's judgment of 30th **July 2011**, for instance, in which no reporter
or columnist of any newspaper; no anchor or guest in live programs
of any TV channel ever felt courage to opine that *the apex court was*
stepping out of their shoes. The PM, the PPP and the PML(Q) had in fact
extracted benefits by apex Court's 'shouting behaviour' over NICL and
Hajj like cases.

Controlling sensitive investigations through judiciary demanded a very
careful handling. Those aforesaid cases could be managed by calling
weekly progress reports by a nominated judge despite FIA's swift
changing hands technique; or by allocating to a judicial commission; or
by appointing a joint investigation team including a member from army
but Pakistani courts resorted to follow a *'media brief' methodology* and
the judges remained happy reading headlines about 'judiciary's powers'.

It was either a 'hands in glove' game with the executive or the simplicity
for which the executive had brewed results suitable to them and the
judiciary got [again & again] humiliated.

In developed democracies the things go different. In UK, during the
corresponding three years the courts dealt numerous cases of corruption
or public importance. Here the wrong doers got punishments irrespective
of their origin. More MPs and less police officers were sent behind the
bars. In UK alone, five MPs and one Lord were sentenced for claiming
benefits which were not justified for their ranks. The financial involvement
in each individual case was less than twelve thousand pounds but all they
got jails; no shouting in courts; no media glamour for judges either. The
people even do not know the names of judges who wrote decisions.

The same happened with media lords in 2011's famous 'hacking
scandals' case in which an empire of *179 years old paper 'News of the*
World' had to shut down their printing and circulation. The paper's chief
had to face interrogations; careers of many ended up in jail, press closed
and hang over continued to haunt many.

But in Pakistan, numerous media anchors, columnists, abbasis and
chaudhries, frequently acted as touts of the superior courts; sometimes
being investigative journalists and sometimes assuming role of the
judiciary's spokesmen; Kamran Khan's live **TV program at GEO dated**
20th **November 2013** is referred in this context.

WHY EXECUTIVE DISOBEYED JUDICIARY:

Since 2009, the SC took cognizance of cases involving over Rs:400 billion and saved tens of billions of the national exchequer; quoting NICL Scam, Hajj Case, Rental Power Plants (RPPs) Case involving Rs:455 million, Bank of Punjab Case AND Evacuee Trust Property Board Case [*blocking controversial sale of 240 acres worth billions of rupees for peanuts in Karachi saving whopping Rs:60 billion for the Pakistan government*]. The SC also had taken up the matter of written off loans and directed the State Bank of Pakistan to submit the list of loan eaters worth Rs:256 billion but when the list was placed just next day, the apex court could not go further for reasons not known to any.

Then the key question: that why PPP government did not respect SC's decisions; let us peep deep in the past political scenario of Pakistan.

After a hilltop task of <u>re-inventing the 'independent judiciary'</u> in March 2009, by taking the whole nation through long march, poor people were of the view that Chief Justice Iftikhar M Chaudhry and his team would bring an end to all injustices, miseries and shortcomings. The CJP could well realize then that the 'ill intentions' of the ruling class, including Zardaris, Sharifs, Gilanis & Rehmans and their 'friends & family members' were the real predicament for the future development of Pakistan; however, the situation worsened day by day.

The top judiciary failed to stand for the expectations of masses as 'independent' in real terms. In some cases the judges tried to settle their old scores by targeting PPP and their leader sitting as president of Pakistan. Some media reports also pointed out towards high judiciary's 'soft attitude' for PML(N), JUI and MQM governments. Allowing Sharif family home before contractual period of ten years, row over the issues of Kh Sharif as the Chief Justice LHC; strictures against the Governor Punjab Late Salman Taseer; eye-wash proceedings in 'big loan' cases and allowing the Punjab government on 'stay order' for four years could be quoted as examples. The people were expecting judges-like behaviour not the score settling.

Through the NRO proceedings, the apex court constantly tried to convince the general populace for five long years that the PPP politicians were corrupt. The people knew it; they believed the scandals but they were expecting punishments for them not gimmicks. No one was punished or even disqualified. The politicians of other political parties were not saints nor were ever so.

When the Supreme Court had taken notice of Justice (Rtd) Malik Qayyum's wrong doings in Zardari's Swiss case, the court should have ordered re-trial or re-opening of 'some old but proven cases' decided by the same J Qayyum Malik in favour of PML, their associates and family members in June-July 1997; as the judgments were managed on gun-point.

Mostly in all the political cases no witness from prosecution was called or recorded because FIA remained under extreme political pressures. [*To mention again: normally one sub-inspector of FIA used to appear in the court, and only once, to tell that 'no witness from prosecution; My Lord' and in all the cases same one phrase*].

That is why the NRO was full of names attached with PPP and no name of PML(N) or PML(Q) or JUI or NAP was there because they had kept judges like Maliks and Parachas with them. They got themselves 'acquitted' in their respective regimes from 1997 till 2007 and since then they are coming '*pawitter & pakeeza*'.

Here PPP's politicians could be the biggest scoundrels but it was not true that they were the only rogues and rascals around and all other parties were comprised of saints and 'imams'. Supreme Court and especially the CJP Iftikhar M Chaudhry could have pondered upon this side of judicious delicacy. If it was sword to be used in battle, it must have two edges equally sharp otherwise it would be termed as knife used for killing (of justice), as one could see the Pakistan of those days. [*An essay published at www.Pakspectator.com on 11th August 2011 is referred*]

Referring to a GEO program dated 4th **August 2011** in which Junaid Jamshed told a hard fact from early Islamic history. Once Hazrat Ali (KAW), then himself fourth Caliph, got stolen his '*zarah*'. He went to the market to have a new one. In market he found his own '*zarah*' lying for sale at the shop of one Jew. Hazrat Ali (KAW) told the shopkeeper that it was his '*zarah*' which he got stolen a day before so he (the Jew) should give it back to him (Hazrat Ali KAW). Arguments developed.

Hazrat Ali (KAW) took that case in Qazi's court. Both, the shopkeeper and the Caliph, were made to sit before Qazi and the hearing started. Qazi asked the complainant, the fourth Caliph, to quote witness to the event. Hazrat Ali (KAW) quoted two witnesses; one (Imam) Hasan (RAU) his son and the other Caliph's servant. There were a series of questions put to the Caliph to ascertain the 'qualifications of witnesses' which were thoroughly narrated in the most humble way.

While concluding, the Qazi rejected Hazrat Ali (KAW)'s petition and exonerated the Jew shopkeeper and gave back that *'zarah'* in question to the Jew saying that *'shahadat'* of son or servant in favour of complainant father were not admissible in judicial proceedings.

The Jew shopkeeper, who had been listening all the question - answers between Qazi and the Caliph, was so impressed with the Qazi's fearlessness, court procedures and the Caliph's satisfied feelings that he immediately asked Hazrat Ali (KAW) to take his *'zarah'* back, recited the *'Kalma Tayyabah'* and accepted Islam saying that:

> *'If such judicial norms and such Qazis and such rulers are accessible in a religion (Islam) it is the whole truth and worth following'.*

Soon after, he was a Muslim.

Need not to compare that uprightness with Pakistan's judicial norms. Pakistan though is an Islamic country having Islamic Constitution but neither those rulers are there nor those *Qazis*. Islam is only to be kept pasted on everyone's forehead here not to be practiced.

Scenario 84

RAYMOND DAVIS,
& BLACK-WATER IN PAKISTAN:

AN MNA MURDERED IN CAPITAL:

Shahbaz Bhatti, an MNA from minority and Christian community, was murdered **on 2nd March 2011,** by gunfire burst in daylight in Pakistan's capital Islamabad. It was a very serious blow to the PPP government writ. From all corners of Pakistan the minority groups launched strikes, came out on roads and the day to day life came standstill all over the country. Immediately, an emergency cabinet meeting was called by Prme Minister Yusaf Raza Gilani. Every member of the cabinet expressed deep concern over law and order situation in the country and especially in Islamabad.

It was the first time that members of the cabinet from the ruling party PPP openly criticized Mr Rehman Malik, the then Federal Interior Minister and demanded resignation from him for his failure. It was a critical moment in the political history of Pakistan that the cabinet members of a ruling party demanded resignation from their own fellow party worker. Rehman Malik, though little ashamed but did not bother to listen the dissident voices. The members went so sentimental over the security issues that at last the Prime Minister himself stood up and offered his resignation instead. The PM was given a pat by the remaining members, the speeches ended in utter grief; most members were tearful when the meeting was called off.

Next day, the same scene was repeated by most of the MNAs in the Parliament. Majority of the members fingered towards the Interior Minister, he took rostrum and made a fiery speech urging that *'such murders do not justify resignations of ministers in-charge; it is not a western democracy, it is Pakistan'.* There was not a single wave of sorrow or grief over his face this time. He simply took Punjab government on horns and criticized them declaring that Punjab was responsible for murder of the MNA Shahbaz Bhatti because of Punjabi Taliban who were allegedly having their sanctuaries in the Southern Punjab.

The Federal Interior Minister Rehman Malik was kind enough to announce a bullet proof car for each member of the cabinet [*comprising of 73 members then, the biggest ever in the history of Pakistan*], of course on public expenses, so that in future no blame of security would come on the Interior Ministry.

It was very strange that when Islamabad Police reached at the scene of occurrence they found posters spread around carrying slogans and manifesto of the Taliban. Apparently it was an effort to make the police and media believe that Shahbaz Bhatti was murdered by the Taliban.

Slicing up the core event once more; born on 9th September 1968 in Lahore, joined PPP in 2002, Shahbaz Bhatti was the first Christian parliamentarian who had taken oath as Federal Minister of Minorities Affairs in Pakistan. His predecessors had been offered only a state minister's portfolio. Mr Bhatti, the cabinet's only Christian minister, had received death threats for urging reform to blasphemy laws. Earlier in January 2011, Punjab Governor Salman Taseer, who had also opposed the said law, was shot dead by one of his security bodyguards.

Pamphlets by *Tehrik e Taliban* Punjab were found at the scene. Tehrik e Taliban had told BBC Urdu they carried out the attack but no conclusive evidence surfaced to prove it. Might be some one else used the name of Taliban because, immediate after the death of Governor Salman Taseer, PM Gilani had made it clear before a large gathering of religious personalities that his government had no intention of reviewing the blasphemy laws, come what may.

Much later; referring to *the 'Dawn' dated 14th January 2012:*

> *'In Mr Bhatti's assassination, confusion about who killed him and why, stemmed from the contradictory statements of government officials. Islamabad police and its Inspector General and Interior Minister made differing statements about the identity of his killer(s), some even contradicting themselves.'*

In the period from his assassination on 2nd March to August 2011, senior police officers insisted the media that 'personal enmity' and 'business rivalry' were felt behind his murder. In August, however, the police declared it was *'an act of terrorism'*. On 23rd August 2011, the IGP informed the Senate Standing Committee on Interior that the Tehrik e Taliban Pakistan (TTP) was behind the murder. Not only he named Malik Abid and Ziaur Rehman as the murderers but said that investigators had obtained red warrants for their arrest from abroad through Interpol.

On 25th December 2011, Interior Minister Rehman Malik came up with his final version: he alleged that the *Sipah e Sahaba Pakistan* (SSP) was behind Mr Bhatti's assassination. The minister also told that the assassins had been identified and had fled to the Middle East after committing the crime. It was known later that the red warrants of the accused were obtained in the third week of December 2011 and not in August when his IGP had given that information to the Senate Committee.

Even more significant was that the two accused were neither identified by eye-witnesses nor nominated by Mr Bhatti's family; and reportedly flew out to Sri Lanka from Islamabad a few hours after committing the crime. According to the earlier police version the two identified killers, Malik Abid and Ziaur Rehman, belonging to Faisalabad were once found running a travel agency in Dubai.

Shahbaz Bhatti, during his time as federal minister, had launched a national campaign to promote interfaith harmony, had moved a proposal of legislation to ban hate speeches and related literature, had strived for introduction of comparative religious studies as a curriculum subject, had demanded quotas for religious minorities in government posts and the reservation of four seats in the Senate for minorities. Bhatti also spearheaded the organisation of a National Interfaith Consultation in July 2010, which brought together senior religious leaders of all faiths from across Pakistan and resulted in a joint declaration against terrorism.

Bhatti had been the recipient of death threats since 2009, when he raised voice for his Christian community attacked in Gojra, a town in central Punjab. The volume of threats increased following his support for another Christian girl, named Aasia, sentenced to death in 2010 for blasphemy.

BBC had reported that Shahbaz Bhatti had just left his mother's home, when his vehicle was sprayed with bullets. At the time of attack he was alone, without any security. His driver reportedly stopped the car and ducked when he saw armed men approaching rather than attempting to evade the threat. After a shower of bullets upon him, Bhatti was taken to the nearby hospital but he was pronounced dead on arrival.

BULK VISAS FOR XE & BLACKWATER:

In the above Shahbaz Bhatti Case, one faction of the police investigators opined that the job had been accomplished by some family members of Raymond Davis, Blackwater from America, to make the western media believe that Pakistan was being ruled by the Taliban. It was deliberately done by some foreign secret agents to make the democratic powers believe that Christians were not being protected by Pakistani government.

In response to Interior Minister Rehman Malik's allegations mentioned in aforesaid paragraphs [*that the Punjab Government was responsible for Bhatti's brutal assassination*] the Punjab government immediately retaliated and counter-attacked Rehman Malik alleging that:

- About **one quarter of Islamabad residences were occupied by the CIA and Blackwater paid agents** those days with connivance of the Interior Ministry.

- The Federal Interior Minister in person had ordered visas for those foreign nationals and had allowed them to accomplish such murderous operations in Pakistan.

- The **Federal Interior Minister in person had ordered to issue visas to 86 Americans and 150 Indians from Pakistani Embassy in Dubai** within four months of 2010.

- Those visas were issued from Dubai whereas Pakistan's Foreign Office had issued policy-instructions that Americans and Indians should only be issued visas from Washington and Delhi respectively.

- When **Pakistani Embassy in Dubai** was asked to explain this violation, they simply **referred it to 'very powerful' person** having base in Dubai also [most probably Mr Zardari, the President].

- It was a fact that **six out of 86 Americans had written 'Zardari House' as their destination and place of stay in Islamabad.**

- It was a fact that **most of those applicants were awarded visas on the same day without necessary verifications.**

- It was a fact that **for some applicants the Pakistan Embassy was specially opened on Fridays,** the official weekend in Dubai.

- It was a fact that most of the visa applications processed in Washington and Dubai were not consulted with the security agencies, neither the ISI nor with IB. In Washington alone **400 visas were issued to Americans in two days in 2010 after 'special security clearance order'** from Islamabad.

- From January to June 2010, in six months period **1895 Americans** were issued Pakistani visas whereas from 14th July to 30th August

2010, in 45 days only, **1445 more Americans were blessed with mostly diplomatic visas.** All of them were belonging to Blackwater Co or XE or similar CIA sponsored agencies.

- The Federal Interior Minister Rehman Malik could not answer that in March 2009, on the direction of the US Ambassador in Pakistan Mrs Anne Peterson, **how many arms licenses of prohibited bores were issued to Blackwater and Xe** companies through a Pakistani security company based in Islamabad.

- It was a fact that the **American 'diplomats' were issued 140 licenses to import AK-47 rifles in 2009 for 'certain special security'** purposes.

When Rehman Malik was asked about his alleged links with Blackwater he told the media that he would quit his job *'if any person brings evidence against him. I have no connection with a foreign security company, Blackwater,'* he had claimed; a blatant lie most persons believed.

To a question from media, Mr Malik said *'he does not own any security firm and all allegations being levelled against him are false.'* Whereas the facts were that he had owned [as per Companies House UK's record] his own security-investigation agency named *Shaffaf Ltd* with following details:

Company's Name: Shaffaf Ltd

Registration Date: 18th January 2000

Co-Registration No: 03908422

Original Address: Crown House North Circular Road London NW10 7PN

2nd Address: Suite 101-102, No: 38 Edgware Road, London W2 2EW

Last Accounts filed: 31st May 2012 [Next due on 28th February 2014]

Activity: Investigation & Security Activities – Code: 7460

Previous Names: No previous name information has been recorded over the last 20 years.

Branch Details: There are no branches associated with this company.

Overseas Company Info: There are no Overseas Details associated with this company

Dr Malik is Managing Director of SHAFFAF LIMITED - dealing in security consultancy and investigation of corporate frauds. He is also Chairman of RODCOM-EUROPE LIMITED, MDI-MEA, Vice Chairman of gfta, President of DM Digital TV and RYSTONE HOLDINGS. [*'The London Post' dated 17*th *April 2011* is referred for more details.]

Shaffaf Ltd had been working for Benazir Bhutto also. Rehman Malik cursed the Blackwater, an American security firm, having no base or existence in Pakistan which was also proved wrong subsequently. In fact the media was trying to find if there was any connection or coordination then going on between Shaffaf Ltd of UK and Blackwater Co.

WHY WERE XE's IN PAKISTAN:

The *'guardian' UK of 11*th *February 2010,* once narrated a controversy about Blackwater regarding fake and false billing for a Filipino prostitute on its payroll in Afghanistan. The company had allegedly employed her in Kabul, billed the government for her plane tickets and monthly salary etc.

Meanwhile, the paper told that *Blackwater, re-named itself as XE Services LLC last year [in 2009] because of the bad publicity* attached to its original name, with company headquarters in North Carolina [USA]. It was among the biggest private security firms employed by the US state department and Pentagon in Iraq and Afghanistan. The most notorious incident involving Blackwater was the shooting of 17 Iraqis in Baghdad in 2007; criminal charges were subsequently dropped in 2009.

Blackwater USA was formed in 1997, by Erik Prince in North Carolina, to provide training support to military and law enforcement organiza-tions. After serving SEAL and SWAT teams, Blackwater USA received their first government contract after the bombing of the USS Cole off the coast of Yemen in October 2000. After winning the bid on the contract, Blackwater was able to train over 100,000 sailors safely. The Blackwater Lodge and Training Centre was officially opened on 15th May 1998 with a 6,000 acre facility and cost of $6.5 million.

In 2002 Blackwater Security Consulting (BSC) was formed. Its first assignment was to provide 20 men with top-secret clearances to protect the CIA HQ & another base [*most probably in Peshawar*] responsible for hunting Bin Laden. In October 2007, Blackwater USA initiated a process of altering its name to Blackwater Worldwide, and unveiled a new logo. On 21st July 2008, Blackwater Worldwide shifted their resources away from security contracting because of extensive risk.

In February 2009, Blackwater announced that it would be changing its name to "XE Services LLC" as part of a company-wide restructuring plan. Subsequently, it reorganized its business units, added a corporate governance and ethics program, and established an independent committee of outside experts to supervise compliance structures.

In December 2011, XE changed its name again to 'Academi'; referring it to Plato's Academi, re-organizing it in ten 'business units'. Immediately after; one of those ten units titled as USTC got contract from the Pentagon to provide *'intelligence analyst support and material procurement'* for NATO in the Afghan drug war.

One of the XE's units titled AWS [*Aviation Worldwide Services*] also provided services to the CIA with three of its aircrafts with tail numbers N962BW, N964BW, and N968BW through a listed owner titled E&J Holdings LLC. Their CASA 212 aircraft, tail number N960BW, operated through Presidential Airways, had crashed on 27th November 2004 in Afghanistan en route from Bagram to Farah. All aboard, three soldiers and three civilian crew members were killed for which the US government faced a 'death lawsuit' filed in the court in October 2005 by the kiths of un-fateful crew. But again in late September 2007, Presidential Airways got a $92m contract from the US Department of Defence for air transportation in Afghanistan, Kyrgyzstan, Pakistan, and Uzbekistan; might be as compensation gesture.

Blackwater Worldwide played a substantial role during the Iraq War as a contractor for the US government; attaining its first high-profile contract of a $27.7 million no-bid contract. Since June 2004 to 2010, Blackwater was paid more than $320 million from the US State Department budget for the Worldwide Personal Protective Service while **in only two years span (between 2005 and September 2007), Blackwater was involved in 195 shooting incidents out of which in 163 cases, Blackwater personnel fired first.**

[*'Newsweek of 15th October 2007'* titled "BLACKWATER IS SOAKED: An arrogant attitude only adds fuel to the criticism" is referred for details]

The US Court documents made public revealed that Blackwater / XE had violated US federal law hundreds of times according to allegations by the federal government. In August 2010, the company agreed to pay a $42 million fine to settle allegations that it unlawfully provided armaments and military equipment overseas. However, the company is still allowed to accept government contracts.

*On 22*nd *September 2007*, US federal prosecutors announced an investigation into the allegations that Blackwater employees had smuggled weapons into Iraq, and that these weapons were later transferred to the Kurdistan Workers Party (PKK), a Kurdish nationalist group designated as a terrorist organization by the United States, NATO and the EU.

While the US government was taking up investigations into those alleged crimes, the FBI snatched those investigations *on 4*th *October 2007* and the progress was reported 'lost'. Ultimately the Iraqi government announced that XE must leave Iraq as soon as a joint Iraqi–US committee would finish drafting the new guidelines. Thus *on 31*st *January 2009*, the US State Department had to notify Blackwater that the agency would not renew its security contract with them.

[*But even then the agreement was renewed in March 2009 for a cost of $22.2 million; The Washington Post of 17*th *March 2009* is referred]

The *New York Times of 19*th *August 2009* reported that the CIA had hired Blackwater "as part of a secret program to locate and assassinate top operatives of Al Qaeda" in Pakistan under specific orders of newly appointed CIA director Leon Panetta. Jeremy Scahill had also reported in *The Nation* in November 2009 that Blackwater operated alongside the CIA in Pakistan in "snatch and grab" operations targeting senior members of the Taliban and Al Qaeda AND that the Blackwater was operating under a US contract in Pakistan. A former Blackwater executive had confirmed that they operated covertly in Pakistan.

May not be out of place to mention that at the end of 2009, a special presidential order from government of Pakistan was issued to give 7000 visas to Americans and was passed on to Mr Haqqani, Pakistan's ambassador in Washington.

When the Pakistan's Foreign Office was asked to comment on the summary containing by-passing the normal procedure to issue visas, the then Foreign Minister Shah Mahmood Qureshi had given a categorical dissenting note. On the basis of that summary and subsequent order, the visas valid for three to six months were issued without the scrutiny or routine security clearance of the ISI or the IB. Later, the Presidency had declined to comment on details of the visa decision, saying only that security clearance was not always needed from the army. The Pakistani army confined to say only that 'we lost control of CIA operatives in Pakistan.'

After deliberations of Federal Interior Minister in the Cabinet, as mentioned in earlier paragraphs, the opposition parties were found roaring in media and on Parliament's floor over an un-precedented move in which government had issued afore-mentioned visas to Americans without security clearances, possibly enabling the CIA to boost its presence. This move had angered Pakistan's military establishment to a considerable extent. More details of those decisions emerged after US operation on Osama in Abbottabad on 2ⁿᵈ May 2011 when the visa issue added fuel to fire between civil and military leadership.

RAYMOND DAVIS KILLED TWO:

Pak-America relationship had reached a low point after Raymond Davis, a CIA contractor and former US Special Forces member, had killed two youngsters in Lahore *on 26ᵗʰ January 2011*. **Raymond Davis, shot two Pakistani men** in what he said was self-defence in a busy market area known as Mozang. Davis called his associates for help which immediately arrived but their vehicle got into a fatal accident with a pedestrian and fled the scene. Onlookers gathered around Davis and took his footage and that of his bullet-ridden vehicle. Police came to the scene and took Davis into custody for onward legal process.

Next day, Raymond Davis was formally declared arrested by the local police for the shootings. Different sources claimed that *Davis was not a diplomat and was not authorised to carry any type of weapons.* The US embassy confirmed his employment as a technical adviser but added that Davis was held-up at gunpoint and reacted in self-defence.

On 29ᵗʰ January 2011 the US officials took turn and claimed that Raymond Davis had diplomatic status in Pakistan and demanded due facilities under the provisions of Vienna Convention but actually Davis did not have diplomatic status per se. Davis was remanded in police custody and PM Gilani did not comment on the Davis's arrest until officials confirmed his identity and status in Pakistan as a foreigner.

On the same day, the then Foreign Minister Shah Mahmood Qureshi was contacted, while he was in Karachi, by the US Ambassador in Islamabad and the US Secretary Hilary Clinton from Washington with the request [subsequently changed to threats] to assign diplomatic status to the

American killer which was refused. The matter was subjudice in the court. Many media personnel were sure that the vague circumstances surrounding Davis could possibly mean that he was a CIA or XE agent.

On 31st January 2011, ABC News in the US also confirmed that Davis was associated with a security firm in Florida, which had a vague background leading to more reports of a possible CIA connection. Next day, President Zardari announced that only Pakistan would decide the fate of Raymond Davis and thereafter the Lahore High Court blocked any moves made by international parties to remove Davis from Pakistan's custody.

On 2nd February 2011, the Federal Interior Minister Rehman Malik stated that Raymond Davis was holding a diplomatic passport but the court extended Davis's remand in police custody. Next day, the US embassy once more agitated that Davis had diplomatic immunity. The Pakistan's Foreign Office, however, affirmed that Raymond Davis's diplomatic immunity appeared to be dubious.

The case was very simple. Davis killed two persons in open day light, was arrested by the Punjab Police and an FIR was registered in local police station of Lahore. As per procedure he was produced before the magistrate who sent him with police on seven days remand.

Immediately the US authorities started threatening the Pakistan government on the pre-text that Davis was enjoying a diplomatic status and Pakistan was refuting the provisions of the Geneva Convention. The matter was again formally referred to the Foreign Office Islamabad for opinion and guidance in the light of the available record. The Foreign Office excavated the whole set of files but could not find any document concerning Davis's diplomatic status nor were the rules there to favour him. The case file was returned to the Punjab government.

On 31st March 2011, a special meeting was called in the Presidency where concerned cabinet members were asked to find out a way to release Raymond Davis in the backdrop of massive pressure from the US government. The strategy to be adopted was to brief the media that pardon to the culprit was being granted on the basis of diplomatic immunity.

The Federal Interior Minister Rehman Malik was proactive to send Davis back to America on the same night. The cabinet members including PM Gilani were aware of Mr Malik's clandestine connections with CIA, *known in public as American Viceroy in Pakistan,* and were looking towards the Foreign Minister who was the concerned and final authority on the issue; Shah M Qureshi straightway refused to go against the rules.

The American lobby present in that mini-cabinet meeting got furious. Arguments developed. Mr Qureshi was asked to tender his resignation from the Foreign Minister's slot. The Interior Minister, who had otherwise no direct connection with the Davis issue, was made the only official spokesman to speak on Davis matters. Mr Qureshi had told there that '..... they (the security establishment) had lost track of most of the people who came in. Their missions were not clearly stated.'

In the same meeting it was told that the US officials made visa requests for *some American Experts* needed to audit the Coalition Support Fund that was established after the 9/11 attacks of 2001 to compensate Pakistan for help in fighting militancy. The Foreign Office had resisted the move by saying that **'You don't need 450 men to audit the funding.'**

However, the Americans managed to get visas in the name of *'other technical people'*. In fact the Pakistani authorities got suspicious after they noticed a large number of people, who appeared to be Americans, driving bullet-proof luxury and utility vehicles in Lahore, Quetta and Peshawar.

The US Embassy declined to comment on the developments suggesting only that the visas might have enabled the CIA to expand its presence in Pakistan, which received billions of dollars in US military aid. What a disgusting reminder it was and a slap on Pakistani nation's face. Raymond Davis was finally taken through certain legal and procedural gimmicks by the court to be sent back to America boarding a special plane from the Lahore Airport; Shahbaz Sharif was in saddles as the Chief Minister.

CIA contractor Raymond Davis was released by Punjab officials reportedly after a deal which was negotiated with the families of the two men he was accused of murdering. Davis was scheduled to be indicted for murder charges. Security forces picked up the families a night earlier and payment of $2 million was apparently made to secure the release. The families remained in police custody till Davis was released and sent to Bagram Air Force Base in Kabul.

Earlier, Senator John Kerry had landed in Pakistan **on 16th February 2011,** met with Punjab's Chief Minister Shahbaz Sharif and PML(N)'s Chief Nawaz Sharif, and announced that the release would occur in a few days. [*Although families of killed persons had refused to meet him*] Rana Sanaullah, Punjab's Law Minister, played the lead role and reportedly received millions dollars for his legal team and the Punjab Police in deal as the CIA payoffs.

One Mr Afzal, the uncle of Shumaila, the widow of one of the slain men and had committed suicide later, told during his interview on a TV Channel that *'family members were told they were being taken to the police station to make statements. Instead, they were taken to a secret location and held in isolation and told that unless they signed a letter pardoning Davis, they would never see daylight.'*

The same evening, Ijazul Haq, Pakistan's former Minister of Religious Affairs, added in a live TV talk, that members of the family and others involved, were given US citizenship to protect them from reprisals.

RELEASE OF RAYMOND DAVIS REWARDED:

Release of Raymond Davis was <u>returned with a big thank you in the form of a drone strike that killed 38 people,</u> the day he was flown away. So what exactly had the PPP government or ISI achieved in their backroom deals with CIA in exchange of his release? The US did so to tell the Pakistani nation that *'stopping the drone strikes was not part of the deal'*, as was widely propagated in media then. The ISI, the military, the Foreign Office and the Presidency were all exposed. *'They do not have a face and can be placed on the same boat; corrupt Generals & politicians - a bunch of horse traders'*, one leading columnist Ayaz Amir opined next day.

One can compare Raymond Davis's event with that of one Pakistani identified for similar activities in America. What Americans had done with him; go through the facts given in the *LA Times dated 24th January 1998*:

'Mir Aimal Kasi, a Pakistani immigrant aged 33, was sentenced to death for gunning down two CIA employees. Kasi had told the Circuit Judge J Howe Brown loudly that 'I don't expect any justice or mercy from your country or this court. The ambush was the result of a wrong policy towards Muslim countries.' He was held guilty by the jury on 10th November 1997 recommending the death penalty.

Mir Aimal Kasi was sentenced for murdering two CIA employees and wounding three others during a shooting rampage in rush-hour traffic outside the agency headquarters [in Langley, Va] in 1993. The conviction of Mir Kasi, capped a lengthy international manhunt by the FBI.

Mir Kasi was captured on 15th June 1996 from a hotel in Pakistan with the active help of Rehman Malik who was Director Immigration in FIA those days. Mr Malik had got signed a statement from Aimal Kasi admitting his guilt while flying back to the United States with American agents.'

Earlier, *LA Times of 23rd June 1997* had published the facts that Rehman Malik was paid $3.5 Million to distribute amongst the 'informants' in Pakistan and Afghanistan to help catch Mir Aimal Kansi. ***Detailed reports were also published in Newsweek and Time magazines.*** Kansi was then held without bail in Fairfax County till the end of trial.

There was a lot of hue and cry and agitation amongst the general populace of Pakistan over Raymond's release. During first week of April 2011, Pakistan had temporarily stopped cooperating with US intelligence officials in the aftermath of detention of Raymond Davis and Cable News Network (CNN) had circulated it as 'Breaking News' but saying that the two countries would continue to share vital intelligence about any imminent acts of terrorism.

At that moment about 40 covert American intelligence operations were going on in Pakistan which were kept hidden from the ISI due to unknown reasons and it was disturbing. The CNN was quoted saying that *'the two nations are "working through differences." The bottom line is that joint cooperation is essential to the security of the two nations. The stakes are too high.'*

An ISI official had told the CNN clearly that:

> *'..... the presence of undisclosed CIA officers amounts to a lack of trust and respect that makes our job very difficult. After incidents like this (referring to Raymond Davis) we do have to take a pause — is it that we are not being trusted? If we cannot be trusted to fight this war on terror on our own turf, then who can?*
>
> *The freezing of cooperation between the two countries is not something the two countries would sustain indefinitely. We want to go back to working with them but we have to work together with trust and respect.'*

This was the atmosphere of mistrust prevailing between the ISI and CIA which brought the American government to decide to strike on Osama on immediate basis which ultimately took place on 2nd May 2011. The first announcement made by the US officials in that context was that:

> ***'We preferred to launch this attack alone because we did not trust the Pakistan any more'.***

The CNN's earlier announcement and ISI officer's briefing was on record that *'mistrust and non cooperation had already prevailed'*.

Soon after, Pakistan sent a written request that the American personnel on CIA's roll as contractors on its soils should leave the country. *A New York Times report indicated that 335 CIA and American special forces had already departed till then.* There were incidents in which Americans had left on their own, probably being coward, *'including some contractors'*.

Coming back, to understand Raymond Davis methodology of performing operations in poor or under-developed states on behalf of the US super power, a few lines from an American journal would be sufficient. An **American retired security official named Robert Anderson** describes his own story at an Online **American News Magazine 'Counter Punch'** and advises the US leadership to shun such activities, as were ordered through Raymond Davis and his team in Pakistan, because the poor Americans normally pay their heavy price afterwards.

Mr Anderson used to perform same like operations in Laos [Cambodia] about four decades ago. During Vietnam War, Laos had the same strategic importance as Pakistan was prevailing then in Afghanistan War. The US had launched certain CIA operations there just as in Pakistan during the last one decade. Mr Anderson was associated with CIA as 'Demolition Technician' but:

> *'.... were equipped with a diplomatic card from the Foreign Office so we were able to claim 'diplomatic Immunity' if captured alive somewhere. We were also told that if we were caught alive or killed, our family in America would be told that we had met a traffic accident in Thailand and our dead bodies were not available. We were briefed to get lost or hide to avoid possible questioning if the media people or UN team would be approaching.*

> *We were made a part of* **'Phoenix Program'** *who were entrusted a job of killing people* **considered disloyal to the US government** *and thus about 60,000 people were murdered in that context.*

> *We had destroyed almost all infra-structure of that country but even then lost the war. Initially, we had ordered our hired men to bring 'ears of the people they had murdered' to claim their remuneration but later we asked them to provide photographs or authentic press reports to claim their bills.'*

If recalled, the same strategy was applied by Raymond Davis in Lahore that after killing the two persons he was seen making photographs of dead bodies with his phone-camera when over-powered by the general populace. Robert Anderson continues to narrate that:

> 'The American Congress had not sanctioned any funds for our horrible program so our local US commanders used to pay us from 'drug money'. We were not part of that side of program but had seen those drug operations from close distance.
>
> It continued till their friend named Oliver North, Chief of Drug Operations in Laos, appeared in a famous court trial named "Iran Contra-Case".'

It is a hard fact of history that since Second World War II the Americans were involved in such activities exactly following the footprints of Nazis of Germany. American leadership had started those secret operations in 1953 by over-throwing Iran's government during the regime of President Roosevelt. It was done so just to control the oil reservoirs of Iran to run the American economy.

America still believes in the same old style of governance all the way through conspiracies and killings through dubious means, as is being done in Pakistan since a decade via drone attacks and Raymond like operations. Now the communication means and media have educated the world and they are able to understand the gimmicks of superpowers though not so empowered to counter them. It brings hatred nothing else.

Pakistan Interior Minister Rehman Malik had told former US envoy Anne Patterson that *'it was not the Army Chief Gen Kayani but the ISI Chief Gen Ahmed Shuja Pasha who was hatching conspiracies against President Asif Ali Zardari'*; a diplomatic cable unveiled by whistle-blower website WikiLeaks had revealed. According to the leaked cable, Mr Malik once sought an urgent appointment to meet with Patterson in November 2009, and said that Pasha was hatching plots against Zardari. Geo News had also reported it the same day but in mild tone.

The real issue cropped up that what arrangements were done by Pakistan's Interior Ministry to keep a track of those Americans who were issued VIP and diplomatic visas. Where were they and how many had actually gone back to States till the end of the PPP government in March 2013; remained a dilemma till today. No body had facts; not even their minister incharge Mr Rehman Malik.

That is where an answer to increasing terrorist activities in Pakistan lies.

Scenario 85

US - OSAMA BIN LADEN OPERATION - I:

On the evening of *26ᵗʰ September 2006,* Gen Musharraf walked into the *Comedy Central's 'Daily Show'* with J Stewart, who offered his guest some tea and cookies and played the perfect host by asking, *"Is it good?"* accompanied by a surprise: *"Where's Osama bin Laden?"* "<u>I don't know,</u>" Gen Musharraf replied, as the audience enjoyed the rare sight of a strong leader apparently cornered. *"You know where he is?"* the General cracked back sarcastically, "<u>You lead on; we'll follow you.</u>" Perhaps Gen Musharraf was being given a cogent hint.

Another scenario:

On *1ˢᵗ December 2009,* the US President Obama, while speaking to the US Army cadets in New York, had chalked out a plan for the US troops to be withdrawn from Afghanistan at the earliest. NATO countries were also pressing hard on US to speak about an exit strategy. An ex US Army General, who had left Afghanistan ten years earlier, told the Americans through his best selling book that:

'America cannot win this Afghan War even in hundred years'.

US economy went shattered due to this war and US owed Trillions of dollars to China alone as debt. 66% voters from Obama's own constituency told him categorically that he would not get their support in next elections [of 2012] due to Afghan war failure.

OPERATION GERONIMO LAUNCHED:

On 2ⁿᵈ May 2011, the US Navy SEALs attacked at a house in Abbottabad and killed Osama Bin Laden [OBL].

The whole Pakistani nation was confused that whether Osama Bin Laden was actually killed in an ambush launched by the American marines in Abbottabad area of Pakistan, about 90 km away from the capital Islamabad. The announcement of Osama's killing was made by the US President Obama himself in the early hours of that day. The entire US nation was delighted over this news. Worldwide, especially in the Western block and NATO member countries, this news was heard with joy and pleasure.

The military operation was carried out by the American SEALs themselves without any involvement of the Pakistan's Army or police [*but whether it was without the information or permission of Pakistan's Army, the ISI, or the Government - was not then ascertained*].

The Pakistani government made announcement for Osama's killing showing a relief that it was sole American operation and Pakistan *had no information on its details.* This was the moment when the things started going wrong. The Opposition parties and their leaders tried to take the Pakistani government on horns by forwarding various theoretical and investigative hypothesis as, according to them Osama had earlier been killed seven times by America starting from their attack in 2001 on Tora Bora mountains in Afghanistan then why a need of killing him 8th time had suddenly cropped up.

[*In American history the event is described as 'Battle of Tora Bora' (Black Cave), fought from 12th December 2001 to 17th December 2001*]

There were about one hundred more questions of investigative and legal nature concerning news about killing Osama BL but the Government of Pakistan had no answer; the US government had broken this news with only little details. The truth was in doldrums and the American people were more inquisitive than Pakistanis as they had paid enormous taxes to go with war option.

America had been investing in Afghanistan since eleven years till then; had been fighting a war which they were unable to win even after hundred years; had been receiving their dead bodies from Afghanistan and had been spending billions of dollars - just to get Osama, dead or alive. Mr Bush had initiated this menace and Mr Obama preferred to continue with Mr Bush's legacy through CIA and Pentagon before whom the Congress and Senate mostly remained helpless.

Pakistan's former military ruler, Gen Musharraf, gave an interview to a London based TV next day and said that:

'*Killing of Osama is OK but the sovereignty of Pakistan has been interfered because the US marines have done this operation whereas the same could have been done by Pakistan Army's SSG (Special Commandoes) unit.*'

The intelligentsia observed that '*as Osama is dead, the US troops should leave Afghanistan at the earliest now.*'

Tehreek e Taliban Pakistan (TTP) confirmed the killing of Osama Bin Laden but also issued a threat that TTP would take its revenge vowing that *'now Pakistani rulers are on our hit-list.'* Pakistan's government continued denying their involvement.

PAKISTAN KNEW IT WELL – A HARD FACT:

A BBC televised evening program categorically stated that the government of Pakistan was not told about the planned attack until the same was completed. But Pakistan's Federal Information Minister Dr Firdaus A Awan told the media that *'how such big operation could take place without the active help and knowledge of our army and intelligence agencies.'* Astonishingly till evening she had gone 180 angles opposite but her original statement was suspiciously correct.

GEO TV's live programs *'Aapis ki Baat with Najam Sethi'* of three next days [*dated 3rd - 5th May 2011*] had told the true story but the political leadership and military elite continued to make [false] statements that Pakistan had not known about the American intentions of Osama's killing.

In the first **TV address of the American President Obama on 2nd May 2011,** immediately after Osama's killing was clear when he said that *'....the success was not possible without the cogent help of Pakistani intelligence agencies; they have led us to the right place and we have succeeded'.*

The US president told his nation and the whole world proudly that the ISI's personnel had taken the SEAL team exactly upto Osama's residence and they made the marvellous achievement to keep the America and their global partners safe.

Secondly, it is still available on record that President Obama rang Mr Zardari immediately to convey congratulations over the success of the said Osama Operation. Same day the US Secretary Hilary Clinton had talked PM Gilani and the US Commander Mike Mullen had told the Army Chief Gen Kayani about the successful raid over Osama Bin Laden.

The most important factor was that the three top American figures had exchanged their good wishes and offered reciprocal congratulations to each other. Both parties were joyful and smiling amidst satisfaction over the development. None of the Pakistani statesmen took it as odd 'NEWS' or unexpected attack; none exclaimed with sorrow nor shown any worries whatsoever. The heads of both the countries talked just in normal way as it was a 'joint task' but accomplished by one party as had been worked out before.

An article in the *'Washington Post' dated 2*nd *May 2011* in the name of Mr Zardari [*said to be written by MNA Farahnaz Ispahani for Mr Zardari*] was sufficient to indicate that top Pakistani leadership knew about the operation; that was why the 'undated' article was placed with the said newspaper in reserve to publish it when the *'Operation Geronimo'* would be successfully completed.

Hussain Haqqani, Pakistan's ambassador in Washington, and Wajid Shamsul Hassan, Pakistani High Commissioner at London, both on the very next day of Osama's killing on 2nd May 2011, had categorically answered media questions on TV that *'Pakistan knew about the operation and it has been carried out as a joint operation of intelligence agencies of both the countries.'*

In this connection one can recall a live TV interview of the then US Secretary State Hillary Clinton in which she had clearly said that *'....many people in Pak-Army and ISI know that where are Osama and Mulla Omar hiding in Pakistan; we also know those people – but it is government of Pakistan's prerogative* [*to do the next appropriate job*]'.

In fact, after getting lead of a high value target's residence [*till then not sure of Osama Bin Laden's presence there*] in Abottabad, the American intelligence had started working on the proposition that:

- Why this lonely house, and so big, suddenly built after 2005 without Municipal Authority's approval for building plans etc. Then it was virtually constructed in open fields.

- So big house but no car or jeep going in or coming out; no telephone cable going in and no mobile registered at this address.

- Why 18ft high walls outside; no windows towards the streets though there were two towards open fields.

- Within that big 18ft walled premises there was another house with 8 ft high walls [it was seen through satellite photography].

- No interaction of residents of that big house with anybody outside; seldom some person coming out or going in without any communication with anyone around.

The answers of above questions lead towards the conclusion that the residence was suspicious thus worth intensive surveillance.

An important question that *'why Pak-Army was not made part of the operation'*. It was because the script was written so. This was the only American [intelligence] operation in Pakistan which was accomplished without the active participation of the Pak-army. The Pak-army refrained and preferred to sit in the back to avoid the Taliban & Al Qaeda's possible revenge and strike backs.

Frequent denials from the Pakistani government and military top-heads, pretending having no prior knowledge of the US operation, were the replica of Pak-US compromise over the 'Drone Attack Policy' [.....*that the Pakistan leadership would stick with issuing press statements for denunciation and disapproval of drone attacks BUT the US government would continue to go by its plans*].

Even when 369 Pakistanis were handed over to the US intelligence & interrogation agencies [*though there was no extradition treaty or diplomatic protocol existing between the two countries*] in the name of WoT; when they were taken to Bagram Base in Afghanistan or to Guantanamo Bay in Cuba; when most of them were killed at either place during interrogation; when the handed over lots also comprised of certain suspects who were ten years old – the Pak-army, ISI, IB & FIA and the American CIA and Pentagon were always seen hands in gloves. However, this time it was planned to be so - it was successfully played.

Then the next question: *when did the leaderships of the two countries, Pakistan & the US, plan to do this operation.* Simply check out the dates within two weeks prior to 2nd May 2011, when the two American war-lords, Gen Mike Mullen and Gen Petreas, were together in Pakistan; one coming directly from Washington and the other through Afghanistan, holding one to one meetings with top civil and military leadership of Pakistan – but then smilingly left for the US without leaving any 'bullshit' note for Pakistan having *'Do More'* instructions.

One more aspect be kept in mind that Pakistan's military elite knew about American tradition or strategy that *'they never try to catch their high value target alive – they are trained to kill that'*. Whereas the Pak-army people are trained otherwise so they did not opt to be part of that killing game.

Another question: *'why the SEAL team preferred to put the dead body of Osama Bin Laden in the sea instead of burying it'*. Here one can believe that the suggestion might have come from the Pakistani leadership because they knew that Muslims and especially the Pakistanis are known for *'dead hero worship'*, little matters how much controversial one would have been in his life; ZA Bhutto & Gen Ziaul Haq can both be quoted as examples.

After Osama Bin Laden's killing in Abottabad, the world media started thinking that:

• Whether the US forces would quit from Afghanistan after declaring WoT over. OR

• The US would remain there, would intensify its operations, using Osama's presence in the region as an excuse.

The answer came immediately after as the very next day, the BBC released a list of 16 die-hard Al Qaeda members, all Arabic speaking, who were allegedly hiding themselves in the Pak-Afghan border region [North Waziristan] on whom similar operations were indicated. It was clearly conveyed to the world that more severe attacks would be launched over the suspected places. The plans were acted upon. Consequently, dozens of suspected hide outs of Haqqani group and Al Qaeda were drone attacked but with no considerable success; civilian women and children were mostly killed.

Daily *'Jang'* dated 7th *March 2012,* gave an account that Gen Musharraf knew about Osama's presence in Abbottabad; while quoting Gen Ziauddin But, the last DG ISI of PML(N) government in 1999. The same fact was corroborated by a well known media guest Gen Amjad Shoaib who had made it open in live TV talk show that during the night of 2nd May 2011, there had been a *telephonic conversation between Gen Kayani and President Zardari and 'there exists a mention of it in the GHQ's log book'.*

The Pakistani people were found jubilant while saying that it was a moment of relief and respite for them because due to Osama's person they had continuously been suffering since eleven years at least. War on terror (WOT) was thrust upon Pakistan which brought drone and terrorist attacks for no fault of the poor people. Pakistan lost about 35000 innocent civilian lives of men, women and children during the last ten years of this 'unholy' war of interests.

'We were fighting other people's war on our lands for no fortune at all', the Pakistani people believed. Pakistan's army lost their 5000 officers

and men on the Pak–Afghan border and tribal areas amidst world criticism and stern threats. Pakistan lost its economy worth 37.5 billion dollars and the estimated loss to their infrastructure escalated to about 67 billion dollars. Who would compensate Pakistan; no one was there to hear their cries.

Media reiterated loudly that Osama bin Laden was a fighter from Saudi Arabia which country had withdrawn their own nationality from this person declaring him an enemy of humanity. He was an illegal migrant in Pakistan. Being a Muslim he might have appealed some but thousands of Muslims were killed in the name of his Al Qaeda in so many Muslim countries; thus why not your sympathies with the killed ones.

Thinking being nationalist; how many Muslim countries came up with help for Pakistani poor people who were suffering from miseries since a decade on account of Muslim 'brotherhood'; no one in fact. Even some Muslim countries refused supply of oil to Pakistan on credit due to his alleged presence there.

Now some material questions that why government of Pakistan was officially denying their hands in this operation. Why Osama's dead body was not shown to the public and was thrown in the sea waters. In a *TV program of DM Digital at Sky 802 dated 2ⁿᵈ May 2011*, the host lady [named Umm e Aadil] gave an opening sermon that Osama was *'shaheed'* (martyr) and the world should be sorry on killing of such a great Muslim. When she was questioned from tens of Pakistani callers that what good he had done for other Muslims or humanity at large or for Pakistan except killing about 40,000 men, she had no cogent answer. She had to quit her stance and then later the TV channel.

Osama's alleged attack on Twin Towers NY coining a 9/11 phrase, had defined the last 10 years history of hostility, chase and violence through the whole world. It shaped US foreign policy leading to two major wars, one of which was continuing till early 2013 on Pak-Afghan borders. It resulted in gross violations of human rights in the name of *'war on terror' (WOT)*. It transformed Pakistan and Afghanistan, dragging them into ideological divides and violence which **claimed thousands of lives, twenty times more than lost on 9/11.**

[*Soon after fighting the Soviets in Afghanistan, around 1992, an Al Qaeda affiliate allegedly attacked American soldiers in Yemen, and in 1996 Osama declared war on America by blowing up US embassies in Africa but it was not until Twin Towers attack that the world had felt his presence. By then it was too late, and in the following years, organisations supported or inspired by him sprang up across the world, slaughtering both Muslims and non-Muslims in their anti-Americanism perspective.*]

On the first anniversary of Osama's killing [2nd May 2012], Pakistan's Federal Defence Minister Ahmed Mukhtar gave a serious press statement that **'the said American Operation was known by both the Pakistan government and army'.** The said statement alerted many concerned because the people were holding mixed opinions about Osama's killing.

An odd situation suddenly cropped up by Defence Minister's deliberations because the intelligentsia had known that the Pak-Army and the ISI had successfully cleared themselves in 13th May 2011's in-camera parliamentary session. However, the people still had in their minds the contents of afore-mentioned Mr Zardari's essay of 2nd May 2011 in American press media; many eye-brows were stunned.

OPERATION - ONLY US PLANNED IT:

In the backdrop of al-Qaeda's alleged attack on the World Trade Centre and the Pentagon on 11th September 2001, the most memorable one-liner came from an US expert Richard Clarke, who said, **'Your government failed you.'** On 15th February 2009, Michael Hayden, George W Bush's last CIA Director said that:

'When's the last time you really knew where he [Osama BL] was? My answer was Tora Bora (Afghanistan) in 2001.'

President Obama's first order to his new CIA boss Leon Panetta was:

'Make the killing or capture of OBL the top priority of the war against al-Qaeda; if we have Osama bin Laden in our sights and the Pakistani government is unable or unwilling to take him out, then we have to act and we will take him out. We will kill bin Laden; we will crush al-Qaeda. That has to be our biggest national-security priority.'

In fact the new capabilities mastered by the CIA & Pentagon after 9/11 gave Obama choices and weapons that were not available to previous Presidents. Had these been available to Bill Clinton in 1998 after al-Qaeda's attacks on US embassies in Africa or to Bush in 2001 when Osama was surrounded at Tora Bora, either chief could order an operation that would have killed bin Laden. Fifteen months after

Obama's above 'Get bin Laden' order, Panetta returned to the White House in August 2010 with good news; the CIA had discovered that house in Abbottabad in which Osama's courier was living.

The US President had to work out: Firstly, when to act; Secondly, who would be called to join the decision-making process; and thirdly, how exactly to go ahead for 100% success. Choices were again:

- Firstly, of predator drones with missiles delivering 500-lb bombs (like those used five months later to kill Anwar al-Awlaki in Yemen);

- Secondly, of B-2 bombers with 2,000-lb laser-guided bombs (like those used in late 2011 against Col Gaddafi in Libya);

- Thirdly, of using special forces on the ground; and

- Fourthly, of a joint military operation in association with Pakistan, the host country. The officers knew Obama was 'betting his presidency' on that issue; if the operation failed, opponents would label him as a 2nd Jimmy Carter, recalling the failed attempt [of 1980] to rescue American hostages in Iran.

Going into details: the joint operation with Pakistan quickly fell off the menu when on 27th January 2011, a CIA contractor Raymond Davis was arrested in Lahore on murder charges; an incident that reminded the White House that its Pakistani allies could turn eyes any time.

Predator plan was shelved because firstly there were doubts whether 500-lb bombs could impact enough punch to guarantee a kill. Secondly Pakistan was unlikely to cooperate in sifting through that they had killed the right man. If al-Qaeda claimed Osama was still alive, how could the US prove otherwise? Thirdly, the US would lose the opportunity to capture valuable evidence from Osama's residence.

The option of B-2 strike [calling for dropping 2000-lb bombs] was thrown away because it would also kill about 20 women and children living with Osama and tens of occupants of neighbouring houses; possibility of escape of the real target was still there.

Thus President Obama was left with no option except to go for the most workable but risky choice of sending SEALs for direct attack. McRaven was directed *on 29th March 2011* to perform a 'full dress rehearsal' of the raid but the final orders were conveyed *on 29*[th] *April 2011*. Interestingly, CIA's Morell had reminded his fellow participants that:

> *'The circumstantial evidence for WMD in Iraq was stronger than the circumstantial evidence for the Abbotabad man's being bin Laden'.*

However, Obama had full confidence in his team and was sure of success too. To cover the questions that if *'some one from within the Pak-army'* unknowingly obstructed the US forces en route or on the ground or took them hostage or if a chopper crashed etc; the team planned to take two more Chinook helicopters with 24 more SEALs for *'backup and fighting their way out.'*

The biggest surprise of the entire operation was that it was a real surprise. **Graham Allison** observed in the *'TIME' of 7*[th] *May 2012* that:

> *'In today's Washington, a week is a lifetime. Secrets are often published overnight, as Obama learned painfully in 2009 when he attempted to consider his options in Afghanistan. He found himself "jammed" when he asked his new Commander in Afghanistan, Gen McChrystal, to assess the situation.*
>
> *When Obama received McChrystal's dire 66-page brief that warned of imminent defeat unless a major initiative was undertaken to "reverse the momentum," the President was shocked.*
>
> *Before he could meet with his national-security team to discuss his options, McChrystal's report appeared in the press.'*

Eventually James Jones, Obama's National Security Adviser was sent aside and his deputy, Tom Donilon was given that top slot. The toughest choice they faced was the time to fire yet they waited five months after getting sure about Osama's hide out. The major issue was of informing, then sharing and lastly winning the confidence of Pakistan's civil and military leadership.

When the decision was taken, astonishingly his Vice President Joe Biden and the Secretary of Defence Robert Gates opposed the raid on the pretext that putting commandos on the ground could risk their being captured or killed; Joint Chiefs of Staff [JCS] Vice Chairman James Cartwright, preferred an air strike. CIA's Deputy Director Michael Morell gave Donilon and Brennan regular [and direct] intelligence updates keeping all others away. Till six months earlier, the CIA was 60% confident of the information about Osama's living in Abbotabad.

About 40 intelligence reviews from August 2010 to April 2011 were placed on record with varying questions and hostile propositions; most important that Osama should be arrested or killed and in the later case what to do with Osama's dead body *'if operation goes successful'*.

Out of six person's team of decision makers, Panetta and CIA's Morell were of the view to go ahead with paramilitary personnel to conduct the raid; it was a painful but realistic decision. Thus, with President Obama's approval, the circle was expanded to include two more players: McRaven and JCS Vice Chairman Cartwright. At this point, Cartwright's boss, JCS Chairman Mike Mullen; Secretary of State Hillary Clinton; Secretary Defence Gates, all were left aside.

At White House, five meetings of NSC members were held in the last six weeks to review all the options and the previous conclusions. Gates and Clinton were called in the meetings alone [without their deputies or staff] and that too after Donilon's personal approval.

OPERATION GERONIMO – MORE DETAILS:

On 2ⁿᵈ May 2011 [Pakistani time], a squad of trained US commandos based in Jalalabad (Afghanistan) had tripped their choppers low and fast through the mountains to launch an attack at Osama Bin Laden's residence in Bilal Town Abbotabad. What's in name: The Operation Geronimo or Operation Neptune's Spear but it went successful.

> [*Though the Americans wrote in their scripts and press briefings that the Operation Geronimo was launched from Jalalabad but subsequent evidence provided enough proof that the US Choppers flew from an army airbase near Tarbela in Pakistan and NOT from Jalalabad. It had also proved the earlier stance that Pakistani elite were part of the said operation.*]

US Vice Admiral William McRaven, Commander of the Joint Special Operations Command (JSOC), was in-charge of that Operation having direct contacts with White House's Sit Room, with Leon Panetta's offices at the CIA headquarters and the Ops Centre in the Pentagon, where a team of some 30 officers was standing by to respond to any contingency.

In White House President Obama was heading the National Security Council members at that particular time of **Sunday 1ˢᵗ May 2011** [US time], however astonishingly, until 24 hours before that US Operation; a majority of those members of the NSC were still unaware of the exact time & *modus operandi* of the attack.

Navy SEAL team, consisting of 23 'operators', a trained dog and an interpreter, boarded two Black Hawk choppers which raised in air at 11.30 PM Abbotabad time carrying photos of Osama and his family members supposed to be there at home.

The MH-60s choppers, modified so as to remain undetected by Pakistani radar stations [though otherwise settled to remain in peacetime mode], flew dangerously low and very fast, only a few feet above the ground, driving over the riverbeds and avoiding trees, reached Abbotabad within 25 minutes whereas the distance was just 50 miles straight run in fact. From the White House Sit Room Brig Gen Marshall Brad Webb, Assistant Commanding General of JSOC was also feeding the choppers through an RQ-170 Sentinel stealth drone which was then flying more than two miles above Abbotabad.

When the helicopters reached their destination, the well planned operation started but the first chopper hit the outer wall while trying to land in Osama's courtyard; it suddenly lost altitude. The tail of the craft clipped one of the compound walls, breaking off the critical tail rotor whereas the SEALs were able to scramble out of the downed machine. Three of those SEALs ran across the small field, blasted the Iron Gate, and entered the garage where [Ibrahim] Kuwaiti had parked his jeep. The Kuwaiti surfaced his head out from behind that metal gate but was shot dead immediately and his wife got a shot in her right shoulder; the silenced weapons made little noise.

In his 3rd floor bedroom, Osama was awake, heard noise and blasts for fifteen minutes but could do nothing in dark. Dressed in *shalwar kameez* [local Pakistani dress], sewn into these were a few hundred euros and two cell-phone numbers but nothing else. The SEALs went from the Kuwaiti's garaged residence into the ground floor of the main house where they shot Abrar, the Kuwaiti's brother, and his wife Bushra, killing them both. As the SEALs ran up to the second floor, they encountered Osama's 23 years old son Khalid, whom they shot too on the staircase.

Over the sound of explosions inside home, Osama's 20 years aged daughter Maryam rushed upstairs to his 3rd-floor bedroom to ask what was going on; she was sent back unhurt.

Osama had got an AK-47 and a pistol in his room but why did not use them was astonishing. He opened the iron door, which could be opened only from the inside, and calmly tried to smell the disorder. Attending noise rushing into their room, a young lady Amal [Osama's youngest Yemeni wife] screamed and stood as shield to her husband; she was pushed aside. She was instructed by her husband 'not to turn on the light' but the electricity feeding transformer of the area had already gone off.

[*The time of one hour power off at particular moment also indicated that the operation had carefully been worked out earlier by both Pakistani and US authorities – it was not a mystery as the media raised their eyebrows next day.*]

It was a moonless night. Amal was then shot in the calf when she fell unconscious on the mattress. Osama offered no resistance when he was given double shots to the chest and left eye. Blood scattered all around on the wall and floor; the game was over.

The Americans had noticed that Osama had no escape plan and there was no secret passage out of his home. He rather died a peaceful death surrounded by his wives and children amidst scattered toys and medicine bottles and not the heap of guns, grenades, or suicide jackets etc.

Osama was leading a 'confined' life there since 2005 when the house was newly built. He was there with three of his wives [ranging from the 28 years aged Amal to the 62 years old Khairiah] and a dozen of his children and grandchildren. Osama had married Khairiah in 1985; she was Ph.D qualified teacher hailing from a wealthy and distinguished real Syed family of Saudi Arabia.

In 2001, Khairiah had fled to neighbouring Iran with her children and had re-joined Osama in 2010 at Abbotabad after harshly managing his journey through North Waziristan. Osama's 2nd wife named Siham bin Abdullah, a 54 years lady with a Ph.D in Koranic grammar was from Sudan; a poet and an intellectual otherwise. His youngest wife Amal was only 17 years aged when married in 2000-01; later bore Osama's five children, including two at Abbotabad.

Practically, Osama was inactive or retired during his whole stay there, certainly leading an unpleasant life. From his computer he used to advise other militant *jihadi* groups not to adopt al-Qaeda's name any more. On 7th August 2010, he wrote to the leader of *al-Shabab* militia in Somalia urging that '*declaring itself part of al-Qaeda would only attract enemies and make it harder to raise money from rich Arabs*'.

In October 2010, as per US version, Osama allegedly sent [*how could he send it without internet or phone facility at home*] a long note to his field commanders that:

'*The Americans had the worst year for them in Afghanistan since they invaded while deepening US budget crisis. But al-Qaeda's long-time sanctuary in Waziristan, in Pakistan's tribal areas, was now too dangerous because of US drone strikes. I am leaning toward getting most of our brothers out of the area.*

Make sure to tell Hamza [Osama's 20 years aged son] that I am of the opinion he should get out of Waziristan ... He should move only when the clouds are heavy; [and preferably] to tiny, prosperous Persian Gulf kingdom of Qatar.

It would be nice if you could nominate one of the qualified brothers to be responsible for a large operation against the US. It would be nice if you would pick a number of the brothers not to exceed 10 and send them to their countries individually without any of them knowing the others to study aviation.'

[This was US official versions to make their people fool otherwise Osama had no connection with the outer world; neither via internet nor through cell-phones – there was no phone line connection at his residence.]

The fact remained that after 7th July 2005's alleged attacks on London Rail Network, al-Qaeda could never launch any successful attack anywhere. Osama's deputy Ayman al Zawahiri had openly conveyed back that *'it was much more realistic to attack American soldiers in Afghanistan than civilians in the US'*.

The independent intelligentsia, however, believed that the whole 'long memo of 48 pages' referred by Peter Bergen in a later issue of the 'TIME' magazine might be coined and framed somewhere in CIA or Pentagon's corner room. Ponder into the facts that:

• There was no telephone or satellite connection available in Osama's premises then how the memo was communicated.

• How the Chief of Al Qaeda, hiding from the world since ten years, could take risk of sending such communications through open 48 pages letter on internet, e-mail or even by hand unto Somalian regions.

• Lastly, see one of the paragraphs: *'He [Osama] instructed his team that the 10th anniversary of the 9/11 attack is coming and due to the importance to this date, the time to start preparing is now. Please send me your suggestions on this.'*

[It was total mockery of realism. The 48-page memo was being written in October 2010 asking for suggestions on 9/11 event of a year after.]

Osama, himself hailing from one of the richest business family of Saudia, was in acute financial crunch throughout his stay at Abbotabad; as was evident from his living standard. His trusted bodyguard and courier Abu Ahmed Ibrahim al-Kuwaiti, courier's brother Abrar and their wives and children were also living in the compound in abject poverty; used to be paid Rs:12,000 a month each [£75] reflecting that *'al-Qaeda's coffers were actually empty'.*

'OPERATION GERONIMO' - MEDIA VERSIONS:

John Brennan, the President's Adviser told the American media that:

'This is different. This intelligence case is different. What we see in this compound is different than anything we've ever seen before. I was confident that we had the basis to take action.'

However, the options were limited as the compound was in a residential neighbourhood in another sovereign country. The American media reports of *3*rd *May 2011* told the official US version that:

'Before dawn, a pair of helicopters left the airbase.... The choppers entered Pakistani airspace using sophisticated technology..... Officially, it was a kill-or-capture mission.

... but shortly after.... one of the helicopters came crashing down. None of the SEALs was injured; the mission continued uninterrupted; with the CIA and White House monitoring the situation.

The SEALs secured ..... then proceeded..... fire - fight ensued. Ahmed and his brother were killed; then, the SEALs killed bin Laden.... Using the call sign for his visual identification, one of the soldiers communicated that "Geronimo" had been killed.

Bin Laden's body.... the US also conducted DNA testing that identified him with near 100% certainty. Photo analysis.... matching physical features.... height all helped confirm the identification. At the White House, there was no doubt.

US forces searched the compound and flew away with documents, hard drives and DVDs....The operation took 40 minutes.

Bin Laden's body was flown to the USS Carl Vinson in the North Arabian sea. There, aboard a US warship, officials conducted a traditional

Islamic burial ritual. Bin Laden's body was washed and placed in a white sheet. He was placed in a weighted bag that, after religious remarks by a military officer, was slipped into the sea.'

US officials maintained that Osama Bin Laden's body was treated with respect and buried at sea, but some Muslims argued there was no good reason for not burying it on land. However, dead Osama, while taking rest in a shrine, could have been more dangerous for the Americans. They did not take risk whatsoever.

Islamic tradition requires the dead to be buried as soon as possible, unless an autopsy is required. The US military took this requirement very seriously, burying the body within hours and the traditional procedures for Islamic burial were followed. On the deck of the US aircraft carrier, the USS Carl Vinson, the last rituals occurred at 0600GMT, approximately 12 hours after Osama was shot in the head. As per **ABC News 'The Blotter'**, after the first shot Osama was shot again, to make sure that he was dead – again no risk was taken.

Osama's dead body was first flown to Afghanistan and Bin Laden's identity was confirmed. Officials say a DNA sample was taken that matched that of several other family members [*hats off to Dr Afridi's fake vaccination campaign*]; facial recognition technology was also used. From Afghanistan, the body was flown to the USS Carl Vinson. *"A military officer read prepared religious remarks, which were translated into Arabic by a native speaker,"* a US defence official later told.

'I think we can all agree this is a good day for America', the President Obama had said.

Justice ® Javed Iqbal's Judicial Commission on 2nd May 2011 event had noted that there was found only one fired bullet mark in the whole campus; in Osama's bed room, where Osama was found dead. That bullet possibly passed through his skull and hit the wall, 8-9 ft above from the floor. It also pointed out that the invader had actually hit Osama from the crawling position.

After this *'Geronimo Operation'*, most intelligentsia believed that this would bring the US policy planners to start an honourable quit from Afghanistan. Every battle or war needs some turning point to make out a logical end; analyse any big event. Killing Osama at last was a shift in the American policy in the Afghan region in fact.

Many tax-payer Americans argued that OBL's death lacked significance because Al Qaeda's terrorist capability had already been zeroed; other organizations were active. Most officers associated with US National Security maintained that Osama's role in Al Qaeda at the time of his death was largely inspirational only; of no practical value being incapacitated since long. It seemed to be plausible because Osama himself was hiding since 2003 at various places without communication with the outer world.

ISI & PAK-ARMY KEPT AWAY:

According to Amal, Osama's third wife, as she told to CIA later that OBL and his family had left the tribal areas in 2003 to live in *Chak Shah Mohammad*, a settled area of Haripur on the highway to Abbotabad, from which place they moved in 2005; Abbotabad house was newly built then.

Osama was killed in Abbotabad but before this operation the Americans took months to confirm that Osama was living in the said compound near Kakul. The event raised a series of questions about the level of cooperation with Pakistani intelligence and the military. Were they taken into confidence? Subsequent official statements issued and interviews released by the US Pentagon and Foreign Office said; NO. Pakistani radars were allegedly dodged in operation but ISPR remained silent on the issue. The ambiguity persisted.

Osama was living in a large house surrounded by high walls topped with barbed wire in a garrison town housing Kakul Military Academy. The idea that the world's most wanted *Jihadi* was spending his days there unnoticed by Pakistani intelligence was never believed by the outsiders. If it was true then it was reflecting a massive failure on the part of many. The oversight was a matter of incompetence or wilful negligence, both needed attention if it was so.

Ten years earlier, Pakistani intelligence and police worked closely with the CIA to dig out a number of Al Qaeda leaders, almost all of whom were found in cities and not in the villages or tribal areas. This time the US got intelligence from Pak-army but no longer trusted Pakistan for a joint operation, because of the involvement of high-stake target.

The US missile strikes on Al Qaeda bases in Sudan in 1998 were launched after tracking a mobile phone of an Al Qaeda member. Since then Osama was not using mobile or even land line phones. Thus CIA planned to interrogate the detainees from Pakistan at Guantanamo Bay with a particular question in sight; to know about the courier in between Al Qaeda and Osama. By 2002, interrogators had sorted out a courier named Abu Ahmed al-Kuwaiti. Later perhaps in 2003, Khalid Sheikh Mohammed had also revealed under interrogation that he was acquainted with al-Kuwaiti.

In 2004, another prisoner named Hassan Gul [*an al-Qaeda agent and a member of Ansar al-Islam, keeping three passports from Yemen, Pakistan and Egypt; captured on 23rd January 2004 by Kurdish police forces at a checkpoint near Kalar, at the Iranian border*] not only confirmed Al-Kuwaiti but also told the Americans about his successor Abu Faraj al-Libi who was captured in 2005 and transferred to Guantánamo in September 2006. Faraj guided the CIA interrogators towards one Maulvi Abdul Khaliq Jan also, a Pakistani by name but not by origin.

In August 2010, CIA's undercover operatives in Pakistan intercepted a wire-trap from which they located al-Kuwaiti and followed him back to Osama's Abbotabad compound.

On 25th April 2011, WikiLeaks leaked certain interrogation files and other classified material from Guantnamo, *especially related with Al-Kuwaiti & Abu Faraj Al-Libi,* which appeared on the front page of the New York Times. One of the documents was carrying the identity of Osama's 'official courier' pointing towards Haripur - Abbotabad's old residence where OBL had moved in mid-2003.

Immediate notice was taken of that situation and *on 28th April 2011,* the team assembled at White House for issuance of green signal for the 1st May attack [as per US time]. Delay might have lost their target pushing all efforts and one year's labour in vain; Gates and Biden again voted no but 'go ahead' was released the next morning.

Pakistan's Army or ISI were not shared or consulted at that moment.

As per CIA claims, Al-Kuwaiti, along with his brother or a cousin, were also killed in 2nd May 2011 attack. The old ID cards found on their bodies told them as Pashtuns named Arshad Khan and Tariq Khan from village Khat Kuruna near Charsadda. Pakistani officials could not find record of the two in Charsadda's said village; however, in June 2011, they were identified by local police as Ibrahim Saeed Ahmed & Abrar Ahmed from Swat Valley, who and their families were living at Osama's compound as domestic servants.

On 7th May 2011, President Zardari, PM Gilani and COAS Gen Ashfaq Kayani met for the second time at Presidency since Osama's operation in Abbotabad and comprehensively reviewed the then prevailing situation in the perspective of Pakistan's national security and foreign policy. The three high ups held this meeting in the backdrop of pressure from the international community on the government to shed light on Osama's hiding near Kakul Military Academy. PML(N) and PPP's former foreign minister Shah Mahmood Qureshi also joined this orchestra.

Coming back; the irony of fate was that the US Attorney General Eric Holder, Secretary of Homeland Security Janet Napolitano, FBI Director Robert Mueller, special assistant to the President for Afghanistan and Pakistan Douglas Lute and many more were told of the perspective raid the same day [29th April 2011]. After the US helicopters escaped Pakistani airspace, Obama made his first calls to former Presidents Bush and Clinton to share the pleasure.

Referring to the *'TIME' of 7th May 2012:*

> *'The most troubling lesson from this case is the dog that hasn't barked. In the aftermath of Abbotabad, we [the US] are left with two possibilities: either the Pakistanis knew that bin Laden was there, or they didn't. .....after intense review of the materials seized in the raid, the brute fact is that not a shred of evidence has been found to suggest anyone in the Pakistani military and intelligence hierarchy knew of bin Laden's whereabouts.*

> *............ Could it be possible that a nation that is unaware that bin Laden lived within its borders for six years, moved five times with three wives and fathered four children (two born in local hospitals) is also a nation that is in control of some 100 nuclear bombs?'*

ISI & PAF ADMITTED FAILURE:

The ISI admitted its failure [or made to admit] that this lack of knowledge brought embarrassment for them. The media was told that Osama's daughter aged 12 was taken in custody who had seen US troops shooting her father to death. There were about 18 people present in compound at the time of US raid. A US chopper crashed amid operation otherwise US marine commandos would have taken all the people in the compound, dead and alive, back to America.

Pakistan's Ministry of Foreign Affairs (MoFA) made fool of Pakistani nation while issuing a statement that the US helicopters had entered

Pakistani airspace making use of blind spots in the radar coverage due to hilly terrain. Moreover, the ISPR release of 5th May 2011 remained silent on the issue of detection of US helicopters there entering and doing operation for forty minutes in Abbotabad.

Pakistan's Air Chief, Rao Suleman Qamar, very next day told open that their radars were not jammed; in fact they were not switched on for western borders due to obvious reasons of **'zero threat'** from that side.

[*When Indians intended to raid Hafiz Saeed's complex near Muridke in the aftermath of the Bombay attacks in November 2008, they had to change their mind when they found that Pakistan's Air Force was ready to hit back the moment Indians crossed the border.*]

Question arose that **'did really the American helicopters come from Afghanistan?'**

Some people doubted it. In their analysis the helicopters flew from the NATO base near Tarbela. From there, the air distance to Abbotabad was 10 kms, only a few minutes away. After returning from Abbotabad, the helicopters flew to Bagram, as normal flights from NATO base to Bagram.

Najam Sethi, in GEO's live program of the same night told that US helicopters flew from Tarbela [*though contradicted himself the next night, not because he was wrong but presumably, because the admission would have forced NATO to leave Tarbela on immediate basis.*]

The US official version given on 2nd May 2011 to the world media by John Brennan, the President's Adviser, however, reiterated that *'the US choppers flew from Jalalabad Afghanistan'*.

Did the helicopters remain unnoticed during the operation?
No. It was just not possible. There were four helicopters; their engines went running all the time during the 40-minute operation; making a lot of noise, even the Stealth type. Their lights were on due to the moonless night; the neighbours did notice them so did the authorities at 500 yards away in Kakul premises.

Were the US helicopters really invisible to our radars?
American helicopters were not invisible and, in fact, no helicopter could be. According to **'Aviation Week'** dated 9th **May 2011,** '... *it is believed that a helicopter cannot yet be made as radar-stealthy as a fixed-wing airplane, as helicopters generally operate at low altitude and against ground clutter.*'

Courageous PAF explained that the country was not expecting any aerial threat from Afghanistan. Air Commodore Tariq Yazdani had also confirmed that the air surveillance system had neither been jammed nor had it been inactive.

Often a question was raised that if *Osama was really killed in Abbotabad on that day.* The live video feed from the Abbotabad operation to CIA headquarters and then to the White House could also be given to CNN for the whole world to watch. However, no doubt that Osama was very much there with his family because it was inconceivable that he would leave them unprotected, without his own reliable guards being present. Osama would have allowed his wives and children to go to their home countries or Saudia if he believed they were not safe with him.

Nevertheless, in Corps Commander's meeting of 5th **May 2011**, Pakistan's army chief ordered an investigation into the intelligence failures that led to Osama's undetected presence, and why US personnel were able to enter Pakistani territory without notice. *The hard fact remains that their investigation report never surfaced up;* and it was not to come up because it was a joint operation [though limited].

In the words of Babar Sattar (ref: *'Dawn' of 7th May 2011*) that:

'....... *We need to rationally approach the concept of sovereignty together with state responsibility to understand why the world views us suspiciously. We need a thorough re-examination of our existing national security doctrine to determine whether it is promoting or jeopardising our security.'*

PAK-ARMY WENT SPLINTED; REALLY?

The media knew that two parallel factions had been working in Pakistan army and especially in the ISI. One faction with pure national interests just to think for Pakistan; COAS Gen Kayani was leading them. The other faction, continuously since two decades, was seeking enlightenment from ex ISI Chief Gen Hamid Gul, encouraged by Taliban's movement and activities in Afghanistan; Gen Zaheerul-Islam, Gen Aziz and partly Gen Mahmud of the then ISI were their silent supporters. From Generals down to ranks, the two philosophies went parallel but equally compelling, effective and strong enough. Thus it was unlikely that Osama was being hosted by Pakistan as a matter of policy.

The nation spends billions on ISI & MI in the name of security and not for spying or 'persuading' the politicians. ISI's fear for certain 'high ups' being chased & followed, taped, photographed, interrogated and coerced had created an impression among the nation that they were 'hawks'. Pakistan lost more civilians and soldiers to terror since 9/11 than all other countries of the world put together; but who thinks nationalism.

The people of Pakistan are simple. So simple that they were not able enough to grasp that if their ISI or MI were real hawks then why there were dreadful attacks on their SSG battalion near Tarbela; why there was an attack on GHQ Rawalpindi; why their 200 soldiers were once taken hostages in the tribal areas; why there prevailed a state of insurgency in Swat for about two years; why a bus full of Army officers was blown in R A Bazar Rawalpindi; why there was an attack on a mosque in Rawarpindi Cantt killing about 18 army officers during Friday prayers; why there were two attacks on two Navy buses in Karachi just a week before 2nd May episode and one after on Naval Base and there were numerous incidents telling attacks on army posts all over the northern part of Pakistan.

Who had caused the above atrocities; more or less their own *Jihadi* colleagues, of course, the Black-water & XE sponsored ones; they knew about Osama's presence or not, but there should have been no loss of lives at least. American authorities pressingly demanded Pakistan to launch an investigation to prove their own opinion, by saying that:

> 'We haven't seen evidence that the government knew about that. Despite the fugitive terror chief hiding for years in a three-storey house near the capital Islamabad, I've not seen evidence that would tell us that the political, the military, or the intelligence leadership had foreknowledge of bin Laden.'

Similarly, the US President Obama said in his first public comments on the issue that Osama had a support network in Pakistan but not clear if the Pakistani government was involved. Obama told the **CBS TV show '60 Minutes'** that:

> 'We think that there had to be some sort of support network for bin Laden inside of Pakistan, "But we don't know who or what that support network was. We don't know whether there might have been some people inside of government, people outside of government, and that's something that we have to investigate and, more importantly, the Pakistani government has to investigate.'

As per White House and CIA versions, the data gathered from the raid was the richest treasure trove on terrorism ever collected, the largest reserve of intelligence derived from the scene of any single terrorist hideout and about the size of a small college library. Mr Donilon of White House cautioned *we can't declare al-Qaeda strategically defeated, they continue to be a threat to the United States, absolutely critical for us to remain vigilant as we continue to press this organization. Killing bin Laden was 'a real blow.'*

On home front, Munawar Hassan, Amir of JI urged, on TV & media, that:

> *'Pakistan Army earned disgrace and humiliation by the US operation in Abbotabad. The nation should reject those who exhibited negligence. ..... That the likes of Osama would keep on coming until and unless unjust and discriminate attitude of the US and West would not change. The Abbotabad operation exposed the inefficiency of the institutions.'*

In short, after this episode, there were processions and protests in various Pakistani cities including Karachi raising slogans of *Jihad* against the US that had entered Pakistan without permission [*how innocent the Pakistanis were*].

The other school of thought was also there to urge that ***Osama, being a Saudi national, had also entered Pakistan without permission, without visa, was also living here without notice; thus was unlawful & equally damaging for Pakistan.*** They maintained that due to his [OBL's] philosophy, Pakistan earned dissociation and hatred from the whole world even from Afghanistan for whom its Generals and political leaders bought poverty and embarrassment.

Pakistan army and government both failed; the people were severely battered; as the stories were true. They urged that the political elite should abandon begging loans and aids from America, IMF, World Bank and other consortiums because the same taken in the name of pseudo development projects or army's needs always made the personal accounts of Generals and politicians more baggy and bulky. The popular demands roared by the media included refusal of dollars to keep America away and push them out; but who bothers about the peoples' cries in Pakistan.

Starting with killing of Osama, America planned to take out their troops from Afghanistan as per White House's plan of December 2009. The US government chalked out their evacuating strategy while standing on Osama's dead body. ***Being a super power the US might not be admitting their defeat, but they deserved an honourable exit at least.***

A popular slogan was developed then: *'Let the Pakistani people live at their own, may be poor but gracefully, we would be better off.'*

FOREIGN PRESS STORIES:

Now the other side of the story; some media persons claimed 'actual':

The whole world including the citizens of Pakistan was told that the Abbotabad compound was not on army's radar. It was not the whole truth. It was on files that the ISI had raided this compound once in 2003 when it was under construction. Then the ISI believed that an al Qaeda operative, Abu Faraj al-Libi, was there. However:

{*As per 'The Telegraph' dated 2nd May 2011, it was Khalid Sheikh Mohammad (KSM), who when repeatedly subjected to methods including "waterboarding" and stress positions, provided the CIA with the name of Osama's personal courier, Al-Libi.*

In December 2009, the government of Tajikistan warned the US that efforts to catch Osama were being thwarted by corrupt Pakistani spies. Gen Abdullo Sadulloevich Nazarov, a senior Tajik counterterrorism official, told the Americans that "many" insider Pakistanis knew where bin Laden was.

In 2010, British PM David Cameron caused a diplomatic furore when he told Pakistan that it should not "look both ways" on terrorism. The Pakistani government issued a strongly-worded rebuttal.}

Referring to *'the guardian' dated 3rd May 2011,* the US might have obtained a clue three years ago [*Ref: Guantanomo's File dated 10th September 2008*] that Osama was hiding in Abbotabad; according to information gathered by interrogators from Abu al-Libi at Guantánamo:

{*Al-Libi had fled to Peshawar and was living there in 2003 when he was asked to become one of Bin Laden's messengers. In July 2003, detainee received a letter from [Osama's] designated courier, Maulawi Abd al-Khaliq Jan, requesting him to take on the responsibility of collecting donations, organising travel, and distributing funds for [Al Qaeda] families in Pakistan.*

Then Al-Libi had moved his family to Abbotabad and worked between Abbotabad and Peshawar. He was captured in Pakistan in May 2005 and the CIA tracked Osama by tracing the network of couriers, one of whom (allegedly) died with him in the US raid of 2nd May 2011.}

Very interesting situation cropped up. The Telegraph (referred above) said that ISI was helping the Al Qaeda and hiding OBL whereas the ISI and the Pakistan government issued a note of strong reaction. The western media also carried the details that *Wikileaks had made the whole matter open during the 2ⁿᵈ half of April 2010 as referred earlier.* That was why the said operation was planned in urgency.

Referring to *'the Daily Mail' dated 3ʳᵈ May 2011:*

> *'WikiLeaks may have triggered the killing of Osama Bin Laden, it was suggested last night. For although the CIA has thought since September [2010] that he [Osama BL] was in hiding in Abbotabad, special forces stormed his fortress only **days after the website published new secret documents.**'*

[One can salute the ISPR, Pakistan's media, MoFA, MoInfo, ISI, IB and all concerned in Pakistan; even then they could not take notes about OBL]

Very strange situation arises that all the three leading newspapers of UK depended upon the same Wikileaks documents released a week before 2ⁿᵈ May 2011 but each paper brewed different interpretations from those documents. More alarming situation it becomes that none of the official from Pakistan's Army, ISI or MoFA or media anchors had caught sight of those Wikileaks and nobody informed Osama to get lost from Abbotabad before operation.

In the backdrop of above discussion, it becomes a futile exercise to suggest that ISI or Pakistan government was kept aloof from 2ⁿᵈ May's operation; and also that whether the later people knew about Osama or not.

Now referring to *'Times of India' dated 24ᵗʰ December 2011;*

> *'Former DG ISI and the Army Chief [for two hours only] Gen Ziauddin Butt, speaking at Pakistan-US Relations Conference on 11ᵗʰ October 2011 said that despite denials, evidences emerge that some elements within Pakistan military harboured Osama Bin Laden with the knowledge of Gen Musharaf & DG IB Ijaz Shah.*
>
> *The then DG IB, Brig (retd) Ijaz Shah, had kept Osama bin Laden in an Intelligence Bureau safe house in Abbotabad. Ijaz Shah was an all-powerful official in the government of Gen Musharraf; Gen Butt added.*

Gen Butt said in the same address that the ISI had helped the CIA to track Osama down and kill him. ....Gen Butt maintained that PM Nawaz Sharif had set up a special task force of 90 US-trained commandos to track down Osama in Afghanistan.'

Though Gen Butt & Gen Musharraf were two diehard opponents to each other in Pak-Army since 1998 but the facts remained visible for all.

QUESTIONS ABOUT OSAMA BL:

There was much hue and cry in Pakistan over killing of Osama Bin Laden in one sided operation without involvement of the ISI though it was later pretended as attack on sovereignty of an independent nation.

MQM also vowed to get a general referendum over 17 questions to mark its score and replies from the public were sought till 17th May 2011. These questions were basically concerned with the post Abbotabad scenario in Pakistan and not with investigative intent. The people considered that America was trying to level the grounds for its next attack on Pakistan. Before that ugly moment the Pakistani people wanted their leadership to answer the following questions:

- Was Osama really active and controlling the Al Qaeda activities all over the world. If so how it was possible for him to control Al Qaeda from premises where there was no facility of telephone or internet available.

- If Osama was actually living in Abbotabad since six years, who used to monitor his residence. Who people monitored him and where were the monitoring reports or videos.

- Why his dead body was not shown to the Americans at least that Osama was really dead for whom they spent trillions of dollars and wasted tens of lives.

- Why Osama's wife and other family members were not taken along to US for further interrogation of hundreds of aspects related with Osama's daily and past activities.

- Why OBL's DNA test report was not made public.

Till late the intelligentsia was continuously briefed that Osama had no links with ISI or Pakistan Army. One can expect any kind of deliberate 'mistake' from Pakistani military institutions but the fact remains that *'Osama had no faith in any Pakistani Intelligence group or bloc'*. He had in his knowledge that:

- Khalid Sheikh Mohammad was arrested from Rawalpindi.

- Abu Zubaidah was arrested from Faisalabad.

- Ramzi Ben Al-Shabih was arrested from Karachi.

- Abu Fraj Al-Labbi was arrested from Mardan.

- Abdul Salam Zaeef, the Taliban's Ambassador, was arrested from Islamabad.

- Dr Gairat Bher, Hikmatyar's son in law and former Afghan Ambassador was arrested from Islamabad.

All the above and many more were arrested by Pakistan's military agencies at their own and were handed over to the Americans; how Osama could have faith in the Pakistan's military spy agencies.

However, it surfaced as hard fact that the Americans could never reach Osama without 'internal' help from within Pakistan; it could either be some very deep military faction of retired ISI officials or might be the civil department depending upon the following coordinating points:

- President Obama's immediate address of 1st May 2011 [US date] to the American nation contained the phrase that *'Osama could not be reached without Pakistan's help and guidance'*.

- The US Secretary of State Hilary Clinton's media statement, given after her tele-conversation with PM Mr Gilani, contained the words of thanks for Pakistan.

- Gen Mike Mullen, the US Commander had issued a press statement after his tele-conversation with Gen Kayani in which there was no mention of any protest from Pakistan side.

- Even the ISPR or the ISI had not issued any formal statement carrying condemnation for the US forces for 2nd May's event if it was one-sided in fact.

- The then Chief of the CIA Leven Penta had given an interview to the CNN immediately after the Abbotabad event, but Pakistan was not criticized at all.

- President Zardari's essay appeared in the American media sharp on 2nd May 2011 NOT condemning US but hailing the attack.

- Wajid Shamsul Hasan, the Pakistani High Commissioner in London, and Hussain Haqqani, Pakistan's Ambassador in Washington, had issued repeated statements to the media that the said Osama Operation was a 'joint task' of America and Pakistan.

- America, without guidance or settled assurances from Pakistan, could not take risk of sending their 'stealth' choppers.

- **On 3rd May 2011,** the Chief Minister of Khyber PK Mr Hoti told the media that *'the concerned SHO of police was not allowed to go inside the premises to complete the required legal formalities'*. This statement of the CM was run on all TV channels but only once. Afterwards it was got removed from the media record.

{Two essays published at *www.criticalppp.com on 8th May 2011 & 14th May 2011* under the titles *'Osama's Episode' & 'Questions About Osama'* are referred}

Scenario 86

US-OSAMA BIN LADEN OPERATION-II:

Killing of Osama Bin Laden [OBL] by the American troops on 2nd May 2011 in Abbotabad triggered a debate in Pakistan and abroad, especially amongst the Americans themselves, that what actual benefits were brewed out of that humiliated operation. There were questions like:

- Osama was in fact not there, he had been killed seven times before; as per Western claims.

- If alive, Osama was not active at all; he was hiding himself since 2005 in Abbotabad.

- Osama had no wireless or electronic communication link with the outer world then how he could influence the war like situations on Afghan soils.

- Al Qaeda, once known as CIA's brainchild, was [perhaps] practically non-operational at least in Afghanistan. Afghan Taliban was a different entity.

- The US has been striving to control this region in the name of *'Al Qaeda eradication'* whereas the Afghan Taliban were fighting to get their homeland free from all foreign forces whether they were Al Qaeda or Americans or NATO or Russians of the past.

In addition to the details given in the previous chapter, the first question was immediately answered by the White House. The US intelligence knew about Osama's presence in Abbotabad since August 2010 but they decided not to share the information with anyone, including their allies such as Pakistan, Britain, Canada and Australia. By mid-February 2011, the officials were convinced that a "high-value target" was hiding in the given compound. President Obama wanted to take action.

WHO ENCASHED OBL's NAME THEN:

Another question arises; where the Al Qaeda was based or centred then and who used to float orders in the name of Osama Bin Laden.

Referring to **John Rollins,** Coordinator US National Security [**Osama bin Laden's Death: Implications and Considerations** dated 5th May 2011] appearing in <u>Congressional Research Service Papers</u>, a cogent policy question was placed before the Congress:

> *'Did the operation necessarily constitute a cover action? Could it have been considered a traditional military activity? Was the role of the CIA Director essential to carrying out the operations? Could it have been carried out by the Secretary of Defence? Other than the role of Director Panetta what was the contribution of CIA officials to carrying out the raid?'*

It may not be out of place to mention that shortly after the attacks of 9/11 of 2001, Congress had passed the Authorization to Use Military Force (AUMF: PL 107 - 40), which authorized the President:

> *'... to use all necessary and appropriate force against those nations, organizations, or persons he determines planned, authorized, committed, or aided the terrorist attacks that occurred on September 11, 2001, or harboured such organizations or persons, in order to prevent any future acts of international terrorism against the United States by such nations, organizations or persons.'*

In this back-drop, one should also ponder upon an article published in the **Washington Post dated 2nd May 2011,** in which the writer, Pakistan's President Zardari had said that:

> *'.... [Although] the events...were not a joint operation, a decade of cooperation and partnership between the United States and Pakistan led up to the elimination of Osama bin Laden as a continuing threat to the civilized world.*
>
> *And we in Pakistan take some satisfaction that our early assistance in identifying an al-Qaeda courier ultimately led to this day.'*

[One can contemplate that how Mr Zardari's article reached the press & editorial staff of the *'Washington Post' of 2nd May 2011*; till then the Operation Geronimo had hardly finished; hats off to Ispahanis & Haqqanis and alikes sitting abroad.]

The last sentence above should be enough to solve the dilemma of ever prevailing question in Pakistani media that *'whether the Pak-Army or the government knew about Osama's living in Abbotabad or not'*. Evidence of knowing by the army was not needed because the above sentence in Mr Zardari's essay had made it clear that *'the government knew about the operation, may not be sure of time';* they were able to identify the Osama's courier through the IB perhaps.

Pakistan's Foreign Office press release of 2nd May 2011 endorsed the international resolve saying that: *'Al Qaeda had declared war on Pakistan and OBL's killing illustrates the resolve of the international community including Pakistan to fight and eliminate terrorism and constitutes a major setback to terrorist organizations around the world'.*

Another question was echoed then that whether killing Osama in a foreign sovereign state was legal by American Law. It was answered by the US government immediately after; saying that:

> *'Although US employees are generally barred from engaging in 'political assassinations' abroad but US policymakers do not apply this prohibition to the targeting of an enemy's command and control structure during periods of armed conflict'.* [CRS Report RL 31133 & 'Declarations of War and Authorizations for the Use of Military Force' by Jennifer K. Elsea and Richard F. Grimmett pp 35-36 are referred]

Earlier, Jeffrey Toobin in his essay 'Killing Osama: Was It Legal?' published in *'New Yorker'* of *2nd May 2011* had also pointed towards the same principle saying *'that the prohibition on political assassinations did not apply to bin Laden or other belligerents in the conflict with Al Qaeda.'*

One should also keep in mind that the power to terminate the military conflict with Al Qaeda reside exclusively with the political branches of government. The American Supreme Court had recognized it decades ago that the termination of a military conflict is a *'political act'* and it historically refused to review the political branches' determinations of when a conflict had officially ended. [*Ludecke v. Watkins, 335 US 168-169 (1948) & Baker v. Carr, 369 US 213-214 (1962)* are referred to in this context]

PAKISTAN NOT ASKED TO JOIN GERONIMO:

Referring to a briefing to the American Congress through *'CRS Report no: 7-5700 [R41809]' dated* 5th *May 2011*, the White House's notes revealed that the said operation was carried out by US Navy SEALs from the US Special Operations Command. It also suggested that the military operation to kill Osama was commanded by the CIA as opposed to the more traditional military chain of command. It was not unprecedented but considered unusual. However, as that arrangement went highly successful and problem-free, the CIA / military command interactions were allowed for similar operations in future.

Why Pakistan, ten years old ally, was not asked to share the said operation. The answer lies in the fact that in 2010, Pakistan started taking a more aggressive approach in peace negotiations and potential reconciliation in Afghanistan. Certain Taliban figures in Pakistan who were pursuing reconciliation with the Karzai government were arrested. Some issues also developed for Pak-Army's purported protection of the hard liner Jalaluddin Haqqani in North Waziristan. Whether there was some truth in it or not but it certainly played a role in widening gulf between the two giant intelligence agencies, CIA and the ISI.

[*Subsequently Gen Pasha, the then DG ISI, confirmed Pak-Army's relations with Haqqani group in his statement before the Abbotabad Commission.*]

On 1st **May 2011** [US time, in Pakistan it was 2nd May], a senior White House Official told the media that:

'OBL was relatively affluent with lots of retired military. The structure of the property [Osama's residence], valued at some $1 million, was roughly eight times larger than surrounding homes. Intelligence analysts concluded that this compound was custom built to hide someone of significance.

OBL's whereabouts led to immediate questioning of Pakistan's role and potential complicity in his refuge; we are "very concerned" about it.'

The **'Foreign Policy' magazine on 2nd May 2011** held that:

'Their worst suspicions confirmed by the fact that Osama bin Laden lived in a large, well protected compound right under the Pakistani military's nose. Either Pakistan's intelligence service is terribly incompetent, fatally compromised, or both, raising questions about its utility as a partner.'

Despite the above given tall statements, the leading US counter-terrorism advisor John Brennan had stated the same day that *'there is no evidence Pakistani officials knew of OBL's whereabouts.'*

With the Osama Killing Operation at Abbotabad, the Americans at once turned their eyes and started counting dollars they gave to

Gen Musharraf in the name of War on Terror (WOT). In post 9/11 era, the Congress [as per their claim] had appropriated about $20 billion in foreign assistance and military 'reimbursements' for Pakistan, placing the country among the top recipients of US financial support over the past decade.

For FYs 2002-10, the US appropriated about $4.43 billion in security assistance, $6.22 billion in economic & humanitarian assistance and $8.88 billion in Coalition Support Fund (reimbursements) for its operational and logistical support of US-led military operations. Nearly $3 billion assistance under 'development' in Pakistan for FY2012 along with about $1 billion under 'reimbursements' to the Pak-Army was also on cards.

After Osama's trace-out, many in Congress started questioning the usefulness of that aid to Pakistan; which sharpened with the early 2011 Raymond Davis affair.

On 3rd May 2011, just the next day Osama was eliminated; the Pakistan Foreign Aid Accountability Act (PFAAA) was introduced in the House; designated to prohibit future foreign assistance to Pakistan unless the Secretary of State certifies that the Pakistani government was not complicit in hiding OBL. The fact remained that funding flows were already hindered by US concerns about corruption and lack of transparency in Pakistan.

The Pak-Army and the intelligence services remained under pressure to answer the above questions of incompetence or complicity; the dynamics provided the Americans an effective leverage to twist Pakistan. Islamabad had to show a stiffened stand expressing their concerns by saying that:

'This event of unauthorized unilateral action cannot be taken as a rule. The Government of Pakistan further affirms that such an event shall not serve as a future precedent for any state, including the US. Such actions undermine cooperation and may also sometime constitute threat to international peace and security.'

Despite the anger and anti-American sentiments amongst general masses in Pakistan, the tone and tenor of Pakistani media did not show any sympathy with Osama; taking him as a foreigner. Some high-profile critics demanded end of US presence in the region but even those did not exhibit any sympathy for Osama. Contrarily, only two notable rallies were seen next day mourning Osama's death [in Quetta and Karachi], comprised of about one thousand participants each, but mainly divulging their Anti-American emotions.

Leaving aside the possible reaction from the so called 'affiliate' groups of Al Qaeda on Osama's killing, the Afghan government's official stand was notable while they held that *'Pakistan's security services should have known about Osama's whereabouts.'* President Karzai had claimed that:

> *'Osama's killing inside Pakistan vindicated his government's opposition to increased US military operations in Afghanistan; the WOT should be focussed on the safe havens of terrorism outside Afghanistan. Osama's death should provide justification for a "premature" US disengagement from the region.'* ['**The guardian' dated 3rd May 2011 is referred**]

Pakistan had also seen a high wave of revengeful attacks from Al Qaeda affiliates like 'Pakistani Taliban (TTP)', experiencing a steep rise in domestic terrorist attacks over government and military installations.

WHY US DID NOT QUIT THE REGION then; was a cogent question.

Another big question: Pondering at President **Obama's speech** on Afghan policy at West Point **on 1st December 2009**, in which 'mission in Afghanistan' was defined as follows:

> *'Our overarching goal [in this Asian region] remains the same: to disrupt, dismantle, and defeat Al Qaeda in Afghanistan and Pakistan, and to prevent its capacity to threaten American and our allies in the future.'*

With Osama's operation accomplished, the US forces could have been withdrawn from Afghanistan but NOT [till immediate after there was no such announcement]. Fresh arguments were developed that *'Al Qaeda's network of operatives and supporters in Afghanistan has gone more robust, though their nominal leader is lost.'* The 99,000 US troops in Afghanistan as such believed that Osama's death had brought minimal effect on the threat profile in Afghanistan; and that the US mission would be jeopardized by a rapid withdrawal.

US Defence Department's report dated 3rd May 2011 carried that *'.... of these groups, Al Qaeda has been among the least materially significant to the fighting in Afghanistan, but may pose the greatest regional threat to the US and its allies.'*

> [The fact remained that Director of Central Intelligence Leon Panetta had earlier said on 27th June 2010 that *'Al Qaeda fighters in Afghanistan itself might number 50-100.'*

ISAF officials said in October 2010 that *'Al Qaeda cells may be moving back into remote areas of Kunar and Nuristan provinces particularly in areas vacated by US-led forces.'*

Gen David Petraeus had said in April 2011 that *'the AQ presence in Afghanistan remains small at less than 100 or so.']*

But the last question arises then that why America needed to launch such offensive operation and why to plan killing Osama. Not so badly needed but the US only wanted to tell the world that *'other nation's sovereignty can be played with any moment, if they are weak; even though it was a compromised operation.'*

Beggars are given no choices, they had to die sooner or later even they are labelled as friends; think Pakistan.

PAK-ARMY'S BRIEFING OF 13TH MAY 2011:

A well played act of historical drama; see the details.

Those were extraordinary moments and it was an unprecedented day. 13th May 2011 will be remembered in the history of Pakistan when the three chiefs of armed forces presented their case in a joint session of the Parliament explaining their shortcomings regarding Osama's event in Abbotabad. PM Gilani was in haste [on 3rd May 2011] for making a pre-determined announcement that *'America has performed an uphill task and has done right'* without appreciating its repercussions ignoring the fact that Pakistan's sovereignty was interfered and country's image was washed out due to their under the table compromise with US.

On the Briefing Day, Federal Information Minister Firdaus Ashiq Awan, could not behave 'minister like' divulging her hatred for a respectable institution. Just a short while after the session started she came out of the Parliament's building and proudly told the media that *'DG ISI Mr pasha has SURRENDERED himself before the PM and Parliament'*.

It was not required to be so jubilant; it was not an occasion to use such derogatory word at all. There were other nice words available in the dictionary with parallel meanings but she did not act 'gracefully'. It was deliberate effort to shoot an impression in air that the general public had gone against 'the army'.

It was not the case and there was no truth in it; the Army as an institution had paid much price for some Generals; more than the people. The session's details indicated that people were more worried about PPP's sitting leadership than army.

Everyone could feel that Gen Ashfaq Kayani was from a different breed. He had the courage to come with proposal, solely his proposal, to call that parliamentary session for putting facts before them. In the last 63 years history, no General did so; not even after 1971's catastrophe.

Mistakes happen every where. Zardari and Gilani did not stand by Benazir Bhutto's pledge and words once uttered at confined CJ's residence that *'Justice Iftikhar M Chaudhry would be our Chief Justice'*; both the President and the PM declined to show wisdom and ultimately *'had to surrender'* before the lawyer's march on 16th March 2009.

It was also a mistake on the part of the PPP. The people ignored it though Justice Iftikhar M Chaudhry could not forget those humiliating moments that is why an unprecedented row between Presidency and judiciary was there. Mistakes happen, the people forget them, give chances to 'some' [but only if they are nationalists], this is democratic way.

ISI's Chief, Gen Ahmed Shuja Pasha also surfaced as an unlike class. He admitted his department's failure, offered his resignation to the COAS and then placed it before the Parliament. Nice gesture it was; very healthy signal but Pakistani politicians would learn something from it or not, let us wait for time. The people should have recalled the stern moments of about two months earlier when Gen Pasha travelled to Washington all the way to have a meeting with his counterpart CIA Chief but then travelled back just after 40 minute's stay there in the US.

What happened there in Washington? That was the starting point of 'going apart' between Pakistan and America. Gen Pasha could only tell his COAS that:

> *'There has been a strong disagreement between us, the two chiefs. I've not agreed with anything he suggested. I told him clearly that we are not under Obama.'*

In the past, our Generals never dared to behave so with CIA Chiefs. Now think about Osama's episode at Abbotabad. It had to be there. A natural outcome of US frustration!

Coming back to the parliamentary session; DG ISI Gen Ahmed Shuja Pasha and DG MI explained the 2nd May's episode and admitted that they failed to keep track of Osama's presence in Abbotabad. The ignorance and guilt was openly confessed.

The Air Chief, when questioned by members, admitted that their radars were working as usual but as the Americans had used 'stealth' choppers in this operation, which could fly at very low level without making any noise or vibration, so their air system could not trace them in Pakistani air space. Pakistan was not yet equipped with latest type of radars to be effective in such situations. In sixty years history of Pakistan, it was the first occasion that the armed forces chiefs were attending a joint Parliamentary session and that too, to admit their guilt what ever it was.

When DG ISI placed his resignation before his Army Chief, unanimously the whole house said 'NO' except Ch Nisar Ali Khan of PML(N) and his handful colleagues who remained mum at that sentimental moment. The army officers remained in the house for more than five hours to answer all the questions relating to the aforesaid event (some were out of context also; it is Pakistan's history).

PML(N) alone asked 47 questions where one lady member tried to drag politics in the session by pointing out, in extra loud voice, that why *'you army people under the command of Gen Musharraf had ousted our beloved Nawaz Sharif'*. Purely it was a point scoring game trying to win her next ticket from PML(N) but asserting at the same time that *'army should shun playing in politics like in Gen Musharraf's era'*. No body gave attention to her.

Most widely asked question from COAS and the Air Chief was that why the drone attacks were not being checked. **During 2011 alone there were 228 deaths till that moment** and three attacks even after 2nd May event, and why so. Some members also indicated that the drone attacks were never checked despite the fact that *'this house had passed a joint unanimous resolution in 2008 that the drone attacks should be stopped with strength and use of force if needed'*.

Then the moment came that whole of the house went silent, mum and astonished when **the army people told them that <u>the resolution passed in 2008 by this Parliament was never forwarded to the GHQ for want of action</u>**. Either it did not come out of the Speaker's Office or the PM Gilani; the head of the executive never bothered to refer it to the GHQ or COAS for implementation.

On the same issue, the Air Chief Rao Suleman Qamar told the house that PAF got the technical equipment, will and know how of shooting the drones in the air but they were never ordered to do so. He again reiterated that even now they promise with the nation that *'there would not be a single drone attack if there is political will"*.

[*When the Air Chief said it loudly, the PM Gilani and the whole cabinet went pale and they pushed their heads into their knees, did not utter a single word and Air Chief's phrase kept on echoing in the house for many minutes.*]

The Pakistani people knew that *the drone attacks in FATA area,* then and since long, killing hundreds of innocent women and children, were being done with the approval and the *connivance of Pakistan government.* Wikileaks had rightly pointed out once that:

'There exists, may be unwritten, a pact between the two governments for continuing drone attacks, hue & cry would also be there in media and newspapers, but the America should never take these protests seriously.'

An MNA from FATA was seen launching a strong protest in this context pointing towards the PPP benches; a fact which was known by all then.

After this particular discussion, the COAS laid down the core announcement that *'from today onwards, the army will take orders from the government, this Parliament and will not go beyond their given commandments'*.

It was the first ever policy statement from the GHQ to strengthen democracy in the country. It was made clear that to give policy directions for army would remain the prerogative of the political government and army's duty would be to obey. The government was urged to tell the army that:

'How we have to take this war on terror and we'll achieve results. [The first step towards this direction was considered and held that] *The government may make an independent commission for Abbotabad event and the required army officers will be there to answer when called'.*

13th May 2011's joint Parliamentary session was an in-camera meeting in which only six guests were invited. Those were chief ministers of all the four provinces, one of AJK and one of Gilgit but they were not permitted to put any question. CM Punjab Shahbaz Sharif did not attend the session on the instance of his party decision. It was an in-camera session but certain members were seen periodically passing the minutes of on-going meeting to the outer world, of course to certain media men dear to them.

There came a moment when an MNA Ata ur Rehman from DI Khan, brother of Maulana Fazalur Rehman of JUI, started questioning and pleading the army that *'Osama was Shaheed (martyr)....'* Immediately DG ISI interrupted and told the house that:

> *'ISI got a full record with proof that you are being regularly paid by Saudi Arabia and Libya in the past and that you label Osama Bin Laden as Shaheed to get more dollars from them'.*

There were roaring voices of 'shame, shame' from the whole house including opposition benches. Maulana Ata ur Rehman had no answer and he preferred to walk out in the wake of humiliation, disgrace, dishonour and sorrow but came back at his own after ten minutes. History will remember those uproarious but hysterical moments, too.

The atmosphere in the joint session remained tense most of the time. S M Zafar, Sh Waqas Akram and Waseem Sajjad succeeded in conveying to the house that *'it is a commendable occasion where historians can see coordination and understanding between the government, army and the people.'* PML(N) had succeeded in achieving that the inquiry committee would be chosen in consultation with the Leader of Opposition in which involvement of judges were also expected.

In the joint Parliamentary session, the best moment appeared when a 12 point unanimous resolution was passed. The salient features were:

• The government should revisit Pak-American relationship in the light of recent developments concerning Pakistan's sovereignty and putting country's interest first.

• If Abbotabad like attack would be repeated in Pakistan, the supply line of NATO and ESAF forces would be permanently blocked; the pact, if any, would stand nullified and facility withdrawn.

• Drone attacks would no more be tolerable. The practice would be discontinued.

• The people of Pakistan and government gave accent of full confidence over the armed forces and would stand behind them in all hours of need.

- Government promised to announce an independent inquiry commission to probe into the lapses of Abbotabad episode which would recommend steps to avoid such misery in future.

- The commission would be framed and announced by leaders of the House and Opposition both in consultancy and mutual agreement.

- The joint session affirmed their concerns over the behaviour of some enemy countries trying to defame Pakistan while nullifying their sacrifices in WOT.

A worrying flash was also seen on the faces of all parliamentarians when, replying a question: if PAF gives assurance that such lapse would not occur again; the Deputy Air Chief instantly nodded his head. He told the house that *'Pakistan does not have the latest radar technology in this regard so they would be helpless if such event occurs again.'*

The house murmured for a while and then asked the government to give immediate attention to the budgetary needs of PAF for their safe future.

At another occasion, when DG ISI conceded their departmental failure in grasping Osama's location in Pakistan since five years, one of the members asked the army team that if there was a likelihood of presence of Mulla Umar and Aiman Azzawahri in Pakistan; the officer told the house that *'the possibility cannot be ruled out.'* The Pakistani nation was united on 13th May 2011 once more but unsure of the next move.

American Senator John Kerry was there in Pakistan the very next week with a new agenda of carrots and stick with him. He was sent back empty handed. He was sent back with his chip of $1.5 billion for current year considering it a peanut comparing with Pakistan's accumulative losses.

Senator Kerry had come to convey a threat that they would launch more attacks for Mulla Umar and Aiman Azzawahri if found in Pakistan but the army did not retaliate those threats. More heads were required to sit together to formulate a nationalistic way-out; no individual decision, neither from Presidency nor from the PM Secretariat alone; the world was told.

JUDICIAL COMMISSION ANNOUNCED:

After the joint Parliamentary session of 13th May 2011, the Pakistan government announced to engage Gen Iqbal with two more army officers to probe into the Abbottabad episode but the PML(N) rejected it out rightly demanding that a judicial commission should be formed. Obliging the opposition's demand when the government announced another commission, the PML(N) Chief Nawaz Sharif rejected it too in the last week of May 2011 on the pretext that they [PML(N)] were not formally consulted.

The 5-member commission announced by PM Gilani was headed by Justice Javed Iqbal, a senior sitting judge of the Supreme Court. Other members of the commission were Justice Fakhruddin G Ebrahim, Lt Gen (retd) Nadeem Ahmed, former police chief Abbas Khan and Ashraf Jahangir Qazi; Cabinet Secretary was designated as Secretary of the Commission.

The main terms of reference included:

• Thorough probe to ascertain facts regarding Osama's presence in Pakistan;

• To investigate the circumstances surrounding the US operation;

• To determine the nature, background and the security lapse on part of the authorities and;

• To make consequential recommendations.

There was an exhausted list of witnesses; just to satisfy the false ego of the Commission's members otherwise useless. To mention a few of them were Chairman CDA Islamabad, Wajid Shamsul Hasan [Pakistan's High Commissioner sitting in London], Sheikh Rashid, Secretary Foreign Affairs, Office bearers of Jama'at e Islami, Amir Haider Hoti [Chief Minister Khyber PK], Nawaz Sharif, Asfand Yar Wali, Imran Khan, Khawaja Asif, Interior Secretary Siddique Akbar, Chief Commissioner ICT Tariq Pirzada, IG Police Islamabad Bani Amin Khan, DG FIA Javed Iqbal, DG Passports Syed Wajid Ali, DG Foreign Affairs on America, Deputy DG Civil Aviation Authority, IG Police Punjab, Home Secretary Punjab, Foreign Minister Hina Rabbani Khar, Defence Minister Ahmed Mukhtar, former ISI chiefs Gen (Retd) Ziauddin Butt and Lt Gen (Retd) Nadeem Taj, Brig (Retd) Ijaz Shah former DG (IB) and tens of media columnists, TV live program analysts, newspaper reporters including Dr Shireen Mazari, Nasim Zahra, Rahimullah Yusufzai, Saleem Bukhari, Fahad Hussain, Farrukh Saleem, Maria Sultan, Asif Ezdi and Saleem Safi etc etc.

Senior Air Traffic Controllers from Islamabad, Lahore, Chaklala and Chirat were called who briefed the Commission on the technical aspects of the whole air-traffic monitoring as well as radar system on ground. If believed that the US choppers flew from Jalalabad (Afghanistan), then only Peshawar air radar could have noticed them but Senior Traffic Controllers from four unconcerned stations were called [for what?] whereas Peshawar's Air Traffic Controller was not seen amongst them.

The intelligentsia were expecting that the Commission would call the decision maker officers from Army, PAF, Presidency, PM Secretariat, ISI, IB, DG MI, the communication officers of concerned offices, Abbottabad's local SHO, DSP, SSP, Special Branch's local officers, Bilal Colony's Wapda and Municipal officers and others but concerned to point out the lapses in national security. The Commission narrated the logic in calling the others like few mentioned above, that *'we called them to know the public opinion'* forgetting that the same was abundantly available in daily media reports then why wasting high official's time and money for extensive travelling and staying in Islamabad and making the whole nation fool.

Brig (rtd) Shaukat Qadir had rightly opined that:

> *'With such high military and political stakes, many Pakistanis believe that the truth will remain as elusive as Bin Laden once was. **You have to ask the right questions to get the right answers.** I doubt this report will explain anything to anyone's satisfaction.'*

The Commission sometimes passed administrative orders also; for instance, during the first week of October 2011, Dr Shakeel Afridi was put on trial for conspiracy against the State and for high treason. The Commission decided that in the light of record and evidence placed before it, prima facie, Dr Afridi did not have a clean slate, and therefore, a case under the relevant law be registered against him.

During the same session, the Commission also withdrew the restraining order against the wives and daughters of Osama after recording their statements and then handed over the OBL compound to the civil administration Abbottabad for disposal in accordance with law. During the night of *25ᵗʰ February 2012*, Osama's whole compound and structure was bull-dozed by Abbotabad Municipality; a chapter closed for ever.

During the first week of December 2011, the Commission declared that the US action in Abbotabad on 2ⁿᵈ May had violated the sovereignty of the country and Osama could have been arrested alive. ***Hussain Haqqani*** *and Rehman Malik were summoned to state that under what law they had issued so big numbers of visas to Americans.* Till then there were more than 20 sessions, more than 100 witnesses examined, 5 field missions conducted and final report was expected to be completed till the end of December but could not. All proceedings of the commission were taken place behind closed doors.

Replying to a media question in a press conference held in PID on 7th December 2011, a member [Lt Gen (retd) Nadeem Ahmad] said that:

'When the ISI was discussed regarding the Abbotabad incident, the Commission had recorded only one statement and I had given my personal opinion that Al-Qaeda declared ISI as their enemy then how they had relations with ISI.'

In July 2011, Gen Nadeem Ahmed had told the Australian journalists that he had firmly believed *'that no intelligence organization in Pakistan would do such a stupid thing as harbouring Bin Laden'.*

2nd January 2012's media reports told that the Commission retrieved 1,87,000 documents from Osama's compound whereas a large number of documents had already been taken away by the US-SEALs on the raiding night. The recovered documents included Osama's diaries, correspondence, and other material in black and white.

BBC Urdu Report [no: 120315] of March 2012, however, narrated that the findings of the Commission were different from the report given by US authorities. It included statements from Osama's family, neighbours and government officials who immediately visited 'the compound' after the US raid. The most crucial finding being that *'the compound had dozens of armed men during the raid, however, only one bullet mark and one bullet shell was found.'*

The bullet mark was found on the wall of the room where Osama used to sleep and there he was killed. The height of the mark suggested that someone had knelt down and taken a shot; the bullet had pierced through Osama's head and struck the wall leaving a mark there with fading splash of blood, the report claimed. Other than this mark, there was no other bullet mark in the entire house, nor was there any other bullet shell. [As per Brig Shaukat Qadir's opinion, *a bunch of bullet holes were marked in the stairs where Osama's 22 years old son was ambushed*]

Six Kalashnikovs recovered from the house were less than a yard away, from deceased's gunmen. The report posed more questions including:

when so many armed men were present in the house during the raid, why did Osama's men not fire even once.

Interior Minister Rehman Malik once told the Commission and the media in early March 2012 that:

> *'Pakistani security agencies were a few days late; they were very close to capturing Osama. We were about to catch Osama when US Navy SEALs raided his compound'.*

Mr Malik was known to release such amusing statements; the media held.

It was also a fact that Osama had undergone a kidney transplant operation in 2002 [*Osama's last and youngest wife, Amal Ahmed al-Sadah had confirmed before the Pakistani interrogators*] and as he survived till 2011, then who has been helping him. During his kidney operation days, Osama had shaved his beard and disguised himself as an ailing Pashtun elder. Osama's elder wife Khairiah Saber, an older woman who occupied a separate floor, was accused by Amal of having betrayed their husband to American intelligence.

The record also pointed out that Osama was 'practically removed' from Al Qaeda's controlling position and was hiding in Abbotabad only waiting for death. Even some officials of White House had known such claims and reports that Osama and his deputy, Ayman al-Zawahri, had suffered serious disagreements that pushed Osama to the sidelines. *'This divide grew with time, and remained a source of tension until the day Bin Laden died; his role was diminished'*, one of the White House summary contained.

Referring to the **NY Times dated 7th March 2012,** several American and Western officials in Washington and Pakistan said that the CIA had scanned millions of documents taken from computer disks found in Bin Laden's house yet found no evidence of official Pakistani support. But for some analysts, that proves nothing. *'There is no smoking gun, but there is also no evidence that firmly rules out complicity,'* said Bruce Riedel, a former CIA officer and Obama's Adviser.

Suggestions to the contrary were the product of American media conspiracy; *'there is a deliberate design to undermine the ISI'*, the Pak-Army believed; and it was proved true subsequently.

Till the first anniversary of the Osama's killing, 2nd May 2012, the Abbotabad Commission was not able to compose its final report despite the day to day working. The speculation amongst the media, however, gave some indications that the Commission had not found any institution or individual responsible for the episode but they were trying to find a neck for the loop they held.

The Abbotabad Commission had in fact made mockery of judicial process and with such inordinate delay the people and the media got so fed up that no political faction or individual would dare to raise a demand of 'judicial probe' in future; share wastage of public funds, poor people's money and hope. The Commission, just to prolong the enquiry for an indefinite period, called so many unconcerned office holders and 'other people' who had virtually narrated and got recorded their statements mostly based on hearsay or media news.

The true accountability demanded that when the Commission's report would be placed before the CJP or the Chief Executive, the expenditure incurred on its proceeding [*remuneration and TA / DA paid to the members, expenditure incurred on the travelling and daily allowances paid to all persons called for 'statements', staying expenses for all in hotels & their transportation and other resources consumed by TV teams, camera men, security officials and journalists for more than a year*] should also be made public – but that day had never seen dawn.

DR SHAKIL AFRIDI FIGURED UP:

After Osama's killing, during investigation process, the fact surfaced that one Dr Shakil Afridi acted as CIA's paid agent and used to keep surveillance over Osama's residence and its inhabitants. The official investigating team detained that doctor for further interrogation.

Afridi was one of several Pakistanis who were detained by the country's security agencies over allegations of working for the CIA. Dr could face the death penalty for collaborating with a foreign spy agency. It was no more mystery that how CIA recruited Afridi to work for the United States.

Dr Afridi came from a humble background, graduated from the Khyber Medical College, Peshawar in 1990 and was working as doctor in-charge of Jamrud Hospital in Khyber Agency of the Federally Administered Tribal Areas of Pakistan. He was in his 40s when arrested in 2011.

The investigations revealed that Dr Afridi's colleagues at Jamrud Hospital in Khyber tribal agency were suspicious of his activities. The hospital's chief surgeon told about his absences which he explained as "business" to be attended in Abbotabad. Dr Afridi was accused of having taken half-dozen World Health Organization cooler boxes without authorization. The containers were for inoculation campaigns, but no immunization drives were underway in Abbotabad or the Khyber agency.

Dr Afridi, after getting married to one Imrana Ghafoor of Multan having American nationality, often visited the US embassy and held meetings with the US officials in different hotels. His colleagues started suspecting the activities of Dr Afridi when he started going absent from duty for days on a stretch. The FATA directorate had issued his transfer orders thrice but he was successful in getting the orders reversed within few days. Imrana Ghafoor was working as headmistress at a government-run Girls High School in Darra Adamkhel.

The record of Jamrud Tehsil Hospital proved that Dr Afridi had taken away six polio kits illegally from the hospital on 17th March 2011 despite the fact that he was not given any such task. Dr Afridi conducted three fake anti-polio campaigns in Abbotabad to reach his target Osama bin Laden. He conducted the first anti-polio campaign on 17th March 2011 and then on 1st April and 20th April to reach Osama's compound. He had succeeded in getting the blood sample from the compound and handed it over to CIA agents for their consumption [in DNA tests].

Within a few days of the last fake polio campaign visit, the US helicopters came and conducted the said operation in Abbotabad. When the operation was completed, Dr Afridi disappeared for some days and did not turn up for duty at the Jamrud Hospital. But 20 days later, Dr Afridi was arrested from Karkhano Market in Hayatabad [Peshawar].

Media sources opined that he was arrested from Torkham border while trying to escape the country [*and only his arrest was shown from Karkhano market Peshawar*]. Soon the Pakistan government was pressurised by the US agencies that Dr Afridi be released which proved the suspicions. Not for the first time, the US was demanding the release of a CIA covered agent in Pakistan, Raymond Davis; the complication this time was that the agent was a Pakistani citizen.

US Secretary of Defence, and former head of the CIA, Leon Panetta, on 22nd February 2012 made his pitch for the release of Dr Afridi, who had, during that fake polio campaign in Abbotabad, obtained DNA evidence confirming the Osama's presence there. Neighborhood residents had confirmed the CNN team that two women who appeared to be nurses visited homes around and offered free vaccinations.

The US Secretary Hilary Clinton's anger and the then CIA Chief, Leon Panetta's chase confirmed the role of Dr Afridi in ascertaining the where-abouts of Bin Laden in Abbotabad but the Americans were hoping to get Afridi released in the back drop of 'the deal' under which the Operation Geronimo was launched – that Pakistan would be a silent party. That was why **on 6ᵗʰ October 2011**, the Commission on OBL recommended that Dr Afridi be charged with "conspiracy against the state of Pakistan and high treason" on the basis of available evidence. Pakistan seized Dr Afridi's assets; his residence was sealed and his family was moved to an undisclosed location. The 15 lady health workers, that assisted Dr Afridi in the fake vaccination program, were also declared not fit for future employment.

FACTS REVEALED -DR PLAYED WELL:

A known Western journalist named *MATTHIEU AIKINS,* based in Kabul, travelled to Pakistan to investigate how one mysterious man [Dr Shakil Afridi] led the US to Bin Laden's doorstep. *On 28ᵗʰ December 2012,* his findings were published at the 'Opinion-Maker' website; see what it concluded.

When did Dr Afridi start working for the CIA? Copies of a sealed court record contained diversified statements; yet its overall gist was confirmed by the US officials offering a window into Dr Afridi's recruitment and handling by CIA agents working undercover in Pakistan.

As per recorded documents, the doctor was recruited in 2008 after attending a workshop for medical professionals in Peshawar, hosted by *Save the Children,* an international NGO that carries out extensive humanitarian operations in Pakistan. There he met with Michael McGrath, the then country director of the said NGO [McGrath left Pakistan in August 2009] who asked Afridi if he was the same doctor who was recently kidnapped by Mangal Bagh, a warlord who headed the militant group called *Lashkar-e-Islam.* Afridi answered that yes; in April that year he had been abducted from his hospital and held for ransom equivalent of around £7500. The incident had made local headlines.

Afterwards, Dr Afridi met McGrath at Saeed Book Bank in Jinnah Super Market Islamabad on one Saturday morning. A week later, they met again in the same busy market; Dr Afridi was picked up and was driven to a residence where he was introduced to 'Kate'; described as a blue-eyed, blond-haired woman in her late thirties. Over dinner, Kate and Afridi talked about his abduction, his family, and the political situation in Khyber Agency, where militants had taken over several main towns. About 90 minutes later, Afridi was dropped off at a gas station down the road.

After Kate, three more CIA handlers named Thoni, Sara, and Sue worked with Dr Afridi; each of them was female - perhaps the CIA knew the doctor's reputation. Dr Afridi used to meet them at gas stations or taxi stands, and then, after driving a short distance to a secluded spot [*he used to get in the back of his handler's vehicle and hide underneath a blanket*] and used to be taken into the US embassy. Eventually, Dr Afridi was given his mission: to create and administer a vaccination program focusing on a specific suburb of Abbottabad.

Due to extreme secrecy of the mission, Dr Afridi was never told the identity of his target. He was given a device capable of communicating by satellite with his handlers - and that the CIA paid him about $55,000 to conduct that fake vaccination campaign; about nine times his official annual salary plus his clinic's income.

It was, **on 21st April 2011**, a grey jeep, an official vehicle with the logo of the Health Department painted on the door, pulled into Abbottabad town and parked in front of one Big House. A doctor stepped down, stood out among the wheat fields and dirt paths of this semi-rural suburb, leaving his driver behind the doctor set off smoothly ahead.

[The people around Osama's residence believed that the said 'big house', [*commonly known as Waziristan House also*] belonged to two brothers, Arshad and Tariq Khan, [*subsequently both names surfaced as fake; their real names were Ibrahim & Abrar*] who lived with their wives and kids, as well as a mysterious uncle who was said to be ill; wasn't all that unusual for conservative *Pashtuns* from the tribal areas.

No one was invited inside the house nor the family ventured outside. Since 2005, they had never caused anyone any trouble either.]

Waiting for him outside the compound's forest-green metal gate were two nurses, Bakhto and Amna, as part of a hepatitis B vaccination team. The nurses had been canvassing the area, knocking on doors and looking for women aged 15 to 45 to cajole into taking the needle. Amna wondered why Dr Shakil was so interested in this house in particular, the only one whose vaccination he had bothered to personally supervise. He rapped sharply on the metal door, they waited, again he knocked, but there seemed to be no one home.

Amna shrugged, Dr Shakil hastily went across the street and called a neighbour, whose son used to do the occasional odd jobs for the Big House. *Dr Shakil had the cell number of one of the Khan brothers*, he dialled it and handed his phone to one of the nurses. The man on the other side had answered that the family was away on a trip, the doctor almost snatched the phone hurriedly.

"Hello?" he said. *"This is Dr Shakil Afridi."* The doctor urgently explained the need for the hepatitis test. *'It was crucial that it happen soon. The vaccine would be very good for them'*, Dr Shakil urged.

Simultaneously, in Washington, President Obama was upset with only one single question: Was Osama bin Laden concealed inside that three-story house? For months, the CIA had conducted intensive surveillance without coming to a definitive answer; their assessment went astray. Such an extraordinarily risky mission - sending a team of commandos deep inside Pakistan without Pakistani political or military's information - could only be argued in vacuum. The operation might have negotiated in principle amongst all but at what time it would be launched – it was not settled. Dr Afridi had helped them to get out of that puzzle.

Due to excessive and 'managed' Pakistani visas issued by Hussain Haqqani and Rehman Malik, a network of Pakistani 'assets' - locals on the CIA payroll – could visibly be seen in Khyber PK and FATA. What exactly Dr Afridi did for the Osama mission, could be judged from American's praise for his key role. *"This was an individual who in fact helped provide intelligence that was very helpful with regards to this operation,"* Defence Secretary Leon Panetta had said. Within a few days of the last fake vaccination campaign visit, the US helicopters accomplished their mission in Abbottabad.

Dr Afridi had actually collected DNA evidence from the Bin Laden house with the help of Amna and Bakhto, the two nurses who had been part of the 22 members' vaccination team; later, the whole team had been arrested, interrogated, and subsequently fired.

[*Any DNA obtained from the people in the compound could then be compared with a sample from bin Laden's sister, who died in Boston in 2010, as evidence the family was in the compound.*]

Nurse Bakhto had first time met Dr Afridi on 16th March, during a short briefing of the vaccination campaign at Abbottabad [especially designed to reach the Bin Laden house]. Then they met on 21st April 2011, amidst the vaccination campaign, at the gate of Osama's residence.

After their investigations, Amna and Bakhto had confirmed to the media that they had indeed gotten into the house and successfully collected blood samples from a young woman, might be bin Laden's daughter. Bakhto in fact had vaccinated seven children for polio there the year before, when one of the brothers brought them to the gate to receive the oral vaccine; this time they were there with hepatitis injections.

Dr Afridi was again in Abbottabad on 27th April, this time driving his personal vehicle, to collect the vaccination records and materials in person. As per ISI's investigation report '...... *that same day Dr Afridi drove with his driver and a social worker to Islamabad. After dropping them off, he met with his CIA handler "Sue" and gave her the used vaccination kits and records, and she paid him for the job.*' All their activities were regularly monitored from a safe house in the neighbourhood of Osama's house since late 2010.

On 28th April 2011, President Obama went 50:50 odds but the Vice President Joe Biden had advised against going ahead. Next day, when DNA test report reached White House, the president ordered the mission to go ahead on immediate basis. Just one day after the Operation Geronimo was to be launched but the Navy SEALs could not proceed due to bad weather reports; however, next day [1st May 2011 as per American calendar] the mission was successfully accomplished.

US PRESSURE STORIES:

Pakistan's military had long grown fed up with the American drone attacks and various other *'unilateral missions,'* in which the CIA operated without its knowledge and consent. Military officials believed the CIA bribed a vast network of local informants inside the country, not only to hunt Al Qaeda and the Taliban but also to spy on Pakistan's nuclear weapons, in the garb of *'falling into the wrong hands'.*

The mistrust between US & Pakistan could be seen at the gates of the US Consulate in Peshawar, where Pakistani armed police guard used to question journalists and anyone leaving the compound and sometimes chased. Pakistani intelligence suspected the Consulate of being a hotbed of spies. ISI's officers maintained that:

> *'Peshawar was just like Berlin at the height of the Cold War; every agency worth their name has people here. We found they were conducting unilateral operations from inside Afghanistan, not just on Osama bin Laden but on so many other issues. We've been restricting access to certain people, tailing them, monitoring them.'*

The spy games had created an atmosphere of extreme paranoia in Peshawar. Not surprisingly, mentioning Dr Afridi's name was not at all liked by many since the Osama incident, and no one was eager to admit any association with the doctor. Dr Afridi's story was wrapped in a protective layer of facts about his secret relationship with the CIA and his mission accomplished at Osama's residence in Abbottabad.

In Dr Afridi's case, one lawyer named Nadeem, in the Peshawar High Court held:

> *"Shakil Afridi was part of a big game; a pawn in the struggle between the US and Pakistan. At stake was the future of CIA operations against Al Qaeda and billions of US dollars in aid to the Pakistani military; he was the hundred – million - dollar man."*

Dr Shakil was later charged not with treason for his work with the CIA but with supplying *Lashkar e Islam* - the militant group - with money and medical treatment for its fighters. Under the tribal code, Dr Afridi was sentenced to 33 years in prison.

The terrorism charges were rightly and intelligently applied in Dr Afridi's case as there was no charge in the Pakistani criminal code for taking money from a foreign government. The actual charge was for waging war against the state; but Pakistan was not in a position of debating that the US was their enemy. The American concern about Afridi might be genuine in the said case but Dr Afridi had not offered his services to the CIA for the sake of humanity [while helping them identify Osama in Abbottabad] but he was in the game for money.

Later a group of lawyers from the tribal areas [*of course financed by the CIA again*] appealed against Dr Afridi's sentence on the basis that he had been tortured into false confessions by the ISI [but what Americans do in Guantanamo Bay – the same story].

Dr Shakil once sent a hand-written letter from the jail:

"I received death threats, I have been tortured, and my body has suffered serious violence. All of this is an untrue story fabricated by the ISI, and they have been telling it to me for the last year."

However, no one going to believe him in an arena of pressures extended on Pakistani Authorities by Hilary Clinton and Leon Panetta AND the statements given by them on live TV talks at various American media channels AND the fact that a bill was moved in American Congress to grant Dr Shakil & his family the American Nationality through naturalization.

[*One can recall here the statement of Gen Pasha, former DG ISI, given before the Abbottabad Commission that the US authorities did their best to get Dr Afridi released through Saudi Arabia's immense pressure; offered him and his family the American nationality straightaway – but the Pak-Army flatly refused to bow down. If Dr Afiridi had no connections with the CIA then how come America went so far to get him bailed out.*]

Rand Paul, the Republican senator from Kentucky, made a lot of noise going to the extent that *"America should not give foreign aid to a country whose government is torturing the man who helped us kill Osama bin Laden."*

Panetta told **CBS's "60 Minutes program on 27th January 2012,"** in a profile to be broadcast that Dr Afridi helped provide intelligence for the raid on bin Laden's compound in Abbotabad, Pakistan. Moving further the US argued that Dr Afridi should be freed and allowed to live in the US.

In early July 2011, Secretary of State Hillary Clinton said that *"his help, after all, was instrumental in taking down one of the world's most notorious murderers"* and had urged for Dr Shakil's release which was rejected.

Desperately then the **US Secretary of State Hilary Clinton had telephoned President Zardari on 28th July 2011 to seek his help in securing Dr Afridi's release;** urging that *'Pakistan has no justification for holding Dr Shakil Afridi'*. It was extremely humiliating for a sovereign nation at least. [*An essay published at www.Pakspectator.com on 2nd May 2012 is referred*]

Dana Rohrabacher asked President Obama to intercede on Afridi's behalf, and moved a bill [H.R.4069 & H.R. 3901] to award a Congressional Gold Medal to Dr Afridi AND declaring him a naturalized US citizen. The two moves were sufficient to prove that Dr Afridi was on CIA's roll thus guilty of high treason charges under Article 6 of the Pakistan's Constitution.

There is no derth of Mir Jaffers & Mir Sadiqs in Pakistan.

On 22ⁿᵈ November 2013; Dr Shakil Afridi was charged with murder, relating to the death of a patient eight years ago at his private clinic in the Khyber Agency region. A woman had come forward blaming Dr Afridi for the death of her son at a clinic in 2005; stating that he operated on her son even though he was not a surgeon, and that caused her son's death.

Earlier, **on 28ᵗʰ August 2013,** a court overturned a previous sentence given to Dr Afridi [*citing procedural errors and ordered a retrial*] in which he had been given a 33-year jail sentence in May 2012 by a court in the Khyber Agency for alleged links to a banned militant group. A 3-member bench comprising its Chairman Shah Wali Khan and two members Pir Fida Muhammad and Akbar Khan reissued notice to Political Agent Khyber Agency to submit original record.

Shakil Afridi, hailed a hero by US officials, was arrested after American SEALs had killed bin Laden on 2ⁿᵈ May 2011 in Abbotabad. Initially he was charged with treason, but court documents showed he was jailed for being a member of a militant group, *Lashkar-e-Islam*.

Scenario 87

ABBOTABAD COMMISSION REPORT:

The Abbotabad Commission on Osama Bin Laden's killing AT LAST submitted its report to the Government of Pakistan in the 2nd week of October 2012. The then Prime Minister Raja Pervaiz Ashraf might have seen it or read it but, placed it on the wheels of bureaucratic order to be dealt with 'in due course'.

High-ups in the government returned the said report back to the Commission to verify certain things in detail. After doing the needful, *on 2nd January 2013*, the Judicial Commission finally handed over their findings again covering that how Osama lived in Pakistan undetected for years until his killing by US special forces on 2nd May 2011 but the report, on this particular aspect, might never be revealed declaring it classified.

However, due to unknown reasons, the PPP government had not opted to make it public; like Hamood ur Rehman Commission Report it was sent to the cold room of the PM Secretariat; the general public also lost sight of it – the country continued to run in routine.

COMMISSION'S REPORT LEAKED:

On 8th July 2013, the Commission's Report suddenly appeared on the official website of **Al-Jazeera**, a middle-eastern media stalwart. On the same evening all the media anchors conducted special talk shows on the subject. Next day's newspapers carried editorials, opinions and excerpts of the Commission's Report cursing openly the then PPP government and the army for their wrong policies relating with Afghanistan and America.

Shortly after the report published, Al-Jazeera website was blocked in Pakistan; Pakistanis were supposed to live in dark – pushed back to the stone age of American Colin Powel of 2001. Hamoodur Rahman Commission Report on 1971's atrocities was also suppressed AND only emerged in portions decades later, in 2000, in leaks to the Indian media from where the Pakistani press had picked links and references.

Suddenly news appeared in print media on 10th July that *'a very responsible bureaucrat of the PM Secretariat had sold the Abbotabad Commission Report to Al-Jazeera for $15,000. The seller bureaucrat* *allegedly tried to sell it to "the Washington Post" & "the New York Times" but failed. Ultimately it was sold to al-Jazeera.'*

Nobody named that bureaucrat; rather no body believed so. Three days later, the PML(N) official spokesman issued statement that the original Abbotabad Commission Report was lying intact and secure in PM Secretariat. On the same evening of 10th July, Dr Shahid Masood in a live talk show at ARY News TV, told the viewers that:

'The said report was openly offered to all TV anchors and bureau chiefs of leading newspapers in Islamabad in clandestine way – for free – but all of them refused to take it as a matter of policy. The media wanted it that the state should make it open OFFICIALLY; at last Al-Jazeera's correspondent accepted it.'

The insiders knew it that the Abbotabad Commission Report had been *purposefully leaked out by the PML(N)* to revengefully hit the Pak-Army and ISI below the belt – due to obvious reasons; recall 12th October 1999's military coup. The then PPP regime was its additional target. The Commission had interviewed senior civilian and military officials and the three widows of bin Laden before they were deported to Saudi Arabia in April 2012.

Pakistan-US ties drastically deteriorated over Osama BL's raid, which had prompted accusations of incompetence or complicity against the military. Relations slumped to more low after botched US air strikes killed 24 Pakistani soldiers *on 26th November 2011* at Salala check post at Pak-Afgan border, but diplomats say the relationship improved when Pakistan re-opened its Afghan land crossings to NATO goods after a seven-month suspension in early January 2013.

The people of Pakistan had high expectations from the Commission of Justice Javed Iqbal but the way it had been wasting time by recording statements of hundreds of local residents, media persons and politicians; it could not deliver anything except disappointment. Commission could have proceeded by collecting evidences through the help of cyber and signal records of mobiles companies and tele-organizations, from the visitors' details and army's record etc. The hearsay statements of general people or of politicians did not serve the purpose.

On either way, the people believed that some of the intelligence personnel of ISI and Army were having actual sympathies with Osama. In ordinary course of nature, the army high command keeps a settled policy and cannot allow adopting different conduits for individuals at their own.

Possibility could be there that some middle level or lower ranks might have known Osama but no cogent evidence was available to believe that.

Fact remained that Osama was living in that premises of Abbottabad; other agencies like Intelligence Bureau, Special Branch of Police, local police station crew, and army's Field Intelligence Unit (FIU) might know the reality. They might have reports that Osama was living there for about five years but never bothered because since 2003 he was going inactive regarding Al Qaeda affairs. The local MNA, MPA and Union Council representatives, postman, water supply, Gas and Wapda officials all took it just a normal residence.

One critic maintained that:

'..... Although leaders of the ISI might not have known about Bin Laden's presence, someone among the country's retired Generals, Military Intelligence or local police must have known something. If Pakistan had taken this breach of sovereignty – by which I mean the head of Al Qaeda sitting in a cantonment so close to the capital — we should have seen a very vigorous investigation. It was a joke.'

Prime Minister Nawaz Sharif had two clear choices. He could forget about the report, and shelve it alongside Hamoodur Rahman's inquiry into the 1971 war, and let the state slide further into chaos and 'Failing State' status. Alternately, he was supposed to [repeatedly] recite and examine the report's contents and heed the clarion call for massive institutional reform - rather than worrying about the source of the leak.

OSAMA'S STAY – BACKGROUND EVENTS:

Osama's family moved from Afghanistan's Kandahar to Karachi shortly after the 11th September 2001 attacks on Twin Towers in America. "They kept a very low profile and lived extremely frugally. They never exposed themselves to public view. They had minimum security. OBL successfully minimised any 'signature' of his presence. His wives, children and grandchildren hardly ever emerged from the places where they stayed. No one ever visited them, not even trusted Al-Qaeda members.

[Whenever OBL felt unwell (unofficial US accounts indicate he suffered from Addison's disease), he treated himself with traditional Arab medicine ... and whenever he felt sluggish he would take some chocolate with an apple.]

Osama Bin Laden spent about two years in a rented house at Haripur; then a piece of land was purchased in Abbotabad through his courier cum personal servant Abrar al-Kuwaiti under a false identity [of Muhammad Arshad], with a fake old style [hand written] national identity card (NIC) in July 2004. During buying process his identity was not verified nor it was a mandatory requirement then [*even now the NICs are not normally verified in routine transactions or buying or selling processes in Pakistan*].

After the completion of construction of the two-storey structure in 2005, an additional, unauthorised storey and 18ft (5.5m) high walls were added in 2005; that unauthorised construction had never been inspected by local Cantonment Board officials, as required by law. In at least one government land survey, the compound, which, at one time, housed 27 people, was listed as being 'uninhabited'. No property tax had been collected on the compound since 2004-05 – a gross negligence on part of the Abbottabad Cantonment Board.

Osama's residence had also been fitted with four separate meters for electricity and natural gas respectively but then how shown as un-occupied – nobody bothered ever. Either Osama BL was extremely fortunate or there was a complete collapse of local governance.

While the IB professed total ignorance about Osama's presence, the ISI, however, had carried out a number of operations in Abbottabad. In January 2011, they captured Umar Patek, the mastermind behind the 2002 Bali bombings in Indonesia. Patek was found in a house in the *Aram Bagh* area of Abbottabad, just three kilometres away from Osama's compound.

Earlier in 2003, ISI had raided a location at two kilometres from Osama's compound in a failed attempt to capture Abu Faraj al-Libi, a known al-Qaeda commander. Al-Libi was later captured from FATA and was handed over to US authorities; he was straightaway sent to Guantanamo Bay.

The Commission noted that the ISI had "closed the file" on Osama BL after the CIA reportedly stopped sharing information on their hunt in 2005. According to ISI assessments, Osama was either dead or inactive, and the lack of intelligence sharing from the CIA was seen as indicative that this was the US view, as well. In fact, the CIA had not stopped chasing Osama - it had just stopped sharing information with the ISI.

When US SEALs had completed their 2nd May 2011's operation, the police were quickly sidelined from carrying out their responsibilities; they were relegated to forming an outer cordon around the site, which was later taken over by the military and ISI, too. None, including senior police officials, demanded that they be allowed to investigate what was ostensibly the scene of at least four additional killings besides Osama BL. NO FIR was filed.

The Commission found that the decision on the FIR had been discussed in a high level meeting between the chief minister, provincial police chief and other senior officials. It was decided there that **it was not** *"in the national interest"* **to register a case, as the matter** *"appeared to be an act of war"*. No written report in the Police Record; hats off to the country's military and their intelligence services as being the responsible authorities.

The Abbotabad Commission Report paints a picture of Pakistan as manipulated and undermined by the Americans.

EXTRACTS FROM COMMISSION'S REPORT:

The Commission's report was fiercely critical of the "illegal manner" in which the US conducted the raid. *"The US acted like a criminal thug,"* the report said.

A US SEAL's raid on 2nd May 2011 that left Osama bin Laden and four other people dead inside his huge residence in Abbottabad had triggered a global controversy on certain key questions regarding the fateful event. On 8th July 2013, as noted in earlier paragraphs, Al Jazeera published an exclusively obtained copy of the findings of the Abbottabad Commission. According to Al Jazeera, the report "was buried by the government and never made public" after it was finished in May 2012.

Here are some fascinating details from the Commission's report.

On his last night, Osama was with Amal al-Sadah, a 28-year-old Yemeni woman who was the youngest of his three wives. Both husband and wife went on the balcony to investigate about the roaring choppers but there was nothing except the moonless sky and pitch black surroundings. When Sadah reached to turn on a light, bin Laden said, "No". After reciting the Kalma and some verses from the Holy Qura'an with some of his children, Osama told his family that American helicopters had arrived and urged them to leave his room.

Ibrahim Al-Kuwaiti, Osama's Pakistani home servant, was shot and killed by US forces when he opened the door after hearing a knock at it [he thought the knock was from his brother Abrar, Osama's courier]. Abrar was also fatally shot during the raid.

Kuwaiti's wife, Maryam, was shot and wounded during show of aggression. Later, when Maryam resisted efforts to comply with her body search, things turned violent; Maryam cursed at the American team, prompting them to slap her.

In 2005, when an earthquake struck the area, the boundary wall of the compound lay collapsed in rubble for months, and yet bin Laden somehow managed to remain unexposed.

An investigator from Abbottabad police swore before the Commission that he was "100% sure" that bin Laden wasn't present in the property, he could have been brought there as part of a "CIA plot." The Commission, however, described that police officer as unprofessional and incompetent.

Some of the police officers simply shrugged that it wasn't their job; the ISI was responsible for security matters.

The ISI maintained that Bin Laden was not operational since 2005 and his Egyptian deputy Ayman al Zawahiri was running al Qaeda's affairs; therefore, everyone, including the US, thought that Bin Laden was dead. The ISI abandoned its search as soon as it thought the US had stopped looking for Ben Laden.

Amongst other items the Americans seized, Osama's purse evidently contained the will of the Al-Qaeda leader. Since then, there have been disputed reports on what it actually contained. Osama's eldest wife, Khairiyyah Sabar, was quoted saying that it dealt only with familial matters. Other accounts suggested that Osama used the will to assert that his children should not assume leadership positions with Al-Qaeda.

Osama kept very few clothing with him; despite having spent six years hiding in Abbottabad, his wardrobe included three pairs of *Shalwar + Kameez* [Pakistani suit] for the summer, three for the winter, a black jacket, two sweaters and one cowboy hat, which he used to wear while strolling in his compound, might be to *"avoid detection from above"*. Osama's wives told the Commission that he was not fond of possessions.

There was in fact a wall separating Osama's family from the families of Ibrahim [Al-Kawaiti] and Abrar. Their children never played with each other and the families did not 'mix or socialize.' Once, Ibrahim's daughter saw Osama's picture on TV, leading her to recognize him as the *'Miskeen Kaka'* [poor uncle] who lived upstairs.

Panic-stricken, Ibrahim attempted to bar the women and kids from watching TV, but his wife argued. He eventually relented and admitted that the man living upstairs was in fact Osama. This had also prompted a hurried security conference inside the compound, which ended with Osama giving up his exercise routine in a covered part of the courtyard.

Before re-locating to Abbottabad, Osama spent some time, about two years, in Haripur where he did not host any guests — he had decided to terminate all contacts with 'Al-Qaeda fellow Mujahideen' in the wake of [allegedly a master mind on 9/11 episode] Khalid Sheikh Mohammed's arrest in March 2003. Sheikh was then shifted to Guantanamo Bay for further interrogation.

In calling on the country's leaders to apologize to the Pakistani people for "dereliction of duty," the Commission's report concluded that:

> '......... *political, military intelligence and bureaucratic leadership cannot be absolved of their responsibility for the state of governance; policy planning and policy implementation that eventually rendered this national failure almost inevitable.'*

In the Nine - Eleven incident of New York, three narratives were made available to the public: that firstly, it was the work of an NGO called al-Qaeda secondly, it was the work of Israeli Mossad; thirdly, it was a 'false flag' operation by a US agency or insider connivance. The media fell in line with the 'official view' that it was the work of an 'Islamist NGO'. The Pakistan Government also endorsed that line but the people of Pakistan continued to believe that it was the work of Mossad or the American insiders.

Several books and innumerable articles were on record discrediting the official US line. Evidence was available to the Commission from Pakistani sources to challenge the credibility of the US narrative. The most important of these was an interview at *Samaa TV* with an eyewitness much later. American writer Paul Craig Roberts had it transcribed by his own sources and published three articles based on its contents on web sites of ICH and elsewhere; the videos were later removed from Youtube.

In a rare inside look at how the Pak-military spies operated, the report detailed the police and other officials being constantly shunted aside.

Referring to the *TIME magazine of 9*[th] *July 2013*:

> '*The work of the commission itself was being tracked. At an invitation-only meeting with local journalists, one spy [of ISI] managed to inveigle entry, before being spotted and asked to leave.*
>
> *The rogue elements within the ISI abetted bin Laden during his stay in Pakistan. "The possibility of some such direct or indirect and 'plausibly deniable' support cannot be ruled out, at least, at some level outside formal structures of the intelligence establishment," the report reads.*'

The lack of a coordinated strategy is said to be one of the reasons behind the failure to catch bin Laden. In one of its hardest-hitting passages, the Commission's report said: ***"It is a glaring testimony to the collective incompetence and negligence, at the very least, of the security and intelligence community in the Abbottabad area. The ISI had perhaps closed its books on bin Laden in 2005."***

The report's authors — a retired Supreme Court judge, a retired army corps commander, a former envoy to Washington and New Delhi, and a retired top cop of Police — described their report as neither a "witch hunt nor a whitewash." Indeed, it was an admirable attempt at collective scrutiny described suitable to all concerned.

PRESIDENT ZARDARI KNEW IT?

Usman Khalid, in his essay dated *10*[th] *July 2013*, available on internet media, pointed out that:

> '*The contradictory statements given before the Commission, intimidation of eyewitnesses to stop them from appearing before the Commission, suspicious death of the entire SEAL team that carried out the Abbotabad operation in an air accident in Afghanistan, were quite adequate to discredit the US narrative.*'

Subsequently it was known to all that:

- President Zardari was 'informed' before hand of the US clandestine operation against a 'high value' target inside Pakistan.

- PAF detected the presence of US F-15 aircraft in the air on Pak-Afghan border and sought instructions but President Zardari could not be contacted until well after the US operation had ended.

However, the military did not issue any statement but the Prime Minister Gilani hailed it as a 'victory' against terrorism.

The press in USA and Canada has been reporting that the top "Special Operations Commander" ordered the files about the Navy SEAL raid on Osama bin Laden's hideout to be washed out from Defence Department's computers and sent to the CIA. The secret move, described briefly in a draft report by the Pentagon's Inspector General, set off no alarms within the Obama administration even though it had violated the federal rules and also the Freedom of Information Act.

The American Press had asked US government for copies of Osama's death certificate and autopsy report as well as the results of tests to identify the body; the Pentagon could not locate the files and the CIA never responded. The AP was informed in March 2012 that they could not locate any photographs or video taken during the raid or showing Osama's body.

The Pentagon also said it could not find any images of bin Laden's body on the USS Carl Vinson, the aircraft carrier from which he was buried at sea. The above detail indicated towards new strategy of the US government to shield its sensitive activities from public scrutiny.

Contrarily, the Pakistani media gave extensive coverage to strong criticism in the Commission's report which accused authorities of complacency, collective failure and negligence that allowed Osama to live undetected in the country for more than nine years and his subsequent killing by the US troops in a covert operation. The said report concluded that:

> 'OBL was able to stay within the limits of Abbotabad Cantonment due to a collective failure of the military authorities, the intelligence authorities, the police and the civilian administration. How the entire neighbourhood, local officials, police and security and intelligence officials all missed the size, the strange shape, the barbed wire, the lack of cars and visitors etc over a period of nearly six years.'

In Pakistan, the general populace took it as a strong evidence of having prior knowledge of the American plans when they saw President Zardari's essay cum tribute in 'the Washington Post' of 2nd May 2011, just twelve hours after Osama's killing in Abbotabad. So quick it was – which transpired that at least Mr Zardari in Pakistan's government had known about the US attack before hand; time might not be in mind. That was why the essay was written and kept ready to be faxed to the top newspaper of the United States and it happened. See some parts of the essay:

- 'His country [Pakistan] provided initial help that ultimately led to al Qaeda leader Osama bin Laden, but he had no clue about the terror mastermind's whereabouts and didn't participate in the US raid to kill the top militant.

- That the raid was *"not a joint operation"* and bin Laden *"was not anywhere we had anticipated he would be."*

- And we in Pakistan take some satisfaction that our early assistance in identifying an al Qaeda courier ultimately led to this day.

- US politicians and military officials have roundly criticized Pakistan for not being more robust in the fight against al Qaeda......[but there stands] *"a decade of cooperation and partnership between the United States and his country that ultimately led to bin Laden's death."*

- He "endorses the words" of and "appreciates the credit" from US President Barack Obama about Pakistan's role.'

> [*In his announcement of bin Laden's death, Obama said "it's important to note that our counterterrorism cooperation with Pakistan helped lead us to bin Laden and the compound where he was hiding."*]

Mr Zardari had further urged in his essay that *"Pakistan had as much reason to despise al Qaeda as any nation. The war on terrorism is as much Pakistan's war as it is America's. And though it may have started with bin Laden, the forces of modernity and moderation remain under serious threat."*

President Zardari had further emphasized in his essay that:

> *"Justice against bin Laden was not just political; it was also personal, as the terrorists murdered our greatest leader, the mother of my children, Benazir Bhutto. The Taliban reacted to bin Laden's death by blaming the government of Pakistan and calling for retribution against its leaders, and specifically against me as the nation's president..... but Pakistanis won't be intimidated."*

Mr Zardari knew another cogent fact that *'the Taliban would react to Osama's death'*, therefore, he got the relevant message incorporated in his essay before hand as can be seen in above lines – hats off to the foresightedness of Pakistani leadership.

On 10th July 2010, while talking to a private TV channel, Justice (retd) Javed Iqbal refuted the foreign media claims [the Commission report being baseless and misleading] saying that the report not only identified those who were responsible for the incident but also reviewed the role of different institutions; the main purpose of the commission was to review performance of country's institutions.

PAK-ARMY'S BOARD OF INQUIRY:

Pak-Army had already completed their enquiries against allegations of lapses and lethargic attitudes of their ISI wing in connection with the Osama's un-noticed living in Abbotabad since six years.

Abbotabad Commission was told that Pak-Army's board of inquiry was established under Lt Gen Javed Iqbal to dig out the reasons and to fix the responsibility. Gen Javed Iqbal told the Commission that the local *Nawan Shehar* police station was located close to Osama's compound; but the police failed to observe anything unusual about the place and no report on anything suspicious was ever filed neither by the police nor Special Branch's contingent, which were responsible to maintain a close watch on the area.

The Board of Inquiry maintained that the police ignored or failed to take note of the visible violation of cantonment regulations; for construction of a third storey at the compound. It was totally a wrong presumption – basically it was the civil administration of Cantonment Executive Office which, under rules, works in liaison with the Army's Station Commander posted there. Yes – local police and the special branch crew were responsible for ignoring the inhabitants of such unique and high walled residence; especially the suspicious activities of the two brothers, Ibrahim and Abrar. However, the special branch was understaffed and under-equipped to do a proficient job.

'Al-Jazeera' dated 9th July 2013 categorically stated that:

> 'Osama was able to evade detection in Pakistan for nine years due to the "collective failure" of the Pakistani state's military and intelligence authorities, and "routine" incompetence at every level of the civil governance structure.
>
> The failure was so complete that, by page 87 of its report, the Commission investigating the circumstances around Bin Laden's killing

in the Pakistani city of Abbotabad in May 2011 was forced to coin a term for it: 'Governance Implosion Syndrome'.

Referring to *'the Express Tribune' dated 10th July 2013*, the Army's Inquiry Board maintained that *'due to poor coordination among agencies, duplication of work, qualitative and quantitative inadequacies of training, skills and equipment were among the reasons that made it possible for Bin Laden to evade detection in Abbotabad.'*

Contrarily, Hussain Haqqani [referring to *'The Economic Times' of Washington dated 10th July 2013*] accused Pakistan's security establishment of its incompetence and lax attitude that allowed Osama bin Laden to live undetected inside Pakistan for nine years.

Haqqani told the Commission during his interview on 19th December 2011 that he was accused of issuing visas to American personnel as the Pakistan's Ambassador in US without any authorisation. He maintained that *'the figures for visas were provided by officials at the embassy and the foreign ministry after he had resigned. Why did the intelligence agencies fail to track down those who were issued visas is another question that has been ignored.'*

{The worthy former ambassador, however, forgot to enlighten that *when the dozens of American visitors were issued the visa with their 'address of stay' as Zardari House F-8/2 Islamabad or Presidency Islamabad* then who fool would keep track of them.}

The **'Gulf News' of 10th July 2013** opined that *'the depth of the distrust between Pakistan and the US is made clear by [Gen] Pasha's assertion that CIA did not share intelligence with ISI because they did not trust it and in fact wanted to use the capture or killing of Bin Laden "to have the ISI declared a terrorist organisation" because of its alleged collusion with Bin Laden.'*

EX-ISI CHIEF BLASTS ALL:

During his briefing to the Abbotabad Commission on Osama, the former DG ISI Gen Ahmed Shuja Pasha opened indiscriminate fire on all. The former spy chief blasted Gen Musharraf for caving in before Americans, the political leadership for ignorance, indifference and its lack of reading culture, all security and intelligence agencies for not performing diligently and *journalists as being 'heavily bribed with money, women and alcohol'* for launching campaigns against the ISI.

The Commission was told that former PM Mr Gilani's statement of 22nd December 2011 at the Parliament's floor calling ISI as *'state within state'* and *asking who had given a visa to Osama bin Laden* had angered the army beyond imagination. Mr Gilani only once asked him for a briefing during his entire premiership. Gen Pasha continued with that:

> *'The Defence Ministry never sent a request for information sharing. No one, including the defence minister [ever] read policy documents on defence and there is no culture of reading among the political leadership. A thinking process does not exist; hence there is no formulation of any policy.'*

Gen Pasha, however, admitted before the Commission that:

- The ISI had brutalised many, even 'decent people' at times as a necessity.

- That *'the ISI had no legal authority for enforced disappearances'*.

- The Americans had pressurised Pakistan through Saudi Arabia for the release of Dr Shakil Afridi but both failed to get him.

- The ISI had *links with Haqqani network* but it was a brain child of ISI and CIA created after the Soviet invasion. Besides Pakistan, other countries like UK and Italy were also in touch with that group in all respects.

- The CIA had infiltrated many foreign NGOs in Pakistan including *Save the Children* that has *'a history of involvement with the CIA'* and concluded that they were NOT CLEAN. The CIA's Director had personally requested him not to expose *'Save the Children's role'* in Pakistan.

- Gen Musharraf *had caved in so promptly and so completely to the US demands that Shamsi Airbase was given to them for drone strikes against people in Pakistan.*

- In Drone Attacks massacre both the *political and military elite were equally responsible for the lapse* throughout the years.

- The *Abbotabad incident was a result of lack of capacity, inadequate knowledge and wrong attitude* on the part of both Generals and politicians in-charge.

- The ISI used to report to the President and the PM but *'the information is shared on a demand basis'*; they never received a demand from the PPP rulers or their Defence Ministry for briefing on any issue.

- The PM had [only] once asked for an update on the security situation.

- *That the ISI knew foreign miscreants lived in Karachi's no-go area* but police dare not venture there.

- *The police protected those who attacked the Qadianis in [Garhi Shahu] Lahore in 2010* and even directed them to the hospital where the wounded were being treated; *'venal political influence intervened everywhere'*.

- That ISI's record was not without blemish; many 'decent people' had been harmed by some of its errors. But the ISI learned from experiences and reformed itself through *'change to its mindset, culture and methodology'*.

- That the journalists were also found involved in the vilification campaign against the ISI launched by the US and many journalists were *'heavily bribed with money, women and alcohol'*; nearly *'every one of our elite was purchasable.'*

- *That the ISI had arrested people without any legal authority, it was a malpractice but the police mostly leaked the information provided to it; thus the ISI preferred to act alone.*

- That all the intelligence agencies must be held accountable for their failure *including Military Intelligence, Air Force Intelligence, Naval Intelligence, Intelligence Bureau, Criminal Investigation Department and the Special Branch.*

  > *'Gen Pasha held that very little coordination exists for terrorism-related information sharing with military intelligence services. The CID, Special Branch and the police have advantage over the ISI because of their spread, area coverage and local knowledge but nothing was done by them.'*

- Pakistan had reached an understanding with the United States on drone strikes targeting militants and those attacks were useful. There were no written agreements - only a political understanding. Admittedly, the drone attacks had their utility, but they represented a breach of the national sovereignty.

- Shamsi Airbase in Baluchistan was being used for US drone strikes against the people in FATA. Pakistan ordered the US personnel to leave the base only after US air strikes killed 24 Pakistani soldiers at Salala check post on 26th November 2011.

- The US arrogance 'knew no limits' and accused the Americans of waging 'psychological warfare' over the whereabouts of Taliban leader Mullah Omar and bin Laden's successor Ayman al-Zawahiri.

While describing Pakistan's conduct with the US, particularly in light of what the Commission deemed "an act of war", Gen Pasha said: *"We are a very weak state, also a very scared state."*

Gen Pasha had understood that the issues the Commission was investigating were not so much of specific individual or institutional failure, but with a problem of collective and systemic failure. He told that the US CIA had 'deeply penetrated' Pakistani society, quoting a US intelligence officer as having allegedly told him: *"You are so cheap... we can buy you with a visa, with a visit to the US, even with a dinner... we can buy anyone."*

Accordingly, Gen Pasha testified that: *"We are a failing state, even if we are not yet a failed state."* Moreover:

- It is not clear if the unscheduled electricity load shedding in Bilal Town Abbotabad at the starting moments of the raid was coincidental or deliberate, suggesting possibly connivance; though the US SEALs had night capability. Osama bin Laden and his family were fumbling in the dark.

- That most of the officers posted in the IB are from police and do not know the basics of intelligence who did not have any intelligence experience either when appointed as DG.

- That the **government never tasked the ISI to deal with counter-terrorism**; the agency had assumed this responsibility *'in response to the dysfunctionality of the prevailing system and the ineffectiveness of other state organs'.*

- That the Haqqani network was jointly created by the CIA and ISI against the Soviet occupation. The ISI was in *'contact with its non-sanctioned members'* who were responsible for administrative and other matters; its fighting factions were under UN control; UK, Italy and some other countries were also in touch with them.

- That the CIA had a history of using NGOs and there were 1300 foreign NGOs working in Pakistan; the CIA was extremely worried that its nexus with NGOs might be publicly exposed, especially of *'Save the Children'.*

In short Gen Pasha opened a barrage of allegations against anyone he could when he appeared before the Abbotabad Commission probing into the US raid that killed Osama bin Laden. He had also hurled a warning, saying there were people who continued criticizing the ISI against national interests, and *that they should fear the ISI*. He had out-rightly rejected the idea of putting ISI under civilian control, saying an earlier attempt to bring it under the Interior Ministry was disastrous.

For intelligentsia, Gen Pasha should have been reprimanded on the issue *'that Pakistan had an understanding with the US on drones'*; seemingly an odd admission for an army General. As said earlier, there was no written agreement, but a political understanding on the drones did exist. National sovereignty was indeed violated by the drones, what were the parameters of 'their utility'.

Meanwhile, talking to Al-Jazeera TV the same day, former US Deputy Secretary of State Richard Armitage said that *'drone attacks could stop if Pakistan so wished'*. He helped give a kind of oblique confirmation to what Gen Pasha told the Commission, that the done attacks were found useful by the Pakistanis, not just in some of the targets they focused on, but also to twist the arm of the frustrated public. One could deeply feel strategic necessities and compulsions under which the security services and armed forces had to operate in the recent past.

The said precarious arrangement, which was constructed by the military itself, needed an urgent correction and visualised direction by a civilian government. The new incumbent PM Nawaz Sharif, holding the defence portfolio himself, was required to speak with knowledge and authority, to keep fears of a civil-military power tussle at bay and to prove the civilians were the rightful leaders of Pakistan's security policy. Going by Abbotabad Commission report, and the bureaucracy, police and intelligence had to mend themselves too, but there was total darkness all lurking around.

QUESTIONS - STILL TO BE ANSWERED:

There are certain questions, of course more volatile, which had never been answered by the Pak Army or by the investigative media of Pakistan. Most important were:

- When Osama evaded American attack on Tora Bora Mountains in Afghanistan in 2002, how he managed to travel into Pakistan along with whole of his family. How he escaped the American hawks around to reach Swat valley straightaway.

• Was it possible that none of the Pak Army troop, or any member of Intelligence community, civil or military, had seen the whole family travelling so long way.

• How he managed to get living in Swat, then travelled to Haripur, settled there for about two years and no intelligence person could take notice of it.

• Since about 2005, he resided in Abbotabad, just at 500 yards from the Pakistan's Military Academy, in big premises having 18 ft high walls and could not be noticed by Military or Civil Intelligence, local police, Wapda people supplying power to the house, Council people supplying water and sewerage facilities etc.

• The local Cantonment authorities had not even completed their routine formalities that whether Osama's house was built according to the approved plan; whether the said property was properly taxed; whether the votes were brought on electoral role; whether the municipal road to that residence was properly maintained or not AND many more things.

• Near Osama's residence in Abbotabad, there was a base office of US Aid, where Dr Shakil Afridi used to roam about and often seen visiting that US Aid Office despite the fact that Dr Afridi was posted in Peshawar.

• Why the PAF leadership failed to provide any rational response to the intruding choppers during this attack.

[*The US SEALs had come there on helicopters. Admitted that the radars were on 'silence mode' but the thundering roar of choppers was loud; they landed on ground, the SEALs walked through, used megaphones, they blasted their damaged chopper – but how the security people around Kakul Academy, the officers inside, Army's Station Commander of the Cantonment or the local police, the Deputy Commissioner or the SSP or the DIG of Police had not heard the roars and rumbles for one hour – very strange.*]

• Why the Joint Staff HQ of Armed Forces was totally missing in action throughout this episode.

- Why no one noticed the preparations on the ground with trees being cut around Osama's residence.

- Why there was an unscheduled power cut at the time of the US attack; the electricity of that area went off at 00.01AM and came back only when the US operation was complete.

- Under what circumstances, Pakistan's High Commissioner at London, Wajid Shamsulhasan, was forced to make that announcement; who was responsible for that dis-information; if it was so.

- Why the 'American Ambassador in Washington', Hussain Haqqani was allowed to play a crucial part in abetting the CIA, allowing the US to gain excessive intrusive accesses in Pakistan and setting up of a vast CIA operative network.

Just 100 yards away from Osama's house, one serving army officer named Maj Amir Aziz was residing. Later it transpired that:

> "At about 00.30 AM that night, Maj Amir heard helicopters roaming over their home, got out curiously, then heard bullets fired in succession; telling that about 150 fires were there. Immediately rang up his Admin Officer Maj Adnan and told the whole event.
>
> Admin Officer passed the worried information to his Commandant Brig Shuja. The Commandant Brigadier heard the event patiently and instructed them 'to calm down as the situation is not clear'."

Maj Amir Aziz told the Commission later that Dr Shakil used to visit that US Aid Office frequently with local and foreign ladies.

It was also available on file that one Col (Rtd) Saeed Iqbal [apparently owning a private security agency] had previously visited Maj Amir Aziz at least thrice in his expensive bullet-proof car. During his short stay with Maj Amir, Col Saeed used to look at Osama's residence through his very modern digital camera, might be making video or taking snaps.

The fact remained that one of the sons of Col Saeed was the ADC to Gen Musharraf during his rule; later worked as Private Secretary of Gen Musharraf. Col Saeed's security agency was mostly comprised of retired ISI personnel, officers and men. Subsequent investigations lead to believe that Col Saeed [might have] provided full ground support to the Americans in association with Dr Shakil Afridi before launching that 2nd May's attack. Dubious roles of Dr Afridi, Col Saeed Iqbal and of Major Amir Aziz could have been scrutinized in detail to find out their criminal intent.

Another hard reality, that after 2ⁿᵈ May 2011, Col Saeed closed his so called security agency, sold out his assets at reduced prices and left Pakistan; most probably to settle in the US – mission accomplished.

OSAMA'S KILLING - LESSONS TO BE LEARNT:

In nut shell, the Abbotabad Commission Report was a derogatory condemnation of Pakistan's civil and military elite - its state institutions.

Referring to Shireen Mazari's conclusion [appeared in *'the News'* of 12ᵗʰ *July 2013*], three aspects of about 337-pages report were striking – and disturbing for Pakistanis:

- About the deep inroads made by the Americans and foreign NGOs into both government and state institutions.

- The then DG ISI Gen Pasha's admission before the Commission that Pakistan had become "too weak" and a US diktat.

- Despite knowing that the US had ended intelligence cooperation after 2005 with the ISI, we continued to give them a free run of the land.

Some media-men, who had once pointed out the questionable US presence near Tarbela, were ridiculed but then one could recall the Raymond Davis episode which had failed to quell our ruling military and civilian elite's passion for servitude to the US. No one questioned the heavy movement of US agents from Islamabad to Abbotabad, Peshawar and back – nor the hundreds of houses rented by the US embassy / USAID in Islamabad.

The Commission observed that the Intelligence Bureau (IB), the country's main civilian intelligence agency, had completely failed to respond to multiple irregularities in the case of Osama's compound in Abbotabad. Instead of being one of the main security institutions of Pakistan, the IB had become little more than a Post Office.

The IB's lack of professionalism was clear from its *'media based'* intelligence reports; only served as a political arm of the PM's office, nothing beyond. The interior ministry had the Americans running its aviation squadron, manned by DynCorp. The ISI was the primary agency responsible for tracing OBL in Pakistan but it miserably failed. Even though the US stopped intelligence cooperation with it, this should not have paralysed the ISI.

The political leadership was equally culpable because it never sought any briefing from the ISI on the issue. The Federal Defence Minister, Ahmed Mukhtar, acknowledged before the Commission that *'he knew little of what went on in his ministry since that was regarded as the domain of the military.'*

On the morning of 2nd May 2011, the Defence Minister came to know of the raid not through the military or government chain of command, but through media reports and a phone call from his daughter in New York.

Ahmed Mukhtar's was not an atypical case. When the US made contact with Pakistan following the raid, it was through a phone call between the then US Chairman of the Joint Chiefs of Staff Committee Admiral Mike Mullen and Pakistani COAS Gen Kayani. It was left to Gen Kayani to then inform the civilian government of what had happened, several hours later.

Abbotabad Commission Report revealed how all institutions, from the lowest rank right to the top, were in a mess with no one owning up to their burden of responsibility. Height of lethargy was that the DGMO informed about the US intrusion to the COAS by 2AM although the choppers were in Abbotabad by 00.25AM. The COAS called the CAS asking him to scramble aircraft at 2.07AM but nothing happened.

Referring to *'the News' dated 1st August 2013,* it emerged from the internal correspondence that members of the Abbottabad Commission had compromised integrity to favour the accused; certain duly verified documents revealed later.

There was seen internal friction among members of the commission; hard-line position taken by one member pitting himself against three colleagues whom he accused of being *'soft on certain institutions.'* One of the members went abroad on the pretext of illness as he was not contented with the report but did not want to write a note of dissent even.

One member of the Commission was considered very critical of his views about army and the ISI. As he wrote a dissenting note, two of his colleagues made all possible efforts to counter his argument and kept the 'bosses in uniform' updated about their continuing efforts to save their skins.

The Commission members prepared their separate drafts in June 2012 which were reduced to two in August that year and were *shared with the GHQ to let them know about intensive efforts to bail them out.* Frustrating efforts were made by two members to convince the colleague of dissenting note in order to come to a point where the note was significantly reduced and certain cogent comments were taken out from the report.

As the IB and ISI people confided with one member over his assessment about the chances of possible reactions, he said he was confident to convince the other members of the Commission about their 'innocence'. While the entire record was opened to the GHQ with regular briefing, no member was ready to face the media on the veracity of allegations that came out of the secret memos.

Chairman of the Commission, Justice (R) Javed Iqbal initially promised to meet the media but later stopped taking calls. AND that was why the Commission did not hold anyone directly responsible; as the report repeatedly stated:

> "........ *the Pakistani military and political leadership displayed a degree of incompetence and irresponsibility that was truly breathtaking and indeed culpable".*

Abbotabad Commission Report [compiled by Justice (Rtd) Javed Iqbal] on Osama Ben Laden's killing on 2nd May 2011 in Pakistan concluded that:

> "...... *It was primarily the intelligence – security failure that was rooted in political irresponsibility and military exercise of authority and influence in policy and administrative areas for which it neither had constitutional or legal authority, nor the necessary expertise and competence."*

Concurrently, most international law experts, even the Americans, including former West German Chancellor Helmut Schmidt, kept the opinion that *'what the US did was illegal and criminal'.* Shamefully, Pakistan's president and the PM welcomed this disgrace.

However, Pakistanis are waiting for a better tomorrow with the same like stuff; is'nt astonishing.

US QUITS – WOT ENDS:

The intelligentsia and historians keep the opinion that the year 2011 contributed much in calling an end to American occupation of Afghan soils and Pakistan's cold shoulders during 2011-12 played a pivotal role in writing that American policy document of 'the US exit till 2014'.

Referring to the *TIME of 14th April 2013*, good days of Pak-US relations took a new start on one evening in June 2009, when Richard Holbrooke [later died in December 2010] paid his first visit [as Obama's envoy for Pak-Afghan lands] to Pakistan's President Asif Ali Zardari at the presidency in Islamabad to know his ideas about how Washington could help. Mr Zardari told Holbrooke that:

> *"Pakistan is like AIG [comparing his country to the US insurance giant that was bailed out in 2008] assuming it 'too big to fail'; the US government had given AIG $100 billion. You should give Pakistan the same."*

And Holbrooke kept on smiling throughout the meeting; he had not liked the image of Pakistan holding a gun to its own head and begging from America.

In 2011, three major incidents brought the Pak-US relationship crashing to its lowest-point ever: a CIA contractor Raymond Davis killed two people in Lahore; US Navy Seals killed Osama without informing the people of Pakistan; and toward the end of the year, 26 Pakistani troops were killed in a cross-border incident at Salala, a check post at Pak-Afghan border.

Till ending 2010, the security relationship worked better when there were other efforts alongside. The US had security interests and Pakistan was concerned with economic and civilian interests. Both countries were better off in 2009-10 when the conversation was not just about drones and terrorists, but it was also about energy and clean water in Pakistan.

The CIA and the Pentagon had seen the benefits of the military cum economic cooperation but Obama's nearest lobby wanted over-night results. They started applying constant pressure that 'threatened to break up the relationship.' At one point, Holbrooke turned to Vali Nasr [his 2nd in command] shaking his head, and said: *"Watch them [the CIA] ruin this relationship. And when it is ruined, they are going to say, 'We told you, you can't work with Pakistan!' We never learn."*

As opined by *Ayaz Amir* in his essay *dated 12*[th] *July 2013* appeared on media pages:

> *"Incompetence and negligence are the two watchwords of the report and those caught by the patriotic fever are using them as ammunition against everything in sight, chiefly the ISI and the army command.*
>
> *There is, however, a fine line between embarrassment and humiliation. ..... The real embarrassment was his presence [here] .... no point in dwelling too much on the loss of national honour in the American assault."*

Osama was a blazing priority for the Americans but not for Pakistanis because for many people in Pakistan he was not a villain but a hero. Even almost every major Al-Qaeda catch – Abu Zubaydah, al-Libbi, Ramzi and Khalid Sheikh Mohammad, were caught here; Pakistan paid for its involvement in Afghan War of 1980s not being complicit with Al-Qaeda. Then *Jihadi* HQ shifted to FATA, Pakistan became major battlefield, even more than Afghanistan, not only did Osama move here much of the Al-Qaeda leadership like Haqqanis did so as well.

Irony of fate was that the leadership, both army and civilian, went happy.

Difficult to differentiate if the America has been Pakistan's friend or foe. The fact remains that he behaved arrogant after his designs and perception of being 'the ONLY super power' after Russia's defeat in 1980s went gradually blurred, tempered and mitigated; it was because of three factors: *'the Sunni resistance to the American occupation in Iraq; the Taliban resistance in Afghanistan; and Iran's refusal to succumb to American threats'*, as Ayaz Amir suggested.

No one knows why Pakistani leadership went on constantly creeping under American's toes then.

Scenario 88

OSAMA'S STORY – ANOTHER ANGLE:

Osama Bin Laden, originally a Saudi national and businessman, earned his welcome in Afghanistan by helping the tribes resist the 1979 Soviet invasion. A conduit for CIA money and weaponry, Osama had recruited Muslims from other countries to fight in the decade-long struggle against the Soviet Army in Afghanistan; thus became an Islamic hero. For him it was a victory if the US attack on Afghanistan had resulted in true Islamic revolution in Pakistan and Saudi Arabia.

OSAMA'S 1ST INTERVIEW AFTER 9/11 2001:

Dr Paul Craig Roberts [an Assistant Secretary of the US Treasury for Economic Policy and Associate Editor of the Wall Street Journal & a well known columnist for Business Week] had once written in his essay *'The Osama Bin Laden Myth'* published *on 26th November 2012* that:

A daily newspaper, Ummat of Karachi dated 28th September 2001 had published an interview of Osama Bin Laden, taken at Kabul (Afghanistan) just 17 days after the [*alleged but unsubstantiated*] al Qaeda attack of 11th September 2001, on the World Trade Centre twin towers New York and Pentagon. The interview was sensational.

The alleged "mastermind" Osama BL of 9/11 said that he and al Qaeda had nothing to do with that attack. The BBC's World Monitoring Service had that interview translated into English and made public on 29th September 2001 for the whole world.

Find here the full text [verbatim] of *daily 'Ummat' newspaper's exclusive interview* with Osama Bin Laden, also available on Weekly Ummat's internet site.

Kabul: *Prominent Arab mojahed holy warrior Usamah Bin-Laden* [the spelling as written in the script] *has said that he or his al-Qa'idah group has nothing to do with the 11 September suicidal attacks in Washington and New York. He said the US government should find the attackers within the country.*

In an exclusive interview with daily "Ummat", he said these attacks could be the act of those who are part of the American system and are rebelling against it and working for some other system. Or, Usamah said, this could be the act of those who want to make the current century a century of conflict between Islam and Christianity.

Or, the American Jews, who are opposed to President Bush ever since the Florida elections, might be the masterminds of this act. There is also a great possibility of the involvement of US intelligence agencies, which need billions of dollars worth of funds every year. He said there is a government within the government in the United States.

The secret agencies, he said, should be asked as to who are behind the attacks. Usamah said support for attack on Afghanistan was a matter of need for some Muslim countries and compulsion for others.

However, he said, he was thankful to the courageous people of Pakistan who erected a bulwark before the wrong forces. He added that the Islamic world was attaching great expectations with Pakistan and, in time of need, "we will protect this bulwark by sacrificing of lives".

Following is the interview in full detail:

Ummat: *You have been accused of involvement in the attacks in New York and Washington. What do you want to say about this? If you are not involved, who might be?*

Usamah [Osama bin Laden]: In the name of Allah, the most beneficent, the most merciful. Praise be to Allah, Who is the creator of the whole universe and Who made the earth as an abode for peace, for the whole mankind. Allah is the Sustainer, who sent Prophet Muhammad for our guidance. I am thankful to the Ummat Group of Publications, which gave me the opportunity to convey my viewpoint to the people, particularly the valiant and *Momin* true Muslim people of Pakistan who refused to believe in lie of the demon.

I have already said that I am not involved in the 11 September attacks in the United States. As a Muslim, I try my best to avoid telling a lie. I had no knowledge of these attacks, nor do I consider the killing of innocent women, children, and other humans as an appreciable act. Islam strictly forbids causing harm to innocent women, children and other people.

Such a practice is forbidden ever in the course of a battle. It is the United States, which is perpetrating maltreatment on women, children, and common people of other faiths, particularly the followers of Islam. All that is going on in Palestine for the last 11 months is sufficient to call the wrath of God upon the United States and Israel.

There is also a warning for those Muslim countries, which witnessed all these as a silent spectator. What had earlier been done to the innocent people of Iraq, Chechnya, and Bosnia?

Only one conclusion could be derived from the indifference of the United States and the West to these acts of terror and the patronage of the tyrants by these powers that America is an anti-Islamic power and it is patronizing the anti-Islamic forces. Its friendship with the Muslim countries is just a show, rather deceit. By enticing or intimidating these countries, the United States is forcing them to play a role of its choice. Put a glance all around and you will see that the slaves of the United States are either rulers or enemies of Muslims.

The US has no friends, nor does it want to keep any because the prerequisite of friendship is to come to the level of the friend or consider him at par with you. America does not want to see anyone equal to it. It expects slavery from others. Therefore, other countries are either its slaves or subordinates.

However, our case is different. We have pledged slavery to God Almighty alone and after this pledge there is no possibility to become the slave of someone else. If we do that, it will be disregardful to both our Sustainers and his fellow beings. Most of the world nations upholding their freedom are the religious ones, which are the enemies of United States, or the latter itself considers them as its enemies. Or the countries, which do not agree to become its slaves, such as China, Iran, Libya, Cuba, Syria, and the former Russia as received.

> *Whoever committed the act of 11 September are not the friends of the American people. I have already said that we are against the American system, not against its people, whereas in these attacks, the common American people have been killed.*

According to my information, the death toll is much higher than what the US government has stated. But the Bush administration does not want the panic to spread. The United States should try to trace the perpetrators of these attacks within itself; the people who are a part of the US system, but are dissenting against it. OR

Those who are working for some other system; persons who want to make the present century as a century of conflict between Islam and

Christianity so that their own civilization, nation, country or ideology could survive. They can be any one, from Russia to Israel and from India to Serbia. In the US itself, there are dozens of well-organized and well-equipped groups, which are capable of causing a large-scale destruction. Then you cannot forget the American Jews, who are annoyed with President Bush ever since the elections in Florida and want to avenge him.

Then there are intelligence agencies in the US, which require billions of dollars worth of funds from the Congress and the government every year. This funding issue was not a big problem till the existence of the former Soviet Union but after that the budget of these agencies was in danger.

They needed an enemy. So, they first started propaganda against Usamah and Taliban and then this incident happened. You see, the Bush administration approved a budget of 40bn dollars. Where will this huge amount go? It will be provided to the same agencies, which need huge funds and want to exert their importance.

Now they will spend the money for their expansion and for increasing their importance. I will give you an example. Drug smugglers from all over the world are in contact with the US secret agencies. These agencies do not want to eradicate narcotics cultivation and trafficking because their importance will be diminished. The people in the US Drug Enforcement Department are encouraging drug trade so that they could show performance and get millions of dollars worth of budget.

General Noriega was made a drug baron by the CIA and, in need, he was made a scapegoat. In the same way, whether it is President Bush or any other US president, they cannot bring Israel to justice for its human rights abuses or to hold it accountable for such crimes. What is this? Is it not that there exists a government within the government in the United Sates? The secret government must be asked as to who made the attacks.

Ummat: *A number of world countries have joined the call of the United States for launching an attack on Afghanistan. These also include a number of Muslim countries. Will Al-Qa'idah declare a jihad against these countries as well*?

Usamah: I must say that my duty is just to awaken the Muslims; to tell them as to what is good for them and what is not. What does Islam says and what the enemies of Islam want?

Al-Qa'idah was set up to wage a jihad against infidelity, particularly to encounter the onslaught of the infidel countries against the Islamic states.

Jihad is the sixth undeclared element of Islam. The first five being the basic holy words of Islam, prayers, fastings, *Zaka'at,* pilgrimage to Mecca, and *Jihad.* Every anti-Islamic person is afraid of it.

Al-Qa'idah wants to keep this element alive and active and make it part of the daily life of the Muslims. It wants to give it the status of worship. We are not against any Islamic country nor do we consider a war against an Islamic country as *jihad.*

We are in favour of armed *jihad* only against those infidel countries, which are killing innocent Muslim men, women, and children just because they are Muslims. Supporting the US act is the need of some Muslim countries and the compulsion of others. However, they should think as to what will remain of their religious and moral position if they support the attack of Christians and the Jews in a Muslim country like Afghanistan.

The orders of Islamic *Shari'ah* jurisprudence for such individuals, organizations, and countries are clear and all the scholars of the Muslim brotherhood are unanimous on them. We will do the same, which is being ordered by the *Amir al-Momenin* the commander of the faithful Mulla Omar and the Islamic scholars. The hearts of the people of Muslim countries are beating with the call of *jihad.* We are grateful to them.

Ummat: *The losses caused in the attacks in New York and Washington have proved that giving an economic blow to the US is not too difficult. US experts admit that a few more such attacks can bring down the American economy. Why is al-Qa'idah not targeting their economic pillars?*

Usamah: I have already said that we are not hostile to the United States. We are against the system, which makes other nations slaves of the United States, or forces them to mortgage their political and economic freedom. This system is totally in control of the American Jews, whose first priority is Israel, not the US.

It is simply that the American people are themselves the slaves of the Jews and are forced to live according to the principles and laws laid by them. So, the punishment should reach Israel. In fact, it is Israel, which is giving a blood bath to innocent Muslims and the US is not uttering a single word.

Ummat: *Why is harm not caused to the enemies of Islam through other means, apart from the armed struggle; for instance, inciting the Muslims to boycott Western products, banks, shipping lines and TV channels.*

Usamah: The first thing is that Western products could only be boycotted when the Muslim fraternity is fully awakened and organized. Secondly, the Muslim companies should become self-sufficient in producing goods equal to the products of Western companies. Economic boycott of the West is not possible unless economic self-sufficiency is attained and substitute products are brought out.

You see that wealth is scattered all across the Muslim world but not a single TV channel has been acquired which can preach Islamic injunctions according to modern requirements and attain an international influence. Muslim traders and philanthropists should make it a point that if the weapon of public opinion is to be used, it is to be kept in the hand.

Today's world is of public opinion and the fates of nations are determined through its pressure. Once the tools for building public opinion are obtained, everything that you asked for can be done.

Ummat: *The entire propaganda about your struggle has so far been made by the Western media. But no information is being received from your sources about the network of Al-Qa'idah and its jihadi successes. Would you comment?*

Usamah: In fact, the Western media is left with nothing else. It has no other theme to survive for a long time. Then we have many other things to do. The struggle for *jihad* and the successes are for the sake of Allah and not to annoy His bondsmen. Our silence is our real propaganda. Rejections, explanations, or corrigendum only waste your time and through them, the enemy wants you to engage in things which are not of use to you. These things are pulling you away from your cause.

> *The Western media is unleashing such a baseless propaganda, which make us surprise but it reflects on what is in their hearts and gradually they themselves become captive of this propaganda. They become afraid of it and begin to cause harm to themselves. Terror is the most dreaded weapon in modern age and the Western media is mercilessly using it against its own people.*

It can add fear and helplessness in the psyche of the people of Europe and the United States. It means that what the enemies of the United States cannot do, its media is doing that. You can understand as to what will be the performance of the nation in a war, which suffers from fear and helplessness.

Ummat: *What will the impact of the freeze of al-Qa'idah accounts by the United States?*

Usamah: God opens up ways for those who work for Him. Freezing of accounts will not make any difference for Al-Qa'idah or other *jihadi* groups. With the grace of Allah, al-Qa'idah has more than three such alternative financial systems, which are all separate and totally independent from each other. This system is operating under the patronage of those who love *jihad*. What to say of the United States, even the combined world cannot budge these people from their path.

These people are not in hundreds but in thousands and millions. Al-Qa'idah comprises of such modern educated youths who are aware of the cracks inside the Western financial system as they are aware of the lines in their hands. These are the very flaws of the Western fiscal system, which are becoming a noose for it and this system could not recuperate in spite of the passage of so many days.

Ummat: *Are there other safe areas other than Afghanistan, where you can continue jihad?*

Usamah: There are areas in all parts of the world where strong *jihadi* forces are present, from Indonesia to Algeria, from Kabul to Chechnya, from Bosnia to Sudan, and from Burma to Kashmir. Then it is not the problem of my person. I am helpless fellowman of God, constantly in the fear of my accountability before God.

It is not the question of Usamah but of Islam and, in Islam too, of *jihad*. Thanks to God, those waging a *jihad* can walk today with their heads raised. *Jihad* was still present when there was no Usamah and it will remain as such even when Usamah is no longer there. Allah opens up ways and creates loves in the hearts of people for those who walk on the path of Allah with their lives, property, and children.

Believe it, through *jihad*, a man gets everything he desires. And the biggest desire of a Muslim is the after life. Martyrdom is the shortest way of attaining an eternal life.

Ummat: *What do you say about the Pakistan government policy on Afghanistan attack?*

Usamah: We are thankful to the Momin and valiant people of Pakistan who erected a blockade in front of the wrong forces and stood in the first file of battle. Pakistan is a great hope for the Islamic brotherhood. Its people are awakened, organized, and rich in the spirit of faith. They backed Afghanistan in its war against the Soviet Union and extended every help to the *mojahedin* and the Afghan people.

Then these are very Pakistanis who are standing shoulder by shoulder with the Taliban. If such people emerge in just two countries, the domination of the West will diminish in a matter of days. Our hearts beat with Pakistan and, God forbid, if a difficult time comes we will protect it with our blood.

Pakistan is sacred for us like a place of worship. We are the people of *jihad* and fighting for the defence of Pakistan is the best of all *jihads* to us. It does not matter for us as to who rules Pakistan. The important thing is that the spirit of *jihad* is alive and stronger in the hearts of the Pakistani people.

OSAMA's DEATH DEBATED:

Coming back to 2nd May 2011's event; the death of Osama BL gave rise to various conspiracy theories and rumours. Keeping aside the above factual interview of 28th September 2001, which was never debated or challenged for complete decade till May 2011, doubts about Osama's death were fuelled by:

- the US military's disposal of his body at sea,

- the decision not to release any photographic or DNA evidence of his death to the public;

- the contradicting accounts of the incident in comparison with the previous American assertions and

- the 25-minute blackout during the raid on Osama's compound due to power cut-off;

- the mysterious crash of a US helicopter in Afghanistan killing 38 persons; 22 SEAL soldiers were amongst them who had taken part in the said Geronimo Operation of 2nd May 2011.

- The images purporting to show a dead Osama on 2nd May, broadcasted on Pakistani TV channels, later picked by the British press and the Associated Press, were swiftly removed from websites after it was exposed as a fake on Twitter.

The **White House on 4th May 2011** announced it would not release any images of Osama's dead body on various pretexts of risks from al Qaeda. Several photos of the aftermath of the raid were given to Reuters by some Pakistani security official, but all were taken after the US forces had left speaking nothing about Osama itself.

On 6th May 2011, reportedly an al-Qaeda website acknowledged Osama's death but the critics came out with more suspicion that it was the same internet site which had been running since years by the CIA in the name of Osama and its activities; also responsible for releasing Osama's fake videos from time to time.

The US government's own refusal to provide any physical evidence to substantiate its claim was a major cause of concern for many. Narrative story was OK but no physical evidence constituting 'actual proof of death' was offered to the public, neither to journalists nor to independent third parties who had requested this information through the Freedom of Information Act (FOIA). Numerous organizations filed FOIA requests seeking at least a partial release of photographs, videos, and DNA test results, including 'The APP, Reuters, CBS News, Judicial Watch, Politico, Fox News, Citizens United, and NPR; but of no avail.

On 26th April 2012, a US federal judge decided in the case *Judicial Watch v. US Department of Defence* that the government did not need to release any evidence to the public. Judicial Watch's president, Tom Fitton, responded to the ruling by saying:

'The court got it terribly wrong. There is no provision under the Freedom of Information Act that allows documents to be kept secret because their release might offend our terrorist enemies. We will appeal.'

Suspicions and qualms about Osama's death flared up by the US military's disposal of his body at sea; US officials maintained that the burial was necessary because arrangements could not be made with any country to bury him within 24 hours, as dictated by Muslim practice. The media had questioned that why America, in the past, had held the bodies of Uday Hussein and Qusay Hussein [sons of Saddam Hussein] for 11 days before being released for burial. [*In that instance, however, several Iraqi cities were reluctant to grant a gravesite for Saddam's sons.*]

Prof Peter Romaniuk of John Jay College of Criminal Justice New York had, commented that:

'..... the burial at sea was to forestall further questions. Obviously they're going to be under pressure to show a body or produce further evidence, but this was a way of taking that issue off the table.

A stated advantage of a burial at sea is that the site is not readily identified or accessed, thus preventing it from becoming a focus of attention or <u>terrorist shrine</u>.'

A number of residents at Abbotabad believed that he never lived among them; some urged that no fire-fight ever took place, and that US forces might have captured Osama alive if at all he was there.

Referring to daily *'Telegraph' dated 3rd May 2011'* one Bashir Qureshi, who lived close to the compound where Osama was shot and whose windows were blown out in the raid, was dismissive while uttering: *"Nobody believes it. We've never seen any Arabs around here, he was not here."*

Hamid Gul, the former ISI Chief of Pakistan, said in an *interview with CNN on 5th May 2011,* that:

"He believed bin Laden had died many years ago, and that the official death story given out by the American media was a hoax. They must have known that he had died some years ago so they were waiting.

They were keeping this story on the ice and they were looking for an appropriate moment and it couldn't be a better moment because President Obama had to fight off his first salvo in his next year's election as he runs for the presidential and for the White House and I think it is a very appropriate time to come out, bring this out of the closet."

A number of Iranians said they believed that bin Laden was working with the US during the entire war on terror. Ismail Kosari and Javad Jahangirzadeh, both members of Irani Parliament believed [referring to *'International Business Times dated 4th May 2011*] that Osama BL:

"....... was just a puppet controlled by the Zionist regime in order to present a violent image of Islam after the September 11 attacks, and his death reflects the passing of a temporary US pawn, and symbolizes the end of one era and the beginning of another in American policy in the region".

Iranian Intelligence Minister Heydar Moslehi, while speaking to *ISNA on 10th May 2011,* claimed to have *"credible information that Bin Laden died some time ago of a disease."*

Iranian President Mahmoud Ahmadinejad had said *"I have exact information that bin Laden was held by the American military for sometime... until the day they killed him he was a prisoner held by them."*

FORMER CIA AGENT SPILLS THE BEANS:

Referring to an interview with Russia's Channel [Press TV dated 19th May 2012] one Berkan Yashar, a Turkish politician but a former CIA agent, revealed that al-Qaeda leader Osama bin Laden had died of natural causes five years before the US announced his death; he was not killed in 2011.

> *"In September of 1992, I was in Chechnya, that's when I first met the man whose name was Bin Laden. This meeting took place in a two-story house in the city of Grozny; on the top floor was a family of Gamsakhurdia, the Georgian president, who then was kicked out of his country. We met on the bottom floor; Osama lived in the same building.*
>
> *He personally knew Bin Laden's three Chechen bodyguards, who had protected him until his death and witnessed his death on 26th June 2006.*
>
> *Even if the entire world believed, I could not possibly believe it. I personally know the Chechens who protected him, they are Sami, Mahmood, and Ayub, and they were with him until the very end.*
>
> *Only three Chechens buried him, according to his will, in the mountains on the Pakistan-Afghan border. The CIA abducted one of the bodyguards, Sami, before they announced killing of Bin Laden last year. The bodyguard disclosed to the US the exact place of burial in the mountains.*
>
> *There was no assault. I know the American operations from the inside: they find the grave, dig out bin Laden and tell everyone about this. They need to show how technologically the security services worked, how each step was controlled, and then present it as a great victory to show that taxpayers are not paying taxes for nothing."*

Now see the America's most prestigious magazine *'TIME' of 30*th *June 2008*, which contained a detailed treatise captioned '**Is Osama Bin Laden Dying again**'. It says that in 2002, Pakistani President Pervez Musharraf said bin Laden had kidney disease, and that he had required a dialysis machine when he lived in Afghanistan. That same year [2002], the FBI's top counter-terrorism official, Dale Watson, said, *"I personally think he is probably not with us anymore."*

CIA produced a report [in 2008] saying that bin Laden had long-term kidney disease and might have only months to live. The agency ostensibly managed to get the names of the medications bin Laden was taking. One US official had concluded, *"Based on his current pharmaceutical intake, [we] would expect that he has no more than six to 18 months to live and impending kidney failure."*

TIME *magazine* referred above, however, had concluded that essay with the phrase *'... given the reliability of past long-distance diagnoses and the continuing threat al-Qaeda poses around the world, that may be the least of America's worries.'*

Cindy Sheehan, the mother of a soldier killed in Iraq, who became a symbol of the opposition to the war, wrote in *'National Review' of* 2nd *May 2011* that:

'I am sorry, but if you believe the newest death of OBL, you're stupid. Just think to yourself – they paraded Saddam's dead sons around to prove they were dead – why do you suppose they hastily buried this version of OBL at sea? This lying, murderous Empire can only exist with your brainwashed consent – just put your flags away and think.'

Travis Shannon opined at **CNN International on** 5th **May 2011** that:

'The only proof of Osama being dead again that we were offered was President Obama telling us that there was a DNA match between the man killed by the Navy SEALs and OBL. Even if it is possible to get DNA done so quickly and the regime did have bin Laden DNA lying around a lab somewhere – where is the empirical proof?'

Davis Richard in *'Economic Voice' program of* 3rd *May 2011 on Russia Today TV*, claimed that:

'.... bin Laden had been dead for nearly ten years, and that his body had been kept in liquid nitrogen so that it can be used as a propaganda tool at a future politically expedient time. In 2002, an anonymous White House source had told him that bin Laden is frozen, literally frozen and that he would be rolled out in the future at some date.'

Referring to Wikipedia; **on** 3rd *May 2011, radio host Alex Jones aired an interview in which Steve Pieczenik* had claimed that:

'Osama Bin Laden had died of 'Marfan syndrome' in 2001 shortly after the September 11 attacks, and that the attacks on the United

States on 9/11 were part of a false flag operation by the American government.'

Alex Jones, a radio personality of Austin, who gives voice to the 9/11 Truth Movement and runs the Web site Infowars.com, also pointed to similar comments made by former Secretary of State Madeleine Albright in 2003:

> *"Yes we have been told by intelligence that they've got him, Bush may roll him out, but because they exposed that at the election they didn't do it".*

Jones had lists of FBI officials and counter-intelligence leaders from Iran, Pakistan and Afghanistan who had said for years that bin Laden was dead. Jones further voiced doubts about the official story of bin Laden's death on his radio show telling his listeners, ***"My friends, this is a complete and total hoax."***

Emily Wax' essay appeared on next day's *'Washington Post' [3ʳᵈ May 2011]* embarked:

> *'Could the public trust bin Laden's DNA samples? Where was bin Laden's body? Why was the most wanted mujahed on Earth buried in an undisclosed location in the northern Arabian Sea?*
>
> *Why the news was announced mere weeks after President Obama's campaign kick-off and just days after his birth certificate was released? Why so late on a Sunday night?'*

Within minutes of the news of bin Laden's funeral at sea, Facebook, Twitter and e-mail lighted up with questions, pointing out discrepancies, motives, cover-ups, comparing photos and videos, voice recordings and FBI most-wanted pinup posters from all over the globe.

9 -11 TRUTH MOVEMENTS:

Steven Jones, a retired professor [in physics] of Brigham Young University and contributor to the **9/11 Truth Movement,** along with other members of the movement, who distrust Washington's version of the attacks, categorically stated that:

> *"This has not put a single of the 9/11 questions to bed; the collapse of the twin towers is best explained as controlled demolition. .... As a scientist, I try to look at the evidence I can get."*

They wrote books and studied the physics of the towers crumbling.

Mike Berger, who works with **911Truth.org**, an organization founded to examine facts around the attack, said:

> *"I don't know how you can have closure, when there are hundreds of contradictions to the stories that you were told. The story doesn't end here because we are told bin Laden is dead. We are living in an endless war of trillions of dollars being spent without any responsibility."*

The Washington Post had added that *'Obama just re-launched his election bid, and nabbing bin Laden is the main kick-off campaign rally. Things aren't going well. So they are bringing back an old staple. ......* *so don't worry, the government got the bad guy.* **This isn't Elvis, man. The government lied to us about weapons of mass destructions [WMDs].'**

The *Iranian network Press TV* interviewed journalist Webster Tarpley [an American author, historian, economist, journalist, lecturer and a critic of the US foreign and domestic policy] and researcher Stephen Lendman **on 5**th **May 2011** who both doubted the official story of bin Laden's death. Tarpley said he believed bin Laden had been dead for a long time. He also claimed that the public was deceived by a staged announcement.

Stephen Lendman said that bin Laden died of natural causes in mid-December 2001 — citing former Pakistani Prime Minister Benazir Bhutto and that bin Laden's supposed death was strategically timed as a distraction so Obama's approval rating would increase, despite a very weak American economy.

Both Tarpley and Lendman suggested that Obama's announcement was also an excuse to involve the United States in wars with Pakistan and Middle Eastern nations.

On the Fox News morning show *Fox & Friends* dated 3rd **May 2011**, co-host Steve Doocy challenged the DNA evidence confirming bin Laden's death, saying that the report was *"just numbers on a piece of paper.*

An article in *'Mediaite' dated 3*rd *May 2011* said that:

> *'Last night Judge Andrew Napolitano agreed that it was good for the monster Osama bin Laden to have been taken out; however, he also*

*warned that Obama killed something that will make our world much more dangerous. **The rule of law also died at the hands of Obama....** Napolitano noticed the joy and unity around the country and claimed he hopes there isn't too much of it.'*

Canadian deputy Leader of the Opposition and MP, Thomas Mulcair, stated in an interview, **dated 4th May 2011**, with Canadian Broadcasting Corporation [CBC]'s TV that *"I don't think from what I've heard that those pictures [of bin Laden's body] exist"*. His remarks were picked up by dozens of US media outlets and criticized by various Canadian politicians; *'National Post'* & *'Toronto Star'* are especially referred.

Andrew Napolitano [a former New Jersey Superior Court Judge & a political and senior judicial analyst for Fox News Channel], the host of the program *Freedom Watch* [aired from 2009 to 2012 with considerable success], said bin Laden's death could not be verified and insinuated that Obama was using the death of bin Laden to save his "lousy presidency"; **CNN of 5th May 2011** is also referred.

An official statement from the Taliban stated, as referred to the *'Indian Express'* **dated 5th May 2011,** that the lack of photos or video footage is suspicious, as their own sources close to bin Laden had not confirmed or denied his death, and that *"when the Americans killed Mullah Dadullah (Taliban's chief military commander) they publicly showed the footage"*

Numerous other conspiracy theories relating to bin Laden's death that were discussed included:

• That bin Laden had been killed a number of years prior in the Tora-Bora Mountains, but that information was kept secret to encourage continued support for the war on terror.

• That bin Laden died much earlier than reported, and the announcement of bin Laden's death was delayed, so as not to clash with the festivities surrounding the wedding of Prince William and Catherine Middleton.

• That the announcement of bin Laden's death was timed to conflict with and take Donald Trump's *Celebrity Apprentice* off the air, to punish Trump for publicly questioning the authenticity of Barack Obama's birth certificate.

That it is suspicious that bin Laden's death occurred almost exactly eight years after George W. Bush's declaration of *"mission accomplished"* in Iraq and Afghanistan; referring to *the 'Telegraph' dated* 3rd *May 2011:*

> '.... *theorists claimed that the terrorist hadn't been killed at all, but his death was announced to give US President Barack Obama a much needed boost in the polls. His death occurred eight years to the day after then US President George W Bush declared "mission accomplished" following intervention in Afghanistan and Iraq.*'

On 9th May 2011, a Canadian scholar Prof Michel Chossudovsky republished the said interview of Osama BL [*just seven days after the US claims of killing him on* 2nd *May 2011 in Abbotabad*] in Global Research, also available at GR's official website with its **Editor's Note** as follows:

> '..... *The authenticity of this interview, which is available in recognized electronic news archives, is confirmed.*
>
> *Osama bin Laden categorically denies his involvement in the 9/11 attacks.*
>
> *Bin Laden's statements in this interview are markedly different from those made in the alleged Osama video tapes.*
>
> *In this interview, Osama bin Laden exhibits an understanding of US foreign policy. He expresses his views regarding the loss of life on 9/11. He also makes statements as to who, in his opinion, might be the likely perpetrator of the September 11 attacks.*'

In his best-seller book *'America's War on Terrorism'*, published in 2005, Prof Chossudovsky had stated that the War on Terrorism [WOT] was a complete fabrication based on the illusion that one man, Osama bin Laden, outwitted the $40 billion-a-year American intelligence apparatus.

> '*The WOT is a war of conquest. Globalisation is the final march to the "New World Order" dominated by Wall Street and the US military-industrial complex'*, the writer said.

SOME US MEDIA MADE SILENT:

The above cited interview of 2001 from Osama BL and his sensational denial was never reported by the US print and electronic media. It was not investigated by the CIA, Pentagon or any executive branch of the White House. No one in the US Congress called attention to

Osama's open denial and refusal of responsibility for one of the greatest humiliations ever inflicted on a superpower, which was dreaming and dying for his *'New World Order'*.

Nothing on media record is available in this regards except a one minute *YouTube* video from CNN in which the anchor, after quoting an al Jazeera report of Osama's denial, concluded that *'we can all weigh that in the scale of credibility and come to our own conclusions'*; a matter of naked disgraceful act on behalf of *'American free press'*.

Through this interview, Osama had outsmarted not only the American National Security Agency, the CIA, the Pentagon's Intelligence, and the FBI, including the other 16 US intelligence agencies, Israel's Mossad, and in addition the National Security Council, NORAD, US Air Traffic Control, and airport security forces etc four times on the same morning of 11th September 2001. The alleged "mastermind" had denied all American perceptions to launch a direct attack on Muslim community the world over.

Paul Craig, in the above cited analysis, referred to the famous Operation Gladio of Europe, a false flag attack sponsored by the CIA; perhaps this was the CIA's way of diverting attention from itself, but it illustrated that *'every intelligence service understands the value to an organization of claiming credit for a successful attack.'*

> [**Operation Gladio** *'In being silent I serve freedom' is the codename for a clandestine NATO "stay-behind" operation in Europe during the Cold War. Its purpose was to continue anti-communist actions in the event of a Soviet invasion and conquest. Although Gladio specifically refers to the Italian branch of the NATO stay-behind organizations, "Operation Gladio" is used as an informal name for all stay-behind organizations, sometimes called "Super NATO".*]

In Nine-Eleven, the same philosophy worked. Although Osama denied responsibility in September 2011 but al Qaeda's some lower rank leaders, realizing the prestige value of the 9/11 attack, claimed credit for the attack.

Only a few Americans were aware of the above given interview of 28th September 2011; many had seen post-event videos in which a person alleged to be bin Laden takes credit for the attacks. ***It is on record that experts had examined them and found them to be fakes,*** and all of the videos released naming Osama were concocted later.

The daily 'Pakistan Observer', the Egyptian press, and the *'Fox News'* had then reported Osama to have died in mid-December 2001, from lung disease. References were made to:

- www.foxnews.com/story/0,2933,41576,00.html

- www.legitgov.org/News-Bin-Ladens-Death-and-Funeral-December-2001

Citing again Global Research's official website [*carrying topic where was Osama on September 11, 2001/3194*]; Osama BL had also suffered from kidney disease. According to a *CBS news report dated 28th January 2002*, Osama bin Laden was hospitalized for dialysis treatment in a Pakistani military hospital in Rawalpindi on 10th September 2001, the day before 9/11.

It remains a normal medical fact that a man suffering from terminal lung and kidney diseases was not able to survive for another decade [and allegedly controlling the al-Qaeda actively] and to be murdered by a US Navy SEAL team in Abbotabad later.

OSAMA'S DEATH - MORE CONTROVERSIES:

Referring to an analysis *dated 27th March 2013*, made on internet media [*Intellihub.com*]; February 2013's Esquire magazine released an interview with a member of Seal Team 6 [alias **'The Shooter'**]. The Shooter claimed to be the one who pulled the trigger and killed OBL while he was in his room standing with "a gun in reach". He had proceeded to shoot the purported Al-Qaeda leader twice in the head.

This was not the first account of the night raid on the Bin Laden compound. Mark Bissonette, writing under the name Mark Owen, claimed to be the one to have pulled the trigger. In his *book: No Easy Day*, Bissonette told a story that conflicted with The Shooters' story.

According to CNN another member of Seal Team 6 came out to speak on the issue declaring *'the Shooter's story of the Esquire as false'*.

The above three controversies agitated the general American minds with questions like *'Is it possible all 3 could be false on that night's act? Is it possible that who ever were killed that night was not Osama Bin Laden?'*

The general US population were referring to **FOXnews.com** dated 26th December 2001:

'*Usama bin Laden has died a peaceful death due to an untreated lung complication, the* **Pakistan Observer** *reported, citing a Taliban leader who allegedly attended the funeral of the Al Qaeda leader.*

Bin Laden was suffering from a serious lung complication and succumbed to the disease in mid-December, in the vicinity of the Tora Bora Mountains. The source claimed that bin Laden was laid to rest honourably in his grave.

About 30 close associates of bin Laden in Al Qaeda, including his most trusted and personal bodyguards, his family members and some "Taliban friends," attended the funeral rites. A volley of bullets was also fired to pay final tribute to the great leader.'

The fact remains that Osama BL had never claimed responsibility for the 9/11 attacks. In fact he vehemently denied being involved. On 28th September 2001, as has been cited before in detail, he had released a statement saying:

"I have already said I am not involved. As a Muslim, I try my best to avoid telling a lie. I had no knowledge... nor do I consider the killing of innocent women, children and other humans as an appreciable act."

The Corbett Report listed a number of proclamations from government officials and researchers around the world claiming Bin Laden to be deceased prior to the official claims made by the US government.

On 18th January 2002, Pakistani President Gen Musharraf announced quite bluntly: *"I think now, frankly, he is dead."*

On 17th July 2002, the then-head of counterterrorism at the FBI, Dale Watson, told a conference of law enforcement officials that *"I personally think he [Bin Laden] is probably not with us anymore; [though] I have no evidence to support that."*

Former US foreign intelligence officer Angelo M. Codevilla, a professor of International Relations at Boston University, stated: '*All the evidence suggests Elvis Presley is more alive today than Osama Bin Laden.*'

Osama Bin Laden never claimed responsibility for the attacks on 9/11; news of his death due to serious illness; burying the dead body 'in deep sea' with no autopsy being done – and lastly, fatal accidents killed members of the elite SEALs team since that fateful night - all lead towards qualms and suspicions nothing less.

One can also consider reporter Josh Gerstein's article, *"CIA, Pentagon fight to keep Osama bin Laden death photos secret"* appeared in the *'politico' of* 27th *September 2011* in which the US government's stance was quoted as *'the 52 unique photographs should not be released publicly because they would reveal military and intelligence secrets and could lead to violence against US personnel.'*

The reporter, in the above article, while breaking down the government's arguments for not releasing any photo related to Bin Laden's capture, death and burial, held that:

> *'Dealing in lies is the CIA's only trade. The US military – industrial – intelligence - national security complex is run on lies, myths, fantasies and illusions. Without them its power, resources, and prestige would go down the toilet.'*

Just for record sake; the argument US President Obama had given to the press was:

> *"It is important for us to make sure that very graphic photos of somebody who was shot in the head are not floating around as an incitement to additional violence. As a propaganda tool, you know, that's not who we are. You know, we don't trot out this stuff as trophies."*

The critics of the Obama Administration, however, held that the real reason for not releasing the photo was because there was no photo; there was no dead body of Bin Laden riddled with American bullets. In their opinion the only dead bodies at that sight were those of American soldiers who were probably sent on a suicide mission by the double-crossing and back - stabbing traitors who control the White House.

22 US SEALs CRASHED TO DEATH:

Dr Paul Craig's research unearthed another fact that:

> *'Shortly after the alleged assassination, 30 members of the SEAL unit died in a mysterious helicopter crash in Afghanistan, and now we learn that not a single one of the thousands of sailors on the aircraft carrier,*

the USS Carl Vinson, witnessed bin Laden's alleged burial at sea from that ship. The press reports with a straight face that for unexplained reasons it was kept secret from the ship's sailors.'

There were some sailor's e-mail accounts available in which they had told their families and friends that they witnessed no burial at sea. Some speculated that the SEALs were bumped off before their questions to one another, *"Were you there on that raid?"*

The media took it strange that the US government captured and killed the terror mastermind without interrogating him and without keeping any evidence or presenting any witnesses to support the assassination claims later. How, the great terror symbol Osama, dying from illnesses in December 2001 in distant Afghanistan, could defeat the US National Security, CIA and the Pentagon [*consuming $40 billion budget a year*], floating a "war on terror" that destroyed US civil liberties and financially ruined the country; who would dare to answer it.

In the first week of October 2001, when President Bush had launched his first attack on Afghanistan after getting green signal from Pakistan's Gen Musharraf through **Colin Powel's infamous 'stoning threat'**, there were 15,000 Muslims serving in the US Armed forces. Capt Abd Al-Rasheed, Imam of Walter Reed Army Medical Centre in Washington DC had to ask the North American Islamic Jurisprudence Council if it was permissible for Muslim troops in the US military to fight other Muslims in the war against terrorism.

The US government had initially manoeuvred to get issued a Fatwa permitting US Muslims to fight if there was 'no alternative' but soon after, on 30th October 2001 perhaps, the Arab clerics had withdrawn that Fatwa, issuing a new one prohibiting US Muslim troops from participating in US attacks on other Muslim forces. History witnessed that the chain of command in the US Army was overtaken by Arab clerics to leave the American nation in rage.

Perhaps due to above controversies, the US government had to announce in July 2013 for reopening of the Navy SEAL's Crash incident. Referring to the *'FP Situation Report dated 24th July 2013'*:

'Congress is looking for answers in the crash that killed 30 Americans, including members of the elite SEAL Team 6. The Congress isn't happy with the answers the Pentagon has provided thus far on the deadly incident which took place on Aug. 6, 2011, three months after Osama bin Laden was killed in Pakistan.'

Republican Rep. Jason Chaffetz of Utah, chair of the House Oversight and Government Reform subcommittee on National Security, met with the victims' families in June 2013 in an "emotional" gathering. He is poised to send questions to the Pentagon and may hold hearings on the matter. The death toll in the crash was the largest of any single incident for the US military during the Afghanistan war.

There were wavering reports that the Congress had launched an investigation of the helicopter crash that killed 30 Americans in Afghanistan, including members of the Navy's elite SEAL Team 6 unit but no concrete result ever surfaced in media or discussed in the Congress sessions.

In a transcript of the Department of Defence, it was stated that *'it was a lucky shot of a low-level fighter that happened to be living [in the area]. He heard all the activity and he happened to be in the right spot.'* Shortly before the CH-47 Chinook helicopter took off on a rescue mission (operation Extortion 17), seven Afghan commandos who were on the passenger list were replaced by other Afghan military officials.

It remained a mystery why the manifest was incorrect, raising red flags among the victims' families. They noted that their sons didn't trust Afghan soldiers. One was quoted as saying, *'They are loyal to the highest bidder.'* In the transcript related to the Pentagon's probe, a Defence official confirmed that all seven names of the Afghan soldiers were incorrect.

Reportedly, the Chinook was shot down by Afghan militants, and all 38 on board perished. Among the dead were 30 Americans, including 22 Navy SEALS, seven Afghan soldiers and one Afghan translator. Their bodies were later recovered, but the helicopter's black box was not. Pentagon officials said that it could not be recovered; citing a flash flood that happened soon after the assault. Chaffetz was of the opinion that *'the Department of Defence's explanation of its failure to find the helicopter's black box seems **awfully odd.'***

All the bodies were cremated because the same were badly burned. Most of the Congress members held that it was a scandal even greater than Benghazi where the US lost four valued American lives; in Afghanistan 30 American soldiers were sacrificed. It is not notified even that how many of the 22 SEALS who died that summer were part of the bin Laden operation in Abbottabad.

During a ceremony at Bagram Air Base for the 38 killed, the deceased Afghan soldiers were loaded onto planes with the bodies of the US forces. An imam spoke an Islamic prayer that included language on US soldiers burning in hell, it was alleged. Chaffetz called those series of events "inappropriate."

A Pentagon spokesman declined to answer detailed questions but said:

'The operational planning and execution of this mission was consistent with previous missions" and "was thoroughly investigated … we share in the grief of all of the families who lost their loved ones. The loss of 38 US and Afghan military personnel was a tragic loss during a difficult campaign.'

OSAMA BL's [SO CALLED] 17 LETTERS:

On the first anniversary of Osama Bin Laden, on 2ⁿᵈ May 2012, the US government released certain papers from Osama's hideout revealing him as a frustrated leader struggling to control an unruly network, Al Qaeda. Some of the documents seized during the raid on the Abbottabad compound were bound by the Research wing of the US Military Academy, West Point and published as '**Letters from Abbottabad: Bin Ladin Sidelined?**' and released it on 3ʳᵈ May 2012.

This booklet was compiled by Don Rassler, Gabriel Koehler-Derrick, Liam Collins, Muhammad al-Obaidi and Nelly Lahoud comprising 17 de-classified documents [out of 6000 in stock] captured during the Abbotabad raid and released to the Combating Terrorism Centre (CTC). The book consisted of electronic draft letters, totalling 175 pages in Arabic and 197 pages in the English translation. The earliest was dated September 2006 and the latest April 2011. These internal al-Qaeda communications were authored by several leaders, most prominently Osama himself.

In contrast to his public statements that focused on the injustice of those he believed to be the "enemies" of Muslims, namely corrupt "apostate" Muslim rulers and their Western "overseers," the focus of Bin Laden's private letters was Muslims suffering at the hands of other *jihadi* factions. The booklet claimed that:

'Bin Ladin's frustration with regional jihadi groups and his seeming inability to exercise control over their actions and public statements is the most compelling story to be told on the basis of the 17 de-classified documents'.

Frank Gardner, BBC Security correspondent commented; it confirmed the popular view that at the time of his death; Osama BL was no longer in operational control of al-Qaeda. The 17 documents were released to an academic institution of the US military so they painted Bin Laden as a loser rather than as a force; there were grievances and causes.

Some documents suggested that Al Qaeda had strained relationship with Iran. Tehran handled the release of detainees, including members of Bin Laden's family, expressing annoyance that the Iranians *"do not wish to appear to be negotiating with us or responding to our pressures."*

[**There was no explicit reference to any institutional support from Pakistan, where the al-Qaeda leader lived for nine years.**]

The papers made mention of *"trusted Pakistani brothers"* but suggested Bin Laden was distrustful of Pakistani intelligence. He gave instructions to his family members travelling to Pakistan to make sure they were not followed. In some papers, Bin Laden and his inner circle emphasised that:

"Even though we have the chance to attack the British, we should not waste our effort to do so but concentrate on defeating America, which will lead to defeating the others. Any arrow and mine we have should be directed against Americans, disregarding all other enemies, including NATO, and concentrating on Americans only," Osama allegedly wrote.

In a letter of 2010, Bin Laden wrote:

"Starting a new phase to correct [the mistakes] we made. In the event that mistakes involuntarily occur and non-combatants die as a result, apologies and explanations should follow."

The said letter reflected that Osama was a bit worried that the people were going away from *Jihad* but *"...... we shall reclaim, God willing, the trust of a large segment of those who lost their trust in the jihadis,"* he wrote.

In its executive summary on the documents, the US military got clues of Bin Laden's frustration with affiliated organisations and his powerlessness to control their actions, including:

- Osama BL was advised by his California - born media adviser Adam Gadahn to distance from al-Qaeda in Iraq because of the later's perceived failures.

- His lieutenants threatened *to take measures against the leadership of the Pakistani Taliban* for their "vile mistakes" including indiscriminate attacks on Muslims.

- Bin Laden wrote a strongly worded letter to al-Qaeda in the Arabian Peninsula urging them to focus on attacking the US, instead of the Yemeni government or their security forces.

- Bin Laden saw little to gain from a pledge of allegiance to al-Qaeda from the Somali radical insurgent group al-Shabab, which he viewed as poorly organised.

The letters revealed that Bin Laden was also cynical of so-called lone missions by home-grown *jihadists;* urging his associates *"not to send a single brother on a suicide operation; they should send at least two"*. Osama had in fact referred to a bungled attack on a British envoy, thus issued chilling guidelines to suicide bombers.

Ambassador Tim Torlot, the then British Ambassador in Yemen, was unharmed after a terrorist disguised in school uniform threw himself at a British convoy and detonated a bomb belt; the bomber failed because he lost his nerve; thus should have had a partner. Osama's guideline narrated:

"*Regardless of the heroism of the brother and his steadfastness, the psychological factors that affect the person in such cases necessitate the presence of a companion that will support and bolster him.*"

Other papers suggest Bin Laden ordered his militants to look out for opportunities to assassinate President Obama or David Petraeus during any of their visits to Pakistan and Afghanistan. He ordered his hit-men to watch airbases for the chance to shoot down Air Force One — and any plane carrying America's military chief in Afghanistan, General David Petraeus.

Mr Petraeus, later CIA director, formerly commanded international forces in Afghanistan. Also warned them not to target Vice-President Joe Biden because "*Biden is totally unprepared for that post [of president], which will lead the US into a crisis.*" Osama wanted him [Joe Biden] to take over because he believed that would spark a disaster in due course of time. One quoted letter found Osama saying:

"*I asked brother Ilyas to prepare two groups — one in Pakistan and the other in the Bagram area of Afghanistan — with the mission of anticipating and spotting the visits of Obama or Petraeus to target the aircraft of either one of them.*

"The reason for concentrating on them is that Obama is the head of infidelity and killing him automatically will make Biden take over the presidency. As for Petraeus, he is the man of the hour in this last year of the war; killing him would alter the war's path."

The said letters suggested that Bin Laden's inner circle closely monitored US and British news media. Al-Qaeda media adviser Adam Gadahn described:

"ABC News as all right, actually it could be one of the best channels as far as we are concerned but the Fox News falls into the abyss and lacks neutrality.

All the political talk in America is about the economy, forgetting or ignoring the war and its role in weakening the economy," wrote Mr Gadahn."

British journalist Robert Fisk of *'The Independent'* was named in a letter from the said spokesman Adam Gadahn; he was on a list of writers. The terror hierarchy was advised to cultivate him to get their message across because his [Robert Frisk's] article expressing his reaction — and other people's — to the attack on a church in Baghdad were liked in Al Qaeda high ups.

Another letter from Osama carried plans of al-Qaeda's media strategy for the tenth anniversary of 9/11. The Chief asked for a courier to pick up recordings he had made, adding: *"Attached to this message is a visual statement to the American people that I hope a copy will be given to the International Al Jazeera."* Allegedly the same tape or disc was sent to some media men in America saying: *"A high quality speech (HD) may receive some interest."*

The released material also contained Ayman al-Zawahiri's complaint to Bin Laden in December 2010 that some people were boasting by claiming to be part of al-Qaeda and making money from it. He added:

"Some figures have emerged collecting money in the name of al-Qaeda, and play at that. Some have abused the money to varying degrees — and then spent it on themselves."

ANALYSIS OF OBL'S PANIC THEORIES:

BBC News dated 3rd May 2012 contributed the final remarks:

> *'Earlier this week, White House counter-terrorism Chief John Brennan said Bin Laden's papers reinforced the view that the US was safer without him.'*

In nut-shell, Osama bin Laden continued to capture the world's imagination even from the depths of the Arabian Sea. On Osama's first anniversary, the US launched what commentators called *"a rare public relations exercise against the late leader of Al Qaeda"*.

Osama's [said to be so called] letters revealed the Al Qaeda to be embroiled in the usual politics of internal strives and bitterness. The US government's intent in revealing the letters at this point was clear:

> *'Discredit the terror network Bin Laden headed, depicting it as weak, bungling and under siege and its leader as desperate to somehow overcome the passing of his global jihad's zenith'*, **'the News'** dated 5th May 2012 is referred.

The said letters also reflected that bin Laden exercised little control over worldwide Al Qaeda splinter groups in Pakistan, Iraq and Yemen, imploring them to stop killing Muslims and overthrowing enemy governments; apply themselves to killing Americans.

In one document, bin Laden gave orders to target aeroplanes known to be carrying President Obama and Gen David Petraeus. So, imagine how good this made President Obama look in election year: he's already enjoying endless mileage from the raid that took out bin Laden and avenged the killing of 3,000 Americans and then, the US president got another opportunity, in the shape of those letters, to remind the world of the dangerous designs OBL continued to harbour against the Americans.

Of course, the Obama administration had refused to release a fuller record of its bin Laden collection, making it difficult to garner larger truths about the terrorist network. However, what made it even more difficult to judge the letters holistically was that they were scrupulously vetted and edited to avoid any breaches of security, caused embarrassment to allies, and jeopardised the on-going peace process in Afghanistan.

The intelligent Americans, however, felt that this 'timely' release was the latest beat in that election year [of 2012] drum roll from the Obama administration. Whosoever did it - did it nicely; drafting 17 letters on computer in an arena of Al Qaeda history was an uphill task for the White House people.

[Never mind; all the 17 letters were 'draft letters'; none of them was shown *'received by some one'*.]

Some more disturbing citations: referring to *'Daily Siasat'* dated 25th *December 2012,* SEAL Team's Commanding Officer W Price, only 42 years old, committed suicide on 22nd December 2012; he was best known for finding and then killing Osama bin Laden on 2nd May 2011. He had sustained an injury while supporting stability operations in Uruzgan Province of Afghanistan. Suicide of the Officer of this grade raises many questions among the media, thus his death remained under investigation for quite some time. Comdr Price was assigned to an East Coast - based Naval Special Warfare unit based in Virginia Beach, VA.

UK's daily *'Independent'* of 25th *December 2012* had also carried a story on W Price's sudden death.

Gordon Duff, Senior Editor of *'Hot Topics'* placed his opinion on the website **on** 7th **August 2011** saying, about the untoward crash of Chinook helicopter killing the all 38 men aboard on 6th August 2011, that:

'Today 31 NATO troops, 22 of them Navy Seals from the Osama bin Laden operation died in what is reported as a helicopter crash in Afghanistan.

The chances of this story being true are almost nil. The chances of this being a staged cover-up is over 80%. We believe these people were murdered to silence them. Why so - we have solid information on two areas:

1. *Osama bin Laden died in 2001 as an active CIA employee and his body was recovered in Afghanistan and taken to "the sand box." We were told it was frozen. We have so much verification from this, CIA, ISI, US military and top officials. I have a direct confirmation from Bin Laden's CIA handler who I grilled mercilessly on this.*

2. *The Abbotabad operation involved numerous American deaths, witnessed, bodies all over, a helicopter crash. These bodies were recovered by land vehicle from Islamabad and*

there was NO "successful" bin Laden operation of any kind. There has been a CIA safe house in Abbotabad where terror suspects were stored for years.'

Not long afterward, Secretary of Defence Leon Panetta announced the near defeat of Al Qaeda, another Bush - fairy tale.

Gordon Duff went another step further to opine that *'Al Qaeda has never existed; there are no magic worldwide terror conspiracies other than those run by governments.'* The government staged this [drama] to accomplish two things:

'We could simply report the truth for those willing to believe it, something we believe is the right thing to do.

We could also support the United States in a very real way, knowing Pakistan would weather this crisis, timed, in some ways, as a face saving move in response to the embarrassing Raymond Davis affair. Crashing of SEAL's helicopter was arranged to stage a cover-up and get rid of any involved.'

The bin Laden killing, the third rate drama of capturing an unarmed frozen dead guy and throwing him into the ocean had probably become an impediment around certain high ranking necks. In the ending paragraphs Gordon had observed that:

'These Americans are casualties in a game, one like 9/11, sacrificial pawns, like Britain's 7/7, all lies, all theatre, and all evil. We aren't anti-American. I am also sick of the fact that Washington can't visit the 'head' without Israel's permission....... We are not going to allow this to stand.

We have a long standing history of "cleaning house" after operations of this kind. Usually its dead senators in plane crashes, heart attacks, car wrecks, like the Minot Barksdale or 9/11 incidents. I could name a dozen more. Does the name Wheeler meaning anything to you? Anyone remember Pat Tillman?'

Some day the historians would be able to dig out the truth but till then President Obama would also be buried under the piles of history itself; who would recall these cruel moments then.

Scenario 89

OSAMA'S KILLING - PAKISTAN SUFFERED:

OSAMA DRAMA – WHY SO:

If at all we believe that Osama was there in Abbotabad and was actually killed in 2nd May's *'Operation Geronimo'*, we can safely presume that he was simply a fugitive, sitting idle in a hide out and waiting for his last breath. He was not controlling Al Qaeda rather somebody else was managing it from somewhere else; how one can run a world level terrorist organisation without a telephone connection or internet. Even a corner grocery shop is not run without such electronic gadgets.

Al Qaeda in original shape may be a dead horse now and dead since long. It had been a decentralized organization, a loose collection of groups distributed throughout the conflict zones, each with its own leaders, programs, tactics and strategies. It was never a centralized international organization dependent on a 'central command' directed by a single person.

It remained a cogent fact that al Qaeda was a brainchild of CIA, used to spread terror for a few occasions and then split into groups; groups concentrated in various countries or different regions of one country, controlled by local group leaders, performed little activities, eaten up their budgets given by CIA and then died at their own. No legend, no history to mention and nothing to leave for perspective hiding criminals commonly labelled as terrorists. Most of these mercenaries were killed by the CIA snappers themselves when their jobs accomplished.

The other face of America could be seen in Libya of 2012-13. Who was fighting with Col Gaddafi in Ben Ghazi, it was Al Qaeda aided and backed by the US forces. There Al Qaeda was good but anywhere else, it remained a curse. When the Libya's war was over, the same Al Qaeda was targeted, attacked and buried in sands by the settling American companyies and soldiers there.

By making extra tall claims what the America wanted to tell the world and at the same time terrifying the poor people of Pakistan. The US wanted to take over the control of Pakistan by playing a broken orchestra of *'Al Qaeda's chase'* and *'hot pursuits'* in Pakistani territories. America was perhaps mistaken; the 84% of Pakistan's population had already marked hatred for the super power but then the leadership went fed up, too. ISI had already nearly dissociated from the CIA intelligence sharing formulae and Pak-army was ready to fire back. All they were determined that AL Qaeda blame would no more be allowed to prevail upon strategies.

An extract taken from 'The Assassination of bin Laden: Its Use and Abuse' written by *James Petras in Axis of Logic* on 5th May 2011 deserves attention here:

> '*Contrary to this immense propaganda campaign and despite whatever symbolic value the killing (of Osama) may have in the eyes of his executioners, there is no evidence that the death will have any impact on the deteriorating military and political position of the US in South Asia, the Middle East, North Africa or elsewhere.*'

Then why that drama of killing Osama, raising slogans so high and blowing Al Qaeda's trumpet loud again. Because America had decided to quit the region in the back drop of its strategic military and political defeats, especially during 2010-11 in Afghanistan. *On 27th April 2011*, nine senior US military officers were assassinated by a 'trusted' Afghan fighter pilot in the high security Kabul airport. Four majors, two captains and two lieutenant colonels were killed in that single event. A big blow and a great catastrophe; in the face of major strategic losses, as evident in such unexpected elimination of top military officials, Obama had to mount a political spectacle; a 'military success story' to satisfy the American public, military and its NATO followers.

In the words of James Petras again:

> '*Several facts mark this out as a strategically important event. It took place in a high security installation, suggesting that no place in Afghanistan is safe from deadly armed attacks by the Taliban or the armed resistance. Secondly, all US military, no matter how high their rank, are vulnerable to deadly attack. Thirdly, no US trained Afghan military official or soldier can be considered 'loyal' – even those most closely in collaboration can and will turn their guns on their mentors.*'

Just two weeks earlier to the above mentioned killing spree; with the collaboration of jail officials, almost 500 jailed Taliban fighters and leaders escaped via a 350 meter tunnel to a dozen waiting trucks. Only two years earlier 900 prisoners had also escaped from the same prison. Karzai government was helpless; perhaps he was also waiting for his end.

SHABQADR ATTAKED – 91 DEAD:

In what appeared to be the first retaliatory attack by Pakistani Taliban [TTP] since the US Navy SEALs killed the al-Qaeda Chief Osama bin Laden in Pakistan's garrison town of Abbotabad, twin-suicide blasts ripped through outside the gate of the Frontier Constabulay [FC]' para-military training centre at Shabqadr in District Charsadda of Khyber PK on 13th May 2011, killing 91 people, most of them paramilitary personnel, and injured more than 120 others.

The Pakistani Taliban [TTP] took the responsibility of the attack to avenge the death of Osama BL earlier that month. The said attack came hours before the country's COAS, Chief of the PAF and the ISI Chief attended the parliament to explain their actions over bin Laden's operation.

The bombings happened as newly trained cadets from the FC were getting into buses after completing their course. They were in plain clothes and were happy that they were going to see their families. Both attacks were of 'suicide nature'; the first suicide bomber came on a motorcycle and detonated his vest among the FC men. When other contingent of the FC came to the rescue to help their dead and wounded colleagues, the second bomber came on another motorcycle and blew him up.

At least 69 of the dead were recruits while the rest of the dying lot was of civilians; twenty-six civilians exactly while four dead bodies were not identified.

"It's the first revenge for the martyrdom of... bin Laden. There will be more," Taliban spokesman Ehsanullah Ehsan had told the Reuters news agency by telephone from an undisclosed location. The security forces had often been the target of such attacks but this bombing was the deadliest attack that year.

PAK-ARMY IMAGE AFTER OSAMA'S KILLING:

Pakistan's armed forces suffered a fatal blow to their respect and honour after Osama bin Laden's killing operation at Abbottabad on 2nd May 2011. The ISI and the Pakistan's Air Force became the first targets. ISI was known as one of the world's competent, proficient and skilled intelligence unit AND PAF was identified as diligent and meticulous hawks before that event but both went utterly disgraced [and exposed too] in Pakistan as well as before the global competitors.

*BBC, in its deliberations of 6*th *May 2011,* displayed text messages allegedly doing the rounds then in Pakistan which were read as:

- *"For Sale: Obsolete Pakistan army radar; can't detect US 'copters but can receive Star Plus; only 999 rupees."* [Star Plus is a popular television channel from India]

- *"What a country! Even Osama is not safe here."*

- *"This is what they are paid for, to defend the borders, not to run bakeries and banks and real estate empires"* [from Nasir Khan, a Swat resident]

- *"Why do we spend more than $6bn (£3.65bn) annually on the army when it can't do its job,"*

For the first time in decades, the powerful Pakistani military establishment had failed to find an excuse to pin the blame on the "bloody civilians" in power. The military took three days to issue a response, and the most prominent part of its statement from the Pakistani point of view was the admission that it did not know about the raid. However, the people believed their contention that it also did not know about bin Laden's presence in Abbottabad.

Pakistani media, though extremely critical of the civilian government at times, steered clear of controversies surrounding the powerful security establishment. It was the media which had first high - lighted the military's role in March [2011] in the aftermath of release of Raymond Davis.

[*While the civilian government made a few passive noises that Mr Davis enjoyed diplomatic immunity, his continued detention was due to the army's intervention. To many, his release came as a shock, and as evidence that even the military had bowed to American wishes.*]

Many people in Pakistan, especially those who live in areas overrun by Taliban militants over the last few years are sure suspected a link between the military and the Islamist militant groups operating in Pakistan and Afghanistan; though they had no tangible proof. In Swat, there was a time when the army and the Taliban running their respective checkpoints literally yards away from each other.

The BBC, however, frankly quoted that *'most people dislike the US, and they feel their own army has let them down.'*

MEHRAN NAVAL BASE ATTACKED:

A fatal loss of men, capital, and honour it was.

On 22nd May 2011, a group of militants assaulted the PNS Mehran Base in Karachi, killing 12 people, injuring 15 others and blowing up at least two P-3C Orion, estimated to be worth $36 million each, used for maritime patrolling, and a helicopter. The attack reportedly started at 10:30 pm and the siege continued for 16 hours.

More than 15 Taliban or Al Qaeda militants [*as per weekly* **TIME** *dated 23rd May 2011*] stormed the said premises with guns and grenades but the government brief said they were six; four killed in encounter while two fled away. {*The Mehran naval base is also the headquarters of the Pakistan navy's air wing*}

The foreign actors, including certain friends of Pakistan in association with the above mentioned, through Pakistani Taliban or Al Qaeda [*'Al-Qaeda had warned of Pakistan strike'* appearing in **ASIA TIMES ONLINE** dated 27th May 2011 is referred here], had carried out this bold and blatant attack on Mehran Naval Base. That attack was launched after a series of talks failed between the navy and al-Qaeda over the release of naval officials arrested on suspicion of TTP / al-Qaeda links in the backdrop of three suicidal attacks done on the navy buses a month earlier.

The said attacks were planned by Ilyas Kashmiri's 313 Brigade, the operational arm of al-Qaeda. Ilyas Kashmiri was later killed in a drone attack in Southern Wazirastan on 5th June 2011; the details of which are given on other pages of this book separately.

The Al Qaeda militants, dressed in black and resembling 'Star Wars characters', had entered from a residential district abutting the base. Using two ladders placed in a spot obscured from security cameras, they scaled the walls and clipped the barbed wire at the top, then headed for the hangar containing American-made P-3C Orion airplanes.

The attackers fired on one plane and the resulting explosion destroyed the second plane too. Pakistani naval commandos and marines eventually cornered the militants in an office building and killed four of them whereas two others might have escaped.

Till 2.30 PM next day, after about 16 hour's siege, the armed forces were able to regain control of that naval base back. One of the worst assault on a military base and arsenal since GHQ Rawalpindi was besieged in October 2009 for two days, killing 22 people and raising serious questions over why it took the military so long to put down the assault.

The said event of Karachi Naval Base had piled further embarrassment for armed forces just twenty days after Osama's episode in Abbottabad. The militants used ladders to climb the boundary walls and dropping them into the naval air base in dark setting off a series of explosions. 11 Chinese and six American maintenance contractors were also there in that naval compound but evacuated safely.

The militants exercised tactics they had been using in previous attacks on other security installations, and even in the March 2009 attack on the visiting Sri Lankan cricket team in Lahore. However, when Pakistani commandos' regained control of that naval air base back after armed fighters launched an audacious attack; almost all the live TV shows were blowing trumpets high that *'it was a successful operation.'*

The official sources confirmed 10 (not 11 as per media news) security personnel were killed, including one navy officer, three navy firemen, three navy commandos, a sailor and two paramilitary soldiers, and 15 others wounded.

By what standards it was successful. The 20-22 years old six men held the whole garrison of world's no:1 army hostage for sixteen hours, killed their 10 men including one commissioned officer, made 15 soldiers to sustain injuries, put two expensive Orion aircrafts on fire and the most importantly made the Pakistan army a laughing stock for the whole world.

The lapses in security issues had turned into talk of the town telling the whole world that our Navy was 'perfectly trained' to keep the multi-million dollars air-fighters in reckless open. So near to the 5 feet high outer boundary that even a child playing in the adjacent street could hurt it with a piece of brick.

Federal Interior Minister Rehman Malik refused to acknowledge any security lapse, saying the "rapid" response had prevented bigger losses. What a positive approach it was. A similar contention was heard on 27th December 2007 after Benazir Bhutto's assassination from the same golden lips of her Chief Security Officer.

Enemies got enough evidence that even Pakistan's army bases were not secure from Al Qaeda's attacks and thus from terrorism. Pakistan placed words in the enemy's lips that Pakistan army was not able to secure their own garages and barracks how they would protect their nuclear arsenal for which the US and the West have been crying since a decade.

A Navy spokesman Commander Salman Ali himself told the media that *'the attack was also likely to raise further concerns about the safety of Pakistan's nuclear weapons, which reportedly number more than 100.'*

The American Congress and Senate were conveyed that their billions of Dollars aid were not being spent under appropriate heads due to certain constraints. Even otherwise the analysis of Dollar-aid accounts portrayed:

> "*The US takes back 64% of this aid back to Washington under the heads of 'expenditure and salaries of American Trainers in Pakistan'. For the residual 36%, the dollar-accounts of their NGOs and Pakistani leadership, civil and military, are considered a safe & better place than schools or water-wells for the poor people.*"

TROUBLE STARTED IN PAK-NAVY:

Karachi is Pakistan's largest city by population and financial hub and the assault was the fourth on the navy in row. Three bombings on Navy buses in the last week of April [2011] had killed nine people. Those three attacks were in fact warning shots for navy officials to accept al-Qaeda's demands over the detained suspects. Pakistan armed forces had shown retaliation to al-Qaeda affiliates within the navy because the naval intelligence had traced an al-Qaeda cell operating inside several navy bases.

> *'Islamic sentiments are common in Pakistan's armed forces and the officers never felt threatened by that. All armed forces around the world, whether American, British or Indian, take some inspiration from religion to motivate their cadre against the enemy. .....*

> *Nonetheless, the higher naval hierarchy observed an uneasy grouping on different naval bases in Karachi. While nobody can obstruct armed forces personnel for rendering Islamic rituals, the grouping was against the discipline of the armed forces as such.*

> *That was the beginning of an intelligence operation in the navy to check for unscrupulous activities.'*

That said alliance was against the then military leadership and opposed to its nexus with the US against Islamic militancy. When some messages were intercepted hinting at attacks on visiting American officials, the Naval Intelligence [PNI] planned their action and after careful evaluation at least 10 people, mostly from the lower cadre, were picked up for interrogation in a series of operations; thus the trouble started.

The arrested ones were held in the PNI office near the Chief Minister House in Karachi, but immediately after, the in-charge of the investigation team received direct threats from the militants thus indicating that militants know the 'detention centre'. The detainees were promptly moved to a safer location, but the threats continued.

Al Qaeda militants feared that interrogation of those ten detainees would lead to the arrest of more of their loyalists in Pakistan Navy [PN]; therefore, they had no choice other than to launch attacks on un-secure naval installations. The thing to be worried the most was that Taliban or Al Qaeda militants were receiving fresh inside information constantly as they always knew where the suspects were being detained and what the interrogation was about. It also proved that sizeable al-Qaeda infiltration within the navy's ranks had already taken place.

Hurriedly, a senior level meeting was called; matters discussed and resolved that the issue be handled with great care; also decided, amongst other steps, to open communication with al-Qaeda. Immediately a Karachite named Samad Mansoori, a former student union activist and later part of 313 Brigade of Ilyas Kashmiri residing in North Waziristan was approached and talks opened.

Al-Qaeda demanded the immediate release of their arrested officials which was straightaway rejected. The detainees were allowed to speak to their families and kept well treated, but the interrogation continued to get information about the strength of al-Qaeda's penetration. The militants were told that they would be discharged from the service and freed once interrogation was completed.

Al-Qaeda rejected PNI's stance and expressed its displeasure by launching attacks on the navy buses on *26th April 2011*. These incidents pointed to more than one al-Qaeda's intelligence cells tracked in the PN. Meanwhile the Americans went more worried and apprised the Pak Armed Forces with the fear that if the problem was not addressed on immediate basis:

- The trade supply lines upwards could face a new threat.

- NATO supply line could be obstructed and damaged.

- The visiting Americans to Pak-naval facilities in the city would be in danger.

Another crackdown was conducted and more people having different ethnic backgrounds were arrested. One naval commando, hailing from South Waziristan's Mehsud tribe, was believed to have received direct instructions from the TTP Chief Hakeemullah Mehsud.

Referring to *MSN News dated 29*th *May 2011:*

> *'The al Qaeda terrorists had managed to gain not only sympathisers, but also recruits in the naval ranks. The Pakistan Navy were worried that how many of these militants were in contact with the navy staff. It was unfortunate that people within their ranks had been found to have links with extremists.*

> *The navy is not the only Pakistani institution whose personnel were found to be involved in terrorism.*

> *A former Army male nurse-turned-jihadi [alias Dr Usman] had played a key role in the October 2009's attack on GHQ, just like some senior Pakistan Air Force (PAF) officers, including one SSG commando, who was found to be involved in the attack on the then army chief Gen Musharraf in 2004.'*

Thus a strategy to deal with the menace was to be worked out by the Pak-army seriously.

Defence analysts offered varying explanations for why the Taliban had struck a naval air base in Karachi, a city that is far from the terrorist bases in the mountainous borderlands but is still viewed as a militant hideout. Some said the American-made airplanes, which were delivered by the US military in the previous summer, were the clear target.

Some opined that the destroyed planes were probably used for surveillance of Indian submarines and thus the attack was Indian sponsored. Others floated the view that as there were 11 Chinese engineers working at that base; the Americans suspected the copying of their surveillance technology by the Chinese, thus that demise.

There were some who surmised that militants sought to discourage the Pakistan Navy's participation in an international coalition that used to monitor the Arabian Sea and waters off North Africa. Nothing clear till today except that it was Ilyas Kashmiri's 313 Brigade of Al Qaeda who had done it; of course for whatever reasons.

Coming back; since the slaying of Osama BL, Al Qaeda militants escalated their terrorism campaign with deadly attacks on the Pakistani paramilitaries on 13th May 2011, killing over 90 recruits, attack on Shabqadr School is referred. Nine days later, they bombed a US consular convoy in the northwest city of Peshawar, killing a bystander. Days after bin Laden's death, the Pakistani Taliban had vowed to exact revenge.

Weekly the 'TIME dated 23rd May 2011' remarked:

'This attack appeared to have been long planned, given its sophistication, even if the cue for its execution was the militants' avowed campaign to avenge Osama's death.

The naval-base attack would serve as a further embarrassment to heavily decorated officers who have long prided themselves on being the guardians of Pakistan's [external & internal] security.'

Osama BL was killed by American Navy Seals in Abbottabad on 2nd May 2011 and Al Qaeda decided to strike back on immediate basis. Of course, they were not strong enough to hit back America in any way because it was beyond their reach. The militants were not capable enough to hit the US Embassy in Islamabad either; nor could they launch attacks of US Consulates in Lahore or Karachi. They opted to attack Pakistan taking plea being America's ally and started from Pakistan's Navy. Within a week, insiders at Mehran Base provided maps, pictures of different exit and entry routes taken in daylight and at night, the location of hangers and details of likely reaction from the Naval security contingents whose strength was also conveyed at times.

Al Qaeda militants were able to enter the heavily guarded facility where one group targeted the aircraft, a second group took on the first strike force and a third finally escaped with the others providing cover - fire. Those who stayed behind were killed.

To add fuel to the Pakistani nation's fury, US President Obama, while on tour to UK those days, told the BBC that he was inclined to order a similar mission (like that of Abbottabad) if another high - value target was discovered in Pakistan, again without notice. The intelligentsia had questioned that threat in the backdrop of unanimous resolution passed by Pakistan's sovereign Parliament on 13th May 2011 and John Kerry's joint statement during his visit to Pakistan a week after [*saying that in future any attack would be launched jointly, if needed*].

NO GIMMICKS; FIND OUT CULPRITS:

An important aspect; that whenever a terrorist activity or suicidal attack was reported, the responsibility was immediately claimed and owned by the Pakistani Taliban [TTP]. Why so; no agency seriously looked into it that who were the actual culprits behind the curtain. Taliban should normally be concerned with the loss and counts of lives and not with the strategic army gadgets. Suicidal attacks on shrines, public gatherings or in busy markets could be attributed to them but what about attack on GHQ, training camp of SSG in Dargai and on two Orion war-planes at Karachi.

The later types of attacks were in fact referred to the state enemies having 'armed skills or militarised minds' on their back. Al Qaeda or Taliban, or a group of youngsters in the name of Taliban, were being used by a very skilful military mind of Pakistan's enemy state. Pakistan mostly felt shy in naming India, Afghanistan or its so-called friend US too.

The three states referred above were openly and jointly playing the orchestra that **'Pakistan is a terrorist state'** whereas the Pakistan government always hesitated to name them. They betrayed each other in the name of 'intelligence sharing' with the US but, simultaneously, continuing talks with India on the bilateral trade. Pakistan army was bent upon reminding Afghanistan about 'Muslim brotherhood', kept on hiding in sheepish skin whereas the wolves continued biting it. Breakfast events were seen around; lunch and dinners were on their way.

It was evident that Osama's killing of 2nd May 2011 in Abbottabad had prompted al-Qaeda contingents in Pakistan to take revenge for the death of their leader. Karachi Naval Base was considered the most easy and vulnerable being un-secure.

Foreign hand in supplying sophisticated weaponry and intelligence gadgets to the militants proved that [might be] India had killed many birds in one shot; so many suicidal attacks and terrorist assaults were in addition. Someone could have taken account of 'gun-powder' (*Barood*) used in all those events and sum up. That killing substance invariably travelled through Pakistan under the garb of NATO supplies or Afghan Trade.

It was enough; Pakistan's Tax Ombudsman Dr Shoaib Suddle's inquiry report was on record that during 2010 only, about 4000 containers were 'lost' on their way to Afghanistan. The ISI and the Pak-Army should have been worried more about those containers and their contents.

Earlier, Bomb attacks hit two buses carrying Pakistani navy officials in Karachi **on 26**th **April 2011,** killing four people in the latest sign of rampant insecurity in the whole nation. Four Naval employees' dead and nearly 60 people were wounded when remote-controlled bombs exploded beside the buses at rush hour at various places in Karachi. The four dead included a lady doctor, a sub lieutenant, a sailor and a civilian employee; and amongst wounded there were 50 navy officials. First bomb was planted on a motorbike parked in the Supermarket of Defence Housing Scheme and the second hidden in rubbish in the Baldia Town neighbourhood; both bombs were triggered by remote control when the buses passed through those target points.

Two days later, **on 28**th **April 2011,** four more navy personnel were killed and about twelve injured when attackers bombed another naval bus taking them to work in Karachi. This attack was launched at Faisal Avenue, one of the main roads of Pakistan's economic capital. A passing motorcyclist was also killed in the blast. Taliban and Al-Qaeda were again officially blamed.

People could recall the moments of 13th May 2011's Parliamentary meeting wherein the Pakistan's Air Chief had openly and loudly pointed out towards the sitting PM Gilani that *'if they tell us to check drone attacks there would be none; you decide and give us orders'.* PM Gilani and whole of the cabinet had gone pale. No decision was conveyed. Result: within one week there were launched five drone attacks leaving behind tens of killings; one had occurred on the same evening.

The speeches, sorrows and *'muzammats'* brought a shining label of a **'failing state'**; with a total of 6,142 persons, including of 2,797 un-identified, 2,580 civilians and 765 Security Forces personnel killed in year 2011 only. This worrying total had constituted an improvement of 17.75% over the preceding year of 2010 when 7,435 persons, including 1,796 civilians and 469 Security Forces personnel, had been killed.

Pakistani people, more or less, were always ready to welcome it but the question was that *'what was the Pakistani political & military elite doing about this?*

Pakistan's foresightedness remained confined up to their Interior Minister Rehman Malik's fiery speeches, as *on 2*nd *August 2011*, he informed the Parliament that the Security Forces had arrested 3,143 alleged terrorists in the country and recovered 4,240 weapons from them over the preceding three years. The irony of fate was that none of them could be convicted by the mighty courts of that country; salute to over delays in submission of charge sheets, frequent adjournments and 150 years old evidence laws being played by millionaire prosecuting and defence counsels in trial courts.

Scenario 90

PAK - US TENSE RELATIONS AT LAST:

On 13ᵗʰ September 2011, the American Embassy in Kabul and the NATO Offices situated nearby were attacked by Afghani Taliban. The international media started portraying that the Karzai government was, perhaps, loosing its control over the capital too.

[**US Embassy Kabul's official statement:** *The attack, which ended on Wednesday morning, (14ᵗʰ Sep) lasted as a 20-hour gun battle, an insurgent attack in the heart of Kabul and finished after a final volley of helicopter gunfire as Afghan police ferreted out and killed the last few assailants who had taken over a half-built downtown building to fire on the nearby US Embassy and NATO compounds.*

The bold assault that started Tuesday (13ᵗʰ Sep) left seven Afghans dead, including four police officers and three civilians, and raised fresh doubts about the Afghans' ability to secure their nation as US and other foreign troops begin to withdraw. No NATO or US Embassy employees were hurt in the attack.

Two or three of the assailants had held out overnight but were killed in the final morning assault by Afghan forces. In all, six attackers had occupied the unfinished, 11-story high-rise at one of the main traffic circles in the Afghan capital. At least one other police officer was killed in an attack in the west of Kabul as suicide bombers tried to strike in a number of neighbour-hoods.

The Taliban claimed responsibility for the attack.]

PAKISTAN BLAMED & THREATENED:

Immediately after, the US Defence Secretary Leon Panetta issued a press statement that the said attack had been launched by 'Haqqani Group' based in Afghanistan but its supplies and logistic support were sent from North Wazirastan.

The Chief of the Haqqani Group, Siraj Haqqani, had then negated the US claims by saying that their logistic centre was based in Eastern Afghanistan and not in North Wazirastan because they were feeling more secure in Afghanistan than in Pakistani area. Siraj Haqqani had also informed the concerned that this attack was not done or aided by Haqqani Group.

Anita Joshua had mentioned in **'The Hindu' dated 18.9.2011** that:

'.......The group's leader Sirajuddin Haqqani on Saturday told Reuters that it no longer had sanctuaries in Pakistan and had moved back to Afghanistan where it felt secure.'

In the blunt remarks by a US official since Pakistan joined the US-led war on militancy in 2001, the outgoing chairman of the Joint Chiefs of Staff, Admiral Mike Mullen, on 22nd September testified before the US Senate that *'the Haqqani militant network is a 'veritable arm' of the ISI'*. US officials alleged there was intelligence, including intercepted phone calls, suggesting those attackers were in communication with people connected to Pakistan's ISI.

Mike Mullen held Islamabad responsible for the Kabul attack, saying Pakistan provided support for that assault. The Pakistan government as well as its army rejected the allegations. John B of the White House, while delivering speech at Harvard Law School, released a statement that:

'Pakistan should attack on Haqqani Group hideouts in North Wazirastan otherwise the US would use its last option'.

Admiral Mike Mullen picked up those words and conveyed a direct threat of launching an armed attack on Pakistan. The Pakistan's civil and military leadership felt the pinch and immediately retaliated by saying big NO to America. They reiterated that Pakistan would not attack its own territory of North Wazirastan nor would they allow any power to enter their territorial limits.

Considering the American threat serious, a high level conference of Sunni Ittehad Council held in Lahore immediately after Mike Mullen's threat, in which fifty (50) Sunni leaders and clergymen jointly issued a *'Fatwa'* (decree) that *'fighting against Americans in this event is 'Jehad' and it is imperative for every Muslim to take part in this holy war'*. It was in fact a big achievement for the PPP government and the Pakistan Army at this moment of distress and agony.

On political front the PPP government immediately contacted chiefs of all political parties and asked them to attend an All Pakistan Political

Parties Conference (APC) at Islamabad *on 30*th *September 2011*. All
the political leaders invariably agreed to assemble in Islamabad so that
the Americans should get a message that their threat had been taken
seriously by the whole nation pushing behind all political rivalries etc.

Another development had already been seen by the nation *on 25*th
September 2011 when a corps commander conference was held in
emergency on Sunday at GHQ where all the strategic plans were considered to deal with any possible foreign attack with an iron hand. The
commanders agreed to resist US demanding Pakistan's Army action in
FATA saying that:

> 'We have already conveyed to the US that **Pakistan cannot go beyond
> what it has already done.** Our army is too stretched battling its own
> Taliban insurgency to go after the network, which has estimated
> 10,000-15,000 fighters. Our military could suffer heavy casualties if it
> were to attempt a crackdown on Haqqani group, which has developed
> extensive alliances with other militant organisations in the region, and
> has mastered the rugged mountain terrain.'

The message was clearly read by the whole world especially our
neighbouring enemies. Same day the Pakistan's Air Force was made
alert and shifting of logistics was accomplished within 24 hours which
inculcated more confidence in the people of Pakistan.

On diplomatic front, the American Ambassador was called in the
Foreign Office Islamabad almost daily and twice on 27th September to
make the US clear about our concerns. The top man of the US Senate
James M, who was in Islamabad at some design or by chance, failed
to convince Pakistani political leadership about the truth of their
threats and at the same time Pakistan's lady Foreign Minister, Hina
Rabbani Khar, also conveyed a comprehensive and lucid message to the
Americans, while speaking in New York, that:

> '**Pakistan cannot be pressurized by such negative means.** The Haqqani
> group that the US holds responsible for last week's attack against
> the American embassy in Kabul was CIA's "blue-eyed boy" for many
> years.'

Responding to questions during an interview with Al Jazeera television,
she had rejected US accusations against the ISI, saying it had no links to
the Haqqani network and that:

> 'If we talk about links, I am sure the CIA also has intelligence links
> with many terrorist organisations around the world and this particular

network has no connections with ISI; it is unsubstantiated allegation. No evidence has been shared with us. Partners and allies do not talk to each other through public statements. If that was the case then we have the right to make our own decision. I think we must not be tested more than we have the ability to bear.'

Strategically speaking, Pakistan Army had taken a wise stance by refraining themselves from any untoward drag in the quagmire of North Wazirastan. Very simple logic that if NATO forces or American soldiers were being attacked in Afghanistan, they could take any measures against them there in Afghan area. Why to thrust upon Pakistan the defeat, shortcomings and follies of their own forces or the failure of their intelligence.

Pakistan had already suffered a lot at the hands of Taliban and Afghan national forces on the charge of being the American ally; and the suffering continued. By initiating armed action against another group like Haqqanis, it did not want to commit its army at another sector in addition to Swat, South Wazirastan and Mohmand Agency. Pakistan had rightly conveyed that after suffering from a loss of $68 billion in economy and sacrificing their 35000 [till then] lives, the country was not in a position to 'do more' in that direction. In fact it was US turn then.

The past behaviour of the Americans had mostly shown their dubious character in that so called war on terror. 'Attack the Haqqani network' was the new slogan of the US Generals but they were not going to stop here. Their next demands were in the crucible; like that:

• *"Search Mulla Omar in the whole FATA otherwise we'll ruin Pakistan.*

• *Taliban's Shoora is in Quetta; smash them; failing to do so would be dealt with severely.*

• *Aiman uz Zawahri is reportedly hiding near Kahuta, allow us to search him.*

• *Mastermind of Mombai Attacks is reportedly running a madrassah near Lahore; close it.*

• *Al Qaeda's new den is reportedly working in Karachi; attack them there."*

And many more excuses like that. Americans were after the Pakistani nuclear arsenals nothing else. Rest of all were stories and excuses.

HAQQANI GROUP TARGETED:

The whole scenario needed revisiting at the American end. The security advisors of President Obama might have asked him to adopt this face-saving policy in the back drop of US defeat on Afghan soils. Next elections were ahead, only a year away, and Mr Obama had totally failed to appraise his nation that they had done better after George Bush. *86 of the Democrats and 56 Republican members were trying on record to bring the White House Admin believe that they were constantly loosing in Afghanistan* so should quit this war as early as possible; much before 2014.

One was unable to understand that why the NATO and American forces were in Afghanistan then if they had failed to achieve their main objectives. They could not handle the Afghan situation in ten years then how the threats of attacking Pakistan would pacify their defeats. Pakistan is another slippery area; it was not like attacking Iraq or Libya or Cambodia. The situation could bring more humiliation for the Americans because on the first day of their attack on North Wazirastan, Pakistan could cut off the NATO supply line and the US or NATO army could not continue fighting beyond a day or two without logistics, they needed.

On the Afghanistan front, the US Command was already facing disgrace and embarrassment due to increasing control of Taliban. The Taliban had proved their armed access up to the American Embassy and the Bagram Airport which was considered the ultimate secure fort of the NATO alliance there. The other indicator was the murder of Burhanuddin Rabbani who was playing a key role in US sponsored negotiations with Afghan Taliban.

(Late) Burhanuddin Rabbani had also paid a diplomatic visit to Iran so that peace talks in South East Asia could be guaranteed but there were other forces in the region which wanted to send back America bleeding and not with victory flags tied on their heads as turbans.

The Americans had also alleged that the murder of Burhanuddin Rabbani was done by the Haqqani Group too whereas the fact remains that the suicidal killer had got the security clearance from the Karzai's top admin incharge who had okayed him to see Mr Rabbani that day.

In fact, the US top brass was pressurising Pakistan to get the Haqqani team join the peace negotiations which their leader Siraj Haqqani had refused many times earlier. Another prevailing truth was that Haqqani Group wanted to expel America from the Afghan soil with a sense and admission of disgusting defeat and not with emblem of success talks.

In the first week of October 2011, National Security Adviser of the White House, *Thomas E Donilon, had secretly met in UAE with Gen Kayani* to deliver a tough message: 'rein in the Haqqani network'. Obama's top adviser on Pakistan, Douglas E Lute was also accompanying him. American officials made veiled threats of increasing drone strikes by the Central Intelligence Agency or conducting cross-border commando raids into Pakistan if the danger to American forces in Afghanistan was not quelled.

Referring to *'The News' of* 7th *October 2011,* just a few weeks before, American officials held a secret meeting with leaders of the Haqqani network to explore how the group might join talks to end the war in Afghanistan. The two meetings, held just over a month apart, underscored the Obama administration's complicated and seemingly contradictory policies in Afghanistan and Pakistan.

The US-talks with the Haqqani network brokered by the ISI illustrated America's recognition that military strikes alone would not end the fighting with the Taliban, the Haqqanis and other insurgents in Afghanistan but those preliminary discussions yielded no results. A little earlier, the Americans had blamed Haqqani fighters for a truck bombing at a NATO outpost south of Kabul on 10th September which killed at least five people and wounded 77 coalition soldiers, of course, along with a 20-hour assault on the US Embassy in Kabul; as has been detailed above.

The US was reviewing whether to designate the entire Haqqani network as a foreign terrorist organisation, even as it had already slapped sanctions against seven of its top leaders, including Badruddin Haqqani who was designated as a global terrorist. Those sanctions targeted kingpins of the Haqqani Network, their financiers, leadership, as well as some of its most dangerous operatives. Earlier, the US had marked Siraj Haqqani, Badruddin Haqqani, Sangeen Zadran and on the Treasury side Nasiruddin Haqqani, Khalil Haqqani, Ahmed Jan Zadran as well as Fazl e Rabi during years 2008-11 as cogent threat for American interests.

The US administration was under new pressure to designate the Haqqanis a terrorist organization alongside 49 others, including al-Qaeda, Lebanon's Hezbollah, the Hamas, the Palestinian Islamist group that controls the Gaza Strip. John Walcott and Viola Gienger, *on 28*th *September 2011*, had placed open their candid opinion on *bloomberg. com* website.

HILLARY CLINTON'S [FRUITLESS] VISIT:

During the third week of October 2011, the US Secretary Hillary Clinton was in Islamabad with a delegation attempting to push Pakistan into action against the Haqqani network. Accompanied by the Director of the CIA, David Petraeus, and the newly appointed military chief, Gen Martin Dempsey, Hillary held long meetings with Gen Kayani, Pakistan's Army Chief, and the political tops on 20th instant.

Hillary talked too much on the issue but Pakistani officials rejected the whole set of criticism, saying *'they have working intelligence links with the Haqqanis, but not operational ones'*. Astonishingly, the White House later rowed back on Mullen's comments; thus the high-level composition of this latest visit seemed designed to place a fresh message of renewed relationship between the two countries. *The Guardian of 20*th *October 2011* had mentioned the key aims as:

> 'Clinton said Pakistan had the capacity to encourage, to push, to squeeze Haqqanis into peace talks. That is what we are looking for. The US had also reached out to the Haqqani network to see if it was ready to talk peace. We are now working among us [Afghanistan, Pakistan and the US] to try to put together a process that would sequence us toward an actual negotiation. There are many ways of doing that. I think it's one of the real successes of the relationship.'

One could note that the whole American delegation led by Hillary Clinton seemed apologetic during the meetings with PM Gilani and COAS Gen Kayani. They were expecting that Pakistan would ask them to eliminate terrorist sanctuaries inside Afghanistan.

> [During the last six months the US had increased their deployments at Pak-Afghan border on eastern side and many attacks were launched on Pakistani security forces.]

The tone and tenor of the delegation sometimes echoed frustration as they made attempts at asserting themselves on Pak-Afghan leaders; though all tactics failed. The Pakistan leadership rather snubbed the Americans telling them about the APC's resolution and the firm reaction it demanded in the case of Americans continuing with their aggressive designs. This firm resolve of the leadership was not lost on Secretary Clinton who had later remarked certain odd things in panic. However, at the same time Hillary tried to convey that '**failing that, US officials suggest they would escalate military strikes**'.

In fact, Hillary Clinton's visit to Pakistan could not provide her much to smile. First time the Americans had felt that the Pakistan's military command had expressed the same words and tone which they had adopted when Gen Ashfaq Kayani had taken Army Chief's slot in early 2008. That was a hard paragraph from Pakistan's history; though lips were of Gen Musharraf but the pushing force was of Gen Kayani's mind.

In ending 2011; very clear message was given to the Americans that Pakistan's President Mr Zardari, the PM Gilani and the Army Chief Gen Kayani had spoken the same bitter language, expressed the same odd tone and the same firm determination. Reportedly, it was Mr Zardari who, with an opening sentence, had embarrassed Hillary by saying that:

> '*Why the US is asking us to take action against Haqqanis in Pakistan. Why don't you take action against them in Afghanistan? You do with them in Afghanistan whatever you like. Secondly, the US command is holding talks with Haqqanis in Kabul and you are asking Pakistan to launch attacks on them.*'

Hillary Clinton had nothing to say much except that '*attacking Haqqanis by you is not the only option; we want to bring them on table and you help us; you can do it, your ISI would help us*'. This time Pakistan's leadership was united, uni-directional and integrated. The priorities were already worked out by civil and military chiefs so were able to convey the same message to the Americans from three different places; the Presidency, the PM House and the GHQ.

During Hillary's meeting with intelligentsia in Islamabad, a Pakistani woman told her that the US acted like Pakistan's mother-in-law; amid the serious talks there was a laugh. The lady said '*we are trying to please you, and every time you come and visit us you have a new idea and tell us that we are not doing enough and need to work harder.*' Hillary Clinton, whose daughter married a New York investment banker this summer, smiled and replied: '*Now that I am a mother-in-law, I totally understand what you're saying.*'

Hillary and her US officials were demanding that Pakistan either deliver the Haqqani network to peace talks, kill its leaders, or pave the way for the Americans to eliminate them; but the Pakistan's leadership did not agree with any of their suggestions. Contrarily, Hillary Clinton's statement that Black-water was not 'directly' working in Pakistan needed a thorough probe.

A day earlier, while in the Afghan capital Kabul, Hillary had told the media there that *'The Haqqani group is considered the greatest threat to American troops in Afghanistan'*. The daily **'Nation' of 22nd October 2011** had pointed out an interesting fact in this regard that:

'The US has an unfortunate history of having propped up leaders like Bhutto, Sukarno, Ben Bella, Qaddafi, Shah of Iran and later when they refused to toe the American line, they were made horrible examples of.

As the US is now pressurising Pakistan to take on groups; which were not long ago bred and reared by the Reagan Administration; the same order seems to be in play. Such a double standard in dealing with the world, one rule for yourself and another for everyone else, is the root cause of mistrust and dislike that the reputation of the world's only Superpower enjoys nowadays.'

In Pakistan, there have been protests in many areas like Multan where a mob burnt an effigy of Hillary Clinton on 20th October when she was holding talks with her Pakistani counterparts in Islamabad. They were demonstrating against the intensified American pressure on them to crack down on militants allegedly destabilising Afghanistan.

Hillary Clinton, while leading an unusually large and powerful US delegation, warned during her four hours of talks with Pakistani officials, that:

'America and Pakistan cannot walk away from their relationship despite frustration on both sides. We are going to stay the course because we both have too much at stake. We cannot walk away.

We should be able to agree that for too long extremists have been able to operate here in Pakistan and from Pakistani soil. No one who targets innocent civilians, whether they be Pakistanis, Afghans, Americans or anyone else should be tolerated or protected.'

The US went increasingly impatient with Pakistan's refusal to take military action against Haqqani network but the super power forgot that according to the US media claims, only 2.7 percent of the total fatalities of 9,000 were estimated to be militants lost in drone attacks during this War on Terror. [*Obviously out of this 2.7 percent, the percentage of actual operatives killed could be far less*] A large number of those killed were innocent men, women and children but Hillary or the US delegation had no regard for that civilian loss of life; they even refused to express remorse at the deaths caused by drone attacks.

American officials warned if Pakistan continued to stay aloof; the US would act unilaterally to end the militant threat. Hillary, while talking to the media at Islamabad urged that:

'Pakistan has a critical role to play in supporting Afghan reconciliation and ending the conflict. We look to Pakistan to take strong steps to deny Afghan insurgents safe havens and to encourage the Taliban to enter negotiations in good faith.

It's like that old story: you can't keep snakes in your backyard and expect them only to bite your neighbours. No policy, that draws distinctions between good terrorists and bad terrorists, can provide long-term security.

What is needed now is to try to agree on how to 'operationalise' efforts to end the threat; this process should take place over the next days and weeks, not months and years.'

Pakistani leadership, both civil and military, simply shelved aside the whole set of overt & hidden threats.

PAK – US GULF WIDENED MORE:

Gen Mike Mullen's declaration before US Senate's Armed Services Committee that Haqqani operatives acted as a proxy for Pakistan's ISI further complicated the question of strategic cooperation between the two countries. While adding Haqqani group to the list of terrorist organizations, the US policy makers pointed towards declaring Pakistan as a terror – sponsoring state; Cuba, Iran, Sudan and Syria were already named.

The above move required halting US aid to Pakistan [though peanuts, and already stood halted] and forced the US to oppose World Bank loans to Pakistan [*the people already wanted so because most of the loans had been pocketed by the ruling elite since decades*]. Pentagon Press Secretary George Little told the media *on 27*th *September 2011* that:

'*The US wants to maintain a relationship with Pakistan that's grounded in common interests, to include going after terrorists that threaten both countries. There are differences from time to time which have been made public, and we continue to discuss those differences in private. We look forward to working with the Pakistanis to try to resolve them.*'

At the same time the Pentagon's summary also kept on record that:

'*Pakistani military officials told reporters in Islamabad on 25*th *September that they had decided not to take action against the Haqqani group because their forces are stretched too thin. If tensions escalated, Pakistan might again, as it did in a previous diplomatic confrontation, cut supply lines to US, NATO and Afghan forces from Karachi. Alternative land or air routes are more costly and difficult.*

The Pakistanis also might abandon secret agreements that permit unmanned US drones to collect intelligence and attack targets in designated areas of Pakistan. They also might expel some or all of the classified number of US intelligence officers and special operations forces who are training Pakistani troops and helping target drone attacks since a decade.'

The American think tanks and research organizations like Heritage Foundation also held that:

'*The Haqqanis probably would continue to get financial support from their allies in the Persian Gulf region and backing from the Pakistan's ISI and there is no likelihood of any change in their policies this time because they (Gulf countries & Pakistan) had no more faith in America now for their continuous betrayals in the past and more American tilt towards India.*'

Interestingly, after hearing Prime Minister Gilani's remarks of 25th September '*that US policy on Afghanistan shows confusion and policy disarray*', Marvin Weinbaum, a former Afghanistan and Pakistan intelligence analyst at the State Department and Director of the Centre for Pakistan Studies at the Middle East Institute in Washington said that:

'*We may just let this ride. We know what direction the US-Pakistan relationship is going, and now we have no idea what the bottom looks like.*'

It was, interalia, held by the opinion makers (referring to **'The Hindu'** **dated 18.9.2011**) that the Pakistani government had successfully rolled the 'do more' phrase back to the US stating that Pakistan had done a lot in the fight against terrorism and now it was time the US should come up for similar sacrifices. Elsewhere in Spain, at the NATO Chiefs of Defence meeting, the Army Chief Gen Kayani underlined Pakistan's sovereign right to formulate policy in accordance with its national interest.

The Haqqani claim of having returned to Afghanistan was in line with the Pakistani establishment's contention that there were terrorist havens west of the Durand Line from where repeated attacks were being launched on its border posts; the latest being of a week ago in Lower Dir. Islamabad, time and again held NATO and Afghanistan responsible for those attacks; stating that negligible security on the Afghan side of the border with Pakistan allowed terrorists to use those areas as safe havens and mount attacks on Pakistani forces and isolated villages along the border.

Commenting on his group if hiding in Pakistan, Sirajuddin Haqqani in his rare interview said:

> *'Gone are the days when we were hiding in the mountains along the Pakistan-Afghanistan border. Now we consider ourselves more secure in Afghanistan besides the Afghan people. Senior military and police officials are with us. There are sincere people in the Afghan government who are loyal to the Taliban as they know our goal is the liberation of our homeland from the clutches of the occupying forces.'*

The American policy makers were, however, unable to understand the facts narrated by the world media including Indian Press, though the Indian government mostly presented distorted facts. Some opinions were there that the Americans and NATO had comprehended the whole game but, just to cover up their humiliation of visible defeat in Afghanistan, they were looking at Pakistan to come up as an scapegoat.

HAQQANIS – HISTORY STANDS BY THEM:

Institute for the Study of Wars (ISW), a non-partisan & non-profitable public policy research organization based at Washington, traced out the history of Haqqani Group as under:

> *'The group is still believed to be led by the old (aged 60+) and ailing Maulvi Jalaluddin Haqqani; a former anti-Soviet Commander. He was*

based in or around Miran Shah, Pakistan's tribal area, since his exile during Sardar Daud's rule in early 1970s. He was initially a part of Hizb e Islami but when it fractured in the late 1970s, Haqqani followed Yunis Khalis rather than Hekmatyar.

When Soviet forces invaded Afghanistan, Haqqani was in Pakistan but, being a field commander in Younus Khalis's Hizb e Islami (HIK), he received significant support from the CIA and ISI to build up a sizable and competent militia force by the mid-1980s.'

That is why the Pakistan never denied its connections with Haqqanis; the same as the CIA held since then. For quite some time the US Ambassador to Afghanistan (1989-1992), Peter Tomsen, used to communicate between the ISI and Haqqanis because all were having common interests.

After the US invasion in October 2001, Haqqani was invited to Islamabad for talks about a post - Taliban government and Gen Musharraf did it on America's stance. **Till May 2008, Haqqanis remained 'a strategic asset' for both America and Pakistan.** One ISI official reportedly used to hold talks with Sirajuddin Haqqani on behalf of the Americans till early March 2009.

[But it is still to be enquired into that whether that ISI official was acting so on behalf of Pakistan Army or used to perform as an under the table paid American Agent.]

It is on record that in a prisoner exchange with Pakistani Taliban led by Baitullah Mehsud, the Pakistani government, once in November 2007, had released three family members of the Haqqani family named Khalil Ahmad (Haqqani's brother), son Dr Fazl – I - Haqqani and brother – in - law Ghazi Khan. If the Pakistan army or ISI had so good relations with Haqqanis then why the three family members of Haqqani remained in Pakistan's custody and had to be released in exchange later.

Maulvi Haqqani and his son Sirajuddin Haqqani run a number of religious schools and due to his father's ill health, Sirajuddin Haqqani run day – to - day operations of the movement as well. The Haqqanis hail from the Zadran tribe, who are mostly, based in Paktia and Khost provinces in the east of Afghanistan but they keep deep relations with their tribesmen in FATA's North Wazirstan since the Soviet War.

The Haqqanis and Zadran tribesmen had been fighting with Soviet forces throughout during 1985-87, sometimes gaining control of Khost through the only built in Khost - Gardez road, but sometimes getting defeated. In 1989, when all Soviet forces left Afghanistan, Haqqani consolidated his military position in Greater Paktia and established a Shura (Council) to coordinate military operations. He was able to capture Khost in 1991 from the communist government of Dr Najibullah; becoming the first mujahideen commander to seize and hold a major Afghan city after the Soviet withdrawal. Haqqani got a ministry in the new government of Burhanuddin Rabbani but defected to the Taliban in 1995.

The relationship between Haqqani and the Taliban government was not smooth but Haqqani nevertheless remained loyal to the Taliban government, becoming Minister of Tribal Affairs. In late September 2001, Mullah Omar appointed Haqqani the Chief Commander of the Taliban armed forces.

Haqqani speaks fluent Arabic and one of his two wives is from the UAE which helped him raise a great deal of funds from Saudi Arabia and the Persian Gulf. Haqqani established a close relationship with Osama Bin Laden in the 1980s and *'the first camp that Osama created in Afghanistan, Lion's Den and similar infrastructure were built in Haqqani's territory.'*

A US military spokesman in eastern Afghanistan, Major Chris Belcher had accused the Haqqanis of inviting foreign fighters from Pakistan, Uzbekistan, Chechnya, Turkey and Middle Eastern countries into Afghanistan. US Army Lt Col Dave Anders, Director Operations of Combined Joint Task Force-82, once wrote to their seniors that:

'Siraj Haqqani is the one who is responsible for kidnappings, assassinations, beheading women, indiscriminate killings and suicide bombings. Siraj is the one dictating the new parameters of brutality associated with Taliban senior leadership. His tribesmen were behind most of the attacks in eastern Afghanistan in 2008 and he commanded them. Khost, Paktia and Paktika are their traditional bases but their influence also extends to other provinces in the east, such as Ghazni, Logar, Wardak and Kabul.'

In addition, the said American report held that the recent simultaneous attacks on government buildings in Kabul in September 2011; a suicide attack on the Indian Embassy on 7th July 2008; an assassination attempt against President Hamid Karzai in April 2008 and many more were also done by Haqqanis. At the same time the Americans also said that the Haqqanis collaborated with the Mullah Omar - led Taliban forces, but tried to keep their leadership in the east.

But, Pakistan had nothing to do with all such details; why these voices were echoed to them.

Of course, Pakistan could not deny the whole set of allegations from America. *On 13th October 2011*, a Haqqani leader named Janbaz Zadran Jamil was killed in a drone attack in Miran Shah. Referring to the **'Express Tribune'** of 14th October, Janbaz was a senior Haqqani leader that was 'taken off the battlefield'; had been playing a central role in helping the Haqqani network attack US and coalition targets in Kabul and south - eastern Afghanistan. It no doubt, pointed towards the US claims that militants in Afghanistan had access to the 'Miranshah - based leadership'; but might be the Pakistan Army not knowing.

Moreover, *need not to tell America that retired and 'off the battlefield' officials are called redundant not the leadership.* US was clearly told by Pakistan to find out their active leadership in Eastern Afghanistan instead of wasting time & money in North Waziristan.

The net result from the whole scenario described above, was that:

- Pakistan's ISI was in contact with the Haqqani group since mid-1970s and those relations were still in line; it was OK.

- Pakistan Army was not in a position to shun those relations just within moments on America's instructions nor could they launch operational attacks on them.

- Pakistan, being a sovereign state, could not allow any other force; American, Afghani or of NATO, to intrude in its territorial limits to launch attacks on their possible sanctuary.

- If Haqqani group was accused of launching attacks anywhere in Afghanistan, the Afghan government or the American network there should have taken appropriate action against them to root out their sanctuaries in Eastern Afghanistan.

- The Americans or the Afghan government could tell Pakistan pin - pointing particular persons and their exact location through their own intelligence spread over in the whole FATA region; Pakistan might take action as per international norms. [Attacking them indiscriminately could cost Pakistan another killed batch of hundreds innocent women and children.]

- Pakistan could only help the Americans as per prevailing customs amongst sovereign nations nothing extra and nothing less.

It is well understood phrase that '**a terrorist for one country may be a freedom fighter for the other nation**'. Haqqanis were terrorists for Americans but for general Afghani populace, they might be their freedom fighters to liberate Afghanistan from Americans. Taliban are specie of another kind in the same scenario. Pakistan had already suffered a lot on that count but Pakistanis in general kept the opinion that the ISI should not be a party in this game anymore; strictly not from any side.

America's quit from Afghanistan was written on the wall, but they set the schedule till ending 2014. Soon the news popped up that bulk of the US men & material had already left the Afghan soils without announcements, till mid 2013 precisely.

PAKISTAN AMIDST GLOBAL CONSPIRACY:

To understand this phenomenon, one has to travel a little back.

Recalling the renowned speech of Obama delivered at the occasion of Cadet's passing out in New York **on 1ˢᵗ December 2009**, Ibrahim Sajid Malick, US correspondent for Sama'a TV, mentions that:

> *'Speaking to a hall full of cadets at the US Military Academy of West Point, President Barack Obama almost seemed like he might be declaring war on Pakistan. Sitting at the back benches of the hall at one point I almost jumped out of my chair when he said: "**the stakes are even higher within a nuclear - armed Pakistan,** because we know that al Qaeda and other extremists seek nuclear weapons, and we have every reason to believe that they would use them." I was shocked because a succession of American officials had recently confirmed that the Pakistani arsenal is secure.'*

The same kind of reason was forwarded by the Americans when they attacked Iraq in 2003 saying that weapons of mass destructions were there. The world knows the tricks the Americans use when they plan to ruin a country. The UN, leave it, it plays the same cards which are handed over to them by the CIA and pentagon. So, President Obama had already started acting his plans of December 2009. Pakistan's dollar thirsty leadership could not follow the words and their body language though the world press including of the US and Western had clearly warned Pakistan on the issue. Pakistan's Interior Minister and financial advisors were already on their pay roll.

In the summer of 2007, Obama, coached by Zbigniew Brzezinski and other controllers, was the originator of the unilateral US policy of using predator drones for assassinations inside Pakistan. This assassination policy was massively escalated along with the troop strength:

"Two weeks ago in Pakistan, Central Intelligence Agency sharpshooters killed eight people suspected of being militants of the Taliban and Al Qaeda, and wounded two others in a compound that was said to be used for terrorist training.. The White House has authorized an expansion of the CIA's drone program in Pakistan's lawless tribal areas, officials said this week, to parallel the president's decision to send 30,000 more troops to Afghanistan.

American officials are talking with Pakistan about the possibility of striking in Baluchistan for the first time - a controversial move since it is outside the tribal areas - because that is where Afghan Taliban leaders are believed to hide."

To achieve that US goal of blame-game, the CIA, the Pentagon, and their various contractors among the private military firms remained on murder spree across Pakistan; it was widely documented in the media. They attacked peaceful villages, community halls, mosques, *Imam-Bargahs*, shrines, police stations and even private wedding parties. Black-water, later called itself as Xe Services and Total Intelligence Solutions, was heavily involved:

'At a covert forward operating base run by the US Joint Special Operations Command (JSOC) in Karachi, members of an elite division of Black-water were at the centre of a secret program in which they planned targeted assassinations, "snatch and grabs" of high-value targets and other sensitive action inside Pakistan. The Black-water operatives also assisted in gathering intelligence and help direct a secret US military drone bombing campaign that ran parallel to the well-documented CIA predator strikes,'

There were persistent charges that a large part of the deadly bombings in Peshawar and other Pakistani cities were being carried out by Black-water; see ***XINHUA's reporting dated 29th October 2010:***

'Chief of Taliban movement in Pakistan Hakimullah Mehsud has blamed the controversial American private firm Black-water for the bomb blast in Peshawar which killed 108 people, local news agency NNI reported Thursday. This was blind terrorism designed for maximum slaughter, especially among women and children.'

Pakistan was deliberately positioned to be the centre of international conspiracy and the enemies in collaboration have been trying to punish it for being the only Muslim nuclear power. The ferocious advisors of Mr Bush had once suggested that:

- Pakistan be declared a failed state and thus should be deprived of their nuclear title and capacity to handle nuclear warheads & equipment.

- The nuclear assets especially the warheads be placed under the custody of a joint task force of US and UK because there was an apprehension that the same could be taken over or approached by the religious extremists sometimes. [*Unfortunately still this presumption prevails*].

- Hilary Clinton had opted to make it her election slogan that she would place Pakistan's nuclear warheads under US control if she would come in power after 2008 US elections.

- The scope of CIA, Pentagon and American intelligence be extended to the tribal areas of Pakistan on the basis of long ago fabricated slogan of 'presence' of Osama [since killed in May 2011], Mulla Omar and Aiman uzZawahri and 'Al-Qaida's training camps' on Pakistani soil etc.

The same dangers were enumerated in Professor *Michel Chossudovsky's paper titled as 'The Destabilization of Pakistan'*. Prof Michel was associated with the 'Global Research' of Canada. In his research paper it was rightly pointed out that the US was pushing Pakistan into accepting the presence of more of its 'special forces' on its soil. The US was expecting this situation because of rising unpopularity of Gen Musharraf in the wake of Ms Benazir's assassination.

To achieve its vicious goal, the American administration wanted to engage a local leader who had a minimal commitment with the Pakistani nation but should be able to further the American objectives, while **'concurrently contributing under the disguise of decentralization'** so that an agenda of weakening the Pakistan Federation's structure be effectively implemented. The report further said:

> *'The political impasse is deliberate. It is part of an evolving US foreign policy agenda, which favours disruption and disarray in the structures of the Pakistani state. Indirect rule of the Pakistani military is to be replaced by the more direct forms of US interference, including an expanded US military presence inside Pakistan, which is also dictated*

by the Middle East Central Asia geopolitical situation and Washington's ongoing plans to extend the Middle East war to a much broader area.'

In the course of 'War on Terror' the US ultimately resolved to hit his ally Pakistan below the belt by floating a slogan that *'the atomic assets of Pakistan are not safe; there is likelihood that the extremists or Taliban might get hold of their control.'* This voice was being maliciously echoed by various candidates running for American presidency. Obama and Hilary Clinton went out of their shoes to convince their gatherings that in case of their success they would prefer to launch an attack on Pakistan to gain control of atomic weapons.

American stalwarts, at last asked Albaradi, Chairman of International Atomic Energy program, to raise slogans in this respect so that the world opinion would go against Pakistan. The world media was already following footprints of the US. These were all speculations specially coined in peculiar situations as were framed against Iraq before regular army was sent there and formal attacks were launched.

Referring to an essay published at *Pakspectator.com* website on *30th September 2011*; the US and their allies in Afghanistan had successfully transferred their battles across the border into the Pakistani territory. Regular attacks on Pakistan's army contingents, members of Frontier Corp, Frontier Militia, Rangers and Police including one on Ms Benazir Bhutto, sponsored and backed by Pakistan's 'Friends' clearly, loudly and stridently told the world that war was at the doorstep of the country; the danger was not over.